The Social Psychology of Emotional and Behavioral Problems

Interfaces of Social and Clinical Psychology

Edited by

Robin M. Kowalski
Mark R. Leary

American Psychological Association

Washington, DC

First printing, March 1999
Second printing, September 2000

Published by
American Psychological Association
750 First Street, NE
Washington, DC 20002

Copies may be ordered from
APA Order Department
P.O. Box 92984
Washington, DC 20090-2984

In the U.K., Europe, Africa, and the Middle East, copies may be ordered from
American Psychological Association
3 Henrietta Street
Covent Garden, London
WC2E 8LU England

Typeset in Goudy by EPS Group Inc., Easton, MD

Printer: Port City Press, Inc., Baltimore, MD
Dust jacket designer: Minker Design, Bethesda, MD
Technical/Production Editor: Amy J. Clarke

Library of Congress Cataloging-in-Publication Data
The social psychology of emotional and behavioral problems : interfaces of social
    and clinical psychology / edited by Robin M. Kowalski and Mark R. Leary—1st
    ed.
        p.   cm.
    Includes bibliographical references and indexes.
    ISBN 1-55798-568-5 (cloth: acid-free paper)
    ISBN 1-55798-760-2 (pbk: acid-free paper)
    1. Social psychiatry.   2. Mental illness—Social aspects.
3. Interpersonal relations.   4. Social psychology.   I. Kowalski, Robin M.
II. Leary, Mark R.
RC455.S6225   1998
155.9′2—dc21   98-33297
                                                                    CIP

British Library Cataloguing-in-Publication Data
A CIP record is available from the British Library.

Printed in the United States of America

The Social Psychology of Emotional and Behavioral Problems

To Tom, for your love and support

—R. M. K.

To Rich, Ed, and Barry for nurturing my early interest in psychology

—M. R. L.

CONTENTS

CONTRIBUTORS

Craig A. Anderson, Department of Psychology, University of Missouri

Roy F. Baumeister, Department of Psychology, Case Western Reserve University

Debora Bell-Dolan, Department of Psychology, University of Missouri

Karen L. Dale, Department of Psychology, University of Plymouth, Plymouth, England

Timothy R. Elliott, Department of Physical Medicine and Rehabilitation, University of Alabama

Donelson R. Forsyth, Department of Psychology, Virginia Commonwealth University

Thomas Gilovich, Department of Psychology, Cornell University

John H. Harvey, Department of Psychology, University of Iowa

Robin M. Kowalski, Department of Psychology, Western Carolina University

Justin Kruger, Department of Psychology, Cornell University

Kimberley D. Kwavnick, Department of Psychology, University of Florida

Brian Lakey, Department of Psychology, Wayne State University

Mark R. Leary, Department of Psychology, Wake Forest University

Penelope Lockwood, Department of Psychology, University of Waterloo, Waterloo, Ontario, Canada

Rowland S. Miller, Department of Psychology and Philosophy, Sam Houston State University

Julia Omarzu, Department of Psychology, University of Iowa

Brian E. Pauwels, Department of Psychology, University of Iowa

Gary L. Rhodes, Department of Psychology, Wayne State University

Peter Salovey, Department of Psychology, Yale University

Kenneth Savitsky, Department of Psychology, Williams College

James A. Shepperd, Department of Psychology, University of Florida

June Price Tangney, Department of Psychology, George Mason University

Joanne V. Wood, Department of Psychology, University of Waterloo, Waterloo, Ontario, Canada

The Social Psychology of Emotional and Behavioral Problems

INTRODUCTION

ROBIN M. KOWALSKI AND MARK R. LEARY

The impetus for this volume began when one of us (Robin M. Kowalski) decided to develop a course that dealt with topics at the interface
of social and clinical psychology. Her excitement about offering such a
course was quickly tempered when she realized that no book existed that
would serve as an appropriate text. All existing books that dealt with topics
at the interface of social and clinical psychology were out of print, out of
date, narrowly focused on one particular topic, or too encyclopedic.

At about the same time, the other editor (Mark R. Leary) was receiving calls from university professors inquiring about the availability of
a book that he had written with Rowland Miller, 10 years earlier. *Social
Psychology and Dysfunctional Behavior* (Leary & Miller, 1986) examines areas
of social psychology that are relevant to the development, diagnosis, and
treatment of psychological difficulties, but like other books in the area, it
too was outdated and out of print. Even so, several instructors had called
to request permission to make copies of the book for use in their classes.
Like Kowalski, they were offering courses that fell at the interface of social
and clinical psychology but had found their options for a course text quite
limited.

The seed for this book was planted as we discussed the lack of a
current book that deals with the social psychology of psychological difficulties. We considered briefly the possibility of writing such a book but
decided instead to edit one, relying on the expertise of a dozen behavioral
researchers whose work has involved a blend of social and clinical psychology. Our goal was to develop a book that provided an up-to-date look
at the ways in which social psychology can help people understand phenomena that were once considered only the purview of clinical and counseling psychologists. We wanted a book that would not only serve as an
appropriate text for relevant undergraduate and graduate courses but also

3

would provide all interested readers—students, researchers, and practitioners alike—with an overview of the important and exciting work being done at the interface of social and clinical–counseling psychology.

Most psychologists would likely agree that many emotional and behavioral problems are essentially social and interpersonal problems. Not only are psychological difficulties typically caused or maintained by interpersonal processes, but also many problems manifest themselves in dysfunctional social behaviors or create difficulties for the troubled individual's personal relationships. This social psychological view does not deny that biochemical and other physiological processes underlie certain psychological problems but highlights the role of interpersonal factors in many disorders. Extreme cases of psychopathology aside, most of the emotional and behavioral problems for which people seek professional help are essentially distortions or exaggerations of normal patterns of behavior or normal behaviors that occur in contexts that other people consider inappropriate (see Maddux, 1987).

Thus, many—if not most—emotional and behavioral problems are rooted in "normal" interpersonal processes, precisely the processes that constitute the content of social psychology. Yet despite the fact that psychologists have acknowledged for many years that interpersonal processes are involved in psychological difficulties, few attempts were made to apply specific social psychological concepts and theories to understanding and treating emotional and behavioral problems until the early 1980s. Since then, however, great strides have been made in integrating aspects of social and clinical psychology. Not only are many researchers now studying psychological difficulties from social psychological perspectives, but graduate programs are becoming increasingly receptive to cross-fertilization between social and clinical psychology (and some graduate programs have even developed programs reflecting the interface of social, clinical, and counseling psychology). Even so, as Forsyth and Leary (1997) observed,

> despite efforts to base psychological practice on a body of scientifically attained knowledge and to make behavioral scientists more responsive to the needs of those who deliver services, the science and practice of psychology continue to lead an uneasy coexistence. (p. 187)

Our hope is that the chapters in this volume will help to make the science and practice of psychology coexist a bit more comfortably and a bit less uneasily.

As we discussed possible chapters for this book, our biggest challenge was deciding which topics to include. When Shelley Taylor of the University of California, Los Angeles, was asked to compile a list of social psychology's contributions to areas that are relevant to the field of mental health, she identified 48 distinct topics (S. Taylor, personal communication, December 23, 1997), but we can include only a dozen or so in this book. The book begins with an opening chapter that provides a brief history and overview of the social–clinical interface. The relationship between psychologists who are interested in basic interpersonal processes (social psychologists) and those who focus on emotional and behavioral problems (chiefly clinical, counseling, and school psychologists) has been a strange and rocky one. These groups have a great deal in common, yet their differences have impeded collaboration between them and the integration of their work.

During the 1980s, the study of *social cognition*—how people think about themselves and their social worlds—dominated experimental social psychology, and researchers devoted a great deal of attention to the processes by which people perceive, process, and act on social information. The chapters in Part I review areas in which work in social cognition has been applied to emotional and behavioral problems. The earliest topic in social–cognition applied to clinical psychology was attribution; Bell-Dolan and Anderson review important parts of this literature within the framework of the attribution process model in chapter 2. In chapter 3, Gilovich, Kruger, and Savitsky explore how *egocentrism*—people's natural difficulty getting beyond their own idiosyncratic perspective—leads to personal distress as well as difficulties with other people. In chapter 4, which deals with social comparison processes, Wood and Lockwood examine the connection between how people compare themselves with others and problems they experience, such as depression and low self-esteem.

The three chapters in Part II each deals with the self. In chapter 5, Dale and Baumeister explore the provocative connection between failures of self-control and psychopathology. They discuss ways in which difficulties in self-regulation can lead to problems as diverse as attention deficit hyperactivity disorder, eating disorders, mood disorders, obsessive–compulsive disorder, and substance abuse. People often seek professional help from psychologists because they are troubled by strong and distressing self-conscious emotions, such as shame, guilt, jealousy, and envy. In chapter 6, Tangney and Salovey examine these problematic social emotions and their relationship to psychological well-being. Chapter 7 provides a reinterpretation of research on self-esteem—a construct that has been linked to a host of psychological outcomes. In this chapter, Leary provides a novel explanation of the function of self-esteem, relying on theory and research from both social and clinical–counseling psychology.

Part III of the book focuses on interpersonal processes in emotional and behavioral problems. Given that how people relate to others can affect their mental health, for better and for worse, many interpersonal topics in social psychology have direct relevance for understanding psychological problems. A fundamental process in human interaction involves disclosures that people make about themselves during the give-and-take of ordinary conversations. In chapter 8, Kowalski examines the self-disclosure process, with an eye on how and why disclosing information about oneself helps to promote one's psychological well-being. Shepperd and Kwavnick extend this theme in chapter 9, as they discuss emotional and behavioral problems that arise as a result of people's concerns with how they are perceived and evaluated by others.

Many of the events that create psychological difficulties for individuals occur in the context of ongoing relationships—those with friends, family members, spouses and other romantic partners, coworkers, and the people who are members of the various groups to which people belong. The chapters in Part IV focus on the effects of these relationships on psychological well-being and distress. In chapter 10, Rhodes and Lakey provide an integrative review of the literature on social support, offering insights into how and why a low degree of support from other people exacerbates a person's psychological disorder. Miller then turns the reader's attention to dysfunctional relationships in chapter 11, discussing various personal, interactive, and relational problems that can make personal relationships psychologically toxic. In chapter 12, Forsyth and Elliott analyze how groups can enhance and undermine the psychological well-being of their members.

The final chapter of the book, coauthored by Harvey, Omarzu, and Pauwels, provides a 20-year retrospective on the interface of social and clinical psychology. Harvey was instrumental in promoting the social–clinical interface during its fledgling days in the 1980s (among other things, he was the founding editor of the *Journal of Social and Clinical Psychology*), thus he is in a unique position to provide an insightful commentary on the field.

As seen from this brief preview, the chapters in this book deal with topics that span the breadth of social psychology, including attribution, social cognition, social comparison, self-regulation, emotions, self-esteem, self-disclosure, impression management, social support, close relationships, and group dynamics. These chapters offer the reader considerable insight into how people's well-being is affected by their interactions and relationships with other people as well as evidence for the usefulness and viability of the interface between social and clinical psychology.

REFERENCES

Forsyth, D. R., & Leary, M. R. (1997). Achieving the goals of the scientist–practitioner model: The seven interfaces of social and counseling psychology. *The Counseling Psychologist, 25*, 180–200.

Leary, M. R., & Miller, R. S. (1986). *Social psychology and dysfunctional behavior.* New York: Springer-Verlag.

Maddux, J. E. (1987). The interface of social, clinical, and counseling psychology: Why bother and what is it anyway? *Journal of Social and Clinical Psychology, 5*, 27–33.

1

INTERFACES OF SOCIAL AND CLINICAL PSYCHOLOGY: WHERE WE HAVE BEEN, WHERE WE ARE

ROBIN M. KOWALSKI AND MARK R. LEARY

Few contemporary psychologists—whatever their formal areas of training and expertise—would question the relevance of social psychology to clinical and counseling psychology. Since the earliest days of the discipline, psychologists with a variety of theoretical bents have recognized that interpersonal factors play an important role in the origin and maintenance of emotional and behavioral problems as well as in the diagnostic and psychotherapeutic activities through which mental health professionals treat psychological difficulties. Yet despite a general recognition that interpersonal processes are relevant to understanding and treating psychological problems, attempts to forge explicit connections between social psychology and clinical psychology evoked little interest among members of either camp for many years. However, over time and with the persistent efforts of a few key figures, an interface between social and clinical psychology began to emerge, and the last 2 decades have seen remarkable advances in theoretical and empirical integrations of the fields.

This chapter provides a look at the relationship between social and clinical psychology, at the notable successes of bridging the fields as well as at the impediments that hinder the integrated kind of psychology that would serve the discipline and the public best. An appreciation of the relationship that currently exists between social and clinical psychology requires an understanding of the development of the two fields, so we begin with an overview of the paths that social psychologists and clinical–counseling psychologists have traveled to meet at the crossroads. We then discuss the status of the interface today from two perspectives: one that examines the substantive content areas that have and have not traversed the schism between the fields and a second that explores the differences between social and clinical psychology that continue to impede their cross-fertilization.

WHERE WE HAVE BEEN: PHASES IN THE DEVELOPMENT OF THE SOCIAL–CLINICAL INTERFACE

We begin with a brief historical overview to provide the reader with a sense of how the relationship between social and clinical psychology has changed over the past 100 years.[1] For convenience, we break the development of social–clinical psychology into five phases that we characterize as the generalist phase (1900–1945), mutual disinterest (1946–1960), early pioneers (1961–1975), early integrations (1976–1989), and incorporation into the mainstream (1990–present).

The Generalist Phase (1900–1945)

Before psychology became splinted into the plethora of subspecialities that exist today, social psychology and clinical psychology interfaced fairly easily. Graduate education in psychology was broader than it is now, and most early psychologists were trained as generalists first and specialists second. Thus, it was not unusual for a particular psychologist's interests and expertise to span what is viewed today as several different fields. Because of their generalist orientation, many early psychologists saw connections between disparate areas that were less obvious to later generations.

Connections between social psychology and the study of abnormal behavior were discussed explicitly during the early part of the century. As early as 1921, when the *Journal of Abnormal Psychology* was transformed into the *Journal of Abnormal and Social Psychology*, Morton Prince argued that researchers in abnormal and social psychology should work closely to understand the role of social factors in the etiology of dysfunctional behaviors and the cultural influences on people's perceptions of what is nor-

---

[1] We refer readers who are interested in more detailed examinations of the history of the social–clinical interface to Leary and Miller (1986) and Snyder and Forsyth (1991a).

mal and abnormal (Hill & Weary, 1983). Furthermore, although psycho-therapy was dominated by psychoanalytic perspectives during the early years of psychology, many of the prominent neo-Freudians—Karen Horney, Alfred Adler, Harry Stack Sullivan, Erich Fromm, and others—began to move psychoanalysis away from its purely intrapsychic roots toward a recognition that interpersonal factors play a role in the instigation and maintenance of dysfunctional behaviors.

Although their roots can be traced to the early part of the century, social psychology and clinical psychology emerged as clearly recognizable specialities in the late 1930s and early 1940s. Although they shared certain elements, they differed in their general approach toward understanding behavior. *Social* psychology, influenced by Kurt Lewin's interactionist perspective, emphasized the role of situational influences, often moderated by personality, in determining people's behavior. *Clinical* psychology, because of its focus on assessment (and, hence, individual differences) and the influence of psychodynamic perspectives, tended to emphasize intrapsychic processes over interpersonal ones. Furthermore, social psychology defined itself as an area interested primarily in "normal" human behavior, whereas clinical psychology emphasized "abnormality." Even so, the lines were not so clearly drawn that psychologists of one ilk could not cross to the other side.

World War 2 was perhaps the single most important influence on the development of both social and clinical psychology. During the war, social psychologists focused heavily on topics of applied importance in the war-time effort. They examined issues such as civilian and soldier morale, the use of persuasion to produce attitude change, and international relations (Cartwright, 1979; Snyder & Forsyth, 1991c). This interest in applied topics provided another point of similarity between social and clinical psychologists of the time. Thus, early on, before social and clinical psychology became specialized and increasingly distinct, an easy interface existed between the two fields. However, after the war, the situation changed rapidly.

Mutual Disinterest (1946–1960)

The period from the mid-1940s until about 1960 was a time of mutual disinterest between social and clinical psychologists. Following World War 2, most clinical psychologists worked alongside psychiatrists in Veterans Administration hospitals. Adopting the prevailing medical model of psychopathology, they emphasized intrapsychic as opposed to interpersonal influences on behavior. In addition, clinical training programs emphasized practice over science as they scrambled to meet the postwar demand for therapists. As clinical psychology oriented toward assessment and practice, clinical researchers thought less about conducting basic research, and research in clinical psychology became increasingly atheoretical (Snyder & Forsyth, 1991c).

Social psychology, however, increasingly leaned toward basic laboratory research, with little thought to the direct application of its research findings whether to clinical and counseling psychology or other domains. Social psychologists prided themselves in their increasing methodological and theoretical sophistication and slowly began to devalue research with an explicitly applied focus. Hendrick (1983) suggested that if it had not been for Kurt Lewin's untimely death in 1947, Lewin's emphasis on "action research" would have promoted continued attention to applied topics in social psychology, thereby promoting closer ties with clinical psychology in the postwar years.

Further compounding the growing division between social and clinical psychology were differences in epistemology and methodology. Social psychologists adopted a "microscopic" approach to studying particular behaviors that contrasted sharply with the more holistic approach of practitioners, and the heavily quantitative, laboratory-based methodology of social psychologists did not interface easily with the qualitative field investigations of practitioners (Forsyth & Leary, 1997; Leary & Maddux, 1987).

One irony of the divergence of social and clinical psychologists is that during this period, the scientist–practitioner model of doctoral training in clinical psychology was established (the so-called *Boulder* model). This model stressed the importance of behavioral science to the practice of clinical psychology, defining a clinical psychologist as both a scientist and a practitioner (Raimy, 1950). Yet although graduate programs required doctoral students in clinical psychology to take courses in research methods and statistics and to conduct empirical dissertations, the scientist–practitioner model did not stimulate clinicians to forge links with other areas of behavioral science, such as social psychology.

As evidence of the growing division between the fields, in 1965 the *Journal of Abnormal and Social Psychology* was split into the *Journal of Abnormal Psychology* and the *Journal of Personality and Social Psychology*. (Although the bifurcation occurred in 1965, the impetus for the separation began somewhat earlier.) Some of the reasons for the split were purely logistical (e.g., the number of manuscripts submitted for review exceeded the capacity of a single journal), but some reasons reflected the increasing specialization and diversification of social and clinical psychology. Most relevant to our discussion is the fact that in spite of some people's feelings that the two fields shared common interests, the articles published in the *Journal of Abnormal and Social Psychology* tended to focus on either social psychology or abnormal psychology, with few articles by writers making any attempt to integrate the two (Hill & Weary, 1983; Snyder, 1997).

Early Pioneers (1961–1975)

In the early 1960s, a few writers began to discuss explicitly the links between social and clinical–counseling psychology. The climate was perhaps right by that time, in that social psychologists had generated some notably successful theories involving attitude change and social influence —topics of obvious clinical relevance. Furthermore, clinical psychologists were beginning to distance themselves from the medical model of psychopathology they had inherited from psychiatry, and counseling psychology was emerging as a subspeciality with an interest in everyday problems of adjustment, those that often had clear interpersonal causes and consequences.

One of the earliest and most influential writers to examine clinically relevant questions from social psychological perspectives was Jerome Frank (1961) in his book *Persuasion and Healing*. (Ironically, Frank had a degree in medicine rather than psychology.) Frank's central thesis was that all instances of psychological change—not only the changes observed in psychotherapy but also the changes that result from experiences such as faith healing and religious conversion—are the result of similar interpersonal and cognitive processes. Frank was instrumental in showing the relevance of nonclinical research, specifically social psychological research, to the practice of psychotherapy. Echoing Frank's sentiment, Arnold Goldstein and his colleagues (Goldstein, 1966, 1971; Goldstein, Heller, & Sechrest, 1966) illustrated the relevance of social psychological research on a variety of topics (including interpersonal attraction, attitude change, group dynamics, and cognitive dissonance) to individual and group psychotherapy.

During this time, ideas from social psychology were incorporated into counseling psychology earlier and more easily than they were incorporated into clinical psychology (Strong, Welsh, Corcoran, & Hoyt, 1992). The most obvious reason for this was that counseling psychologists were typically more interested than clinical psychologists in "normal" adjustment problems rather than psychopathology, and these everyday problems in living seemed more amenable to social psychological analysis than did many of the more severe disorders. One unifying theme in early efforts was a focus on counseling as a social influence process—a message that was stated most forcefully and effectively by Stanley Strong (1968) in an article entitled, "Counseling: An Interpersonal Influence Process." Applying the Hovland, Janis, and Kelley (1953) model of attitude change—a bulwark social psychological theory of the time—Strong demonstrated how characteristics of the counselor, the client, and the counselor's message influenced a client's change. Strong and other counseling psychologists were instrumental in showing the relevance of social psychology to the theory and practice of counseling (see Strong et al., 1992, for a review).

Links between social and clinical–counseling psychology were further promoted during this time by the realization that some psychological symptoms reflect interpersonal strategies designed to influence the reactions of other people (Braginsky, Braginsky, & Ring, 1969; Carson, 1969; Fontana & Gessner, 1969; Fontana & Klein, 1968). A classic example of this line of work is a study by Braginsky and Braginsky (1967), who showed that people hospitalized with a schizophrenia diagnosis increased or decreased their psychotic symptoms as a function of their goals. At the same time, Robert Carson applied transactional approaches to the study of personality. He suggested that deviant behavior emerges from disordered social interactions and that psychological difficulties are best explained by interpersonal rather than intrapersonal processes. Indeed, conceptualizations of what is regarded as abnormal can be made only in reference to the behaviors of others in social situations. Theoretical and empirical approaches such as these demonstrated that certain features of psychopathology could be understood in terms of social psychological processes and interpersonal behaviors.

As these early prophets—Frank, Goldstein, Strong, Carson, the Braginskys, and others—cried out in the wilderness for others to heed their call, social psychology began to experience a "crisis of confidence" (Elms, 1975). Disillusioned with the traditional emphasis on basic laboratory research and the seeming irrelevance of much research in social psychology to the solution of real-world problems, many social psychologists redirected their research attention to topics that were relevant to real social and personal problems. Although the relevance of social psychology to applied concerns had been apparent during World War 2, not until the 1960s did the movement toward applied social psychology gain momentum. One applied area that beckoned these disillusioned social psychologists involved what had previously been viewed as topics of clinical interest.

Early Integrations (1976–1989)

Prior to the mid-1970s, most research that borrowed concepts from both social and clinical psychology involved the application of specific social psychological principles—for example, attribution, social influence, self-presentation, or attitude change—to topics of interest to clinical and counseling psychologists. Thus, the interface was fairly limited in scope and only relevant to researchers who were specifically interested in these clinically relevant topics.

In *The Application of Social Psychology to Clinical Practice*, Sharon Brehm (1976) took a broader view of the clinical relevance of social psychology, showing how dominant social psychological theories of the day— reactance, dissonance, and attribution theories—could contribute to understanding and treating psychological problems. Thus, her volume not only showed the clinical relevance of particular theories but also advocated the usefulness of social psychological theories more generally. Brehm's intent was to carry on the work of the early social–clinical pioneers, but she perceived that her book was met with "a deafening roar of indifference" (Brehm, 1991, p. 800). Yet in terms of helping to create a climate that fostered connections between social and clinical psychology, Brehm's book was clearly a catalyst.

Another influential figure in this period was Seymour Sarason (1981a), who in his article, "An Asocial Psychology and a Misdirected Clinical Psychology" (as well as a book with a similar theme; S. B. Sarason, 1981b), advocated that clinical psychology cannot exist independent of considerations of individuals' social worlds. As Sarason (1981a) put it, "a clinical psychology not rooted in a realistic social psychology . . . is a misdirected clinical psychology" (p. 835). This article may have been particularly influential because it appeared in the *American Psychologist,* one of the most widely circulated journals in psychology.

In an attempt to bring together some of the early work at the emerging interface of social and clinical psychology, Weary and Mirels (1982) edited a volume, *Integrations of Clinical and Social Psychology.* Their book was important not only because it provided a venue for work at the interface but also because it brought the interface to the attention of a wider audience. Other books by Leary and Miller (1986) and by Maddux, Stoltenberg, and Rosenwein (1987) also provide early reviews of areas in which social psychological concepts and theories had been applied to understand the origin, diagnosis, and treatment of emotional and behavioral problems.

During the 1980s, research that spanned social and clinical psychology began to take on a different flavor than previously. Whereas research in the 1960s and 1970s focused primarily on the applications of social psychology to the practice of counseling and psychotherapy, the focus shifted in the 1980s toward social factors involved in the etiology and maintenance of dysfunctional behaviors (Weary, 1987). One particularly active and fruitful arena involved social psychological processes in health and illness. The emerging area of health psychology was, in large part, fueled by the recognition that social psychology was quite relevant to understanding and promoting wellness and to helping people to deal psychologically with illness and injury (Meyerowitz, Burish, & Wallston, 1986; Snyder & Ford, 1987). This shift in emphasis was both a cause and an effect of social psychologists becoming increasingly interested in clinically relevant topics.

Nearly 20 years after the *Journal of Abnormal and Social Psychology* split into two separate journals, John Harvey (1983) founded the *Journal of Social and Clinical Psychology* (JSCP) to provide a "forum explicitly dedicated to work representing the rich and extensive interface of social and clinical psychology" (p. 1). As new journals often do, JSCP concretized social–clinical psychology as a legitimate, identifiable specialty and provided an outlet for work that had occasional difficulty being published in established journals in social and clinical psychology.[2] The nature of the interface during this period was reflected in the topics that appeared most frequently in JSCP, including attribution, relationships, ego defenses, emotion, health, and the self (Snyder, 1988). Interest in social–clinical psychology was reflected in publication trends at other journals as well. A historical study of clinically relevant research in social psychological journals showed that the primary journals in social psychology also began to see an increase in social–clinical articles at about the same time (Leary, Jenkins, & Shepperd, 1984).

This advocacy phase also witnessed a flood of articles about the interface itself. Many writers during the 1980s surveyed the territory, marked its boundaries, discussed the state of the relationship between social and clinical psychology, and rallied the troops to join the call for further integration (Brehm & Smith, 1982; Forsyth & Strong, 1986; Harari, 1983; Harvey, Bratt, & Lennox, 1987; Hendrick, 1983; Langer, 1982; Leary, 1987; Leary & Maddux, 1987; Maddux, 1987; Maddux, Stoltenberg, Rosenwein, & Leary, 1987; Weary, 1987; Weary, Mirels, & Jordan, 1982).

Incorporation Into the Mainstream (1990–Present)

In looking back at these articles from the 1980s, one is struck by their spirited, evangelical tone. Recognizing the benefits to be gained from fostering closer connections between social and clinical psychology, these writers exhorted their readers to enlist in the integrative effort. Knowing that most of their readers were entrenched in traditional views of what constituted social psychology versus clinical–counseling psychology, the authors took every opportunity to convince them of the merits of interfacing the two.

By 1990, proponents of the interface no longer felt the need to justify efforts to pull aspects of social and clinical psychology together. Research and theory at the interface of social and clinical–counseling psychology had become increasingly visible, and researchers on both sides of the divide seemed more willing to wander into one another's territory than they were a decade earlier. Social psychologists' interest in emotional and behavioral problems had increased to the point where they no longer felt traitorous or out of the mainstream to investigate such topics. Likewise, clinical–counseling psychologists had seemed to recognize that at least some theory and research in social psychology might inform clinical research and prac-

---

[2]More than one author whose work spanned the gulf between social and clinical psychology experienced the frustration of being told by the editor of a social psychology journal that a submitted paper was not acceptable because it was clinical and by the editor of a journal in clinical or counseling psychology that the same paper was, in fact, not appropriate and should be submitted to a social psychological one.

tice, although many of them continued to see its relevance as minor. By the early 1990s, in the *Handbook of Social and Clinical Psychology*, Snyder and Forsyth (1991a) had no difficulty filling 40 chapters and over 800 pages with material that interfaced the fields. The interface had rapidly matured to the point where, like any political or intellectual "revolution," it was becoming part of the established mainstream.

WHERE WE ARE, PART I: TOPICS AT THE INTERFACE

Having traced the development of the social–clinical interface, we turn our attention to its current state. In this section, we focus specifically on the degree to which particular areas of investigation within social psychology have (or have not) had an impact on theory, research, and practice in clinical and counseling psychology. We acknowledge from the outset that our discussion here is unidirectional—exploring the influence of social psychology on clinical–counseling psychology—and more-or-less ignores the reciprocal influences of clinical–counseling psychology on social psychology. However, there are good reasons for this one-sided approach, which we address later in this chapter. To facilitate our discussion of the current status of the interface, we rely here on the suggestion that the topics that constitute the social–clinical interface focus on three relatively distinct types of phenomena (Leary, 1987):

- Social-dysgenic processes—interpersonal processes involved in the development, maintenance, and exacerbation of dysfunctional behavior and emotions.
- Social-diagnostic processes—interpersonal processes involved in the identification, classification, and assessment of psychological problems (by both professionals and laypeople).
- Social-therapeutic processes—interpersonal processes involved in the prevention and treatment of emotional and behavioral difficulties.

Table 1 presents a grid in which the columns reflect these three foci of the interface and the rows represent general topic areas in social psychology.[3] (For ease of discussion, we also classified the social psychological topics themselves into three general categories reflecting social-cognitive, interpersonal, and personality processes.) The three broad foci (social-dysgenic, social-diagnostic, and social-therapeutic processes) and the numerous social psychological topics that fall within each domain highlight the substantive content areas of the social–clinical interface. For each con-

---

[3]We do not claim that these topics constitute all of the domains of social psychology. However, an inspection of both textbooks and recent issues of journals in social psychology suggests that these 12 topics incorporate most contemporary social psychological research.

TABLE 1
The Interface Content Areas of Social–Clinical Psychology

Social psychological processes	Type of research		
	Social dysgenic	Social diagnostic	Social therapeutic
Social-cognitive processes			
Attribution	✚	✔	✚
Social perception and cognition	✚	✔	✔
Attitudes	✔	○	✚
Interpersonal processes			
Social influence	○	○	✚
Self-disclosure and self-presentation	✔	✔	✔
Interpersonal relationships	✔	○	✔
Aggression	✔	na	na
Prosocial behavior	○	na	✔
Group processes	○	○	✔
Personality processes			
The self	✚	○	✔
Emotion	✚	○	○
Individual differences	✚	✔	✚

Note. This table shows the amount of theoretical and empirical progress that has been made in various topics at the interface of social and clinical–counseling psychology. ✚ = extensive progress has been made in this area; ✔ = some progress has been made in this area; ○ = little or no progress has been made in this area; na = not applicable (social psychological process cannot be applied easily to this area).

tent area, we indicated (with a zero, check, or plus sign) the degree to which we believe theoretical and empirical progress has been made in understanding the social psychological processes involved. Admittedly, these are our own impressions of the current state of affairs, and some readers may disagree with our assessment. But these impressions provide a starting point for discussing the current state of knowledge in these areas.

Social-Cognitive Processes

Without question, areas within social psychology that focus explicitly on cognitive processes—for example, attribution, social perception and cognition, and attitudes—have most easily crossed the narrow bridge between social and clinical psychology. In fact, the cognitive revolution in psychology was an important impetus to the interface, as social and clinical psychologists alike recognized the usefulness of cognitive approaches to understand behavior.

Attribution

Much of the early research that spanned social and clinical psychology dealt with attributional processes. For example, Abramson, Seligman, and Teasdale (1978) applied an attributional analysis to depression, resulting in a highly influential theory (i.e., learned helplessness theory) and stimulating a great deal of important research. Attributional approaches were also applied early on to understand how people's interpretations of their (and others') reactions can foster psychological distress (Valins & Nisbett, 1972). Much of the work that directly applies social psychological perspectives to treatment also is based on attributional theories (Murdock & Altmaier, 1991; Rabinowitz, Zevon, & Karuza, 1988). Because researchers interested in attribution got a jump start on many other areas, we know a great deal about the attributional processes that underlie the development, diagnosis, and treatment of psychological problems (Bell-Dolan & Anderson, this volume, chapter 2).

Social Perception and Cognition

Within the social-dysgenic realm, a considerable body of theory and research deals with how people's perceptions and ways of thinking can set them up for emotional and behavioral problems (Gilovich, Kruger, & Savitsky, this volume, chapter 3). Researchers have also devoted attention to the social-diagnostic processes by which clinicians and laypeople draw inferences about other people's personalities and mental health (e.g., Cantor, 1982; Kayne & Alloy, 1988; Salovey & Turk, 1991). To the extent that clinical inference is, at heart, an exercise in person perception, much can be gained by applying what is known about social perception and cognition to the processes by which clinicians draw conclusions about their clients.

Clinical and counseling psychology have always emphasized the importance of changing clients' thoughts to produce psychological change, but until recently, little attention has been devoted to the processes by which such cognitive changes occur. Models arising from social cognition have begun to elucidate these processes and offer suggestions to how they may be expedited (see Abramson, 1988).

Attitudes

Social psychological theory and research involving attitudes have been applied to the study of ways to change clients' attitudes in the course of counseling and psychotherapy. As noted earlier, Brehm (1976) was among the first to discuss the importance of social psychological theories of attitude change, such as dissonance and reactance theory, for understanding and promoting client change. More recently, the elaboration likelihood model has received a great deal of attention by researchers in counseling psychology (see Cacioppo, Claiborn, Petty, & Heesacker, 1991).

Researchers have also examined the consequences of holding certain attitudes on psychological difficulties, for example, the effects of women's attitudes toward abortion on their reactions to having an abortion themselves (Conklin & O'Connor, 1995). Given that people's attitudes can predispose them to emotional–behavioral problems as well as either promote or impede their progress, more attention to the clinical relevance of attitudes is needed.

Interpersonal Processes

Social psychological theory and research on interpersonal interactions and relationships have clear implications for clinical–counseling psychology. Not only do many psychological difficulties arise from interpersonal processes, but the therapeutic encounter itself is, after all, a social interaction.

Social Influence

We noted earlier that many of the early applications of social psychology to practice involved social influence processes (Strong, 1968), and more recently researchers have continued to investigate interpersonal processes that underlie effective (and ineffective) counseling and psychotherapy. However, relatively little attention has been directed toward the role of social influence processes in either the development or the diagnosis of psychological problems. For many years, psychologists have recognized that social influence processes—those that underlie conformity and socialization, for example—are involved in the development of many psychological problems. However, few efforts have been made to apply specific social psychological formulations to the study of emotional and behavioral problems.

Nor has much attention been paid to social influence processes in diagnosis and assessment. Clinicians' judgments about clients are undoubtedly affected by what they think other people (laypeople or other professionals) believe. A great deal of psychological assessment now occurs in teams of professionals, raising the possibility that one professional's assessment will be biased by other members of the team, either through simple "informational" influence or direct pressure to subscribe to another member's judgment. The effect of social influence processes in such situations is obvious.

Self-Disclosure and Self-Presentation

Despite their close conceptual similarity, the research literatures on self-disclosure and self-presentation have largely remained distinct. Although the relevance of self-presentational perspectives to clinical psychology was recognized in the 1960s (e.g., Braginsky et al., 1969), the area lay fallow for over a decade. More recently, researchers have revisited the idea that some psychological symptoms may reflect people's efforts to manage others' impressions of them in ways that will be personally beneficial (Leary, 1995; Shepperd & Kwavnick, this volume, chapter 9; Snyder, Smith, Augelli, & Ingram, 1985). Self-presentational perspectives have also been applied to understanding socially based forms of anxiety (Leary & Kowalski, 1995; Miller, 1996; Schlenker & Leary, 1982), excuse making (Snyder, Higgins, & Stucky, 1983), and health risk behaviors (Leary, Tchividjian, & Kraxberger, 1994) as well as explicitly clinical topics, such as assessment (e.g., malingering) and the therapeutic encounter (Kelly, McKillop, & Neimeyer, 1991).

Researchers interested in self-disclosure have investigated the consequences of disclosing information about oneself—whether in everyday life or therapy settings—on psychological distress and well-being (Kowalski, this volume, chapter 8; Pennebaker, 1997). The beneficial effects of self-disclosure on mental health depend on a number of factors, including the nature of the disclosure, characteristics of the confidant, and situational constraints.

Interpersonal Relationships

The study of interpersonal relationships became a dominant topic of study in social psychology during the 1980s. At the same time that many researchers became interested in the fundamental processes through which relationships are established, maintained, and terminated, other researchers became interested specifically in dysfunctional relationships—both the factors that contribute to relationship difficulties per se and the ways in which dysfunctional relationships can contribute to problems in living (Bradbury & Fincham, 1991; Miller, this volume, chapter 11). The literature on social support processes is noteworthy in this regard. A great deal of theory and research addresses the relationship between social support and psychological problems (Rhodes & Lakey, this volume, chapter 10; B. R. Sarason, Sarason, & Pierce, 1990).

The reactions of other people to those with psychological problems have also received attention. Psychological problems affect how people respond to the troubled individual, and their reactions have implications for the relationship between the individuals and for the individual's difficulty itself. Coyne's (1976) interactional theory of depression is an excellent example of an approach that examines the effects of psychological problems on interpersonal interactions and relationships (Segrin & Dillard, 1992).

Counselors and psychotherapists have been interested from the beginning in the relationship between therapists and their clients, recognizing that the nature of this relationship is fundamental to the outcome of counseling and psychotherapy (Goldstein, 1971). However, relatively few efforts have been made to examine the therapeutic alliance from the standpoint of social psychological perspectives.

Aggression

Given that hostility and aggression are often clinical problems in their own right, theory and research on the determinants of aggression are quite relevant to counselors and clinicians. Perhaps most notable is work on the interpersonal determinants of sexual aggression. White and Kowalski (1998) proposed an integrative contextual developmental perspective on male violence against women. In addition to historical and sociocultural factors, this model examines the relationship of the social network, dyadic relationships, and situational and interpersonal variables to the psychological processes underlying violence against women (see also Koss et al., 1994).

Prosocial Behavior

Work that deals with helping and other forms of prosocial behavior, although not particularly relevant to social-dysgenic or social-diagnostic processes, does appear relevant to understanding the psychological helping process itself. Specifically, social psychologists have been interested in factors that determine whether people seek help from others and how they react to help that is offered (Wills & DePaulo, 1991). Such work is obviously relevant to the therapeutic relationship, although few efforts have been made to apply it directly.

Group Processes

Perhaps the most glaring omission from the social–clinical interface has been the topic of group processes. Virtually no work investigates how group processes influence the development and maintenance of psychological problems (see, however, Forsyth & Elliott, this volume, chapter 12).

Even more surprising has been the lack of attention to group processes in psychological treatment. Group counseling and psychotherapy have been popular modes of treatment for many years, and much has been written in the clinical literature about them. Yet rarely has the extensive body of social psychological theory and research on group dynamics made its way into these discussions or have social psychologists specifically studied therapeutic groups. If not for the efforts of Forsyth and his colleagues, this territory would remain virtually unexplored (Forsyth, 1990 [chapter 15], 1991).

Personality Processes

During the 1980s, the emerging hybrid area became known as *social–clinical* psychology, due in no small part to the titles of early books (Brehm, 1976; Weary & Mirels, 1982) and the *Journal of Social and Clinical Psychology*. It is interesting to note, however, that much of the work in the area has been neither social nor clinical. Instead, a substantial part of it focuses on personality variables and processes (Snyder, 1997). This work has a decidedly social–psychological orientation, in that the variables of interest involve attributes and processes related to people's social lives (vs. purely intrapsychic constructs), yet this work deals more clearly with cognitive, motivational, and emotional processes within the individual than with the interpersonal events that transpire between people. So, for example, we have clinically relevant research on personality processes, such as ego defense, coping, and affect regulation, and on individual differences, such as attributional style, self-consciousness, and negative affectivity.

We are not ones to draw sharp lines between social and personality psychology. The boundaries between subareas of psychology are somewhat arbitrary, and a complete understanding of virtually any behavioral phenomenon requires attention to both situational and dispositional factors; thus, both social and personality psychology are relevant. Our point is that much of the work that attracts the label of social–clinical psychology involves personality processes and variables and is conducted by behavioral scientists who would identify themselves as personality psychologists rather than social psychologists.[4]

The Self

Three topics involving personality stand out. The self has been a central topic in personality and clinical psychology for many years and has regained respectability within mainline social psychology in the past couple of decades. Recent theory and research on self and identity is truly voluminous, and much of it has clear implications for understanding and treating psychological problems. Influential work on the self includes such topics as self-esteem (particularly the dysfunctional manifestations of ego defense and low self-esteem), self-handicapping, self-efficacy, self-verification, and assorted processes involving self-attention and self-regulation (Dale & Baumeister, this volume, chapter 5; Epstein, 1991; Leary, this volume, chapter 7; Moore, Britt, & Leary, 1997; Swann, 1997).

Emotion

Research on emotion has also become prominent in social–personality psychology and, again, much of it is applicable to clinically relevant phenomena. Researchers have examined fundamental emotional processes as well as specific dysphoric emotions that often bring people to seek profes-

---

[4]Similarly, much of the work at the interface has come from researchers and writers who identify themselves as counseling psychologists rather than clinical psychologists. Their work may be characterized as clinical in a broad, generic sense but not narrowly. Thus, much of what we call social–clinical psychology could just as easily be termed *personality–counseling psychology*.

sional help, such as depression, jealousy, loneliness, social anxiety, and shame (Tangney & Salovey, this volume, chapter 6). In contrast, relatively little attention has been directed toward the role of emotion in counseling and psychotherapy—a surprising state of affairs, given the importance that many clinical theories place on emotional experience and expression in therapy (see Safran & Greenberg, 1991).

Individual Differences

The study of individual differences has always been important in clinical–counseling psychology. However, traditionally, the focus has been on assessing and understanding psychopathological personalities, as measured by standard clinical instruments such as the Minnesota Multiphasic Personality Inventory. The contribution to the interface of individual difference researchers in social–personality psychology has been to highlight personality variables in normal people that predispose them to emotional or behavioral difficulties. Clinically relevant individual differences that have attracted attention in integrative social–clinical research include trait self-esteem, depression, social anxiety, Type A personality, attributional style, defensive pessimism, negative affectivity, interpersonal dependency, narcissism, loneliness, hope, and self-consciousness. With growing awareness that the effectiveness of therapy is moderated by the client's personality, researchers are devoting more attention to individual differences in preferences for and responses to particular therapeutic approaches (Beutler, Clarkin, Crago, & Bergen, 1991).

Summary

Even a cursory glance at Table 1 reveals that many areas of social psychology have been applied to topics involving the development, diagnosis, and treatment of psychological problems. It is important to realize that virtually all of this research has appeared since 1976. From the table, one can also see areas in which cross-fertilization has been less apparent. In particular, despite the importance of assessment and diagnosis to clinical–counseling psychology, the social-diagnostic processes by which practitioners obtain, integrate, and use information to make decisions about clients have received relatively little attention.

WHERE WE ARE, PART II: INTERDISCIPLINARY ISSUES

Despite impressive changes in the social–clinical landscape in recent years, many social and clinical psychologists continue to keep a safe distance from one another's areas of interest and expertise. Like families of in-laws who admit that they ought to get along yet often are cooly indif-ferent or even mildly critical toward one another, social and clinical psy-chologists have tended to have ambivalent feelings about some of their closest professional relatives. Proponents of the social–clinical interface have come to realize that fostering connections between the areas is a considerably more complex matter than simply encouraging social and clin-ical psychologists to read one another's journals and use one another's con-structs in their research. The impediments to the interface run deeper than either simple inertia or a stubborn reluctance to adopt ideas from other fields.

Instead, by virtue of their goals, training, and professional worldviews, social and clinical psychologists differ in several fundamental ways that have made it difficult for them to be completely open to one another's work. The differences between social and clinical psychology have been discussed at length, so we do not reiterate the discussion here (see Forsyth & Leary, 1991, 1997; Leary & Maddux, 1987; and Snyder & Forsyth, 1991c). However, a few points are germane to understanding why the in-terface does not run as deep as many believe that it should.[5]

Theory and Metatheory

Traditionally, social psychologists have explained phenomena by using theories that originated in social psychology, and clinical psychologists have explained phenomena by using theories that have emerged from clin-ical psychology. This insular theoretical approach is quite understandable when one field has not made inroads into a particular topic of interest to the other, but it is more difficult to understand when social and clinical psychologists study the same phenomena. Yet with a few exceptions, social and clinical psychologists have strongly preferred their own theoretical per-spectives. As a case in point, Moore et al. (1997) noted that "although both social and counseling psychologists have devoted a large amount of effort to studying self-processes, only occasionally have researchers from the two disciplines drawn on the others' theories and research" (p. 221).

Several writers have pointed out that social psychologists have been much slower to actively adopt theories and constructs from clinical–counseling psychology than vice versa. By and large, the interface has rep-resented a one-way exchange of information from social psychology to clinical–counseling psychology. One possible reason is the greater inherent

---

[5]We acknowledge that any generalization that compares and contrasts social psychologists with clinical or counseling psychologists is inherently an overgeneralization. Members of each area differ widely among themselves, and some representatives of each area are more like those of the other field than modal members of their own. Nonetheless, we think that certain differences in goals, training, and worldviews can be identified that are relevant to understanding the interface.

difficulty involved in applying theories that focus on dysfunction to the study of "normal" interpersonal processes than the application of knowledge about basic interpersonal processes to the study of dysfunction. This is why we did not attempt to present a companion table to Table 1 that described the areas in clinical psychology that have affected social psychology. Instances in which social psychologists have adopted theoretical perspectives from clinical or counseling psychology for use in their own work are virtually nonexistent.

Granted, social psychologists have begun to investigate many phenomena that have traditionally been the purview of clinical and counseling psychologists, and in that sense, social psychology is far more clinically oriented than it was even a few years ago. Yet this infusion of clinically relevant topics into social psychology is purely a function of social psychologists expanding the range of topics they investigate rather than adopting particular theories and constructs from clinical or counseling psychology. To their credit, social psychologists have become much better about incorporating findings from clinical and counseling psychology in their literature reviews than they were previously. Even so, this is typically in the service of discussing social psychological constructs and theories rather than incorporating clinical or counseling ones.

When bemoaning the shortage of theoretical integrations, we must realize that the problem runs deeper than simple parochialism. Forsyth and Leary (1991, 1997) pointed out that social and clinical psychologists carry with them implicit metatheoretical assumptions about the nature of the phenomena they study that determine how they approach theorizing and research. These differences in metatheory, most of which are rarely articulated or even recognized, predispose them to develop different kinds of theories that emphasize different sorts of processes. In general, for example, social psychologists prefer theories that emphasize situational and interpersonal factors, whereas clinical and counseling psychologists prefer theories that stress dispositional and intrapersonal ones (Forsyth & Leary, 1997). (This is why clinical and counseling psychologists traditionally have favored theories originating in developmental and personality psychology over those in social psychology.) As a result of these preferences, many members of each field simply do not find one another's perspectives particularly useful.

Approaches to Research

Social and clinical psychologists have also differed in their preferred approaches to collecting data. Social psychologists have typically focused on methodological rigor and controlled experimentation, whereas clinical and counseling psychologists have more frequently used field studies and decried the deception so often used by social psychologists. Whereas social psychologists rely on laboratory research that includes as many participants as possible, clinical and counseling psychologists often rely on field investigations with much smaller sample sizes (Snyder & Forsyth, 1991c). As a result of these differences in how social and clinical psychologists typically conduct research, psychologists in each field have viewed the findings of those in the other field with mild suspicion. Clinical and counseling psychologists have often questioned the relevance of highly controlled laboratory experiments for understanding psychological problems and their treatment, and social psychologists have questioned the methodological rigor of inherently "messy" field studies of clinical samples.

Although they may dismiss or criticize one another's ways of conducting research, social and clinical psychologists have nonetheless benefited from one another's methods. The methodological and statistical expertise of the social psychologists has been a valuable resource to practitioners, and clinical researchers' solutions to methodological problems encountered in applied settings have provided social psychologists, who increasingly conduct such research themselves, with useful methodological skills. Furthermore, attempts to increase the interdisciplinary focus of many graduate programs has led to some clinical psychologists receiving their research training from social psychologists and vice versa (Harvey, Omarzu, & Pauwels, this volume, chapter 13; Weary, 1987). Given that the so-called *experimenter's dilemma*—the inherent trade-off between internal and external validity—is a constant one, one tactic would be to have social psychologists and clinical–counseling psychologists jointly investigate phenomena by using both basic and applied methodologies.

Graduate Education

Training in clinical psychology has long operated from the scientist–practitioner model, which advocates "an integrated approach to knowledge that recognizes the interdependence of theory, research, and practice" (Meara et al., 1988, p. 368). Indeed, the original recommendations for graduate training (American Psychological Association, 1947) stated that the education of a clinical psychologist "should be directed to research and professional goals, not to technical goals" (p. 543). Most doctoral programs fulfill the aims of the scientist–practitioner model, at least minimally, in terms of providing students in clinical and counseling psychology both with a basic education in research methods and statistics and with exposure to theory and research across diverse areas of psychology, including social psychology.

However, simply taking a graduate course in social psychology does little to promote the integration of the fields. Without an explicit attempt to show the applications of social psychological principles to understanding, assessing, and treating clinical problems, few clinical students will see the inherent relevance of social psychology to them. So, for example, if a clinical student learns about attributions without examining the role that attributions play in exacerbating problems in dysfunctional relationships, little is gained.

We might take solace in the fact that students in clinical and counseling psychology are at least being exposed to social psychology because the reverse is seldom true. Not only has little theory or research from clinical or counseling psychology found its way into courses in social psychology, but graduate students in social psychology are seldom encouraged (or even permitted) to take courses in the clinical or counseling program. In addition, rarely are students trained to conduct research on social psychological processes that maintain or exacerbate psychological problems.

To address these issues, graduate programs in clinical and counseling psychology should include a broader array of courses related to social psychology, specifically courses that explicitly address clinically relevant theory and research. Similarly, social psychology students should be encouraged to take courses that expose them to topics in psychopathology, assessment, and therapy. In addition, classes that focus specifically on the interface should be offered. Some universities do offer such courses, but they are typically special topics seminars offered only irregularly.

Even more to the point, more integrative interdisciplinary graduate programs should be created. The call for programs in social–clinical psychology extends back 2 decades (Harvey & Weary, 1979) but has met with less success than proponents originally hoped (Harvey et al., 1987, and this volume, chapter 13). However, a few such programs do exist, and although specifically geared toward social or clinical psychology, others allow students to easily move across areas in terms of research.

Professional Contact

Increasing specialization within psychology has accentuated the perceived differences among its subdisciplines. Although social, clinical, and counseling psychologists share a professional identity as psychologists, many have difficulty stepping beyond the traditional boundaries of their fields. With the pressures to publish and to maintain expertise in a particular area, many academicians find themselves tied to the literatures with which they are most familiar. Time constraints frequently do not allow investigations into other related but nonprimary areas. Conferences are typically designed for one area or another, and even those that cater to different kinds of psychologists (e.g., the American Psychological Association's Annual Convention) splinter into factions who attend different sessions and, often, stay in different hotels. For these and other reasons, the two sides of the interface face logistical hurdles to establish and maintain the professional contact that would foster communication between them.

Psychological Practice

In many ways, the bottom line for the interface may be the degree to which the practice of psychology, broadly defined, is enhanced by theory and research from social psychology. It is all well and good to integrate social and clinical psychology in ways that help psychologists better understand emotional and behavioral problems, but we would hope that the knowledge gained through an integrative approach would improve the quality of psychological services, broadly defined, that psychological professionals provide to both well and disturbed individuals. Theoretical discussions regarding the implications of social psychology for clinical practice can take us only so far without efforts to show on a practical level that knowledge and interventions based on social psychological principles enhance counseling and psychotherapy (Snyder & Forsyth, 1991b).

Many practitioners acknowledge that they rarely, if ever, consider research findings in the course of their practices, relying instead on knowledge gained from interactions with clients and colleagues (Cohen, Sargent, & Sechrest, 1986; Maddux, Stoltenberg, Rosenwein, & Leary, 1987; Morrow-Bradley & Elliott, 1986). Part of the reason for this may be that many practicing psychologists fail to see the direct relevance of social psychological research for their work with clients. In many instances, the application of particular social psychological findings to mental health goes unstated in the article and, therefore, unrecognized by practitioners (Ruble, Costanzo, & Higgins, 1992).

But the issue is larger than this. In our view, the goal of applying social psychological research to the practice of psychology seriously misses the point. To suggest that practicing psychologists should consider the findings of particular studies as they conduct counseling and psychotherapy is to misconstrue the purpose of this research. The reason that psychologists conduct basic research is to test the viability of hypotheses—in the case of clinically relevant research, hypotheses regarding the development and maintenance of psychological problems or approaches to their treatment. If the results of accumulated studies lend support to a particular theory, hypothesis, or conceptualization, then that conceptualization—not the empirical studies themselves—should be what is of interest to the practicing psychologist. To insist that practicing psychologists read articles that describe basic social psychological studies and apply the results of those studies to their practice is not only unrealistic but also fundamentally misguided.

CONCLUSIONS

Those who believe that there should be extensive cross-fertilization between social and clinical–counseling psychology likely conclude that the interface remains in its infancy and that great strides need to be made before we can talk about a true interface between the fields. However, those who conceptualize the interface as a sharing of ideas and a respect for the work of other researchers and practitioners see the interface as relatively well developed if not mature.[6]

Our view falls somewhere in between. Social psychology and clinical psychology have had a pronounced effect on one another in recent years —an effect that has been far greater than any of the pioneers of the 1960s might have foreseen. Their cross-fertilization has been a healthy development for both fields and perhaps for the science and practice of psychology more generally. Social psychologists have markedly enhanced the quality and scope of their theories by broadening their attention to the social psychological processes that underlie emotional and behavioral problems. Likewise, clinical and counseling psychologists have broadened their horizons, both by developing a greater appreciation of the effects of interpersonal factors on dysfunctional behavior and by occasionally using theories and research that originated in social psychology.

In the process, we have all seen that the lines that divide the psychological specializations are arbitrary and that venturing beyond one's own traditional territory provides fresh perspectives that inform one's own work. Not only are ideas shared across the backyard fence, but the conversations generate entirely new perspectives that could not have come about without the contributions of experts with differing goals, interests, and areas of expertise.

REFERENCES

Abramson, L. Y. (1988). *Social cognition and clinical psychology: A synthesis.* New York: Guilford.

Abramson, L. Y., Seligman, M. E. P., & Teasdale, J. D. (1978). Learned helplessness in humans: Critique and reformulation. *Journal of Abnormal Psychology, 87,* 49–74.

American Psychological Association. (1947). Recommended graduate training program in clinical psychology. *American Psychologist, 2,* 539–558.

Beutler, L. E., Clarkin, J., Crago, M., & Bergen, J. (1991). Client–therapist matching. In C. R. Snyder & D. R. Forsyth (Eds.), *Handbook of social and clinical psychology: The health perspective* (pp. 699–716). New York: Pergamon.

---

[6]We concur with other writers who have suggested that the interface of social and clinical–counseling psychology is stronger, deeper, and more developed than is readily apparent on the surface (Harvey & Weary, 1991; Snyder, 1988; Snyder & Forsyth, 1991c). Many researchers and practitioners are actively involved with the interface but unaware that they are. In addition, among those who are aware of the interdisciplinary approach of their work, many are reluctant to openly flaunt such cross-fertilization for fear of being viewed as operating on the periphery of their own subspeciality.

Bradbury, T. N., & Fincham, F. D. (1991). Clinical and social perspectives on close relationships. In C. R. Snyder & D. R. Forsyth (Eds.), *Handbook of social and clinical psychology: The health perspective* (pp. 309–326). New York: Pergamon.

Braginsky, B., & Braginsky, D. (1967). Schizophrenic patients in the psychiatric interview: An experimental study of their effectiveness at manipulation. *Journal of Consulting Psychology, 30,* 295–300.

Braginsky, B., Braginsky, D., & Ring, K. (1969). *Methods of madness: The mental hospital as a last resort.* New York: Holt, Rinehart, & Winston.

Brehm, S. (1976). *The application of social psychology to clinical practice.* Washington, DC: Hemisphere.

Brehm, S. S. (1991). On winning battles and losing wars. In C. R. Snyder & D. R. Forsyth (Eds.), *Handbook of social and clinical psychology: The health perspective* (p. 800). New York: Pergamon.

Brehm, S. S., & Smith, T. W. (1982). The application of social psychology to clinical practice: A range of possibilities. In G. Weary & H. L. Mirels (Eds.), *Integrations of clinical and social psychology* (pp. 9–24). New York: Oxford University Press.

Cacioppo, J. T., Claiborn, C. D., Petty, R. E., & Heesacker, M. (1991). General framework for the study of attitude change in psychotherapy. In C. R. Snyder & D. R. Forsyth (Eds.), *Handbook of social and clinical psychology: The health perspective* (pp. 523–539). New York: Pergamon.

Cantor, N. (1982). "Everyday" versus normative models of clinical and social judgment. In G. Weary & H. L. Mirels (Eds.), *Integrations of clinical and social psychology* (pp. 27–47). New York: Oxford University Press.

Carson, R. C. (1969). *Interaction concepts of personality.* Chicago: Aldine.

Cartwright, D. (1979). Contemporary social psychology in historical perspective. *Social Psychology Quarterly, 42,* 82–93.

Cohen, L. H., Sargent, M. M., & Sechrest, L. B. (1986). Use of psychotherapy research by professional psychologists. *American Psychologist, 41,* 198–206.

Conklin, M. P., & O'Connor, B. P. (1995). Beliefs about the fetus as a moderator of post-abortion psychological well-being. *Journal of Social and Clinical Psychology, 14,* 76–95.

Coyne, J. C. (1976). Toward an interactional theory of depression. *Psychiatry, 39,* 28–40.

Elms, A. C. (1975). The crisis of confidence in social psychology. *American Psychologist, 30,* 967–976.

Epstein, S. (1991). Cognitive-experiential self-theory: An integrative theory of personality. In R. C. Curtis (Ed.), *The relational self: Theoretical convergences in psychoanalysis and social psychology* (pp. 111–137). New York: Guilford.

Fontana, A. F., & Gessner, T. (1969). Patients' goals and the manifestation of psychopathology. *Journal of Consulting and Clinical Psychology, 33,* 247–253.

Fontana, A. F., & Klein, E. B. (1968). Self-presentation and the schizophrenic "deficit." *Journal of Consulting and Clinical Psychology, 32,* 110–119.

Forsyth, D. R. (1990). *Group dynamics* (2nd ed.). Belmont, CA: Brooks/Cole.

Forsyth, D. R. (1991). Change in therapeutic groups. In C. R. Snyder & D. R. Forsyth (Eds.), *Handbook of social and clinical psychology: The health perspective* (pp. 664–680). New York: Pergamon.

Forsyth, D. R., & Leary, M. R. (1991). Metatheoretical and epistemological issues. In C. R. Snyder & D. R. Forsyth (Eds.), *Handbook of social and clinical psychology: The health perspective* (pp. 757–773). New York: Pergamon.

Forsyth, D. R., & Leary, M. R. (1997). Achieving the goals of the scientist–practitioner model: The seven interfaces of social and counseling psychology. *The Counseling Psychologist, 25*, 180–200.

Forsyth, D. R., & Strong, S. R. (1986). The scientific study of counseling and psychotherapy: A unificationist view. *American Psychologist, 41*, 113–119.

Frank, J. D. (1961). *Persuasion and healing*. New York: Schocken Books.

Goldstein, A. P. (1966). Psychotherapy research by extrapolation from social psychology. *Journal of Counseling Psychology, 13*, 38–45.

Goldstein, A. P. (1971). *Psychotherapeutic attraction*. New York: Pergamon Press.

Goldstein, A. P., Heller, K., & Sechrest, L. B. (1966). *Psychotherapy and the psychology of behavior change*. New York: Wiley.

Harari, H. (1983). Social psychology of clinical practice and in clinical practice. *Journal of Social and Clinical Psychology, 1*, 173–192.

Harvey, J. H. (1983). The founding of the *Journal of Social and Clinical Psychology*. *Journal of Social and Clinical Psychology, 1*, 1–3.

Harvey, J. H., Bratt, A., & Lennox, R. D. (1987). The maturing interface of social–clinical–counseling psychology. *Journal of Social and Clinical Psychology, 5*, 8–20.

Harvey, J. H., & Weary, G. (1979). The integration of social and clinical psychology training programs. *Personality and Social Psychology Bulletin, 5*, 511–515.

Harvey, J. H., & Weary, G. (1991). Foreword: Maturing of an interface. In C. R. Snyder & D. R. Forsyth (Eds.), *Handbook of social and clinical psychology: The health perspective* (pp. xvii–xxii). New York: Pergamon.

Hendrick, C. (1983). Clinical social psychology: A birthright reclaimed. *Journal of Social and Clinical Psychology, 1*, 66–77.

Hill, M. G., & Weary, G. (1983). Perspectives on the *Journal of Abnormal and Social Psychology*: How it began and how it was transformed. *Journal of Social and Clinical Psychology, 1*, 4–14.

Hovland, J., Janis, I. L., & Kelley, H. H. (1953). *Communication and persuasion: Psychological studies of opinion change*. New Haven, CT: Yale University Press.

Kayne, N. T., & Alloy, L. B. (1988). Clinician and patient as aberrant actuaries: Expectation-based distortion in assessment of covariation. In L. Y. Abramson (Ed.), *Social cognition and clinical psychology: A synthesis* (pp. 295–365). New York: Guilford.

Kelly, A. E., McKillop, K. J., & Neimeyer, G. J. (1991). Effects of counselor as audience on internalization of depressed and nondepressed self-presentations. *Journal of Counseling Psychology, 38,* 126–132.

Koss, M. P., Goodman, L. A., Browne, A., Fitzgerald, L. F., Keita, G. P., & Russo, N. F. (1994). *No safe haven: Male violence against women at home, at work, and in the community.* Washington, DC: American Psychological Association.

Langer, E. J. (1982). The value of a social psychological approach to clinical issues. In G. Weary & H. L. Mirels (Eds.), *Integrations of clinical and social psychology* (pp. 3–5). New York: Oxford University Press.

Leary, M. R. (1987). The three faces of social–clinical–counseling psychology. *Journal of Social and Clinical Psychology, 5,* 168–175.

Leary, M. R. (1995). *Self-presentation: Impression management and interpersonal behavior.* Boulder, CO: Westview.

Leary, M. R., Jenkins, T. B., & Shepperd, J. A. (1984). The growth of interest in clinically-relevant research in social psychology. *Journal of Social and Clinical Psychology, 2,* 333–338.

Leary, M. R., & Kowalski, R. M. (1995). *Social anxiety.* New York: Guilford.

Leary, M. R., & Maddux, J. E. (1987). Progress toward a viable interface between social and clinical–counseling psychology. *American Psychologist, 42,* 904–911.

Leary, M. R., & Miller, R. S. (1986). *Social psychology and dysfunctional behavior.* New York: Springer-Verlag.

Leary, M. R., Tchividjian, L. R., & Kraxberger, B. E. (1994). Self-presentation can be hazardous to your health. *Health Psychology, 13,* 461–470.

Maddux, J. E. (1987). The interface of social, clinical, and counseling psychology: Why bother and what is it anyway? *Journal of Social and Clinical Psychology, 5,* 27–33.

Maddux, J. E., Stoltenberg, C. D., & Rosenwein, R. (Eds.). (1987). *Social processes in clinical and counseling psychology.* New York: Springer-Verlag.

Maddux, J. E., Stoltenberg, C. D., Rosenwein, R., & Leary, M. R. (1987). Social processes in clinical and counseling psychology: Introduction and orienting assumptions. In J. E. Maddux, C. D. Stoltenberg, & R. Rosenwein (Eds.), *Social processes in clinical and counseling psychology* (pp. 1–13). New York: Springer-Verlag.

Meara, N., Schmidt, L. D., Carrington, C. H., Davis, K. L., Dixon, D. N., Fretz, B. R., Myers, R. A., Pidley, C. R., & Suinn, R. M. (1988). Training and accreditation in counseling psychology. *The Counseling Psychologist, 16,* 366–384.

Meyerowitz, B. E., Burish, T. G., & Wallston, K. A. (1986). Health psychology: A tradition of integration of clinical and social psychology. *Journal of Social and Clinical Psychology, 4,* 375–392.

Miller, R. S. (1996). *Embarrassment: Poise and peril in everyday life.* New York: Guilford.

Moore, M. A., Britt, T. W., & Leary, M. R. (1997). Integrating social and counseling psychological perspectives on the self. *The Counseling Psychologist, 25*, 220–239.

Morrow-Bradley, C., & Elliott, R. (1986). Utilization of psychotherapy research by practicing psychotherapists. *American Psychologist, 41*, 188–197.

Murdock, N. L., & Altmaier, E. M. (1991). Attribution-based treatments. In C. R. Snyder & D. R. Forsyth (Eds.), *Handbook of social and clinical psychology: The health perspective* (pp. 563–578). New York: Pergamon.

Pennebaker, J. W. (1997). *Opening up*. New York: Guilford.

Rabinowitz, V. C., Zevon, M. A., & Karuza, J., Jr. (1988). Psychotherapy as helping: An attributional analysis. In L. Y. Abramson (Ed.), *Social cognition and clinical psychology: A synthesis* (pp. 177–203). New York: Guilford.

Raimy, V. C. (1950). *Training in clinical psychology*. New York: Prentice-Hall.

Ruble, D. N., Costanzo, P. R., & Higgins, T. (1992). Social psychological foundations of mental health. In D. N. Ruble, P. A. Costanzo, & M. E. Oliveri (Eds.), *The social psychology of mental health* (pp. 1–23). New York: Guilford.

Safran, J. D., & Greenberg, L. S. (Eds.). (1991). *Emotion, psychotherapy, and change*. New York: Guilford.

Salovey, P., & Turk, D. C. (1991). Clinical judgment and decision making. In C. R. Snyder & D. R. Forsyth (Eds.), *Handbook of social and clinical psychology: The health perspective* (pp. 416–437). New York: Pergamon.

Sarason, B. R., Sarason, I., & Pierce, G. R. (Eds.). (1990). *Social support: An interactional view*. New York: Wiley.

Sarason, S. B. (1981a). An asocial psychology and a misdirected clinical psychology. *American Psychologist, 36*, 827–836.

Sarason, S. B. (1981b). *Psychology misdirected*. New York: Free Press.

Schlenker, B. R., & Leary, M. R. (1982). Social anxiety and self-presentation: A conceptualization and model. *Psychological Bulletin, 92*, 641–669.

Segrin, C., & Dillard, J. P. (1992). The interactional theory of depression: A meta-analysis of the research literature. *Journal of Social and Clinical Psychology, 11*, 43–70.

Snyder, C. R. (1988). On being where you already are: An invitation to the social/clinical/counseling interface. *Journal of Social and Clinical Psychology, 6*, i–ii.

Snyder, C. R. (1997). State of the interface between clinical and social psychology. *Journal of Social and Clinical Psychology, 16*, 231–242.

Snyder, C. R., & Ford, C. E. (Eds.). (1987). *Coping with negative events: Clinical and social psychological perspectives*. New York: Plenum.

Snyder, C. R., & Forsyth, D. R. (Eds.). (1991a). *Handbook of social and clinical psychology: The health perspective*. New York: Pergamon.

Snyder, C. R., & Forsyth, D. R. (1991b). The interface toward the year 2000. In C. R. Snyder & D. R. Forsyth (Eds.), *Handbook of social and clinical psychology: The health perspective* (pp. 788–806). New York: Pergamon.

Snyder, C. R., & Forsyth, D. R. (1991c). Social and clinical psychology united.

In C. R. Snyder & D. R. Forsyth (Eds.), *Handbook of social and clinical psychology: The health perspective* (pp. 3–17). New York: Pergamon.

Snyder, C. R., Higgins, R. L., & Stucky, R. J. (1983). *Excuses: Masquerades in search of grace*. New York: Wiley.

Snyder, C. R., Smith, T. W., Augelli, R. W., & Ingram, R. E. (1985). On the self-serving function of social anxiety: Shyness as a self-handicapping strategy. *Journal of Personality and Social Psychology, 48*, 970–980.

Strong, S. R. (1968). Counseling: An interpersonal influence process. *Journal of Counseling Psychology, 15*, 215–224.

Strong, S. R., Welsh, J. A., Corcoran, J. L., & Hoyt, W. T. (1992). Social psychology and counseling psychology: The history, products, and promise of an interface. *Journal of Counseling Psychology, 39*, 139–157.

Swann, W. B., Jr. (1997). The trouble with change: Self-verification and allegiance to self. *Psychological Science, 8*, 177–180.

Valins, S., & Nisbett, R. E. (1972). Attribution processes in the development and treatment of emotional disorders. In E. E. Jones, D. E. Kanouse, H. H. Kelley, R. E. Nisbitt, S. Valins, & B. Weiner (Eds.), *Attribution: Perceiving the causes of behavior* (pp. 137–150). Morristown, NJ: General Learning Press.

Weary, G. (1987). Natural bridges: The interface of social and clinical psychology. *Journal of Social and Clinical Psychology, 5*, 160–167.

Weary, G., & Mirels, H. L. (Eds.). (1982). *Integrations of clinical and social psychology*. New York: Oxford University Press.

Weary, G., Mirels, H. L., & Jordan, J. S. (1982). The integration of clinical and social psychology: Current status and future directions. In G. Weary & H. L. Mirels (Eds.), *Integrations of clinical and social psychology* (pp. 297–302). New York: Oxford University Press.

White, J. G., & Kowalski, R. M. (1998). Male violence toward women: An integrated perspective. In R. G. Geen & E. Donnerstein (Eds.), *Human aggression: Theories, research, and implications for social policy* (pp. 203–209). San Diego, CA: Academic Press.

Wills, T. A., & DePaulo, B. M. (1991). Interpersonal analysis of the help-seeking process. In C. R. Snyder & D. R. Forsyth (Eds.), *Handbook of social and clinical psychology: The health perspective* (pp. 350–375). New York: Pergamon.

I

SOCIAL–COGNITIVE
PROCESSES

2

ATTRIBUTIONAL PROCESSES: AN INTEGRATION OF SOCIAL AND CLINICAL PSYCHOLOGY

DEBORA BELL-DOLAN AND CRAIG A. ANDERSON

"Why did Dad yell at me?"
"Why did you push your sister?"
"Why did the boss not promote me?"

Understanding causality seems central to human experience (Weiner, 1986). *Why* is there such focus on "why"? Psychologists and philosophers of science (e.g., Hempel, 1966) have long addressed this question and have contended that the interest in causality serves a number of functions for people, lay citizens and scientists alike, including increasing people's mastery and control over the environment and satisfying their desire to understand the world around them. Causal explanations can be generated for virtually any event of interest (e.g., why do the hydrogen and oxygen atoms in a molecule of water bind so strongly?). More specifically, however, attributions refer to causal statements made by "ordinary" individuals (noting that even scientists, in the conduct of their daily lives, can be considered ordinary!) about events involving humans. Although we believe that the same basic psychological processes are involved in all types of explanations, attributions are particularly important in understanding human behavior and a wide range of clinical phenomena. Thus, we focus our examples and discussions on this more limited type of explanation.

Psychologists have taken a keen interest in attributions. In fact, several empirically supported theories outline the relationship of people's attributions to their thoughts, feelings, and behavior. Attribution theories (e.g., E. E. Jones & Davis, 1965; Kelley, 1967, 1973; Weiner, 1986) have emphasized the types of causal explanations that people make, the processes by which they make them, and the impact of specific attributions on subsequent cognitive, affective, and behavioral functioning. One goal of this chapter is to summarize the literature on attributional processes. However, an exhaustive review of the literature would be redundant with the many excellent reviews already in existence (see, e.g., Anderson, Krull, & Weiner, 1996; and Kelley & Michela, 1980). Thus, a more central goal is to examine the contributions that both social psychology and clinical psychology have made to attribution research and the implications of this area of research for social and clinical practice. The attribution literature provides a useful illustration of the interface between social and clinical psychology, as attribution processes are relevant to the concerns of both areas; understanding attribution processes allows social psychologists to better understand phenomena such as interpersonal attraction, aggression, and self-handicapping and allows clinical psychologists to explain and intervene more effectively with problems such as depression, shyness, and marital discord.

To meet the goals of this chapter, we first provide a brief overview of basic attribution theory, focusing on the current thinking about the "what" and "how" of attributions. Second, we discuss why attribution theory is important, focusing on the consequences of attributional processes and products that individuals face in their daily lives. These consequences are considered on two levels. *Proximal* (or immediate) *consequences* refer to the momentary, often immediate, and short-term effects that making a specific attribution can have on a person's thoughts, feelings, and behavior. *Distal*, or longer term, *consequences* refer to the ways in which making certain types of attributions repeatedly over time may be related to a person's long-term adjustment. Finally, we discuss implications of the existing research and possible future directions.

THE "WHAT" OF ATTRIBUTIONS

Understanding the structural characteristics of attributions provides the foundation for then understanding the process and the function, or consequences, of making attributions. Thus, we first describe several relevant characteristics of attributions, including the personal and situational characteristics on which attributions may be based and the dimensions on which they can vary.

Defining a Common Mental Process

Attributions can be defined as the causal explanations that people offer about a variety of intrapersonal and interpersonal events in their lives. For example, if Sam learns that Jack has become unemployed, Sam may come up with the explanation that Jack is lazy. On what is this attribution (and other attributions) based? People's personal explanations are based on a set of general personal beliefs or principles, such as "only lazy people are unemployed in a booming economy," as well as an assessment of the specific circumstances (e.g., "the economy is currently booming"). Of note is that the accuracy of these principles is irrelevant to the process of making attributions. Sam's attribution is a logical extension of his principles, and the attribution will guide his attitudes and actions toward Jack, regardless of "truth" or accuracy.

Thus, to make an explanation or attribution, the person must identify the relevant general principles and specific circumstances. This identification is sometimes specified explicitly, to an audience, and sometimes only implicitly, to oneself. In making an attribution statement, some of the principles and circumstances are frequently left implicit, on the assumption that the audience will understand what is meant without explicit reference to it. For example, in explaining why he robbed banks, Willie Sutton reputedly replied "because that is where the money is." This attribution for his bank-robbing behavior implicitly assumes a host of general principles and particular circumstances. It assumes that the audience believes that acquiring money is a basic motive guiding the behavior of many individuals, that Sutton had this goal, and so on.

Another factor to keep in mind is that attributions can range from being highly automatic to being the result of controlled, careful, logical thought. For example, some attributions are generated so rapidly, automatically, and without awareness that some researchers prefer to think of them as being part of the perceptual process rather than the attribution process (e.g., Erickson & Krull, 1994). First impressions often have this automatic character. At the other end of this dimension are attributions that take much time, effort, and explicit gathering and processing of information, such as jury members' attributions in murder trials.

Dimensions of Attributions

Causal attributions can vary on a number of dimensions. Although the exact number of relevant dimensions is still a subject of debate, at least three valid dimensions, and perhaps as many as five, have been identified (Anderson & Weiner, 1992; Weiner, 1985, 1986). Probably the most researched dimension is that of *locus* (e.g., Rotter, 1966). Events can be ascribed to causes that are internal (e.g., "I hit my sister because I was angry") or external (e.g., "I hit my sister because she was being mean) to the actor. Attribution locus is tied to several emotional and behavioral adjustment outcomes (Holtzworth-Munroe, 1992; Moore & Schultz, 1983; Silverman & Peterson, 1993). For example, depression and loneliness is associated with making internal attributions for negative events (e.g., failing an examination) but external attributions for positive events (e.g., getting a job). Aggression is associated with making a particular kind of external attribution for a perceived injury (e.g., "He did that on purpose!"). *Stability* of causes can also vary, ranging from causes that would be expected to fluctuate over time, such as luck (e.g., being in the right place at the right time), to causes that show temporal consistency (e.g., intelligence or ability). Stability of attributions is related to expectations of success and achievement motivation (Weiner, 1986). *Controllability* refers to an individual's determination of whether the actor could have behaved differently. Controllability encompasses attributions of blame and is associated with emotions such as guilt and shame (Weiner, 1986). In addition to these three dimensions, some researchers have also advanced globality (i.e., how consistent across situations a causal factor is expected to be; Abramson, Seligman, & Teasdale, 1978) and intentionality (i.e., whether the actor's behavior was purposeful; Weiner, 1986) as meaningful attribution dimensions. These causal dimensions have been used successfully to predict cognitive, emotional, and behavioral functioning in a wide variety of domains. We provide specific examples later in this chapter.

THE "HOW" OF ATTRIBUTIONS: THE ATTRIBUTION PROCESS MODEL

The attribution model we present has been described in more detail by Anderson et al. (1996). This model is based on work by many attribution and social inference scholars, including work by Cheng and Novick (1990), Gilbert (1989), Hilton, Mathes, and Trabasso (1992), Krull and Erickson (1995), Trope (1986), Uleman (1987), and Weiner (1985). The specific details of the various current attribution models differ, of course, but these differences are relatively unimportant to the understanding and treatment of clinical problems that involve maladaptive attributions.

Figure 1 shows our model of the attribution process. As indicated in Figure 1, some event must first occur for this process to be activated. It may be a personal failure of some kind (e.g., a fight with one's spouse), a brief conversation with a stranger, or an opening statement in a trial.

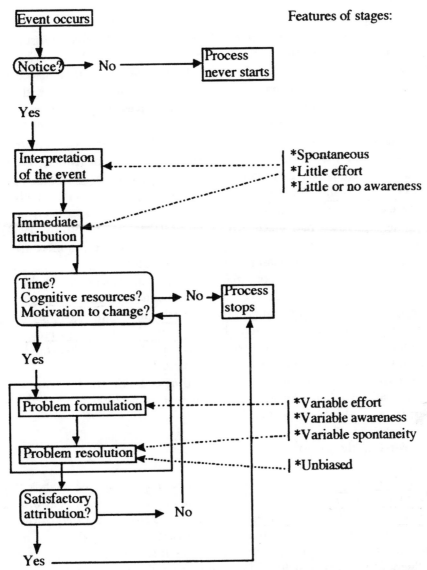

Figure 1. The attribution process. From "Explanations: Processes and Consequences," by C. A. Anderson, D. S. Krull, and B. Weiner, 1996, in E. T. Higgins and A. W. Kruglanski (Eds.), *Social Psychology: Handbook of Basic Principles* (p. 274), New York: Guilford Press. Copyright 1996 by Guilford Press. Adapted with permission.

Noticing the Event

The event must be *noticed* for the attribution process to start. Many factors influence the noticeability of an event, such as its loudness or brightness (James, 1890; see also Fiske & Taylor, 1991 [chapter 7]). A silent, unmarked police car is much less likely to attract attention than a marked police car with a screeching siren and flashing lights. The characteristics of the person also play a role. Arthur Conan Doyle's character Sherlock Holmes trained himself to notice details (or their absence) that other perceivers would overlook. Clinical training similarly includes teaching future therapists to notice certain types of details in clients' lives or interactions.

In addition, the importance of the event to the perceiver will influence its noticeability. For instance, hearing one's name may capture attention when said loudly, but less self-relevant stimuli do not (Moray, 1959). Finally, the temporary or chronic activation of particular cognitive categories may influence the noticeability of an event. For example, perceivers more easily recognize success- or failure-related words, respectively, after learning that they had succeeded or failed (Postman & Brown, 1952). Similarly, a police officer (or the spouse of a police officer) is more likely to notice a distant siren than is the average citizen.

The noticeability of potential causes also influences the likelihood that they will be adopted as attributions of events. Stimuli that are particularly novel, visually dominant, unusual, or relevant to one's goals are more likely to be assigned a causal role than less attention-grabbing stimuli. For instance, perceivers tend to attribute causality to actors who stand out visually against a relatively pallid background (McArthur & Post, 1977), who have red hair or a leg brace (McArthur & Solomon, 1978), or who are visually dominant by virtue of their seating position relative to the perceiver (Taylor & Fiske, 1975).

Interpreting the Event

After perceivers notice an event, they must decide what it is that they have noticed. Perception is not a pure encoding of reality but instead a construction by the perceiver (e.g., Neisser, 1976). People frequently fail to appreciate that others do not perceive events in exactly the same manner that they do. Of course, the perceiver's interpretation of an event is influenced by the event itself, but the perceiver's prior mental state (e.g., expectations) also plays an important role.

People often see what they expect to see, but they do not recognize this influence on their own perceptions. Most importantly, social and personal events have an element of ambiguity and so can be interpreted in more than one way. Ambiguous events are likely to be interpreted in terms of the more accessible cognitive category (e.g., Higgins, 1996). Thus, perceivers may be more likely to interpret a shove as hostile if the actor is Black rather than White (Sagar & Schofield, 1980), a facial expression as fear if it occurs in the presence of a cobra (E. E. Jones, 1990), and a guest lecturer as "warm" if he or she has previously been described as such (Kelley, 1950).

Immediate Attribution

As noted earlier, some attributions are made quickly and automatically. These immediate attributions tend to be spontaneous, requiring little effort and little or no awareness. Some of these immediate attributions appear to be based on three perceptual cues. First, perceivers use temporal order. If a perceiver sees one boxer throw a punch and the other dodge it, the perceiver may automatically infer that the thrown punch was the cause of the dodge. In an extended interpersonal interaction, the sequence of cause and effect is less apparent and is influenced by additional factors such as perspective. For instance, perceivers tend to see their own behavior as responses to others' actions rather than viewing others' behavior as reactions to their own actions (Swann, Pelham, & Roberts, 1987). Second, perceivers use temporal and spatial contiguity cues. For example, people are more likely to explain a friend's elation by a current potential explanation than by one from the distant past (Zebrowitz, 1990). Third, perceivers use similarity cues. Events are frequently attributed to causes that are similar in some way. For instance, people tend to think that "big" events require "big" causes (Taylor, 1982). Thus, a person may be less likely to attribute uncontrollable crying and major depressive feelings to minor daily hassles than to the death of a loved one, even though major events are frequently caused by seemingly small causes. The power of similarity cues can also be seen in various prescientific medical theories in which a remedy resembles an illness (e.g., red stones stop bleeding, yellow substances cure jaundice) and in the psychodynamic practitioners' use of resemblance criteria in inferring associative links among elements in their patients' dream and waking lives (Frazer, 1959; Nisbett & Ross, 1980). However, even Freud is reputed to have warned fellow analysts about the overuse of similarity criteria by noting that "sometimes a cigar is just a cigar."

In addition to perceptual cues, immediate attributions may result from an individual's personal beliefs or *social theories* being applied to the event (e.g., Fiske & Taylor, 1991 [chapter 4]). In the simplest and perhaps most automatic type of social-theory-based explanation, the explanation is simply drawn from prior knowledge about why the target event occurs. Thus, when people learn that a valuable racehorse was found dead, the possibility of foul play may immediately pop into their head because of previous foul-play cases (Abelson & Lalljee, 1988). In a more clinical context, when some depressed individuals with low self-esteem receive failure feedback, they tend to automatically think about their personal shortcomings. It is interesting to note that people from different cultures or subcultures may have different intuitive social theories about the causes of certain types of outcomes and that these knowledge structure differences may produce different immediate attributions for an observed event. For instance, perceivers in independent cultures (e.g., United States, England) may immediately attribute events to the person rather than to situational forces because their social theories suggest the importance of personal characteristics in explaining behavior (Dill, Erickson, & Krull, 1994). Perceivers from interdependent cultures (e.g., India, China, Africa, Latin America) may immediately make situational (or group) attributions because their social theories emphasize the importance of situational and group context (e.g., Fletcher & Ward, 1988; J. G. Miller, 1984; Shweder & Bourne, 1982; see also the work on implicit theories by Dweck, Hong, & Chiu, 1993).

After the immediate attribution is made, several process constraints come into play, as shown in Figure 1. If there are enough time, cognitive resources, and motivation to further examine the event, then a more effortful explanation process is started; otherwise, the attribution process stops and the perceiver uses the immediate attribution.

Problem-Based Attribution

In many cases people have the time, cognitive resources, and motivation to further examine the event being explained. This leads to a more resource-intensive *problem-based attribution process*. Figure 1 depicts this as consisting of two discrete stages: problem formulation and problem resolution (see also Anderson, 1983).[1] For instance, most people who experience serious marital difficulties spend considerable time and effort trying to understand the causes of those difficulties. The first step in such complex problem-based explanations is to formulate the problem.

Problem Formulation

This step involves gathering information about the to-be-explained event from many different sources. Problem formulation is controlled by a guiding knowledge structure (Anderson, 1983; Anderson & Slusher, 1986; see also Abelson & Lalljee, 1988; Read & Miller, 1993), a type of schema that contains information about the type of event, possible attributions for the event, the type of information needed to assess these possible attributions, and the likely effects or implications of these attributions. The additional information may come from memory, from a directed search in the immediate environment, and from more effortful search procedures such as asking other people or going to the library.

Many guiding knowledge structures might be applied to a given event. Chronic person factors and acute situational factors influence which one is selected. For example, one chronic characteristic of highly aggressive

---

[1]Figure 1 shows a sequential process with the capability of recycling multiple times. An alternative formulation might involve a more complex set of parallel processes. We have no preference for one or the other, and there are presently no data distinguishing between the two. We present the sequential version because of its simplicity.

people is their readiness to perceive more "aggression" in the behavior of others than there really is (Dill, Anderson, Anderson, & Deuser, 1997; Dodge, 1985). Similarly, certain situational cues, such as being punched in the face, demand an aggressive interpretation. The most accessible guiding knowledge structure that meets some criterion of fit is most likely considered first. This is how individual differences in formulation of the same event come about. The goals of the perceiver also influence which guiding knowledge structure is used. Sometimes the goal is accuracy, but other goals are also common. For instance, sometimes people tire of the attribution process and become more interested in reaching an explanation quickly—they want to be free of the attribution task and are not particularly concerned about the accuracy of their explanation. At other times, people may have an impression management goal—certain attributions may create or maintain a desired impression (for self or others) better than other attributions (see Kruglanski's, 1989, discussions of the need for closure and the need for specific closure).

Even though the problem formulation process is complex and resource intensive, much of it takes place at automatic levels that are not conscious to the perceiver. For this reason, it is valuable to have people with different perspectives contribute to the same attribution generation process, be it clinical or judicial. People with different perspectives have disparate biases (i.e., accessible knowledge structures) and thus provide a better reality check than any single individual can accomplish.

Problem Resolution

This step involves integrating the various pieces of information collected during problem formulation into a "best" attribution. A match is sought between the attribution possibilities brought to mind in the problem formulation stage and the relevant information also brought to mind during that stage. The attribution with the best match is tentatively adopted (see L. C. Miller & Read, 1991, and Read & Miller, 1993, for a description of how such a matching process probably operates).

Evaluation of Satisfaction

At least one additional judgment is then made (this judgment could be construed as a part of problem resolution, but for clarity we discuss it separately). The perceiver must decide whether the best attribution is satisfying enough. If the attribution is not satisfactory, either because none of the causal candidates generated in problem resolution sufficiently fits the information or because other goals for the explanation are not met, the perceiver cycles back to the process constraints question and reassesses his or her motivation and ability to consider the event further. If time, resources, and the need to come up with a better explanation are sufficient, then a new formulation of the problem is attempted. This may result in different causal candidates being considered and new relevant information being recruited from memory or gathered from other sources. Alternatively, the explainer may simply execute the process again with relaxed standards (Abelson & Lalljee, 1988). In either case, the problem resolution process is engaged once again, and the resulting best match undergoes the satisfaction test. Eventually, either the explainer arrives at a satisfactory attribution or constraints stop the process and the event remains unexplained beyond the immediate attribution.

Motivational Influences

Motivational variables obviously influence the attributions that people generate, although not necessarily in the simple ways proposed in the early days of attribution work. We believe that motivational factors are important at each step, except problem resolution. In our view, motivationally relevant variables (e.g., need states, goals) frequently have their impact through purely cognitive processes. For instance, at the noticing step, the ego relevance of impinging stimuli influences the perceptual readiness (i.e., accessibility) to receive these stimuli.

The immediate attribution is strongly influenced by the currently accessible knowledge structures, but what is currently accessible depends on many factors and includes variables traditionally thought of as motivational. Thus, prejudice against a particular racial group will influence which knowledge structures are accessible when a person is in a mixed-race bar; an unintentional bump by a member of a disliked racial group may be interpreted as an intentional personal affront (e.g., Duncan, 1976; Sagar & Schofield, 1980; see also Dodge & Crick, 1990).

Motivational variables can also influence the selection of guiding knowledge structures and relevant information in the problem formulation stage. For instance, ego-involvement manipulations influence what kind of information is seen as relevant (Anderson & Slusher, 1986). Once the information set judged to be relevant by a perceiver is properly specified, then the generated attribution (at problem resolution) reflects that information (see also Eisen, 1979; Novick, Fratianne, & Cheng, 1992; and Rusbult & Medlin, 1982).

At the two choice points (constraints and satisfaction), motivational variables essentially turn the attribution process on or off. At both of these steps, motivational variables influence the decision concerning whether a new attribution is needed. If there is no motivation to change the current state of knowledge about the event, then the process stops (see Kruglanski, 1989).

To summarize, attributions are people's causal explanations for human-relevant events. Although these explanations can range from relatively automatic judgments to carefully considered conclusions, we maintain that individuals go through the same basic multistep process in forming initial attributions and that given the time, resources, and motivation, a more detailed explanation process occurs. At the end of this process, the person has what he or she considers the best possible attribution for an event and is then geared to respond to that event.

THE "SO WHAT" OF ATTRIBUTIONS

It is interesting and informative to understand the process of making attributions: how and under what conditions individuals make certain types of causal judgments. Although for many researchers and practitioners, the ultimate interest in examining attributions stems from their relationship to the subsequent cognitive, affective, or behavioral experience of the attributor. For example, the teacher is interested in how his or her students' attributions for test performance affect motivation to attend class and study; the coach is interested in how the athlete's attribution for winning or losing a game affects his or her confidence and effort in training; and the therapist wants to know how the client's attribution for his wife's behavior affects the subsequent marital interactions. Researchers of the attributional model have examined the relationship of attributions to the immediate thoughts, feelings, and behaviors of the attributor as well as to his or her longer term functioning.

Proximal Consequences: The Attributional Process Model

Proximal consequences can be thought of as a person's immediate, or near immediate, responses to a specific event and his or her attributions of that event. These responses include thoughts, feelings, and behaviors. Although many thought–feeling–behavior associations are multidirectional in nature, theory and evidence support specific directional relationships in the attributional process. Our attributional process model (adapted from Anderson & Weiner, 1992) delineates a process by which a person moves from event to attribution to cognitive, affective, and behavioral response. The initial step from event to attribution has been discussed previously. The remainder of the model is discussed in the next few sections.

Thoughts

The attribution process, involving an explanatory judgment, makes an explicit statement regarding the attributor's thoughts about the current event. For example, when Fred says "I failed the examination because I'm not smart," he is making explicit his thoughts about the causes of the examination score. Additionally, however, the attribution makes an implicit statement about the attributor's belief about future events. For example, attributing a failed examination to a lack of ability implies Fred's belief that examination failure is likely to occur again in the future. If Sarah makes a characterological attribution for an argument with a coworker (e.g., "I'm very opinionated"), this implies her belief that she may get into similar arguments with others, whereas an external attribution (e.g., "She's narrow minded) may imply that the coworker is likely to get into future arguments. These thoughts about future events have been investigated in success expectancy research.

Success expectancy has been found to relate to two attributional dimensions, locus and stability. Specifically, internal locus is more predictive of success expectancy than external locus. People who make internal attributions for success are likely to show increases in expectations of future success relative to people who make external attributions for success. Likewise, internal attributions for failure are associated with decreases in success expectancy relative to external attributions for failure (Anderson & Weiner, 1992; Rotter, 1966). However, external attributions for success and failure are not consistently related to expectation of future success or failure. Stable attributions also result in more changes in success expectancy than do unstable attributions (Weiner, 1986), with stable attributions for success leading to increases in success expectancy, stable attributions for failure leading to decreases in success expectancy, and unstable attributions for either success or failure not leading to any consistent changes in success expectancy.

The bidirectional nature of these relationships is demonstrated by evidence that success expectancies also influence subsequent attributions (Anderson & Weiner, 1992). For example, in the context of high success expectancy, a person is more likely to make a stable attribution for a success experience and an unstable attribution for failure. However, a person with low success expectancy is likely to make a stable attribution for subsequent failure and an unstable attribution for success. Both failure for a person with high success expectancy and success for a person with low success expectancy are unexpected outcomes. Therefore, an unstable attribution is logical. However, making stable attributions for expected outcomes and unstable ones for unexpected outcomes creates a self-perpetuating cycle, frequently resulting in self-serving or self-defeating biases that are difficult to alter (Anderson & Weiner, 1992; Harvey & Weary, 1981).

The potential implications of success expectancies are obvious, then. The person who expects to succeed, and whose success experiences confirm this expectancy, will likely approach tasks much differently than the person who expects to fail. The relationship of this attribution–expectancy link to responses such as achievement strivings and learned helplessness is discussed later.

Emotions

According to our model, emotions can result directly from events as well as from people's attributions and success expectancies after those events. Weiner, Russell, and Lerman (1978, 1979) suggested that the direct event–emotion path results in primary emotions, such as happiness or sadness, depending on whether the event was positive or negative. These primary emotions are thus similar to unconditioned responses, resulting directly and automatically from the environmental event, and not dependent on interpretations or attributions about the event. More distinct emotions, however, are associated with specific attributions. For example, locus is associated with self-esteem and pride (Weiner, 1986), with internally attributed success serving an esteem-enhancing function and internally attributed failure damaging self-esteem. External attributions for failure, in the forms of excuse making and rationalization, can protect individuals from decrements in self-esteem (Snyder & Higgins, 1988). Stability, by virtue of its temporal dimension, is related to time-based emotions such as hope and fear (Weiner, 1986; Weiner et al., 1978).

The controllability dimension also is associated with specific emotional responses. For negative events in which the person attributes the outcome to causes he or she could have controlled, guilt has been found to result (Hoffman, 1975; Weiner, Graham, & Chandler, 1982). For negative events that are attributed to uncontrollable causes (e.g., intelligence), shame is the likely affect (Brown & Weiner, 1984). Emotions have also been examined for events attributed to causes perceived to be within another person's control. For example, attributing a negative outcome to causes another person could have controlled are associated with anger toward that person (Averill, 1982, 1983), whereas uncontrollable attributions are related to feelings of pity or sympathy (Anderson & Weiner, 1992; Weiner et al., 1982) and decreased feelings of hostility (Brewin, 1992).

Behaviors

Behavior can be predicted from a variety of sources, including a person's attributions, success expectancy thoughts, and emotions, as well as from his or her motivation or desire to achieve a certain outcome. However, much of the research on behavioral reactions focuses on attribution–emotion–behavior links. For example, anger-invoking attributions (in which the event is attributed to causes within another person's power) typically yield retaliation and neglect. However, people tend to respond to sympathy-inducing events and attributions by offering assistance (Betancourt, 1990; Rohrkemper, 1985; Trivers, 1971; Weiner, Perry, & Magnusson, 1988). For guilt-inducing events, in which people see the negative outcomes as being due to internal and controllable causes, apologies and attempts to remediate are the most likely result (Anderson & Weiner, 1992; Niedenthal, Tangney, & Gavanski, 1994). However, uncontrollable shaming attributions are associated with withdrawal (Anderson & Weiner, 1992; Lindsay-Hartz, de Rivera, & Mascolo, 1995; Tangney, 1995). Success expectancies, influenced by locus and stability attributions, influence task persistence. For example, students who attribute school failures to their lack of ability (an internal, stable cause) are more likely than peers to give up easily (Covington & Omelich, 1984; Dweck & Leggett, 1988).

Summary

The attributional process model addresses links among events and the attributions that people make for them, to the subsequent thoughts, feelings, and behaviors that individuals experience and express. Locus and stability of attributions are related to success expectancy thoughts, and locus, stability, and controllability are associated with emotions about a person's own behavior as well as the behaviors of others. Success expectancy can predict behavior, such as an individual's quality of subsequent performance, as well as the likelihood of persisting versus giving up on a task. Emotions can also influence a person's tendency to approach or withdraw from a situation or task; guilt and shame are associated with reparation versus withdrawal, respectively, and pity and anger are associated with helping versus neglecting others.

We may be implying in this section that the human experience fits neatly into models with a finite (and relatively small) set of directional relationships. However, we know that life is not that simple or rigidly organized. In the next section, we acknowledge some of the complexities of people's attributions and their relationships to cognitive, affective, and behavioral adjustment, addressing some of the applications of the attributional model to personal and interpersonal issues of interest to clinical psychology.

Long-Term Functioning: Clinical Applications of the Attributional Process Model

Clinical psychologists are usually faced with issues that make up the latter portions of our attributional process model. People do not come to therapy complaining about their thoughts and attributions; they complain about feeling depressed, anxious, or lonely; about having difficulty with school or job performance; or about dissatisfaction or dysfunction in relationships. However, from our attributional process model, it is possible that these problems in living are associated with, and perhaps stem from or are exacerbated by, maladaptive attributions. Thus, in the next few sections, we cite several common problems in living with their associated affective and behavioral features and examine whether certain characteristic attributional styles can be identified. Note that we do not even begin to address all the problems in living for which attributional processes may be relevant. For additional coverage of adjustment issues, the other chapters in this book and several other sources (e.g., Anderson et al., 1996; Harvey, Orbush, & Weber, 1992; Weary, Stanley, & Harvey, 1989; Weiner, 1995) provide excellent information. Here, we include a sampling of the possible applications of attributional theory and research.

Academic Achievement

Most parents spend at least part of their parenting years worrying about the adequacy of their children's academic achievement. Adults (especially parents) recognize the importance of working up to one's potential, yet many students seemingly do not understand the importance of this or do not care to achieve academically. Research investigating achievement-related attributions sheds significant light on children's achievement motivation and strivings. In particular, Dweck and colleagues (see Dweck & Leggett, 1988, for a review) have demonstrated that children who view ability as internal and unstable (i.e., ability is changeable because of factors such as effort) tend to maintain positive mood, motivation, and performance after failure. However, children who view ability as stable and unchanging (e.g., due to intelligence) and so attribute failure to internal, stable, and uncontrollable causes are likely to show less effective performance after failure or to give up entirely. Similar effects of attributional stability and controllability have been found for students of all ages (e.g., Covington & Omelich, 1984; Powers, Douglas, Cool, & Gose, 1985; Stipek & Mason, 1987; Wilson & Linville, 1982). Global attributions for failure also are associated with lowered task persistence in the form of increased off-task behavior (Mikulincer & Nizan, 1988).

Researchers of success expectancy have taken the understanding of academic achievement problems one step further, demonstrating that negative attributions are associated with low success expectancy and a learned helpless style of approaching academic tasks (Diener & Dweck, 1978). These children focus on failure, do not consider ways to remediate failure, and avoid future learning situations in which failure is expected to recur. Not surprisingly, the academic attainment of these children is frequently disappointing to the children themselves as well as to other people around them and may be associated with feelings of inadequacy or depression.

Depression

Depression is an affective state that most people experience, at least transiently, at some time. The feeling and, in more severe cases, the disorder are associated with sad mood, feelings of guilt or shame, low self-esteem, low motivation, and social withdrawal or ineffective social interactions. Maladaptive thoughts, including attributions, are also characteristic of depression and in fact are considered to be a central feature of depression by some theorists. For example, according to the Abramson et al. (1978) reformulated learned helplessness theory of depression, depression results when an individual experiences a number of negative events and explains them with primarily negative attributions. Specifically, depressive attributions for negative or failure events are likely to be internal, stable, and global, and attributions for positive events are external, unstable, and specific. The subsequent expansion of this theory (Abramson, Metalsky, & Alloy, 1989) implicates the combination of negative experiences and this depressive attributional style in the development of pessimism about the future or "hopelessness" depression. Therefore, according to Abramson et al. (1978, 1989), when answering one of the questions that opened this chapter, "Why did the boss not promote me?," a person who is depressed may respond, "because I am an inadequate employee," reflecting an internal, stable (ability), and global (all employee skills) attribution. Additionally, the hopelessly depressed person will expect this sort of event to recur in the future.

Although not an attributional theory per se, Beck's (Beck & Clark, 1988; Clark, Beck, & Brown, 1989) cognitive theory of depression also implicates negative attributional processes in the development and maintenance of depression. Beck suggested that depressive thinking is characterized by a variety of cognitive errors, including catastrophization, overgeneralization, personalization, and selective attention to negative events. Personalization corresponds to making internal attributions, whereas overgeneralization is similar to stable and global attributions, in which causes are generalized across time and situation. The catastrophization and selective attention cognitive errors refer to the tendency to focus on failure and negative aspects of events, again suggesting the globality of negative events.

Research on attributional style and depression is largely consistent with both basic research on maladaptive processes and the cognitive theories of depression. Several studies indicate that both youths and adults with depressive symptoms showed more internal, stable, and global attributions for negative events and more external, unstable, and specific attributions for positive events than their nondepressed counterparts (Blumberg & Izard, 1985; Quiggle, Garber, Panek, & Dodge, 1992; Seligman et al., 1984), although whether attributions for positive events (e.g., Benfield, Palmer, Pfefferbaum, & Stowe, 1988) versus negative events (e.g., Crocker, Alloy, & Kayne, 1988) are more important in understanding depression is currently unclear. Individuals with depressive disorders have shown the same pattern, differentiating them from individuals with nondepressive psychiatric disorders and individuals with nonpsychiatric medical conditions

(Rapps, Peterson, Reinhard, Abramson, & Seligman, 1982; Silverman & Peterson, 1993).

The controllability dimension proposed by Anderson and Arnoult (1985a) has received less attention than the other dimensions, but it appears to hold promise for understanding depression. Depressed people generally make relatively more uncontrollable attributions for both positive and negative events. In two studies comparing the statistical power of various attributional dimensions to predict problems such as loneliness and depression, controllability attributional style proved to be the most important (Anderson & Arnoult, 1985a; Anderson & Riger, 1991).

Experimental and longitudinal researchers have examined possible causal relationships between attributions and depression. Our model suggests that maladaptive attributions should give rise to depressed affect and responding. However, the reverse (or no direct causal relationship) is also possible. Findings are consistent with our hypotheses, suggesting the development of depression subsequent to negative attributions. The experimental induction of particular attributions has been more successful in leading to mood change than mood induction has been in leading to attribution changes (Anderson, 1983; Golin, Sweeney, & Schaeffer, 1981). Longitudinal research also suggests that maladaptive attributions predate depression (Metalsky, Abramson, Seligman, Semmel, & Peterson, 1982; Panek & Garber, 1992; Seligman et al., 1984).

Anxiety

Anxiety, especially social anxiety, and shyness have also received a great deal of attention from both social and clinical psychologists. Similar to depression, anxiety is a fairly common negative mood state in its mild form and is frequently associated with low self-esteem, low success expectancy and achievement motivation, and an avoidant behavioral style. Similar maladaptive attributions have also been proposed. For example, Beck (1986) suggested that anxious individuals overperceive the likelihood and magnitude of threat and doubt their ability to respond effectively. Although attributions were not specifically proposed by Beck, the overwhelming threat appraisal suggests that attributions of externality, uncontrollability, and globality for negative events play a role in anxiety production and maintenance. Other theorists have included uncontrollable attributions for negative events as an additional causal factor (e.g., Cheek & Melchior, 1990; Hope, Gansler, & Heimberg, 1989). It is interesting to note that Schlenker and Leary (1982) suggested that success events may also result in external and uncontrollable attributions by highly anxious individuals.

As might be expected based on theoretical disagreement about the role of internal attributions, findings regarding internal attributions are somewhat inconsistent. Using nonclinical samples, several researchers have found shyness and social anxiety to be associated with internal attributions for failure and external attributions for success (Anderson & Arnoult, 1985a, 1985b; Arkin, Appleman, & Burger, 1980; Girodo, Dotzenroth, & Stein, 1981; Teglasi & Hoffman, 1982). Test anxiety and more general trait anxiety are also related to internal attributions for failure in both adults and children (Diener & Dweck, 1978, 1980; Fincham, Hokoda, & Sanders, 1989; Hedl, 1990; Leppin, Schwarzer, Belz, Jerusalem, & Quast, 1987). However, researchers testing participants with clinical anxiety disorders, panic disorder in particular, have often failed to find effects on the internal dimension (Brodbeck & Michelson, 1987; Ganellen, 1988; Heimberg et al., 1989). However, Heimberg et al. found that individuals with social phobia did display maladaptive internal attributions.

Globality and stability have received more consistent support in both clinical and nonclinical samples. Anxiety and shyness is associated with stable attributions for personal failure (Fincham, Hokoda, & Sanders, 1989). Patients with panic disorder, agoraphobia, and social phobia also are more likely than nonanxious individuals to attribute negative events to stable and global causes (Brodbeck & Michelson, 1987; Heimberg et al., 1989).

As with depression, controllability has received less attention than other attribution dimensions. Anderson and Arnoult (1985a, 1985b) found that shy individuals tended to propose internal uncontrollable attributions for interpersonal failure. Indirect evidence for the importance of a controllability dimension, particularly as it interacts with internality, comes from research on anxious children's interpretations of peer provocation. When faced with ambiguous peer provocation, anxious children tended to assign hostile rather than accidental intent to their peers' behavior (Bell-Dolan, 1989; Bell-Dolan & Suarez, 1997). In other words, peers behaving intentionally are presumed to have control over their actions, thus implying that the event was not controllable from the victim's perspective. These findings are consistent with the overperception of threat and uncontrollable attributions theorized to characterize anxiety.

Relationship Satisfaction

Relationship satisfaction encompasses several areas of research, including the loneliness and friendship literature and the marital satisfaction literature. Loneliness resembles both anxiety and depression, involving a negative affective state, frequent dissatisfaction with oneself, and social withdrawal or ineffectiveness. In fact, research demonstrates empirical links of loneliness to both depression and anxiety (W. H. Jones, Rose, & Russell, 1990; Moore & Schultz, 1983; Yang & Chum, 1994). Thus, not surprisingly, the attributions of lonely people are similar to those reported by depressed and anxious individuals. Specifically, loneliness is associated with internal, stable, and controllable attributions for negative events (Anderson & Arnoult, 1985a, 1985b; Anderson, Miller, Riger, Dill, & Sedikides, 1994; Anderson & Riger, 1991; Renshaw & Brown, 1993). Like anxious individuals, lonely people also attribute hostile intent to others' behavior (Hanley-Dunn, Maxwell, & Santos, 1985).

The marital satisfaction literature examines how attributions for events within the marital relationship relate to happiness in that relationship. Marital dissatisfaction is related to a person's tendency to blame his or her partner for relationship difficulties (Bradbury & Fincham, 1990; Fincham & Bradbury, 1988, 1992; Sabourin, Lussier, & Wright, 1991; Townsley, Beach, Fincham, & O'Leary, 1991), in other words, to attribute difficulty to external and other-controllable causes. The globality and stability of these blaming attributions has also been documented (Fincham & Grych, 1991; Sabourin et al., 1991).

Note that although marital dissatisfaction may be associated with depression, the specific attributional styles associated with depression and marital dissatisfaction are distinct. Whereas depressive attributional style involves self-focused internal, stable, and uncontrollable attributions, relationship dissatisfaction involves other-focused, blaming attributions that serve to highlight the partner's negative qualities and minimize his or her positive qualities (Baucom, Sayers, & Duhe, 1989). Researchers have documented the distinctiveness of these two attribution styles (Fincham, Beach, & Bradbury, 1989; Townsley et al., 1991) and in fact have shown the attributing marital problems to oneself rather than to one's partner predicts depression (Heim & Snyder, 1991).

The shift from self-focused negative attributions, which are associated with internalizing symptoms such as depression, anxiety, and loneliness, to other-focused negative attributions as seen in relationship dissatisfaction is accompanied by a change in the predominant form of behavioral responding. Whereas the self-focused and self-blaming negative attributions are associated with withdrawal and avoidant responses, we discuss in the next section on aggression the frequent results of other-focused negative attributions.

Aggression

Much research focuses on understanding why people behave in aggressive and violent ways. Recently, attribution researchers have suggested that the attributions people make may serve to justify and perpetuate their aggression. Because aggression is relatively common and overt in youngsters, much of the understanding comes from research on childhood aggression. Dodge and colleagues have found that children who are aggressive are more likely than their nonaggressive peers to overinterpret hostility, attributing even nonhostile provocation from a playmate (i.e., an accidental shove) to hostile intent (Dodge, 1985; Lochman & Dodge, 1994). This finding extends beyond traditionally defined, overly aggressive children to include children who are relationally aggressive (i.e., those who use social exclusion, gossip, etc. to harm another's relationships) and whose aggression is primarily reactive (Crick, 1995; Crick & Dodge, 1996). Delinquent adolescents have also been found to show maladaptive attributions, with their level of physical aggression being associated with a tendency to attribute social failure (e.g., a peer blocking goal attainment) to controllable causes (Guerra, Huesmann, & Zelli, 1990, 1993). Guerra et al. (1993) also found a relationship between aggression and external attributions for social failure.

Among aggressive adults, similar external and controllable attributions have been found. For example, violent husbands tend to make external and controllable attributions, blaming their wife's intentionally negative behavior for the marital violence (Holtzworth-Munroe, 1992; Shields & Hanneke, 1983). When internal attributions are made, they tend to refer to unstable causes, such as alcohol intoxication (Holtzworth-Munroe, 1992; Senchak & Leonard, 1994). It is interesting to note, however, that Dutton (1986) found that violent husbands who self-referred for therapy tended to offer internal attributions for their violence, highlighting the relevance of attributions for an individual's openness to change in therapy.

IMPLICATIONS FOR INTERVENTION

Ultimately, psychologists care about attributions and their associated affective and behavioral responses because of the implications for enhancing people's functioning and adjustment. If the models are accurate, then modifying an individual's attributions should lead to changes in his or her momentary affect (e.g., guilt, shame, anger), predominant mood (e.g., irritability, depression), success expectancy, and behavioral responding (e.g., aggression, withdrawal, helping). Of course, clinicians could change attributions in many directions, but most treatment and research programs have focused on changing the attributions associated with problematic mood and behavior. Thus, for depressed individuals who tend to view negative events as being primarily internal, stable, and uncontrollable, treatment would focus on helping them to see external and unstable causes for particular negative events (e.g., social rejection from a peer would be attributed to the peer having a bad day rather than to the unlikability of the depressed person) and to see controllability in the events around them (e.g., the same social rejection could perhaps be modified or avoided through some proactive pleasant behavior on the part of the depressed person). For angry and aggressive individuals who tend to blame negative events on the intentionally (controllable) negative behavior of others, treatment would help them to see the unintentional nature of some of the behavior of others (e.g., the person who cut them off on the freeway was not being a jerk but was trying to avoid a tire in the road) and to share some responsibility for negative interactions (e.g., a marital argument resulted from both partners' lack of patience with the other). In fact, this attribution therapy approach has served as the basis for several cognitive therapies for depression (e.g., Beck, Rush, Shaw, & Emory, 1979), anxiety (e.g., Freeman & Simon, 1989; Kendall, Chansky, Kane, & Kim, 1992), and marital problems (e.g., Epstein & Baucom, 1989) as well as numerous other intrapersonal and interpersonal problems.

On the whole, such attribution retraining programs have shown promising results. Evaluation of attribution-oriented therapies demonstrates their effectiveness in reducing dysfunctional attributions and behavior in areas such as depression (e.g., Beck, Hollon, Young, Bedrosian, & Budenz, 1985; Kammer, 1983) and academic functioning (Carr & Borkowski, 1989; Dweck, 1975; Reid & Borkowski, 1987; Reiher & Dembo, 1984). Cognitive–behavioral therapies, which frequently incorporate attribution retraining as a component of their treatment, have been shown to provide superior treatment outcomes to other forms of therapy (e.g., Weisz, Weiss, Alicke, & Klotz, 1987). Note, however, that few of these treatment programs offer attribution retraining in isolation but instead include it in a multicomponent treatment involving direct attention to thoughts, behavior, and emotional and physical responding. Nonetheless, we believe that attending to maladaptive thought patterns is a crucial component of successful intervention and change.

SUMMARY AND CONCLUSION

Attributional processes have captured the attention of social and clinical psychologists alike because of their relationship to people's personal adjustment, interpersonal relationships, occupational effectiveness, and social responsibility. The potential utility of attribution theory is indeed far reaching, being relevant to the trial lawyer or jury consultant who attempts to predict how a group of 12 men and women will respond to various possible defense arguments, to the schoolteacher who is attempting to motivate a group of underachieving students, to the therapist who is working to alleviate a client's depression, and to the public fundraiser who wants to plan the most effective campaign for soliciting donations from the community. The appeal of attribution theory for understanding, changing, and motivating adaptive behavior is also compelling. The fact that attributions are internal to the attributors, carried with them wherever they go, suggests that changing attributions is more promising and potentially more cost effective than controlling external factors, such as the environment. People move from one environment or context to the next, and with these moves the demands and supports of the environment shift. It is not always possible to keep children in supportive environments, for example, where their efforts are rewarded with success. However, if parents can maximize children's tendency to make internal, effort attributions for success, then their ability to withstand and persevere in the face of failure will likewise be maximized. Similarly, employees will not always have understanding and competent bosses, but if employees can attribute the praise they get from bosses to their own competent performance, and attribute the outbursts to the bosses' poor interaction skills, then the ability to go to work every day and derive some job satisfaction will be enhanced. Thus, helping people to develop their "portable" arsenal of adaptive attributions arms them for a multitude of challenges in daily life.

Despite the promise of contemporary attribution theory, the work of attribution researchers is not complete. Further refinement of attribution models, particularly with respect to cleanly identifying the most relevant attribution dimensions (which may be different for different situations) and clarifying directionality, is still needed. The relation between attributional accuracy and adaptiveness is another issue needing future research attention. Although wildly inaccurate attributions (and attributional styles) are certainly maladaptive in the long run, it is less clear that this positive relation between accuracy and adaptiveness holds true in all situations or at less extreme levels of inaccuracy. Attribution therapies also merit continued refinement and testing, especially in terms of their unique contributions in multicomponent treatment packages. Central to these advances will be the continued cross-fertilization of the area by diverse fields within psychology as well as from other disciplines. It is easy for social psychologists to talk to other social psychologists and for clinical psychologists to talk to others of "their kind." True advancement of attribution theory, research, and treatment will come from talking to each other and building on the complementary bodies of knowledge.

REFERENCES

Abelson, R. P., & Lalljee, M. G. (1988). Knowledge structures and causal explanation. In D. J. Hilton (Ed.), *Contemporary science and natural explanation: Commonsense conceptions of causality* (pp. 175–203). Brighton, England: Harvester.

Abramson, L. Y., Metalsky, G. I., & Alloy, L. B. (1989). Hopelessness depression: A theory-based subtype of depression. *Psychological Review, 96,* 358–372.

Abramson, L. Y., Seligman, M. E. P., & Teasdale, J. (1978). Learned helplessness in humans: Critique and reformulation. *Journal of Abnormal Psychology, 87,* 49–74.

Anderson, C. A. (1983). The causal structure of situations: The generation of plausible causal attributions as a function of type of event situation. *Journal of Experimental Social Psychology, 19,* 185–203.

Anderson, C. A., & Arnoult, L. H. (1985a). Attributional models of depression, loneliness, and shyness. In J. H. Harvey & G. Weary (Eds.), *Attribution: Basic issues and applications* (pp. 235–280). New York: Academic Press.

Anderson, C. A., & Arnoult, L. H. (1985b). Attributional style and everyday problems in living: Depression, loneliness, and shyness. *Social Cognition, 3,* 16–35.

Anderson, C. A., Krull, D. S., & Weiner, B. (1996). Explanations: Processes and consequences. In E. T. Higgins & A. W. Kruglanski (Eds.), *Social psychology: Handbook of basic principles* (pp. 271–296). New York: Guilford Press.

Anderson, C. A., Miller, R. S., Riger, A. L., Dill, J. C., & Sedikides, C. (1994). Behavioral and characterological attributional styles as predictors of depression and loneliness: Review, refinement, and test. *Journal of Personality and Social Psychology, 66,* 549–558.

Anderson, C. A., & Riger, A. L. (1991). A controllability attributional model of problems in living: Dimensional and situational interactions in the prediction of depression and loneliness. *Social Cognition, 9,* 149–181.

Anderson, C. A., & Slusher, M. P. (1986). Relocating motivational effects: An examination of the cognition–motivation debate on attributions for success and failure. *Social Cognition, 4,* 270–292.

Anderson, C. A., & Weiner, B. (1992). Attribution and attributional processes in personality. In G. Caprara & G. Heck (Eds.), *Modern personality psychology: Critical reviews and new directions* (pp. 295–324). New York: Harvester Wheatsheaf.

Arkin, R. M., Appleman, A. J., & Burger, J. M. (1980). Social anxiety, self-presentation, and the self-serving bias in causal attribution. *Journal of Personality and Social Psychology, 38,* 23–35.

Averill, J. R. (1982). *Anger and aggression: An essay on emotion.* New York: Springer-Verlag.

Averill, J. R. (1983). Studies on anger and aggression. *American Psychologist, 38,* 1145–1160.

Baucom, D. H., Sayers, S. L., & Duhe, A. (1989). Attributional style and attributional patterns among married couples. *Journal of Personality and Social Psychology, 56,* 596–607.

Beck, A. T. (1986). Cognitive approaches to anxiety disorders. In B. F. Shaw, Z. V. Segal, T. M. Vallis, & F. E. Cashman (Eds.), *Anxiety disorders: Psychological and biological perspectives* (pp. 115–136). New York: Plenum.

Beck, A. T., & Clark, D. A. (1988). Anxiety and depression: An information processing perspective. *Anxiety Research, 1,* 23–26.

Beck, A. T., Hollon, S. D., Young, J. E., Bedrosian, R. C., & Budenz, D. (1985). Treatment of depression with cognitive therapy and amitriptyline. *Archives of General Psychiatry, 42,* 142–148.

Beck, A. T., Rush, A. J., Shaw, B. F., & Emory, G. (1979). *Cognitive therapy of depression*. New York: Guilford Press.

Bell-Dolan, D. J. (1989). Social cue interpretation of anxious children. *Journal of Clinical Child Psychology, 24*, 1–10.

Bell-Dolan, D. J., & Suarez, L. (1997, April). *Anxious children's social perceptions: Responses to provocation, peer group entry, and social failure situations*. Paper presented at the biennial meeting of the Society for Research in Child Development, Washington, DC.

Benfield, C. Y., Palmer, D. J., Pfefferbaum, B., & Stowe, M. L. (1988). A comparison of depressed and nondepressed disturbed children on measures of attributional style, hopelessness, life stress, and temperament. *Journal of Abnormal Child Psychology, 16*, 397–410.

Betancourt, H. (1990). An attribution-empathy model of helping behavior: Behavioral intentions and judgments of help-giving. *Personality and Social Psychology Bulletin, 16*, 573–591.

Blumberg, S. H., & Izard, C. E. (1985). Affective and cognitive characteristics of depression in 10- and 11-year-old children. *Journal of Personality and Social Psychology, 49*, 194–202.

Bradbury, T. N., & Fincham, F. D. (1990). Attributions in marriage: Review and critique. *Psychological Bulletin, 107*, 3–33.

Brewin, C. R. (1992). Attribution and emotion in patients' families. In J. H. Harvey, T. L. Orbuch, & A. L. Weber (Eds.), *Attributions, accounts, and close relationships* (pp. 194–208). New York: Springer-Verlag.

Brodbeck, C., & Michelson, L. (1987). Problem-solving skills and attributional styles of agoraphobics. *Cognitive Therapy and Research, 11*, 593–610.

Brown, J., & Weiner, B. (1984). Affective consequences of ability versus effort ascriptions: Controversies, resolutions, and quandaries. *Journal of Educational Psychology, 76*, 146–158.

Carr, M., & Borkowski, J. G. (1989). Attributional training and the generalization of reading strategies with underachieving children. *Learning and Individual Differences, 1*, 327–341.

Cheek, J. M., & Melchior, L. A. (1990). Shyness, self-esteem, and self-consciousness. In H. Leitenberg (Ed.), *Handbook of social and evaluation anxiety* (pp. 47–82). New York: Plenum.

Cheng, P. W., & Novick, L. R. (1990). A probabilistic contrast model of causal induction. *Journal of Personality and Social Psychology, 58*, 545–567.

Clark, D. A., Beck, A. T., & Brown, G. (1989). Cognitive mediation in general psychiatric outpatients: A test of the content-specificity hypothesis. *Journal of Personality and Social Psychology, 56*, 958–964.

Covington, M. V., & Omelich, C. L. (1984). Controversies or consistencies? A reply to Brown and Weiner. *Journal of Educational Psychology, 76*, 159–168.

Crick, N. R. (1995). Relational aggression: The role of intent attributions, feelings of distress, and provocation type. *Development and Psychopathology, 7*, 313–332.

Crick, N. R., & Dodge, K. A. (1996). Social information-processing mechanisms in reactive and proactive aggression. *Child Development, 67,* 993–1002.

Crocker, J., Alloy, L. B., & Kayne, N. T. (1988). Attributional style, depression, and perceptions of consensus for events. *Journal of Personality and Social Psychology, 54,* 840–846.

Diener, C. I., & Dweck, C. S. (1978). An analysis of learned helplessness: Continuous changes in performance, strategy and achievement cognitions following failure. *Journal of Personality and Social Psychology, 36,* 451–462.

Diener, C. I., & Dweck, C. S. (1980). An analysis of learned helplessness: II. The processing of success. *Journal of Personality and Social Psychology, 39,* 940–952.

Dill, K. E., Anderson, C. A., Anderson, K. B., & Deuser, W. E. (1997). Effects of aggressive personality on social expectations and social perceptions. *Journal of Research in Personality, 31,* 272–292.

Dill, K. E., Erickson, D. J., & Krull, D. S. (1994, May). *When do perceivers draw situational attributions for behavior? Effects of stability, majority, multiple targets, and behavior type.* Paper presented at the Midwestern Psychological Association Convention, Chicago.

Dodge, K. A. (1985). Attributional bias in aggressive children. In P. C. Kendall (Ed.), *Advances in cognitive–behavioral research and therapy* (Vol. 4, pp. 73–110). Orlando, FL: Academic Press.

Dodge, K. A., & Crick, N. R. (1990). Social information-processing bases of aggressive behavior in children. *Personality and Social Psychology Bulletin, 16,* 8–22.

Duncan, S. L. (1976). Differential social perception and attribution of intergroup violence: Testing the lower limits of stereotyping of Blacks. *Journal of Personality and Social Psychology, 34,* 590–598.

Dutton, D. G. (1986). Wife assaulters' explanations for assault: The neutralization of self-punishment. *Canadian Journal of Behavioral Science, 18,* 381–390.

Dweck, C. S. (1975). The role of expectations and attributions in the alleviation of learned helplessness. *Journal of Personality and Social Psychology, 31,* 674–685.

Dweck, C. S., Hong, Y., & Chiu, C. (1993). Implicit theories: Individual differences in the likelihood and meaning of dispositional inference. *Personality and Social Psychology Bulletin, 19,* 644–656.

Dweck, C. S., & Leggett, E. (1988). A social cognitive approach to motivation and personality. *Psychological Review, 95,* 256–273.

Eisen, S. V. (1979). Actor–observer differences in information inference and causal attribution. *Journal of Personality and Social Psychology, 37,* 261–272.

Epstein, N., & Baucom, D. (1989). Cognitive–behavioral marital therapy. In A. Freeman, K. M. Simon, L. E. Beutler, & H. Arkowitz (Eds.), *Comprehensive handbook of cognitive therapy* (pp. 491–513). New York: Plenum.

Erickson, D. J., & Krull, D. S. (1994, May). *To be caused or to be inferred: The distinctiveness of inferences and causal attributions.* Paper presented at the Midwestern Psychological Association Convention, Chicago.

Fincham, F. D., Beach, S. R., & Bradbury, T. N. (1989). Marital distress, depression, and attributions: Is the marital distress–attribution association an artifact of depression? *Journal of Consulting and Clinical Psychology, 57,* 768–771.

Fincham, F. D., & Bradbury, T. N. (1988). The impact of attributions in marriage: An experimental analysis. *Journal of Social and Clinical Psychology, 7,* 147–162.

Fincham, F. D., & Bradbury, T. N. (1992). Assessing attributions in marriage: The Relationship Attribution Measure. *Journal of Personality and Social Psychology, 62,* 457–468.

Fincham, F. D., & Grych, J. H. (1991). Explanations for family events in distressed and nondistressed couples: Is one type of explanation used consistently? *Journal of Family Psychology, 4,* 341–353.

Fincham, F. D., Hokoda, A., & Sanders, R. (1989). Learned helplessness, test anxiety, and academic achievement: A longitudinal analysis. *Child Development, 60,* 138–145.

Fiske, S. T., & Taylor, S. E. (1991). *Social cognition* (2nd ed.). Reading, MA: Addison-Wesley.

Fletcher, G. J. O., & Ward, C. (1988). Attribution theory and processes: A cross-cultural perspective. In M. H. Bond (Ed.), *The cross-cultural challenge to social psychology* (pp. 230–244). Beverly Hills, CA: Sage.

Frazer, J. G. (1959). *The new golden bough.* New York: Criterion Books.

Freeman, A., & Simon, K. M. (1989). Cognitive therapy of anxiety. In A. Freeman, K. M. Simon, L. E. Beutler, & H. Arkowitz (Eds.), *Comprehensive handbook of cognitive therapy* (pp. 347–366). New York: Plenum.

Ganellen, R. J. (1988). Specificity of attributions and overgeneralization in depression and anxiety. *Journal of Abnormal Psychology, 97,* 83–86.

Gilbert, D. T. (1989). Thinking lightly about others: Automatic components of the social inference process. In J. S. Uleman & J. A. Bargh (Eds.), *Unintended thought: Limits of awareness, intention, and control* (pp. 189–211). New York: Guilford Press.

Girodo, M., Dotzenroth, S. E., & Stein, S. J. (1981). Causal attribution bias in shy males: Implications for self-esteem and self-confidence. *Cognitive Therapy and Research, 5,* 325–338.

Golin, S., Sweeney, P. D., & Schaeffer, D. E. (1981). The causality of causal attributions in depression: A cross-lagged panel correlational analysis. *Journal of Abnormal Psychology, 90,* 14–22.

Guerra, N. G., Huesmann, L. R., & Zelli, A. (1990). Attributions for social failure and aggression in incarcerated delinquent youth. *Journal of Abnormal Child Psychology, 18,* 347–355.

Guerra, N. G., Huesmann, L. R., & Zelli, A. (1993). Attributions for social failure and adolescent aggression. *Aggressive Behavior, 19,* 421–434.

Hanley-Dunn, P., Maxwell, S. E., & Santos, J. F. (1985). Interpretation of interpersonal interactions: The influence of loneliness. *Personality and Social Psychology Bulletin, 11,* 445–456.

Harvey, J. H., Orbush, T. L., & Weber, A. L. (Eds.). (1992). *Attributions, accounts, and close relationships*. New York: Springer-Verlag.

Harvey, J. H., & Weary, G. (1981). *Perspectives on the attributional process*. Dubuque, IA: Brown.

Hedl, J. L. (1990). Test anxiety and causal attributions: Some evidence toward replication. *Anxiety Research, 3,* 73–84.

Heim, S. C., & Snyder, D. K. (1991). Predicting depression from marital distress and attributional processes. *Journal of Marital and Family Therapy, 17,* 67–72.

Heimberg, R. G., Klosko, J. S., Dodge, C. S., Shadick, R., Becker, R. E., & Barlow, D. H. (1989). Anxiety disorders, depression, and attributional style: A further test of the specificity of depressive attributions. *Cognitive Therapy and Research, 13,* 21–36.

Hempel, C. G. (1966). *Philosophy of natural science*. Englewood Cliffs, NJ: Prentice Hall.

Higgins, E. T. (1996). Knowledge activation: Accessibility, applicability, and salience. In E. T. Higgins & A. W. Kruglanski (Eds.), *Social psychology: Handbook of basic principles* (pp. 133–168). New York: Guilford Press.

Hilton, D. J., Mathes, R. H., & Trabasso, T. R. (1992). The study of causal explanation in natural language: Analyzing reports of the *Challenger* disaster in the *New York Times*. In M. L. McLaughlin, M. J. Cody, & S. J. Read (Eds.), *Explaining one's self to others: Reason-giving in a social context* (pp. 41–59). Hillsdale, NJ: Erlbaum.

Hoffman, M. L. (1975). Developmental synthesis of affect and cognition and its implications for altruistic motivation. *Developmental Psychology, 11,* 607–622.

Holtzworth-Munroe, A. (1992). Attributions and maritally violent men: The role of cognitions in marital violence. In J. H. Harvey, T. L. Orbush, & A. L. Weber (Eds.), *Attributions, accounts, and close relationships* (pp. 165–175). New York: Springer-Verlag.

Hope, D. A., Gansler, D. A., & Heimberg, R. G. (1989). Attentional focus and causal attributions in social phobia: Implications from social psychology. *Clinical Psychology Review, 9,* 49–60.

James, W. (1890). *The principles of psychology* (Vol. 2). New York: Holt.

Jones, E. E. (1990). *Interpersonal perception*. New York: Macmillan.

Jones, E. E., & Davis, K. E. (1965). From acts to dispositions: The attribution process in person perception. *Advances in Experimental Social Psychology, 2,* 219–266.

Jones, W. H., Rose, J., & Russell, D. (1990). Loneliness and social anxiety. In H. Leitenberg (Ed.), *Handbook of social and evaluation anxiety* (pp. 247–266). New York: Plenum.

Kammer, D. (1983). Depression, attributional style, and failure generalization. *Cognitive Therapy and Research, 7,* 413–423.

Kelley, H. H. (1950). The warm–cold variable in first impressions of persons. *Journal of Personality, 18,* 431–439.

Kelley, H. H. (1967). Attribution theory in social psychology. In D. Levine (Ed.), *Nebraska Symposium on Motivation* (Vol. 15, pp. 192–238). Lincoln: University of Nebraska Press.

Kelley, H. H. (1973). The process of causal attribution. *American Psychologist, 28*, 107–128.

Kelley, H. H., & Michela, J. L. (1980). Attribution theory and research. *Annual Review of Psychology, 31*, 457–501.

Kendall, P. C., Chansky, T. E., Kane, M. T., & Kim, R. S. (1992). *Anxiety disorders in youth: Cognitive–behavioral interventions*. Boston: Allyn & Bacon.

Kruglanski, A. W. (1989). *Lay epistemics and human knowledge: Cognitive and motivational bases*. New York: Plenum.

Krull, D. S., & Erickson, D. J. (1995). Inferential hopscotch: How people draw social inferences from behavior. *Current Directions in Psychological Science, 4*, 35–38.

Leppin, A., Schwarzer, R., Belz, D., Jerusalem, M., & Quast, H. (1987). Causal attribution patterns of high and low test-anxious students. *Advances in Test Anxiety Research, 5*, 67–86.

Lindsay-Hartz, J., de Rivera, J., & Mascolo, M. F. (1995). Differentiating guilt and shame and their effects on motivation. In J. P. Tangney & K. W. Fischer (Eds.), *Self-conscious emotions: The psychology of shame, guilt, embarrassment, and pride* (pp. 274–300). New York: Guilford Press.

Lochman, J. E., & Dodge, K. A. (1994). Social-cognitive processes of severely violent, moderately aggressive, and nonaggressive boys. *Journal of Consulting and Clinical Psychology, 62*, 366–374.

McArthur, L. Z., & Post, D. L. (1977). Figural emphasis and person perception. *Journal of Experimental Social Psychology, 13*, 520–535.

McArthur, L. Z., & Solomon, L. K. (1978). Perceptions of an aggressive encounter as a function of the victim's salience and the perceiver's arousal. *Journal of Personality and Social Psychology, 36*, 1278–1290.

Metalsky, G. I., Abramson, L. Y., Seligman, M. E. P., Semmel, A., & Peterson, C. (1982). Attributional style and life events in the classroom: Vulnerability and invulnerability to depressive mood reactions. *Journal of Personality and Social Psychology, 38*, 704–718.

Mikulincer, M., & Nizan, B. (1988). Causal attribution, cognitive interference, and the generalization of learned helplessness. *Journal of Personality and Social Psychology, 55*, 470–478.

Miller, J. G. (1984). Culture and the development of everyday social explanation. *Journal of Personality and Social Psychology, 46*, 961–978.

Miller, L. C., & Read, S. J. (1991). On the coherence of mental models of persons and relationships: A knowledge structure approach. In G. J. O. Fletcher & F. Fincham (Eds.), *Cognition in close relationships* (pp. 69–99). Hillsdale, NJ: Erlbaum.

Moore, D., & Schultz, N. R. (1983). Loneliness at adolescence: Correlates, attributions, and coping. *Journal of Youth and Adolescence, 12*, 95–100.

Moray, N. (1959). Attention in dichotic listening: Affective cues and the influence of instructions. *Quarterly Journal of Experimental Psychology, 11*, 56–60.

Neisser, U. (1976). *Cognition and reality*. New York: Freeman.

Niedenthal, P. M., Tangney, J. P., & Gavanski, I. (1994). "If only I weren't" versus "if only I hadn't": Distinguishing shame and guilt in counterfactual thinking. *Journal of Personality and Social Psychology, 67*, 585–595.

Nisbett, R. E., & Ross, L. (1980). *Human inference: Strategies and shortcomings of social judgment*. Englewood Cliffs, NJ: Prentice Hall.

Novick, L. R., Fratianne, A., & Cheng, P. W. (1992). Knowledge-based assumptions in causal attribution. *Social Cognition, 10*, 299–334.

Panek, W. F., & Garber, J. (1992). Role of aggression, rejection, and attributions in the prediction of depression in children. *Development and Psychopathology, 4*, 145–165.

Postman, L., & Brown, D. R. (1952). The perceptual consequences of success and failure. *Journal of Abnormal and Social Psychology, 47*, 213–221.

Powers, S., Douglas, P., Cool, B. A., & Gose, K. F. (1985). Achievement motivation and attributions for success and failure. *Psychological Reports, 57*, 751–754.

Quiggle, N. L., Garber, J., Panek, W. F., & Dodge, K. A. (1992). Social information processing in aggressive and depressed children. *Child Development, 63*, 1305–1320.

Rapps, C. S., Peterson, C., Reinhard, K. E., Abramson, L. Y., & Seligman, M. E. P. (1982). Attributional style among depressed patients. *Journal of Abnormal Psychology, 91*, 102–108.

Read, S. J., & Miller, L. C. (1993). Rapist or "regular guy": Explanatory coherence in the construction of mental models of others. *Personality and Social Psychology Bulletin, 19*, 526–540.

Reid, M. K., & Borkowski, J. G. (1987). Causal attributions of hyperactive children: Implications for teaching strategies and self-control. *Journal of Educational Psychology, 79*, 296–307.

Reiher, R. H., & Dembo, M. H. (1984). Changing academic task persistence through a self-instructional attribution training program. *Contemporary Educational Psychology, 9*, 89–94.

Renshaw, P. D., & Brown, P. J. (1993). Loneliness in middle childhood: Concurrent and longitudinal predictors. *Child Development, 64*, 1271–1284.

Rohrkemper, M. M. (1985). Individual differences in students' perceptions of routine classroom events. *Journal of Educational Psychology, 77*, 29–44.

Rotter, J. B. (1966). Generalized expectancies for internal versus external control of reinforcement. *Psychological Monographs, 80*(1, Whole No. 609).

Rusbult, C., & Medlin, S. (1982). Information availability, goodness of outcome, and attributions of causality. *Journal of Experimental Social Psychology, 18*, 292–305.

Sabourin, S., Lussier, Y., & Wright, J. (1991). The effects of measurement strategy on attributions for marital problems and behaviors. *Journal of Applied Social Psychology, 21,* 734–746.

Sagar, H. A., & Schofield, J. W. (1980). Racial and behavioral cues in Black and White children's perceptions of ambiguously aggressive acts. *Journal of Personality and Social Psychology, 39,* 590–598.

Schlenker, B. R., & Leary, M. R. (1982). Social anxiety and self-presentation: A conceptualization and model. *Psychological Bulletin, 92,* 641–669.

Seligman, M. E. P., Peterson, C., Kaslow, N. J., Tanenbaum, R. L., Alloy, L. B., & Abramson, L. Y. (1984). Explanatory style and depressive symptoms among children. *Journal of Abnormal Psychology, 93,* 235–238.

Senchak, M., & Leonard, K. E. (1994). Attributions for episodes of marital aggression: The effects of aggression severity and alcohol use. *Journal of Family Violence, 9,* 371–381.

Shields, N. M., & Hanneke, C. R. (1983). Attribution processes in violent relationships: Perceptions of violent husbands and their wives. *Journal of Applied Social Psychology, 13,* 515–527.

Shweder, R. A., & Bourne, E. (1982). Does the concept of the person vary cross-culturally? In A. J. Marsella & G. White (Eds.), *Cultural conceptions of mental health and therapy* (pp. 97–137). Boston: Reidel.

Silverman, R. J., & Peterson, C. (1993). Explanatory style of schizophrenic and depressed outpatients. *Cognitive Therapy and Research, 17,* 457–470.

Snyder, C. R., & Higgins, R. L. (1988). Excuses: Their effective role in the negotiation of reality. *Psychological Bulletin, 104,* 23–35.

Stipek, D. J., & Mason, T. C. (1987). Attributions, emotions, and behavior in the elementary school classroom. *Journal of Classroom Interaction, 22,* 1–5.

Swann, W. B., Jr., Pelham, B. W., & Roberts, D. C. (1987). Causal chunking: Memory and inference in ongoing interaction. *Journal of Personality and Social Psychology, 53,* 858–865.

Tangney, J. P. (1995). Shame and guilt in interpersonal relationships. In J. P. Tangney & K. W. Fischer (Eds.), *Self-conscious emotions: The psychology of shame, guilt, embarrassment, and pride* (pp. 114–142). New York: Guilford Press.

Taylor, S. E. (1982). Social cognition and health. *Personality and Social Psychology Bulletin, 8,* 549–562.

Taylor, S. E., & Fiske, S. T. (1975). Point of view and perceptions of causality. *Journal of Personality and Social Psychology, 32,* 439–445.

Teglasi, H., & Hoffman, M. A. (1982). Causal attributions of shy subjects. *Journal of Research in Personality, 16,* 376–385.

Townsley, R. M., Beach, S. R., Fincham, F. D., & O'Leary, K. D. (1991). Cognitive specificity for marital discord and depression: What types of cognition influence discord? *Behavior Therapy, 22,* 519–530.

Trivers, R. L. (1971). The evolution of reciprocal altruism. *Quarterly Review of Biology, 46,* 35–57.

Trope, Y. (1986). Identification and inferential processes in dispositional attribution. *Psychological Review, 93*, 239–257.

Uleman, J. S. (1987). Consciousness and control: The case of spontaneous trait inferences. *Personality and Social Psychology Bulletin, 13*, 337–354.

Weary, G., Stanley, M. A., & Harvey, J. H. (1989). *Attribution*. New York: Springer-Verlag.

Weiner, B. (1985). An attributional theory of achievement motivation and emotion. *Psychological Review, 92*, 548–573.

Weiner, B. (1986). *An attributional theory of motivation and emotion*. New York: Springer-Verlag.

Weiner, B. (1995). *Judgments of responsibility: A foundation for a theory of social conduct*. New York: Guilford Press.

Weiner, B., Graham, S., & Chandler, C. (1982). Causal antecedents of pity, anger, and guilt. *Personality and Social Psychology Bulletin, 8*, 226–232.

Weiner, B., Perry, R. P., & Magnusson, J. (1988). An attributional analysis of reactions to stigmas. *Journal of Personality and Social Psychology, 55*, 738–748.

Weiner, B., Russell, D., & Lerman, D. (1978). Affective consequences of causal ascriptions. In J. H. Harvey, W. J. Ickes, & R. F. Kidd (Eds.), *New directions in attribution research* (Vol. 2, pp. 59–88). Hillsdale, NJ: Erlbaum.

Weiner, B., Russell, D., & Lerman, D. (1979). The cognition–emotion process in achievement-related contexts. *Journal of Personality and Social Psychology, 37*, 1211–1220.

Weisz, J. R., Weiss, B., Alicke, M. D., & Klotz, M. L. (1987). Effectiveness of psychotherapy with children and adolescents: Meta-analytic findings for clinicians. *Journal of Consulting and Clinical Psychology, 55*, 542–549.

Wilson, T. D., & Linville, P. W. (1982). Improving the academic performance of college freshmen: Attribution therapy revisited. *Journal of Personality and Social Psychology, 42*, 367–376.

Yang, B., & Chum, G. A. (1994). Life stress, social support, and problem-solving skills predictive of depressive symptoms, hopelessness, and suicide ideation in an Asian student population: A test of a model. *Suicide and Life Threatening Behavior, 24*, 127–139.

Zebrowitz, L. A. (1990). *Social perception*. Pacific Grove, CA: Brooks/Cole.

3

EVERYDAY EGOCENTRISM AND EVERYDAY INTERPERSONAL PROBLEMS

THOMAS GILOVICH, JUSTIN KRUGER, AND KENNETH SAVITSKY

People turn to psychotherapists for help with a variety of psychological challenges. Some do so to be liberated from depression; others to cope with the death of a loved one; still others to overcome a personal failing, such as procrastination, sloth, or a tendency to eat to excess—or to eat barely anything at all. However, more clients enter a clinic to resolve problems with interpersonal relationships than for any other reason (Veroff, Kulka, & Douvan, 1981)—an ungratifying marriage, a conflict with an in-law, a rebellious teenager. Although everyone has shortcomings and a share of life's misfortunes, people seek professional assistance to deal with them mainly when such problems impede on their interpersonal relationships.

There are, in turn, many causes of interpersonal stress and conflict. Personalities clash. Values collide. Self-interests diverge. In this chapter, we examine a subtle but pervasive cause of interpersonal conflict: the difficulty people have in getting beyond, not their own interests, but their own perspective. Although people differ in the importance they place on maximizing their own well being, everyone is necessarily the center of his or her own world. Being at the center of one's world, furthermore, creates

69

a unique vantage point from which everything else is seen. And therein lies a fertile source of interpersonal difficulty. When two people with the best of intentions see the world differently, the possibility of interpersonal conflict exists. Indeed, to say that two people "see things differently" or that they "don't see eye to eye" is to say they are not getting along.

The failure to see things eye to eye can lead to trouble in a number of ways; we focus on three in this chapter. First, we explore how being at the center of their own world leads people to exaggerate how much they are responsible for joint projects. This bias, furthermore, can lead people to believe that they are being shortchanged and that others are slighting them for selfish reasons. Second, we examine how everyday, "normal" egocentrism leads people to overestimate the extent to which their appearance and behavior are noticed, evaluated, and remembered by others. This *spotlight effect* can inhibit people from taking certain actions that are in their best interests to take and therefore—later on—lead to nagging feelings of regret. In more extreme cases, the spotlight effect can start individuals down the path to social phobia and even paranoia. Finally, we discuss the related phenomenon of the *illusion of transparency*, the tendency for people to think that their internal states are more transparent and available to others' inspection than is actually the case. This can lead to interpersonal conflict when people think they have communicated their reactions more clearly than they truly have, and it can exacerbate such problems as speech anxiety and stuttering for which the fear that others can detect one's nervousness only serves to intensify one's symptomatology.

EGOCENTRIC ASSESSMENTS OF CREDIT AND BLAME

What happens when a married couple tries to assess whether the amount of work each is doing is "fair"? To do so, of course, requires an accurate assessment of the amount of work each person typically does—how much time and effort each spends doing the dishes, taking out the garbage, handling the finances, and so on. How accurate are such assessments?

This question was originally addressed by M. Ross and Sicoly (1979), who asked married couples to divide responsibility between themselves and their spouse for a series of joint activities. The authors then added together the proportions the two respondents claimed for themselves. If the couples were accurate in their assessments, the two estimates should have totaled 100%. They did not. The couples collectively tended to claim more than the maximally allowable 100% for a wide variety of joint marital activities. For example, the husband might estimate that he walks the dog 70% of the time, whereas his wife reports that she walks the dog 50% of the time. Together, these estimates total 120%—more than even the most energetic dog could have walked. This finding has been replicated by a number of researchers using several, slightly different methodologies (Christensen, Sullaway, & King, 1983; Deutsch, Lozy, & Saxon, 1993; Kruger & Gilovich, in press; Thompson & Kelley, 1981).

Why do couples overestimate? Part of the phenomenon doubtless stems from a motivated desire to claim as much as is reasonably possible for oneself. Greater assigned responsibility, after all, allows one to stake a greater claim to future benefits. Also a person's self-esteem may be enhanced by the belief that he or she is the primary agent in joint marital tasks. Thus, people may search harder to come up with instances in which they contributed to a given task than instances when their spouse bore the brunt of the effort, or they may weigh their own contributions more heavily than those of their spouse. Indeed, people have been found to claim more responsibility for successful than unsuccessful enterprises (Beckman, 1970; Forsyth & Schlenker, 1977; M. Ross & Sicoly, 1979, Study 2), a finding clearly consistent with this motivational interpretation.

But self interest is not the only thing that distorts people's attributions of responsibility. Married couples tend to overestimate their contribution not only to activities that reflect positively on the person who did them but also to those that reflect negatively on the responsible party. Motivated reasoning cannot account for this pattern of data. Furthermore, for couples at least, the magnitude of the overestimation is only weakly correlated with the desirability of the activity (Kruger & Gilovich, in press; M. Ross & Sicoly, 1979; Thompson & Kelley, 1981).

The other important variable at work then is an egocentric bias in the cognitive availability of information. Simply put, people have a much easier time remembering their own inputs than those of their partner. It is a lot easier to remember the times we did the dishes, fed the cat, or reigned in our anger than the times our spouse did. There are doubtless many reasons for this asymmetry in cognitive availability. For one, we are always present to witness our own contributions, not so for the contributions of others. We cannot fail to notice the instances when we vacuumed the living room, but our partner may have chosen to vacuum when we were at the beach, the ballpark, or the ballet; unless our powers of observation are keen, our partner's efforts may fail to register. Furthermore, even when we are aware of another person's contributions, we are unlikely to encode them as deeply or as richly. With more information concerning our own inputs to draw on, we recall them disproportionately.

It is also the case that many contributions to joint efforts are cognitive contributions—planning, obsessing, reviewing. They involve "stewing" rather than doing. For this type of effort, of course, the asymmetry in the availability of one's own and another's contributions is particularly pronounced. Finally, people may retrieve more of their own inputs when they apportion responsibility because they may frame the question or begin the search by asking "How much have I contributed?" rather than "How much has my spouse contributed?"

Regardless of the cause, the ready availability of people's own contributions results in a reliable egocentric bias in judgments of responsibility. Because the ease with which specific instances come to mind is used to estimate frequency (Tversky & Kahneman, 1973), individuals are prone to inflated views of their own relative contributions. A number of findings support this availability explanation. For one, experimental instructions that manipulate whether people focus on their own or the other person's contributions produce corresponding differences in responsibility allocations (Burger & Rodman, 1983; M. Ross & Sicoly, 1979, Experiment 5). In addition, the difference between the number of self and other inputs recalled (a measure of differential availability) is correlated with attributions of responsibility (M. Ross & Sicoly, 1979, Experiment 1; Thompson & Kelley, 1981). Finally, people report using information about themselves more than information about others when making such judgments (Brawley, 1984; Thompson & Kelley, 1981, Study 3).

Not surprisingly, egocentrically biased allocations of responsibility can have important interpersonal implications. Social and business relationships often require joint decisions and coordinated action. Overestimating one's role in such endeavors is likely to create conflict. According to equity theorists (e.g., Walster, Walster, & Berscheid, 1978), people desire proportionality between inputs and outcomes, for both themselves and others. It is this proportionality—this fairness—that determines people's satisfaction with their social and business interactions. But if people consistently overestimate their inputs, they may feel they are doing more than their share —and that others are doing less than theirs. Unfortunately, they are wrong, and to make matters worse, so is everyone else.

Consider the case, courtesy of M. Ross and Sicoly (1979), of determining authorship of a collaborative paper:

> You have worked on a research project with another person, and the question arises as to who should be "first author" (i.e., who contributed more to the final product?). Often, it seems that both of you feel entirely justified in claiming that honor. Moreover, since you are convinced that your view of reality must be shared by your colleague (there being only one reality), you assume that the other person is attempting to take advantage of you. Sometimes such concerns are settled or prevented by the use of arbitrary decision rules, for example, the rule of "alphabetical priority"—a favorite gambit of those whose surnames begin with letters in the first part of the alphabet. (p. 322)

Sound familiar? M. Ross (1981) described several historical examples of such disputes. John Banting and Fred Macleod, for instance, were awarded the Nobel Prize in 1923 for their discovery of insulin. On receiving the prize, Banting contended that Macleod, who was the head of the laboratory, had been more of a hindrance than a help. Macleod, however, managed to omit Banting's name in his speeches describing the research that led to their discovery (Harris, 1946).

Note that such disputes may create interpersonal discord for two very different reasons. First, people may feel underappreciated or underacknowledged because they have overestimated their own role. Second, should perceptions of responsibility become explicit (as they inevitably do in determining authorship, e.g.), people may fail to realize that differences in judgment could arise from honest evaluations of information that is differentially available. Instead, they may interpret the other party's views not as an attempt to get what they perceive as fair but as a calculated effort to take advantage of them. We discuss each of these sources of potential conflict in turn.

Before we do so, however, it is important to acknowledge that the consequences of inflated attributions of responsibility are not all bad. Recall, for example, that couples also overestimate their relative agency in negative or unsuccessful endeavors. Those who underestimate their partner's culpability for negative activities may hold more favorable impressions of one another. Indeed, researchers have found that the more that spouses underestimate their partners' contribution to negative events (and overestimate their own), the happier they are with their marriage (Fincham & Bradbury, 1989).

There are corresponding advantages to overestimating one's agency in the workplace. The feeling that one is carrying the weight of a joint endeavor may increase feelings of efficacy and control. Such beliefs are likely to energize increased effort and productivity. Indeed, people who possess a strong sense of personal control respond more vigorously to challenging tasks and persist at them longer (Bandura, 1986; Kamen & Seligman, 1986; Seligman & Schulman, 1986). Of course, such a strong sense of personal control is sometimes bittersweet, as it can come at the price of excessively blaming oneself for negative events. One need only consider the executive who takes too much responsibility for his company's bungled business opportunity, the graduate student who castigates herself excessively for a failed study, or the athlete who unrealistically assumes the entire blame for his team's loss.

"It's Not Fair": Interpersonal Consequences of Inflated Responsibility Estimates

Anecdotal evidence aside, the claim that inflated assessments of responsibility can have important interpersonal consequences has received much empirical support. People who claim more than their fair share of credit are not likely to win any popularity contests. Forsyth, Berger, and Mitchell (1981) conducted a study in which participants engaged in a group discussion, divided responsibility for the outcome, and ostensibly learned how the other group members had divided their responsibility. In actuality, the feedback had been previously crafted so that some participants appeared to overattribute. Participants who had ostensibly taken the "lion's share" of the responsibility for a success were less well liked than participants who had taken less credit. Furthermore, participants assumed these selfish individuals were harder to get along with and found them to be less desirable coworkers.

Returning to the context of marriage, a number of investigators have found that the more responsibility spouses claim for themselves for joint activities such as "initiating discussions about the relationship," the less satisfied they are with one another (Fincham & Bradbury, 1989; Thompson & Kelley, 1981). Of course, this finding is correlational, so the usual caution applies. Nevertheless, biased responsibility allocation might give rise to marital dissatisfaction for at least two reasons. In keeping with equity theory, a couple's dissatisfaction may stem from feelings of inequity or injustice. People tend to become disgruntled with a relationship if they believe they are doing more than their fair share to maintain it. In addition, overestimating their role in marital activities may lead people to believe that they "call the shots" or "wear the pants" in the relationship more than is actually the case. This, in turn, may cause people to undervalue their spouse. In support of this contention, research indicates that perceived control of marital decision making is related to lower evaluations of one's spouse (Kipnis, Castell, Gergen, & Mauch, 1976).

Biased allocations of responsibility may likewise generate problems in the business world. It is a basic tenet of human resource management that employees tend to be satisfied only when the balance between inputs (i.e., work) and outputs (i.e., salary) is perceived as equitable. People tend to be happiest when everyone is paid in accordance with his or her contributions. Indeed, perceived compensation fairness is one of the strongest predictors of job satisfaction among workers in the United States and around the world (DeConinck, Stilwell, & Brock, 1996; Heneman & Schwab, 1985; Scarpello & Jones, 1996; Singh, 1994). Of course, if people demand proportionality between work inputs and rewards yet overestimate their own inputs, they are unlikely to view their own compensation as fair. As a result, employees will tend to feel underpaid and underacknowledged.

The same sort of egocentrism that gives rise to biased assessments of responsibility may likewise have important implications for bargaining and negotiation. Consider the case of two civil disputants attempting to arrive at a fair out-of-court settlement or a company negotiating its take-over price. The salience of one's own inputs may lead to an exaggerated belief in the strength of one's side or the value of one's company. The arguments that one's attorney develops to sway the judge or jury, for example, are likely to be particularly available and can lead to inflated assessments of what constitutes a fair settlement. Such beliefs, in turn, can impede successful negotiation.

Babcock and Loewenstein (1997) examined the impact of negotiators' *interesting study* beliefs about the strength of their side and found that when disputants overestimate the strength of their own position, settlement is often delayed or precluded. In one study, participants were assigned the role of plaintiff or defendant and were asked to negotiate a settlement in a mock court case arising from an automobile accident. All participants received the same materials about the case (e.g., witness testimony, police reports) and faced substantial financial incentives to settle. The participants were asked, individually and anonymously, what they considered a fair amount for the plaintiff to receive in an out-of-court settlement. In particular, they were asked to estimate a settlement price that would seem fair to a neutral third party.

Two important findings emerged. First, both sides tended to overestimate the strength of their case. Plaintiffs' assessments of a fair settlement price were, on average, $17,709 higher than the defendants', even though both had access to the exact same information about the case. Second, the extent of this bias was related to the ability to reach a settlement. The more the two sides overestimated the strength of their case, the less likely they were to settle. In a follow-up study designed to establish the causal link between bias and settlement, the experimenters manipulated whether participants learned of their role as plaintiff or defendant before reading the case materials or after. When participants learned their roles after reading the materials, they were less likely to overestimate the strength of their case, and more likely to settle.

Why does exaggerating the strength of one's own side inhibit settlement? The answer appears to be the same reason that workers are unhappy with wages that fall below what they feel they deserve, and that married couples are unhappy with their partner's contributions: fairness or, rather, the perception of fairness. If both sides distort the strength of their own positions, it is hard to find a compromise that both perceive to be fair. In keeping with this notion, researchers have found that negotiators are strongly averse to settling even slightly below the point they view as fair (e.g., Loewenstein, Thompson, & Bazerman, 1989).

"They're Not Being Fair": Biased Perceptions of Bias

The extent to which egocentrically biased perceptions of responsibility might harm everyday social relationships also depends on how people explain any such discrepancies of judgment that become apparent. If one's partner assumes more credit than one thinks is fair, one is unlikely to get too worked up if one thinks it is due to an honest difference in perspective and cognitive availability. However, one does not take so kindly to a divergence of opinion if one thinks it stems from a deliberate attempt to gain favor. Exaggerated claims by coauthors that are seen as strategic attempts to improve authorship position rarely go over well and often result in the end of the collaboration.

How do people resolve discrepancies in judgments of responsibility? Kruger and Gilovich (in press) examined this question in several recent studies. In one, married couples were asked to divide responsibility between themselves and their spouse in a manner similar to other research in this area—but with one twist: Afterwards, couples were asked to predict their spouse's estimates, that is, how they thought their spouse would allocate responsibility between the two of them. Kruger and Gilovich found that couples correctly anticipated that their spouse would claim more than their fair share of credit for activities that reflect positively on the person who performs them. Thus, it did not surprise participants that their spouse would overestimate responsibility for "spending time on appearance to please one's partner." This result suggests that social perceivers may have at least some understanding that judgments of responsibility may be biased—so far, so good. Unfortunately, other data suggest that people only get part of the story right and, furthermore, that when they are right, they are right for the wrong reasons.

As noted above, married individuals correctly expect their partners to claim more than their fair share of credit for activities that reflected positively on the person who did them. However, they also expect—incorrectly—that their partners will avoid the blame for negative activities, such as "causing arguments that occur between the two of you." Thus, they predict the bias correctly for positive activities but get it backwards for activities that reflect negatively on the person who performed them. Kruger and Gilovich's (in press) participants, in other words, were not purely *self-interested agents*—they did not give themselves credit for the good while blaming others for the bad—but they were strong *self-interest theorists*—they expected others to do just that (cf. Miller & Ratner, 1996).

The participants were mistaken in another way as well: Even when they were correct about the direction of bias, they misgauged its magnitude. Married individuals in these studies overestimated the extent to which their partners would claim responsibility for positive activities. This is consistent with a finding by Robinson, Keltner, Ward, and Ross (1995), who assessed the attitudes of self-described liberals and conservatives about a racial discrimination case. They found that although liberals and conservatives did differ in their interpretation of the politically charged incident, they did not differ as much as they thought they would.

It also appears that people assume that others, rather than themselves, are prone to bias. People seem to believe that they are privy to a knowable, objective reality and that those who claim to see things differently must be biased. This *naive realism* (L. Ross & Ward, 1996) was apparent in the study by Robinson et al. (1995), described above. Both liberals and conservatives believed that the other side's judgments had been more influenced by political ideology and less influenced by the available evidence than their own. Thus, people are likely to believe that their own assessments of responsibility are accurate whereas the judgments of others are not. We examined this possibility explicitly by asking participants who had played a series of videogames with a teammate to divide responsibility between the two of them for several outcomes of the game (e.g., points earned). Afterwards, participants indicated how they thought their teammate and an unbiased observer would apportion responsibility between themselves and their teammate. Participants believed that their teammate's judgments would be quite different from their own—but naively assumed that a neutral observer would see things just as they themselves did (Kruger & Gilovich, 1998).

In his 1981 chapter, M. Ross posited that a simple appreciation of the tendency to allocate responsibility in a biased manner might serve to ameliorate some of the "negative effects of self-centeredness" (p. 320). Sadly, the data suggest that although people may have some appreciation of this bias, they intuit neither its cause nor their own susceptibility. In fact, people's intuitions about bias appear less forgiving than their actual biases.

"I Can See Clearly Now": Overcoming Biased Responsibility Allocation

There may be ways to ameliorate the everyday problems that biased responsibility allocations create. One approach is to change the differential availability of people's personal contributions. By targeting the extent to which one remembers one's own contributions more easily than the contributions of another, inflated responsibility allocations may be lessened. Toward this end, M. Ross and Sicoly (1979, Experiment 5) asked graduate students to divide responsibility for their bachelor theses between themselves and their undergraduate supervisors. Students indicated either the relative percentage for which they were responsible or the relative percentage for which their supervisor was responsible. Despite the underlying equivalence of the two questions, the students' responses were quite different in the two conditions: The students assigned themselves less personal responsibility when they were asked for their supervisor's relative contribution. Apparently, this version of the question caused participants to search their memories for their supervisors' inputs more than they would have done otherwise and thus lessened the differential availability of their own contributions.

A second approach seeks not to eliminate the biased responsibility allocating but to alter people's explanations for it. This approach is based on the assumption that "knowledge will set one free" and that knowing about the bias will lessen its troublesome impact. If one knows that people in general tend to claim too much credit for themselves, not just one's partner, the behavior is normalized and can seem less irksome. In addition, if one recognizes that the behavior is often the product of an honest cognitive bias, not a motivated grab for credit, it is easier to respond more temperately. The need to "stand one's ground" and react defensively is lessened. After all, much of the conflict that stems from this bias is tied not to the bias itself but to people's explanations for it. Successful intervention then may consist of getting people to substitute a benign cognitive explanation for the more explosive motivational theories they entertain naturally.

A final intervention aims to circumvent biased responsibility allocation rather than lessen its magnitude or alter how it is explained. This technique applies most readily to people in on-going, long-term relationships and is based on the premise that egocentric biases in retrospective assessments of who did what may be too hard to overcome. It is better to avoid such biases altogether by deciding in advance on what constitutes a fair division of labor and agreeing beforehand on which tasks are to be performed by whom. Judgments of fairness are then made in the clear light of foresight rather than under the dark cloud of retrospection. This technique can be enhanced by using the same technique that one often recommends to children who must share a cookie: One breaks the cookie in half, and the other picks the half he or she prefers. In this case, one person might devise two equal menus of chores, and the other person then chooses one set to perform. By using such techniques, the differential availability in memory never comes into play and potentially acrimonious accusations of selfishness are avoided.

THE SPOTLIGHT EFFECT: EGOCENTRIC ASSESSMENTS OF THE SALIENCE OF ONE'S ACTIONS AND APPEARANCE

The work on responsibility allocation that we just reviewed is concerned with people's estimates of what transpired or "who did how much." As we just saw, such estimates are commonly biased in an egocentric direction, with people claiming more responsibility for both positive and negative outcomes than is objectively warranted (M. Ross & Sicoly, 1979; Thompson & Kelley, 1981). But what happens when people are asked not about general outcomes or processes but about particular actions? Specifically, how salient do people think their own actions are in the eyes of others? It does not take great powers of derivation to propose that the same egocentrism that gives rise to biased responsibility allocation may likewise generate biased assessments of how clearly one's actions stand out and are available to others. People may assume, in other words, that their actions, because they command so much of their own attention, are likely to occupy the attention of others as well.

Consider the activity of dining alone in a restaurant. If you are like most people, it is a decidedly unpleasant experience, primarily because of the sense that "all eyes are on you"—eyes that are likely to size you up as a friendless outcast. Indeed, many people go to great lengths to portray their isolation in a more favorable light (to an audience that may or may not be attending). Some bring work to the table, others ask for a seat in a remote corner of the restaurant, and still others—the boldest—ostentatiously take notes like a discriminating restaurant critic. Mercifully, some restaurants provide assistance to solo diners by offering an eating counter that simultaneously seats them facing away from those eating with friends and family and offers the opportunity to connect socially to the cooking staff and to others eating alone (Goffman, 1963).

Of course, this feeling of sticking out like the proverbial "sore thumb" is not limited to dining alone in a restaurant. People feel it whenever they are momentarily caught with no one to talk to at a cocktail party, when they fumble for change or have to ask for directions at the front of a bus, or when their hair is having one of its recalcitrant, unmanageable days. To flesh out this feeling still further, we turn not to "the literature" but to literature, that is, fiction, and a passage from Tom Wolfe's (1987) *The Bonfire of the Vanities*. In one scene, the book's protagonist, Sherman McCoy, finds himself without a conversational partner at a Manhattan cocktail party:

> Now what would he do? All at once he was alone in this noisy hive with no place to roost. Alone! He became acutely aware that the entire party was now composed of these [conversational] bouquets and that not to be in one of them was to be an abject, incompetent social failure.
>
> He moved on . . . Alone! . . . He felt the pressure of social failure . . . What could he do to make it appear as if he *meant* to be by himself, as if he were moving through the hive by choice?
>
> Near the doorway . . . were models of the seating arrangement for dinner . . . It struck Sherman, the leonine Yale man, as another piece of vulgarity. Nevertheless, he looked. It was a way of appearing occupied, as if he were alone for no other reason than to study the seating arrangement. (p. 353)

It is entirely possible, of course, that Sherman McCoy, like many who find themselves in such situations, is appropriately concerned about the image he is projecting and the need to "put up a good front." Perhaps Sherman's fellow Manhattan socialites noticed his predicament and—what is more—formed lasting opinions of his social skills, his character, or his status on that basis. A large literature in social psychology attests to people's tendency to form strong dispositional inferences about others on the basis of the flimsiest behavioral evidence. That is, people are inclined to jump to conclusions about what someone is like by observing that person's behavior, not granting appropriate weight to mitigating situational factors (Gilbert & Jones, 1986; Jones & Harris, 1967; L. Ross, 1977; L. Ross, Amabile, & Steinmetz, 1977).

Still, we suspect that this is often not the case in situations like the one confronting Sherman McCoy. On the whole, fewer people may notice one's isolation than one suspects; fewer still may view it in a negative light. Indeed, recent research suggests that because individuals are so caught up in monitoring their behavior in such situations, they have difficulty gauging how prominent their actions are in the eyes of others. In particular, people overestimate the likelihood that those present will notice and remember their own actions, whether those actions reflect positively or negatively on them.

In one set of studies (Gilovich, Medvec, & Savitsky, 1998), for example, participants engaged in a group discussion on a sensitive topic for a 30-min period and were then led to separate cubicles and asked to rank everyone in the group, themselves included, on a number of positive and negative dimensions. Who contributed the most to the group discussion? Who made the greatest number of speech errors? Who made the most comments that others would be likely to judge critically? They were asked to rank everyone both as they themselves thought appropriate and as they thought the group as a whole would rank everyone. This allowed a comparison between how participants thought their fellow group members would see them and how the rest of the group actually did see them. The results revealed substantial egocentrism. Participants thought they would be ranked higher by others than they actually were on all dimensions, whether positive or negative. It seems that people believe the social spotlight shines more brightly on them than is actually the case.

Several additional studies document this *spotlight effect* in a very different paradigm—one that captures the embarrassment a person often feels when caught in the spotlight (Gilovich, Medvec, et al., 1998). Participants arrived at a laboratory individually and were told—without explanation —to "put on this shirt." The experimenter then handed the participant an oversized T-shirt with a large picture of the pop singer Barry Manilow on the front (a figure of dubious renown on college campuses). The experimenter then explained that the remainder of the study would be run in a laboratory down the hall and would be conducted by a different experimenter. The participant was led to the new laboratory and told to knock on the door, where the second experimenter would "take it from there."

After entering the new lab, the participant was confronted by a second experimenter and five other participants who were filling out questionnaires. The experimenter gestured to a chair opposite of everyone else and told the participant to be seated. But just as he or she was about to do so, the experimenter interjected that "on second thought," the others were too far ahead and maybe it would be best if the participant waited outside for a moment. The participant then went outside and was soon joined by the experimenter, who explained that the study was concerned with incidental memory. In particular, the experimenter wanted to compare the incidental memories of the five individuals still in the room with the participant's intuitions about incidental memory. Accordingly, the participant was asked to estimate how many of the others would recall accurately the participant's hair color, whether he or she was wearing glasses, and (the real item of interest) who was pictured on the participant's shirt.

As expected, the participants thought they (and their questionable T-shirt) stood out more than they actually did. Participants estimated that nearly 50% of their fellow participants would notice who was pictured on their shirt, when in reality less than 25% did so (Gilovich, Medvec, et al., 1998). People often occupy less of the social spotlight than they think.

"I Could've Been a Contender": The Spotlight Effect and the Experience of Regret

When asked to review their entire lives and think of their biggest regrets, most people report regretting things they have failed to do rather than things they have done: not going to college, not reconciling with a parent or child, not learning to play a musical instrument or to speak a foreign language. Many of these regrets of inaction, furthermore, seem to stem from a failure to act because of a concern about the prospect of failing and how it would look to others. "I never asked her out because I thought she might say no and everyone would think less of me." "I could never summon the courage to play at my piano teacher's recitals, and now I can't play in front of anyone." "I knew the moment was ripe, but I was afraid of what others would think" (Gilovich & Medvec, 1994, 1995; Hattiangadi, Medvec, & Gilovich, 1995).

It is not difficult to see the role of the spotlight effect in such decisions. People may fail to act because of a concern—an exaggerated concern—that if they fail, everyone else will know about it and view them critically. In fact, however, the research on the spotlight effect that we just reviewed suggests that much of this concern about what others may think is misplaced—others are less likely to notice or think much about one's failures than one suspects. Over time, these failures to act can lead to the pain of regret, particularly as one's confidence that one would have succeeded grows and one's concern over others' reactions shrinks (Gilovich, Kerr, & Medvec, 1993).

Does this mean that people should throw caution to the wind and act boldly whenever possible? Not necessarily. There may be sound, functional reasons for an *omission bias*—a reluctance to depart from the status quo (Spranca, Minsk, & Baron, 1991). Adherence to the status quo has at least kept one alive—up to the point of the decision, at any rate. Rash actions, however, can put one's survival at risk. Thus, people may benefit from a reluctance to rush in too soon; if a degree of existential angst and regret over failing to seize the moment is the price to be paid for caution, so be it.

But what knowledge of the spotlight effect should encourage is a different attitude toward those actions that one truly wants to take but hesitates from doing so out of a concern of what others will think if one fails. In these situations, the spotlight research suggests that one should be more bold. Even if one does fail, the social consequences are generally not as severe as people think. As important as one's failures are to oneself, they are less so to others. Others are often too busy with their own concerns to even notice.

"What Will Everyone Think?": The Spotlight Effect, Social Phobia, and Paranoia

So far, our focus in this chapter has been on how everyday egocentrism can play a role in everyday interpersonal difficulties—miscommunication, hurt feelings, social awkwardness, intractable disagreements, and so on. Sometimes, however, such egocentrism can lead to more severe conditions as well. Consider, for instance, the spotlight effect that we just described. Most people would acknowledge that the feeling of being in the spotlight can be uncomfortable and aversive and that the fear of others' evaluations may be responsible for a few missed opportunities. For some, however, the fear that people are paying attention to them and perhaps judging them critically goes much further. At its most extreme, this fear translates into the paralyzing condition of social phobia or social anxiety disorder. "The essential feature of Social Phobia is a marked and persistent fear of social or performance situations in which embarrassment may occur" (American Psychiatric Association, 1994, p. 411). In some performance situations, of course, such a fear may be warranted because the spotlight is indeed on. In other circumstances, however, the fear is out of proportion to the actual risk; many fewer people are likely to notice and evaluate the phobic individual's actions than he or she suspects. Indeed, one promising form of therapy with socially phobic individuals involves getting them to make more realistic assessments of the scrutiny they are likely to receive from others (Heimberg, 1990).

The spotlight effect also has obvious connections to the phenomenon of paranoia. As Fenigstein and Vanable (1992) pointed out, it has long been a clinical insight that a heightened sense of self-consciousness is associated with paranoia, dating back at least to the seminal theorizing of Kraepelin (1915). Fenigstein and Vanable examined this relationship in a series of experiments and suggested that a seemingly paranoid tendency for individuals to overperceive the extent to which others' behavior is directed at them, a tendency they refer to as the *self-as-target bias*, is rather common in college student populations (Fenigstein, 1984; Fenigstein & Vanable, 1992). An awareness of the self, particularly an awareness of oneself as a social object, appears to be intertwined with the concern—pathological or not—that one is the focus of others' attention and scrutiny. As Fenigstein and Vanable (1992) put it, "ordinary individuals, in their everyday behavior, manifest characteristics—such as self-centered thought, suspiciousness, assumptions of ill will or hostility, and even notions of conspiratorial intent—that are reminiscent of paranoia" (p. 130). Thus, the difference between clinical paranoia and the kind of egocentric biases that are our chief concern here may be one of degree, not of kind.

THE ILLUSION OF TRANSPARENCY

We just saw how the thought and attention people devote to monitoring their actions and appearance can lead them to overestimate how salient they are to others. But what about their covert behavior—their thoughts, feelings, and internal sensations? These too are often the object of a person's attention and the subject of rumination. Does the attention people devote to such inner states distort their assessment of how apparent such states are to others?

We believe so. In particular, we propose that people are prone to an illusion of transparency, believing that their thoughts, feelings, and emotions are more apparent to others than is actually the case. Although most people realize, on some level, that others cannot "read their minds" and have no direct access to their internal sensations, they may fail to correct adequately for this realization when attempting to determine how they appear to others. The net result of this process then is that people may not only overestimate the extent to which others take note of them, as we discussed in the previous section, but also exaggerate the extent to which others can detect their internal sensations.

Gilovich, Savitsky, and Medvec (1998) documented this illusion in several experiments. In one taste test experiment, volunteers came to the laboratory individually and were videotaped as they tasted a series of five drinks, one by one. Before each participant arrived, the experimenters had concocted one of the five drinks to be quite distasteful and then had randomly placed the offensive drink amidst the other four. Tasters were told to expect one foul-tasting drink in the set, but they did not know which it would be (despite tasting markedly different, the foul-tasting drink looked identical to the other four). Of critical importance, the tasters were instructed to conceal their reactions to the foul-tasting drink so as to prevent any onlookers from guessing which one it had been.

After the last drink, the tasters were asked to indicate how well they thought they had been able to follow this instruction, that is, how well they had succeeded in holding their feelings in or how much of their disgust over tasting the foul-tasting drink had "leaked out," despite their best attempts to conceal it. In particular, tasters estimated the proportion of observers who would be able to tell which of the five drinks had been the foul-tasting one solely on the basis of the taster's videotaped facial expressions. In fact, groups of judges watched videotapes of the tasters and attempted to do just that. The tasters' estimates of their own leakage could then be compared with the observers' actual ability to identify the foul-tasting drink.

How accurate were tasters' estimates? As anticipated, tasters succumbed to an illusion of transparency. They overestimated the extent to which their internal feelings of disgust had been apparent to others and consequently overestimated the number of observers who could identify the foul-tasting drink. In fact, tasters expected about twice the accuracy rate that observers were able to muster. Put simply, tasters' disgust was not as apparent as they suspected—they were far less transparent than they thought (Gilovich, Savitsky, et al., 1998).

Analogous results have been obtained in a variety of other experiments. In one, participants who were told to lie believed that they had leaked more cues to deception than they actually had and thus overestimated the extent to which their lies were detectable to others (Gilovich, Savitsky, et al., 1998). In another study, participants who were alarmed over a potential emergency situation believed that their concern was more apparent to others than was actually the case (Gilovich, Savitsky, et al., 1998). How might this illusion of transparency contribute to everyday interpersonal problems? We highlight two potential sources of difficulty, one intrapersonal and one interpersonal.

From Bad to Worse: The Illusion of Transparency and Self-Exacerbating Syndromes

Many problems have the property that worrying about them makes them worse. This may be particularly true of the problem of covering up thoughts and feelings that one would prefer to remain hidden. In this case, the thought that others might be able to detect one's internal states can lead a person to focus undue attention on such states. Thus, what begins as a troubling concern can spiral into a debilitating obsession. The mistaken belief that one's problematic internal sensations are leaking out, in other words, and the focus of attention that results can lead to a perpetuation and exacerbation of those very sensations.

Consider the anxiety many people feel over the prospect of delivering a public speech—anxiety that has been shown to be often less apparent to others than the speaker believes (Savitsky, 1997). For many people, speech anxiety is a significant concern and a consequential affliction. In one survey of individuals with public speaking anxiety, many reported that their fear was so great that it forced them to change jobs or interfered with their education (Stein, Walker, & Forde, 1996).

But fears over public speaking also possess a component that goes beyond simply being frightened or nervous over the prospect of speaking in front of people. In the survey cited above, fully 80% of the respondents with public speaking fears indicated being concerned that they would "tremble, shake, or show some other signs of anxiety" (Stein et al., 1996, p. 172) while speaking. In other words, they indicated being anxious over the possibility that they might appear to be anxious to others. They were nervous about looking nervous. Given that people are prone to an illusion of transparency, it is easy to see how speech anxiety can become self-perpetuating. An individual may experience some amount of nervousness when giving a speech, feelings that he or she may believe are more apparent to the audience than is actually the case. This thought—that the audience is aware of just how nervous he or she feels—may then ironically serve to make the speaker all the more nervous. The speaker then believes that this newfound nervousness is itself apparent to others, leading to still more nervousness, and so on.[1]

Speech anxiety may thus be an example of what Storms and McCaul (1976) have termed *self-exacerbating syndromes*. According to these authors, the experience of many conditions can itself lead to an increase in those very conditions. Storms and McCaul (1976) cited the example of a tennis player with doubts about the quality of her game: "Her serve, for no particular reason, has a tendency to fall apart in the midst of a match. She gets angry and frustrated, curses her athletic inadequacy, and double-faults her way through the rest of the set" (p. 143). Her thoughts about her own apparent shortcomings, it seems, only make matters worse. Storms and McCaul discussed numerous examples of such syndromes, including stuttering, insomnia, and writer's block, and link the phenomenon to a variety

---

[1] In fact, the individual need not even experience any bona fide anxiety to set this cycle in motion. Normal preparatory arousal, stemming from the simple need to "get with it" and mobilize whatever cognitive and motor programs are required to perform, may be misattributed as pangs of anxiety and self-doubt. That is, the individual may reason heuristically and conclude "if I am feeling these feelings of arousal, I must be nervous about giving this speech" (Savitsky, Medvec, Charlton, & Gilovich, 1998; Schwarz, 1990; Schwarz & Clore, 1983). The concern that such feelings are apparent to others then may give rise to a more genuine experience of nervousness and anxiety, which the individual may then think is also leaking out, and so on, as before.

of attentional and attributional mechanisms. The phenomenon of *stereotype threat*, whereby members of stigmatized groups ironically come to fulfill the negative stereotypes held about their group through their worries and concerns about fulfilling those very stereotypes, may also be a manifestation of this process (Steele & Aronson, 1995).

To this list then we can add the fear of public speaking as well as more generalized social anxiety. The literature on social anxiety suggests that like speech anxiety, it is often characterized by a profound concern that one's privately experienced distress is readily observable to others (Marks, 1969; Nichols, 1974)—concerns that are largely illusory (Clark & Arkowitz, 1975; McEwan & Devins, 1983). One can readily imagine, for example, the same spiral described above plaguing an individual who is chronically shy and nervous about approaching potential romantic partners. The conviction that his or her nervousness is more apparent than it actually is can serve, once again, to heighten his or her experience of nervousness, ultimately jeopardizing the whole endeavor.

In general, we suggest that any time people are nervous over the very prospect of appearing nervous, the illusion that they are more transparent than they actually are can send them into a spiral of ever-heightening anxiety and worry over the leakage of that anxiety. In the end, a person's nervousness may reach a "fevered pitch" and become just as apparent to others as initially feared. In this way, the illusion of transparency can render an individual's fears self-fulfilling and can turn what is initially a troubling concern into a severe and debilitating affliction.

"You Should Have Known How I Felt": The Illusion of Transparency and Interpersonal Conflict

The illusion of transparency, like its close cousin, the spotlight effect, can instigate interpersonal conflict. Consider the results of one additional experiment, a facial expressions study (Savitsky, 1997). Participants in this experiment were given sets of six emotions and asked to portray—through their facial expressions alone—one emotion from each set as they were videotaped. After each facial expression, they were asked how successful they thought they had been. In particular, they were asked to predict the proportion of observers who would be able to identify the emotion they had portrayed. How many observers would be able to tell, for example, that it was confusion rather than hatred, worry, frustration, fatigue, or embarrassment that they had tried to express?

As in the taste test study discussed above, Savitsky (1997) then showed the videotapes to observers. The observers were simply asked to identify the emotion the expressor had attempted to convey in each instance. Their ability to do so could then be compared with the expressors' predictions. As before, this comparison revealed a substantial illusion of transparency: Expressors thought they had been able to convey their emotional states through their facial expressions with far greater clarity than they actually had. That is, observers' actual ability to recognize the expressors' emotional expressions fell far short of the expressors' expectations.

Note that unlike the taste test study and the other results discussed above, in which participants attempted to conceal their internal states from others, these results demonstrate that the illusion also applies to instances in which people attempt to communicate their internal states. Here too the strength and richness of a person's own experience of an emotional state may not come across in his or her attempts to communicate it to others. It can be difficult to distill the complex nature of emotional states, such as envy, excitement, or jealousy into an adequate facial expression. But because these states may be felt so clearly, the individual may lose sight of this fact. It is easy to confuse the clarity of one's internal experience with the clarity of one's expressive behavior. Because adjustments from judgmental starting points are often insufficient (Jacowitz & Kahneman, 1995; Tversky & Kahneman, 1974), people may fail to correct adequately for the discrepancy between their internal experience and its external manifestations, even when they are aware that such a correction is necessary. As a result, the attempt to communicate particular thoughts, feelings, and other internal states can fall short of how well one thinks one has communicated them, leaving others with little idea of one's intended meaning.

This tendency can shed light on certain types of interpersonal conflict. Consider, once again, two individuals in a marital relationship. Research shows that the ability to read one another's nonverbal communications is related to marital satisfaction (Gottman & Porterfield, 1981; Kahn, 1970; Noller, 1980). We suggest, further, that people's beliefs about how well they communicate their inner thoughts and emotions may have a similar effect. If people overestimate the clarity with which they have sent certain signals ("that's annoying," "I need some attention," or "my mind is made up"), they may interpret their partners' failure to take appropriate action as evidence of moodiness, a lack of caring, or, worse, open hostility. This can lead, in turn, to accusations that their partner is insensitive or "just doesn't care." In general, an exaggerated view of how well one has communicated one's inner states or an unrealistic expectation that one's partner is able to "read one's mind" can give rise to misunderstanding. In this way, the illusion of transparency may be one source of interpersonal discord, and couples especially prone to the illusion may be particularly prone to conflict.

An exaggerated sense of the clarity of one's attempted communications undoubtedly contributes to a host of other interpersonal difficulties in a host of other contexts. Disagreements related to perceived transparency may be particularly common in the workplace, where a sense of decorum can prevent individuals from speaking their minds with complete candor, relying instead on insinuation and the belief that others will "know what I mean." Managers, for instance, may tend to overestimate the degree to which they have communicated their pleasure or displeasure to their subordinates or may believe they have stated their expectations more clearly than is actually the case. This can lead to a host of inefficiencies, as the subordinate's output does not match what is truly needed. It can lead also to an explosive "chewing out" of the subordinate, which is likely to produce resentment and a sense that the supervisor is petty, capricious, and unpredictable. Poor morale, slacking, and even deliberate sabotage can result.

Workers, for their part, may likewise fail to sufficiently apprise their supervisors of their thoughts, such as their reservations about certain policies. This too can lead to waste, as the failure to provide feedback can send a company down a dead end, with resources squandered on a product or policy with unspoken shortcomings. This is analogous to the phenomenon of *groupthink*—the tendency for individuals in a group to suppress their inner doubts about a policy out of the desire not to "rock the boat" and disrupt group harmony (Janis, 1972, 1982; Mullen, Anthony, Salas, & Driskell, 1994). We can only wonder whether the illusion of transparency has a hand in this potentially destructive process as well. Individuals who are afraid to challenge the group openly may try to communicate their reservations nonverbally. If they believe they have done so more effectively than they actually have, they may feel no need to do what really needs to be done, namely, to communicate their concerns explicitly, clearly, and forcefully. What is more, workers may perceive others' failures to heed their advice as an implicit signal that their opinions—or even they themselves—are not valued, when in reality it reflects a simple failure to communicate.

The illusion of transparency may also play a role in that much-discussed and particularly vexatious problem of the modern workplace, sexual harassment. If the object of an individual's amorous advances believes that he or she has sent a clearer message of "not interested" than is actually the case, then he or she may interpret continued pursuit as harassment. The resultant accusation may then come as something of a shock to the pursuer, as he or she may think that both were engaged in a consensual flirtation. We do not mean to suggest, of course, that such misperceptions on the part of targets are involved in all cases of sexual harassment. Boorish, insensitive sexual predators do exist. Nevertheless, issues of sex and attraction (and the lack thereof) are issues that people often refrain from discussing directly. Communication in this area is often nuanced, indirect, and nonverbal. It is, in other words, precisely the type of domain in which the illusion of transparency is likely to be pervasive and pronounced.

CONCLUSIONS, SUGGESTIONS, AND
UNANSWERED QUESTIONS

One of the most productive areas of psychological research over the past 30 years has been the examination of everyday human judgment. This research shows clearly that people's judgments are prone to systematic biases and, as a result, people often misevaluate the evidence of their everyday experience and render faulty judgments, form dubious beliefs, and embark on unwise courses of action (Dawes, 1988; Gilovich, 1991; Kahneman, Slovic, & Tversky, 1982; Nisbett & Ross, 1980). In this chapter, we examined some of the faulty judgments people commonly make about how they are seen by others. Correctly anticipating how one is viewed by others is not easy because one can never truly "get out of one's skin" and view oneself from another's vantage point. Although one occupies the center of one's own "lifespace" (Lewin, 1951), one seldom is so prominent in the lifespace of others. This difference in vantage points can lead to misperception and misunderstanding.

We examined three of the most common difficulties people encounter when trying to get beyond the self. First, we discussed how the salience of one's own contributions to a joint effort—to oneself at least—can lead to an innocent bias in estimates of how much one has contributed. People tend to assign themselves more credit than their partners are willing to grant them. We saw how this can lead to conflict, as both partners may think that they are being shortchanged and that the other person is deliberately slighting them out of selfish motives. We also examined how the care and attention that people devote to monitoring their own actions and appearance can lead them to overestimate how salient a stimulus they are to others. People tend to believe that the social spotlight is directed at them more than actually is the case. This often leads to a degree of self-consciousness that is debilitating. At its most benign, it gives rise to missed opportunities and a nagging sense that one has not lived one's life to the fullest; at its most troublesome, it paves the way to extreme social reticence and phobia. Finally, we reviewed the parallel phenomenon of the illusion of transparency, the belief that one's inner states are more apparent to others than is actually the case. Here too the bias stems from the difficulty of getting beyond the self: Because one's inner thoughts and feelings are such a powerful part of one's own experience, it is difficult to appreciate how unavailable they are to others. The illusion of transparency can lead to problems at home and the office as people think they have communicated better than they have, so the unresponsiveness of others is attributed to insensitivity or a lack of concern.

In our discussion of these three egocentric biases, we emphasized how they tend to affect the thoughts of just about anyone and how they give rise to a variety of everyday interpersonal difficulties. Beyond our discussion of paranoia and social phobia, we gave scant attention to the pronounced individual differences in egocentrism that one observes in the normal course of social interaction and the more extreme pathological conditions that excessive egocentrism can create. This is not to suggest that such extreme individuals or such debilitating conditions do not exist. They do, as the literature on narcissism (Kernberg, 1975), depression (Ingram & Smith, 1984; Smith & Greenberg, 1981), and alcoholism (Hull & Young, 1983; Hull, Young, & Jouriles, 1986), to cite just a few examples, makes clear. But a complete account of such people and conditions requires an analysis of a host of causes and conditions that lie beyond the straightforward cognitive biases that have been our concern in this chapter.

We also declined to address whether there are any developmental trends in the magnitude of the egocentric biases we discussed. This question is perhaps most pertinent to the spotlight effect. As any parent or high school teacher can attest, adolescents are unusually concerned with how they are seen by others and absolutely convinced that they *are* seen by others—that all eyes are on them (Elkind, 1967). Irrational thoughts that "I could never live it down" or "I would rather die" abound. Indeed, all too many adolescent suicides are precipitated by a sense of humiliation brought on by some perceived loss of face (Shaffer, 1974, 1988). To the extent that such a loss of face is more apparent than real—that is, the potential suicide victim has an exaggerated sense of the extent to which others will notice, remember, and judge his or her shortcomings—research on the spotlight effect has something important to say about this pressing problem of modern life (Garland & Zigler, 1993).

In addition to the issues of individual differences and developmental trends in egocentrism, there is the question of whether the egocentric biases we discussed are likely to be moderated by cultural or subcultural differences in perspectives on the self. We emphasized the kind of cognitive biases that are likely to plague the judgments of nearly everyone in just about any culture. People have their sense organs oriented outward and away from themselves, so everyone can be expected to have some difficulty in accurately perceiving how they appear to others. Still, cultures vary in how the self is conceptualized and how much the self dominates the organization of one's experience (Markus & Kitayama, 1991; Triandis, 1989). Although it has yet to be empirically examined, there is every reason to believe that such differences in how the self is organized might be correlated with the magnitude of the type of egocentric biases we examined in this chapter. It is not lost on us, of course, that in Western culture a strong sense of self and self-esteem is carefully nurtured. Indeed, some have argued that never before in human history has the autonomous self been as cultivated, celebrated, and glorified as it is in the current Western world (Lasch, 1979). This implies that such phenomena as the biased responsibility allocations, the spotlight effect, and the illusion of transparency might be particularly pronounced in members of contemporary Western society. When the self is emphasized and accentuated in everyday discourse and common socialization practices, the groundwork is laid for strong egocentric biases.

REFERENCES

American Psychiatric Association. (1994). *Diagnostic and statistical manual of mental disorders* (4th ed.). Washington: American Psychiatric Association.

Babcock, L., & Loewenstein, G. (1997). Explaining bargaining impasse: The role of self-serving biases. *Journal of Economic Perspectives, 11*, 109–126.

Bandura, A. (1986). *Social foundations of thought and action: A social cognitive theory.* Englewood, NJ: Prentice-Hall.

Beckman, L. J. (1970). Effects of students' performance on teachers' and observers' attributions of causality. *Journal of Educational Psychology, 65*, 198–204.

Brawley, L. R. (1984). Unintentional egocentric biases in attributions. *Journal of Sport Psychology, 6*, 264–278.

Burger, J. M., & Rodman, J. L. (1983). Attributions of responsibility for group tasks: The egocentric bias and the actor–observer difference. *Journal of Personality and Social Psychology, 45*, 1232–1242.

Christensen, A., Sullaway, M., & King, C. E. (1983). Systematic error in behavioral reports of dyadic interaction: Egocentric bias and content effects. *Behavioral Assessment, 5*, 129–140.

Clark, J. V., & Arkowitz, H. (1975). Social anxiety and self-evaluation of interpersonal performance. *Psychological Reports, 36*, 211–221.

Dawes, R. (1988). *Rational choice in an uncertain world.* San Diego, CA: Harcourt Brace Jovanovich.

DeConinck, J. B., Stilwell, C. D., & Brock, B. A. (1996). A construct validity analysis of scores on measures of distributive justice and pay satisfaction. *Educational and Psychological Measurement, 56*, 1026–1036.

Deutsch, F. M., Lozy, J. L., & Saxon, S. (1993). Couples' reports of contributions to child care. *Journal of Family Issues, 14*, 421–437.

Elkind, D. (1967). Egocentrism in adolescence. *Child Development, 38*, 1025–1034.

Fenigstein, A. (1984). Self-consciousness and the overperception of self as a target. *Journal of Personality and Social Psychology, 47*, 860–870.

Fenigstein, A., & Vanable, P. A. (1992). Paranoia and self-consciousness. *Journal of Personality and Social Psychology, 62*, 129–138.

Fincham, F. D., & Bradbury, T. N. (1989). Perceived responsibility for activities in marriage: Egocentric or partner-centric bias? *Journal of Marriage and the Family, 51*, 27–35.

Forsyth, D. R., Berger, R. E., & Mitchell, T. (1981). The effects of self-serving vs.

other-serving claims of responsibility on attraction and attribution in groups. *Social Psychology Quarterly, 44,* 56–64.

Forsyth, D. R., & Schlenker, B. R. (1977). Attributing the causes of group performance: Effects of performance quality, task importance, and future testing. *Journal of Personality, 45,* 220–236.

Garland, A. F., & Zigler, E. (1993). Adolescent suicide prevention: Current research and social policy implications. *American Psychologist, 48,* 169–182.

Gilbert, D. T., & Jones, E. E. (1986). Perceiver-induced constraint: Interpretations of self-generated reality. *Journal of Personality and Social Psychology, 50,* 269–280.

Gilovich, T. (1991). *How we know what isn't so: The fallibility of human reason in everyday life.* New York: Free Press.

Gilovich, T., Kerr, M., & Medvec, V. H. (1993). The effect of temporal perspective on subjective confidence. *Journal of Personality and Social Psychology, 64,* 552–560.

Gilovich, T., & Medvec, V. H. (1994). The temporal pattern to the experience of regret. *Journal of Personality and Social Psychology, 67,* 357–365.

Gilovich, T., & Medvec, V. H. (1995). The experience of regret: What, when, and why. *Psychological Review, 102,* 379–395.

Gilovich, T., Medvec, V. H., & Savitsky, K. (1998). *The spotlight effect in social judgment: An egocentric bias in estimates of the salience of one's actions and appearance.* Unpublished manuscript, Cornell University.

Gilovich, T., Savitsky, K., & Medvec, V. H. (1998). The illusion of transparency: Biased assessments of others' ability to read our emotional states. *Journal of Personality and Social Psychology, 75,* 332–346.

Goffman, E. (1963). *Behavior in public places.* New York: Free Press.

Gottman, J. M., & Porterfield, A. L. (1981). Communicative competence in the nonverbal behavior of married couples. *Journal of Marriage and the Family, 43,* 817–824.

Harris, S. (1946). *Banting's miracle: The story of the discovery of insulin.* Philadelphia: Lippincott.

Hattiangadi, N., Medvec, V. H., & Gilovich, T. (1995). Failing to act: Regrets of Terman's geniuses. *International Journal of Aging and Human Development, 40,* 175–185.

Heimberg, R. G. (1990). Cognitive behavior therapy. In A. S. Bellack & M. Herson (Eds.), *Handbook of comparative treatments for adult disorders* (pp. 203–218). New York: Wiley.

Heneman, H. G., & Schwab, D. P. (1985). Pay satisfaction: Its multi-dimensional nature and measurement. *International Journal of Psychology, 20,* 129–141.

Hull, J. G., & Young, R. D. (1983). Self-consciousness, self-esteem, and success–failure as determinants of alcohol consumption in male social drinkers. *Journal of Personality and Social Psychology, 44,* 1097–1109.

Hull, J. G., Young, R. D., & Jouriles, E. (1986). Applications of the self-awareness model of alcohol consumption: Predicting patterns of use and abuse. *Journal of Personality and Social Psychology, 51,* 790–796.

Ingram, R. E., & Smith, T. W. (1984). Depression and internal versus external focus of attention. *Cognitive Therapy and Research, 8,* 139–152.

Jacowitz, K. E., & Kahneman, D. (1995). Measures of anchoring in estimation tasks. *Personality and Social Psychology Bulletin, 21,* 1161–1166.

Janis, I. (1972). *Victims of groupthink.* Boston: Houghton Mifflin.

Janis, I. (1982). *Groupthink* (2nd ed.). Boston: Houghton Mifflin.

Jones, E. E., & Harris, V. A. (1967). The attribution of attitudes. *Journal of Experimental Social Psychology, 3,* 1–24.

Kahn, M. (1970). Nonverbal communication and marital satisfaction. *Family Process, 9,* 449–456.

Kahneman, D., Slovic, P., & Tversky, A. (1982). *Judgment under uncertainty: Heuristics and biases.* Cambridge, UK: Cambridge University Press.

Kamen, L. P., & Seligman, M. E. P. (1986). Explanatory style and health. *Current Psychology Research and Reviews, 6,* 207–218.

Kernberg, O. F. (1975). *Borderline conditions and pathological narcissism.* New York: Aronson.

Kipnis, D., Castell, P. T., Gergen, M., & Mauch, D. (1976). Metamorphic effects of power. *Journal of Applied Psychology, 61,* 127–135.

Kraepelin, E. (1915). *Psychiatrie: Ein lehrbuch* [*Psychiatry: A textbook*] (7th ed.). Leipzig, Germany: Barth.

Kruger, J., & Gilovich, T. (in press). "Naive cynicism" in everyday theories of responsibility assessments: On biased assumptions of bias. *Journal of Personality and Social Psychology.*

Lasch, C. (1979). *The culture of narcissism: American life in an era of diminishing expectations.* New York: Norton.

Lewin, K. (1951). *Field theory in social science.* New York: Harper.

Loewenstein, G., Thompson, L., & Bazerman, M. (1989). Social utility and decision making in interpersonal context. *Journal of Personality and Social Psychology, 57,* 426–441.

Marks, I. M. (1969). *Fears and phobias.* New York: Academic Press.

Markus, H. R., & Kitayama, S. (1991). Culture and the self: Implications for cognition, emotion, and motivation. *Psychological Review, 98,* 224–253.

McEwan, K. L., & Devins, G. M. (1983). Is increased arousal in social anxiety noticed by others? *Journal of Abnormal Psychology, 92,* 417–421.

Miller, D. T., & Ratner, R. K. (1996). The power of the myth of self interest. In L. Montada & M. J. Lerner (Eds.), *Current societal issues about justice: Critical issues in social justice* (pp. 25–48). New York: Plenum Press.

Mullen, B., Anthony, T., Salas, E., & Driskell, J. E. (1994). Group cohesiveness and quality of decision making: An integration of tests of the groupthink hypothesis. *Small Group Research, 25,* 189–204.

Nichols, K. (1974). Severe social anxiety. *British Journal of Medical Psychology, 47*, 302–306.

Nisbett, R. E., & Ross, L. (1980). *Human inference: Strategies and shortcomings of social judgment.* Englewood Cliffs, NJ: Prentice-Hall.

Noller, P. (1980). Misunderstandings in marital communication: A study of couples' nonverbal communication. *Journal of Personality and Social Psychology, 39*, 1135–1148.

Robinson, R., Keltner, D., Ward, A., & Ross, L. (1995). Actual versus assumed differences in construal: "Naive realism" in intergroup perception and conflict. *Journal of Personality and Social Psychology, 68*, 404–417.

Ross, L. (1977). The intuitive psychologist and his shortcomings: Distortions in the attribution process. In L. Berkowitz (Ed.), *Advances in experimental social psychology* (Vol. 10, pp. 174–221). New York: Academic Press.

Ross, L., Amabile, T. M., & Steinmetz, J. L. (1977). Social roles, social control, and biases in social-perception processes. *Journal of Personality and Social Psychology, 35*, 485–494.

Ross, L., & Ward, A. (1996). Naive realism in everyday life: Implications for social conflict and misunderstanding. In E. Reed, E. Turiel, & T. Brown (Eds.), *Values and knowledge* (pp. 103–135). Hillsdale, NJ: Erlbaum.

Ross, M. (1981). Self-centered biases in attributions of responsibility: Antecedents and consequences. In E. T. Higgins, C. P. Herman, & M. P. Zanna (Eds.), *Social cognition: The Ontario Symposium* (pp. 305–321). Hillsdale, NJ: Erlbaum.

Ross, M., & Sicoly, F. (1979). Egocentric biases in availability and attribution. *Journal of Personality and Social Psychology, 37*, 322–336.

Savitsky, K. (1997). *Perceived transparency and the leakage of emotional states: Do we know how little we show?* Unpublished doctoral dissertation, Cornell University.

Savitsky, K., Medvec, V. H., Charlton, A. E., & Gilovich, T. (1998). "What, me worry?": Arousal, misattribution, and the effect of temporal distance on confidence. *Personality and Social Psychology Bulletin, 24*, 529–536.

Scarpello, V., & Jones, F. F. (1996). Why justice matters in compensation decision making. *Journal of Organizational Behavior, 17*, 285–299.

Schwarz, N. (1990). Feelings as information: Informational and motivational functions of affective states. In E. T. Higgins & R. Sorrentino (Eds.), *Handbook of motivation and cognition: Foundations of social behavior* (Vol. 2, pp. 527–561). New York: Guilford Press.

Schwarz, N., & Clore, G. L. (1983). Mood, misattribution, and judgments of well-being: Informative and directive functions of affective states. *Journal of Personality and Social Psychology, 45*, 513–523.

Seligman, M. E. P., & Schulman, P. (1986). Explanatory style as a predictor of productivity and quitting among life insurance sales agents. *Journal of Personality and Social Psychology, 50*, 832–838.

Shaffer, D. (1974). Suicide in childhood and early adolescence. *Journal of Child Psychology and Psychiatry, 45,* 406–451.

Shaffer, D. (1988). The epidemiology of teen suicide: An examination of risk factors. *Journal of Clinical Psychiatry, 49,* 36–41.

Singh, P. (1994). Perception and reactions to inequity as a function of social comparison referents and hierarchical levels. *Journal of Applied Social Psychology, 24,* 557–565.

Smith, T. W., & Greenberg, J. (1981). Depression and self-focused attention. *Motivation and Emotion, 5,* 323–331.

Spranca, M., Minsk, E., & Baron, J. (1991). Omission and commission in judgment and choice. *Journal of Experimental Social Psychology, 27,* 76–105.

Steele, C. M., & Aronson, J. (1995). Stereotype threat and the intellectual test performance of African Americans. *Journal of Personality and Social Psychology, 69,* 797–811.

Stein, M. B., Walker, J. R., & Forde, D. R. (1996). Public-speaking fears in a community sample: Prevalence, impact on functioning, and diagnostic classification. *Archives of General Psychiatry, 53,* 169–174.

Storms, M. D., & McCaul, K. D. (1976). Attribution processes and emotional exacerbation of dysfunctional behavior. In J. H. Harvey, W. J. Ickes, & R. F. Kidd (Eds.), *New directions in attribution research* (Vol. 1, pp. 143–164). Hillsdale, NJ: Erlbaum.

Thompson, S. C., & Kelley, H. H. (1981). Judgments of responsibility for activities in close relationships. *Journal of Personality and Social Psychology, 41,* 469–477.

Triandis, H. C. (1989). The self and social behavior in differing cultural contexts. *Psychological Review, 96,* 506–520.

Tversky, A., & Kahneman, D. (1973). Availability: A heuristic for judging frequency and probability. *Cognitive Psychology, 5,* 207–232.

Tversky, A., & Kahneman, D. (1974). Judgment under uncertainty: Heuristics and biases. *Science, 185,* 1124–1131.

Veroff, J., Kulka, R. A., & Douvan, E. (1981). *Mental health in America: Patterns of help-seeking from 1957 to 1976.* New York: Basic Books.

Walster, E., Walster, G. W., & Berscheid, E. (1978). *Equity: Theory and research.* Boston: Allyn & Bacon.

Wolfe, T. (1987). *The bonfire of the vanities.* Toronto, Ontario, Canada: Bantam.

4

SOCIAL COMPARISONS IN DYSPHORIC AND LOW SELF-ESTEEM PEOPLE

JOANNE V. WOOD AND PENELOPE LOCKWOOD

A 1st-year university student, feeling isolated and despondent because she is away from her friends and family, frequently compares herself with her cheerful, popular roommate. She wonders why she is not adjusting as well to university life, which only deepens her feelings of inadequacy. In contrast, when a salesperson notes how much more she is selling than her coworkers, her spirits and her self-confidence rise. Both of these individuals have made *social comparisons*: They have compared themselves with other people.

In the original theory of social comparison, Leon Festinger (1954) argued that human beings have a drive to evaluate their opinions and abilities; to function effectively, they need to know what their capacities and limitations are, and they must be accurate in their opinions. Festinger thought that people best serve this need for self-evaluation by comparing

We thank several people who provided helpful comments on an earlier version of this chapter: Rick Gibbons, Robin Kowalski, Mark Leary, Stephen Swallow, Gifford Weary, and Richard Wenzlaff. We are especially grateful for the comments of Tony Ahrens, Lisa Aspinwall, and Tom Wills.

themselves against objective standards, but when such standards are unavailable, they compare themselves with other people. His central proposition was the *similarity hypothesis*, according to which people prefer to compare themselves with other people who are similar. Although Festinger discussed social comparison processes involving opinions and abilities, researchers have studied social comparisons involving all types of personal attributes, such as physical attractiveness, personality characteristics, and emotions.

In the two examples that began this chapter, social comparisons seemed, in the case of the university student, to deepen feelings of dysphoria and, in the case of the salesperson, to boost self-confidence. Do social comparisons play such roles in depression and self-esteem? In this chapter, we examine this question. We consider depression and low self-esteem together because the two constructs overlap a great deal. Depressed people often have low self-esteem, even when their depression is in remission, and correlations between measures of the two variables range from about .40 to about .60. Considerable research indicates that depressed and low self-esteem people respond to failure in similar ways and that nondepressed and high self-esteem people exhibit similar self-serving biases (see Wood & Dodgson, 1996, for references). For convenience, we sometimes refer to the combination of depressed and low self-esteem people as *low self-worth people*.

SOCIAL COMPARISON IN DEPRESSION AND LOW SELF-ESTEEM

There is ample reason to believe that social comparison processes could be pivotal in people who are low in self-worth. First, a major characteristic of depression (Beck, 1976) and, by definition, of low self-esteem is a negative self-view, and people's self-evaluations are believed to be based in part on social comparison processes. A classic illustration is the "Mr. Clean–Mr. Dirty" study, in which job applicants faced another applicant who was either well groomed and very organized or disheveled and disorganized (Morse & Gergen, 1970). Those in the company of Mr. Dirty had higher self-evaluations than did those who thought they were competing with Mr. Clean. Researchers also have pointed to more global and long-term effects of social comparisons on the self-concept (see Wood, 1989, for a review). For example, one study indicates that children's self-evaluations are dependent on the competence of their classmates; those with higher ability classmates had lower aspirations than did those with lower ability classmates (Marsh & Parker, 1984). As researchers such as Swallow and Kuiper (1988) have suggested then, social comparisons that are unflattering to the self may lead to or help maintain the negative self-evaluations of depressed and low self-esteem individuals.

Social comparisons also may promote other cognitive or emotional concomitants of depression and low self-esteem. For example, comparisons with others who are superior to the self in some way—*upward comparisons*—can dampen one's morale or mood, whereas comparisons with others who are inferior to or less fortunate than oneself—*downward comparisons*—can improve one's moods (see Major, Testa, & Bylsma, 1991, for a review). Comparisons also may affect one's feelings of optimism (Gibbons & Gerrard, 1991), hope (Ahrens & Alloy, 1997), and motivation (Lockwood & Kunda, 1997), all of which are dampened in depressed people. In addition, social comparisons may serve the motives thought to be important to depressed and low self-esteem individuals, as we describe shortly.

In keeping with the view that social comparisons may be important in depression and low self-esteem, social comparison also has played a role in some prominent theories of depression (e.g., Beck, 1976). For example, in their reformulated learned helplessness model, Abramson, Seligman, and Teasdale (1978) proposed that depressed people suffer a loss of self-esteem if they believe that other people can exert greater control than they can over desired outcomes.

THEORETICAL PERSPECTIVES

Next, we identify various theoretical perspectives that focus specifically on whether high and low self-worth people differ in their social comparison processes. The perspectives revolve around the motivations that may prompt social comparisons and whether differences between the motivations of low and high self-worth people lead to differences in their selections of and their reactions to social comparisons. After identifying the perspectives, we review the evidence to see which are supported.

Self-Evaluation Perspective

As described earlier, Festinger's (1954) theory emphasizes that social comparison is crucial to self-evaluation or self-assessment. Weary has proposed that because depressed people have been exposed to many uncontrollable life events, they are highly uncertain about their ability to detect or understand cause and effect relations (e.g., Weary, Elbin, & Hill, 1987). Hence, they are especially motivated to engage in social comparison, and they are especially sensitive to social comparison feedback (e.g., Weary, Marsh, Gleicher, & Edwards, 1993). Although Weary has focused on causal uncertainty, we expand this perspective to refer to any type of uncertainty.

Depressed people seem to experience heightened uncertainty in many domains (see Weary et al., 1987, for references). In addition, people with low self-esteem seem more uncertain and unstable in their self-concepts than are people with high self-esteem (Campbell, 1990).

The self-evaluation perspective, then, suggests that low self-worth people seek more social comparison information than do high self-worth people and are more sensitive to such information. In addition, lows should be especially interested in comparisons with people who can help them to reduce their uncertainty.

Self-Enhancement Perspective

A second motive that should be prominent among people who are depressed or low in self-esteem is *self-enhancement*—to improve their moods, to feel better about themselves, and to cope with stressors. Although Festinger's (1954) theory emphasized accurate, unbiased self-evaluation as the purpose behind social comparison, a great deal of research focuses on the self-enhancing function of social comparison. Identifying most strongly with the self-enhancement position is Wills's (1981) theory of downward comparison. Wills proposed that when people are low in subjective well-being—either because of temporary threats or because of dispositionally low self-esteem—they seek to compare themselves with people who are less fortunate than themselves or inferior to themselves and that such downward comparisons make them feel better. Considerable evidence has been cited in support of this theory (see Gibbons & Gerrard, 1991; and Wills, 1991, for reviews). According to this perspective, then, low self-worth people should be especially likely to seek downward comparisons and to benefit from them.

Self-Protection Perspective

People also may use comparative strategies that are not aimed for self-enhancement but for self-protection. Whereas in self-enhancement one tries to bolster one's self-view though such strategies as drawing favorable attention to one's talents, in *self-protection* one tries to avoid exposure of one's weaknesses (Baumeister, Tice, & Hutton, 1989). According to Baumeister et al., people with low self-esteem primarily aim for self-protection, whereas people with high self-esteem primarily aim for self-enhancement.

In the context of social comparisons, self-protection may take the form of avoiding unflattering comparisons, which are often upward, or avoiding comparisons altogether (e.g., Brickman & Bulman, 1977; Smith & Insko, 1987). Swallow and Kuiper (1990) have argued that some depressed people seek less social comparison information than do nondepressed people because they have negative expectancies for what comparisons will reveal. Note that the self-protection hypothesis that low self-worth people may avoid comparisons altogether opposes the self-evaluation perspective, which predicts that such people are especially eager to compare themselves with others.

Self-Validation Perspective

Unlike the self-evaluation perspective, the *self-validation* perspective holds that low self-worth people know their own position but seek support for it. Like the self-enhancement perspective, the self-validation perspective assumes that low self-worth people want to feel better, but unlike the self-enhancement perspective, it does not emphasize that low self-worth people hope to see themselves as superior to someone else. Instead, they seek company or reassurance through seeing themselves as similar to others. In his downward comparison theory, Wills (1981, 1991) also noted that people who are experiencing problems may feel better by comparing themselves with someone who is also experiencing problems but who is at the same level as themselves, which he called *lateral comparisons*. Several other researchers have suggested that low self-worth people may seek comparisons for validation (Aspinwall & Taylor, 1993; Gibbons & Boney-McCoy, 1991; Locke & Horowitz, 1990).

Failure-to-Self-Protect/Self-Enhance Perspective

Several depression theorists have suggested that depressed people are characterized by a lack of motivation to protect their self-esteem. In the context of social comparisons, then, this view holds that people who are depressed or low in self-esteem fail to use the self-protective comparison strategies used by people who are not depressed or high in self-esteem (e.g., Alloy, Albright, & Clements, 1987; Swallow & Kuiper, 1987). For example, whereas high self-worth people may avoid unflattering upward comparisons, low self-worth people may not.

Self-Depreciation Perspective

The *self-depreciation* perspective goes a step further to hold that depressed or low self-esteem people not only fail to avoid unfavorable comparisons, but they also actually seek out such comparisons: They characteristically make dysfunctional or maladaptive social comparisons (e.g., Beck, 1976; Swallow & Kuiper, 1993). For example, after one has failed a test and there is no chance to remedy the failure, one may "rub one's own nose in it" by seeking information about people who performed well on the test.

We should note at the outset that self-depreciation motives are very difficult to establish definitively. What may appear to be a maladaptive comparison may actually be driven by other motives or may even be beneficial in the long term. For example, people may make upward comparisons to self-depreciate, but they also may be seeking to improve themselves (Wood, 1989), to verify their negative self-views—which may lend stability and clarity to their worlds (Swann, 1987)—or even to self-protect by maintaining vigilance to possible sources of threats to their self-esteem.

Indeed, interpreting the selection of any comparison target as supporting a particular perspective is hazardous. In recent years, social comparison researchers have become increasingly sophisticated in their predictions about the direction of comparison. Beginning with the work of Buunk, Collins, Taylor, VanYperen, and Dakof (1990) and Major et al. (1991), researchers increasingly have recognized that comparisons may have multiple effects—that not all downward comparisons are self-enhancing and that not all upward comparisons are self-deflating. For example, cancer patients may feel threatened, rather than fortunate, when they compare themselves with other patients whose conditions are worsening. Similarly, when people identify with others who are superior, upward comparisons can be self-enhancing rather than demoralizing (Collins, 1996). Researchers have begun to identify moderators of these effects, such as a person's expectations for whether he or she will improve or worsen on the comparison dimension (Aspinwall, 1997; Lockwood & Kunda, 1997; Wood & VanderZee, 1997). Although the literature has become more sophisticated in this respect, we can draw simple upward–downward predictions from each perspective because the vast majority of studies conducted in this area were designed to test these more simple predictions and because, given the comparison contexts used, these predictions are usually appropriate.

WHAT IS THE EVIDENCE?

Which of these theoretical perspectives is supported empirically? Before we review the evidence concerning social comparisons and depression and low self-esteem, we should offer two caveats about this research. First, virtually all of the depression evidence that we cite involves as research participants not clinically depressed people but dysphoric university students. Debate has raged over whether studies of dysphoric students truly inform one's understanding of clinical depression (e.g., Coyne, 1994; Vredenburg, Flett, & Krames, 1993). We refer to such participants as *dysphoric*, rather than depressed, and we emphasize that our interpretations may not apply to clinical depression. Likewise, participants who are identified as having low self-esteem in university samples probably would not be below the median in self-esteem in the general population (Swann, 1987). They may not harbor predominantly negative self-views, just less positive self-views than those of high self-esteem people (Baumeister et al., 1989). Hence, conclusions from such studies may not apply to people who are low in self-esteem in the general population.

In addition, as Ahrens and Alloy (1997) have noted about this literature, most of the research uses cross-sectional rather than longitudinal designs. Hence, it is not clear whether social comparisons preceded the dysphoria or vice versa. Any differences shown between dysphoric and nondysphoric people's social comparisons do not necessarily point to a causal role of social comparison; they may reflect only concomitants of dysphoria or perhaps even attempts to recover from dysphoria. We organize our review of the evidence in terms of studies of the overall degree of comparison seeking, studies involving the selection of specific targets, and studies of the effects of comparison.

Studies of the Overall Degree of Comparison Seeking

Most of the theoretical perspectives outlined above implicitly assume that people do make social comparisons, and the perspectives make predictions about which targets dysphoric or low self-esteem people select for comparisons. This situation mirrors that of the social comparison literature generally where there are surprisingly few studies of the degree to which people make social comparisons (Wood, 1996). However, two perspectives concerning low self-esteem or dysphoria also make a prediction about the overall degree of comparison seeking: The self-evaluation perspective predicts that people who are low in self-worth are especially likely to seek social comparisons to resolve their uncertainty, and the self-protection perspective may be interpreted as implying that dysphoric people avoid social comparisons (Flett, Vredenburg, Pliner, & Krames, 1987; Swallow & Kuiper, 1990). Both of these perspectives also make predictions about target choice, but first we review studies that speak to the overall degree of comparison seeking. Studies of the degree of comparison seeking examine social comparison through global self-report measures, self-report measures that are less global, and measures of actual comparison seeking.

Global Self-Reports

Several studies in which researchers have examined low self-worth people's self-reported degree of comparison seeking support the self-evaluation perspective. Two studies indicate that the more depressed older women were, the more frequently they reported that they made social comparisons (Heidrich & Ryff, 1993, Study 1), both upward and downward

(Study 2). Similarly, undergraduates with low self-esteem reported that they used more social comparison information than did respondents with high self-esteem (Wayment & Taylor, 1995). VanderZee, Buunk, and Sanderman (1996) found that people high in neuroticism reported a greater need to socially compare. Gibbons and Buunk (in press) have recently developed a self-report measure of social comparison tendencies, with items such as "I always pay a lot of attention to how I do things compared with how others do things." Across multiple samples from the United States and the Netherlands, the authors consistently found that self-esteem and social comparison were negatively correlated and that both neuroticism and depression were positively correlated with social comparison. (Further analyses also suggest that the relations of both self-esteem and depression with social comparison may be due to their shared association with neuroticism.) Clearly, then, low self-worth people tend to report that they are especially interested in social comparisons.

Unfortunately, however, global self-report measures may be vulnerable to several problems (Wood, 1996). First, they may be inaccurate. As H. T. Reis and Wheeler (1991) have argued about global self-report measures of social interactions, respondents may be selective about the events they report, their memory may be distorted by such factors as their moods and recency effects, and they may have difficulty aggregating their past experiences into a global impression. A second problem involves social desirability; people often do not want to admit that they engage in social comparison (see Wood, 1996, for a review). They also may not want to report that they have made certain types of comparisons, such as downward comparisons, for fear that they would appear to have gloated over someone else's misery (Wills, 1981). A third problem is that often people may be unaware that they have made social comparisons because comparisons may be subtle, almost automatic, and fleeting (Brickman & Bulman, 1977; Wood, 1996). A fourth problem with global self-report measures is that they may reflect participants' theories or beliefs about their social comparisons rather than their actual comparisons.

Such problems may bias self-report studies in favor of detecting more comparison making by low self-worth people than high self-worth people. For example, people who are depressed or low in self-esteem generally seem to respond in less socially desirable ways than people who are high in self-worth (Paulhus, 1991). Hence, lows may be more willing than highs to report social comparisons. In addition, high self-worth people's belief that they are self-reliant may lead them to say that they have little need to compare, whereas low self-worth people's uncertainty may lead them to guess that they often seek comparisons. Thus, the global self-report measures cited above may well indicate that low self-worth people make more social comparisons but they also may reflect other factors.

Self-Report Measures That Are Less Global

Less global forms of self-report also may reflect the operation of participants' theories rather than their actual comparison behaviors. In one study, high and low self-esteem undergraduates were asked to identify their motives for a social comparison they had just selected. Both groups identified motives in the following order of frequency: self-evaluation, common bond (measured by such items as "so I won't feel alone or isolated"), self-improvement, self-enhancement, altruism ("to help them"), and self-destruction ("to confirm my fear of getting worse"; Helgeson & Mickelson, 1995, Study 2). Thus, low self-esteem participants' stated motive was self-evaluation, which supports the self-evaluation perspective. However, that perspective also predicts that lows should be more likely than highs to have self-evaluative needs, yet self-esteem differences appeared on only one motive: Self-destruction was more commonly reported by participants with low than with high self-esteem. Although this finding is fascinating, it may not reflect low self-esteem participants' true motives but a theory that they harbor about their self-destructiveness.

Similarly, in a study in which participants imagined that they had just received feedback on a test, dysphoric participants who were high in dysfunctional attitudes (e.g., "If I fail partly, it is as bad as being a complete failure") said they would be especially interested in looking at the scores of other students (Swallow & Kuiper, 1990). The role-play nature of this study permits the possibility that dysphoric participants with dysfunctional attitudes merely have the theory that they will seek many social comparisons. Perhaps, when faced with a real exam, dysphoric individuals avoid comparisons or certain types of comparisons.

Measures of Actual Comparison Seeking

Indeed, two rare real-world studies of interest in social comparison by Flett et al. (1987, Studies 1 and 2) suggest exactly this: Dysphoric undergraduates who had taken a psychology exam spent less time looking at other students' scores than did nondysphoric students, regardless of how they had performed on the exam. These results contradict the self-evaluation view that depressed people seek more social comparisons. It could be argued, however, that because participants had received their own scores on the exam, they were not uncertain and hence had little need to self-evaluate through social comparisons. This possibility seems unlikely, in that the students had received little information about their relative standing, so social comparisons could have been helpful. Flett et al. suggested that their results point to self-protection; because dysphoric people have negative expectations, they have refrained from social comparisons to avoid embarrassment or a blow to their self-esteem. However, it is puzzling that performance did not interact with dysphoria in predicting comparison seeking. Dysphoric participants who had performed well on the exam should have had high expectations.

Section Summary

Although researchers have not found differences between low and high self-worth people in every study of the overall degree of comparison seeking (Northcraft & Ashford, 1990), most studies generally offer more support for the self-evaluation perspective than for the self-protection perspective. Global self-report or related measures suggest that in comparison with their high self-worth counterparts, dysphoric or low self-esteem people report that they do seek more social comparisons and that they seek more social comparisons for the purpose of self-evaluation. However, more studies like Flett et al.'s (1987) are needed to determine whether participants' beliefs correspond with actual comparison behaviors.

We have recommendations for such research. First, in studies of actual comparison selections, measures of participants' expectations for those comparisons should be administered. If dysphoric people do seek more social comparison information, they may do so not to reduce their uncertainty but to confirm their negative self-views (Swann, 1987). Second, if dysphoric or low self-worth people harbor self-protective motives in addition to self-evaluative motives, studies may have the greatest chance of revealing interests in self-evaluation if they provide a private context for participants' comparison seeking. For example, in Flett et al.'s (1987) study of actual comparison seeking, perhaps dysphoric participants inhibited their comparison seeking because they were in the presence of an experimenter as they looked at other students' scores. They may have wanted to avoid drawing the experimenter's attention to their own relative standing.

Studies Involving Specific Targets for Comparisons of Opinions

We now turn from studies of the overall degree of comparison seeking to studies involving specific comparison targets. Although most of these focus on comparisons of personal attributes, two studies involve comparisons of opinions. These two studies are relevant to the self-evaluation perspective, which predicts that dysphoric individuals especially value comparison targets who can help them reduce their uncertainty. In keeping with this idea, Weary et al. (1987) found that dysphoric participants were especially likely to evaluate positively a target who had made judgments that were similar to their own. As the authors pointed out, however, this finding also may mean simply that dysphoric individuals like people who agree with them because such people bolster their self-esteem.

Similarly, Weary, Marsh, and McCormick (1994) found that relative to nondysphoric participants, dysphoric participants were more likely to choose as a discussion partner someone who would provide the most accurate appraisal of their opinions, namely, someone who was generally similar to themselves but who disagreed with them on the specific issue under discussion (Goethals & Darley, 1977). This result supports the authors' reasoning that dysphoric individuals are more interested than nondysphoric individuals in reducing uncertainty. However, both groups' top choice was the similar agreer—the target who, as the authors pointed out, bolstered their esteem the most. One also must keep in mind the measure used when interpreting these results: Choosing a discussion partner may reflect not only participants' social comparison motives but also their desires to be liked or to have a harmonious discussion. It is possible that a "purer" measure of social comparison may have yielded more evidence of uncertainty-reduction motives in dysphoric individuals. The problems with this type of measure are described further in the section on affiliation measures. In summary, two studies involving specific targets on an opinion dimension support the self-evaluation perspective but are open to other interpretations.

Studies of the Selection of Specific Targets for Comparisons of Personal Attributes

Next, we review the studies involving participants' selections of specific comparison targets along dimensions of personal attributes, such as ability or personality. These studies speak to all of the theoretical perspectives that we identified. Specifically, the self-enhancement perspective predicts that low self-worth people are especially likely to select downward targets. The self-protection perspective predicts that they are especially likely to avoid upward or unfavorable comparisons. The *failure-to-self-enhance/self-protect* perspective, in contrast, predicts that it is high self-worth people who make these self-enhancing or self-protective comparison choices and that low self-worth people do not. The self-depreciation perspective predicts that low self-worth people select comparisons that are upward or unfavorable to themselves. Both the self-evaluation and self-validation perspectives predict that low self-worth people select similar comparison targets. We organize our review of these studies in terms of the operationalization of social comparison used: comparative ratings, self-reported selections, self-recorded comparison diaries, choice of comparison target, and affiliation.

Comparative Rating Studies

Two types of comparative rating measures ask respondents to judge their standing relative to other people on some dimension. In *self-versus-other ratings*, respondents are asked to rate themselves against some other person or people, such as the "average college student," along some dimension. In *consensus measures*, respondents are asked about some characteristic and are asked to estimate what percentage of other people would share that characteristic. On both of these types of measures, people typically—when they are not selected for being dysphoric or low in self-esteem—respond in ways that are flattering to themselves. On self-versus-other ratings, they rate themselves as superior to others; on consensus measures, they judge others to be similar to themselves (Wood, 1989). Perceiving similarity between the self and others is thought to be reassuring and to increase one's sense of belonging (Swallow & Kuiper, 1987). Respondents also often claim that they are special or different from others when that judgment is more flattering (e.g., Goethals, 1986).

Considerable evidence suggests that people who are dysphoric or low in self-esteem exhibit a very different pattern on these measures. On self-versus-other ratings, they are less flattering to themselves than are non-dysphoric or high self-esteem people. Studies indicate that they rate themselves as (a) inferior to others, (b) similar to others, or (c) higher than others but to a lesser degree than do nondysphoric or high self-esteem people. Similarly, on consensus measures, dysphoric people are less likely than nondysphoric people to see others as similar to themselves (see Alloy et al., 1987; and Swallow & Kuiper, 1993, for reviews).

Such evidence has been widely viewed as opposing Wills's (1981) downward comparison theory and as suggesting instead that people who are high in self-worth, rather than low, are especially likely to make downward comparisons. Researchers have reached this conclusion by interpreting comparative ratings in two different senses. The first sense is that the comparative ratings represent evaluations drawn from one's previous social comparisons (e.g., Swallow & Kuiper, 1987). For example, a dysphoric woman who seeks comparisons with people who are superior to her (Ahrens & Alloy, 1997) may rate herself as inferior to others on a comparative rating. In contrast, high self-worth people may seek many downward comparisons, which would result in a rating of themselves as superior to others.

The other sense in which comparative ratings are interpreted does not involve the effects of previous comparisons. Instead, the mere act of making a judgment about oneself relative to others is called *social comparison* (e.g., Alloy et al., 1987). In this sense, a judgment by nondysphoric people that they are superior to a target would be called a downward comparison, even if the nondysphoric people did not consider that target's attributes and how they measure up to their own. As Wood (1996) has argued, this second sense in which comparative ratings are interpreted does not comport with the traditional understanding of social comparison. Social comparison is understood to involve taking into account information concerning another person or other people in relation to the self. This second sense of interpreting comparative ratings, in contrast, sees them as reflecting the rater's own cognitive biases. For example, low self-esteem people's tendency to judge themselves as inferior to others is seen as reflecting a breakdown in depressed people's self-protective motives (e.g., Alloy et al., 1987).

Comparative ratings involve the traditional definition of social comparison only when they are interpreted in the first sense, as reflecting the effects of social comparisons either in a veridical or biased fashion. Accordingly, we focus on that interpretation of comparative ratings. Unfortunately, even if we restrict ourselves to this interpretation, two problems jeopardize our understanding of what comparative ratings mean. First, researchers often have assumed that they reflect cognitive biases, when instead they may reflect accurately one's past comparisons. High self-esteem people may truly be superior to many other people on a variety of dimensions, hence their rating that they are superior may be veridical.

The second problem is the opposite: Researchers may assume that comparative ratings reflect the effects of previous social comparisons when they do not. Some evidence suggests that when people make comparative ratings, they typically do not think about the supposed objects of comparison, much less consider them in relation to the self (e.g., Diener & Fujita, 1997; see Wood, 1996, for a review). It is easy to see how this could come about in the case of depressed or low self-esteem people. Very frequently dysphoric people, and by definition low self-esteem people, experience feelings of unworthiness and inferiority. Hence, when they rate themselves unfavorably relative to others, they may not mean that they have actually compared themselves with the people they are rating themselves against, but instead they may base their ratings on their own feelings of happiness or self-worth or lack thereof (cf. Wills, 1991; Wood & Taylor, 1991).

Accordingly, we believe that global comparative ratings disconnected from any specific comparison do not speak clearly to the question of what types of comparisons low self-worth people make. Comparative ratings more clearly reflect actual social comparisons when respondents make comparative ratings right after receiving specific comparison information in the laboratory or in everyday life. This is not to say that the global comparative rating findings described above are not fascinating or not relevant to the study of depression and low self-esteem. The pattern of evaluating oneself unfavorably relative to others may, as researchers have suggested, reflect a breakdown in dysphoric people's motivation to protect their self-esteem. Our point is that the relevance of global comparative rating measures to social comparisons is not clear.[1]

---

[1]We also do not review articles that concern self-esteem or dysphoria in relation to processes of derogating others. Although studies concerning other derogation are fascinating and may well have implications for the maintenance of self-esteem (e.g., Crocker, Thompson, McGraw, & Ingerman, 1987) and depression (Pelham, 1991), it is not clear that they truly reflect social comparison in the sense of considering social information in relation to the self.

Self-Reports of Selections of Comparison Targets

Bearing in mind the problems with global self-report measures described earlier, we now turn to four studies in which researchers examined participants' self-reports of with whom they compared themselves. These studies offer no agreement: A study of arthritis patients supports the self-enhancement view, in that people high in negative affect, as measured by a combination of a depression measure and a self-esteem measure, were especially likely to report that they preferred downward comparisons (DeVellis et al., 1990); a study of undergraduates supports the self-depreciation view that low self-esteem people seek upward comparisons (Wayment & Taylor, 1995); the self-depreciation view is also supported by a study of a community sample, which found that people high in neuroticism reported more upward comparisons (VanderZee et al., 1996); and a study of cardiac rehabilitation patients found no difference between those with low and high self-esteem (Helgeson & Taylor, 1993).

Self-Recorded Comparison Diaries

Wheeler and Miyake (1992) invented a way of capturing social comparisons in everyday life that relies on both self-reports and comparative ratings but that uses them in ways that are likely to avoid the major problems of both methods. Specifically, Wheeler and Miyake asked respondents to record social comparisons as they occurred in their daily lives; after each comparison, they were asked to complete questions about such matters as with whom they compared themselves, the dimension on which they compared, and their moods before and after the comparison. Some of the problems inherent in global self-report methods described above, such as the difficulty of remembering and then integrating one's experiences into a summary impression, are avoided with this method because respondents describe each social comparison soon after it occurs. The self-recording method also may be somewhat less susceptible to the problems of social desirability and lack of awareness of comparisons because respondents are trained to recognize their comparisons and because such training suggests that social comparisons are normative. The comparative rating element of Wheeler and Miyake's study is that participants rated their own standing relative to their comparison target after each comparison. Rating the target as inferior to the self constituted a downward comparison; rating the target as superior constituted an upward comparison. Unlike the more abstract comparative ratings reviewed earlier, this rating measure does not seem susceptible to the possibility of not reflecting social comparisons because they are connected explicitly to the comparison the respondent just made. A recent study by Giordano and Wood (1997) supports the validity of the Wheeler and Miyake method.

Wheeler and Miyake's (1992) results are intriguing. They show that contrary to the self-enhancement perspective, people with high self-esteem were more likely to make downward comparisons than were people with low self-esteem (on certain dimensions, e.g., academic matters). Even under threat (as operationalized by negative mood), lows were no more likely than highs to seek downward comparisons. Using a modified version of Wheeler and Miyake's self-recording method, Giordano and Wood (1997) replicated these findings.

By suggesting that people with low self-esteem are less likely than those with high self-esteem to make downward comparisons, these results challenge the self-enhancement perspective and support the failure-to-self-protect/self-enhance perspective. At the same time, two features of this method should be considered when interpreting these results. Whether respondents made downward comparisons was determined by their ratings of their standing relative to the other, which may reflect not only what comparisons they sought but what conclusions they drew from such comparisons. People with low self-esteem may have sought downward comparisons, but after having made comparisons, they may have concluded that they were not truly superior to the comparison targets after all.

Indeed, lows may not have sought comparisons at all; Wheeler and Miyake (1992) did not distinguish between comparisons that people sought and the comparisons they were "forced" to make with people they unintentionally encountered. People may receive unsolicited comparative information from many sources, such as their TV sets and people they pass on the street (e.g., Wood, 1989). Perhaps low self-esteem people seek or prefer downward comparisons, but they are especially likely to experience upward comparisons involuntarily. In contrast, when high self-esteem people notice other people, they may more readily conclude that they are superior in some way. Wood and Giordano (1998) tested this idea in their self-recording study. When participants recorded a comparison, they indicated whether the comparison was voluntarily chosen or forced; they reported their motive for comparing as well. Results indicated that the correlation that Wheeler and Miyake and Giordano and Wood (1997) found between self-esteem and downward comparisons was qualified by whether the comparison was voluntary or involuntary; the correlation was significant only for involuntary comparisons. This result suggests that high self-esteem people involuntarily make more downward comparisons than do low self-esteem people but that highs and lows may be equally likely to seek downward comparisons voluntarily.

However, lows made surprising choices when they selected comparisons voluntarily (Wood & Giordano, 1998). When they were unhappy, they were not especially inclined to seek downward comparisons, as the self-enhancement model predicts. Instead, it was high self-esteem people who sought more downward than upward comparisons. Low self-esteem people reported that they voluntarily sought downward comparisons for self-enhancement when they were happy rather than unhappy. We return to this finding later in the chapter.

Laboratory Target Selection Studies

In several studies conducted in a laboratory, participants were presented with an array of possible comparison targets and were asked to choose among them. Typically, self-worth is examined in combination with a threat manipulation of some sort. This type of study includes the classic *rank order paradigm*, in which participants are led to believe that their score ranks in the middle of a group of about seven others who are also participating. Then they are given the opportunity to see the score associated with one other participant's rank. This measure allows researchers to examine whether participants choose upward, downward, or similar comparisons by whether they choose to see the scores of others whose scores ranked higher, lower, or at similar ranks, respectively.

In three rank order studies, researchers examined participants who varied in self-esteem (Smith & Insko, 1987; Wilson & Benner, 1971) or in terms of a construct called *fear of negative evaluation*, which is related (inversely) to self-esteem (Friend & Gilbert, 1973). In one of these studies, researchers found a main effect for self-worth, such that participants lower in self-worth were less likely to choose the highest ranked score (Smith & Insko, 1987). In another study, researchers found that self-worth interacted with a manipulation of threat, such that low self-worth participants who were also threatened were least likely to choose to see a higher ranked score (Friend & Gilbert, 1973). In a third study, Wilson and Benner (1971) obtained more complicated interactions involving self-esteem, gender, certainty of the validity of the test, and the public versus private nature of the comparison context (which was operationalized as choosing a discussion partner or choosing to observe the other), but whenever a self-esteem effect emerged, low self-esteem participants selected comparisons that were more downward than those selected by high self-esteem participants.

These studies have been cited as supporting downward comparison theory (e.g., Wood, 1989), and they do in the sense that people who are lower in self-esteem generally choose comparisons that are more downward than do high self-esteem people. Two of the studies show that low self-esteem people are especially likely to make such downward choices when they have been threatened in some way, either by being told that they performed poorly on a test (Friend & Gilbert, 1973) or that the comparison context will be a public one (Wilson & Benner, 1971). However, as Wheeler and Mikaye (1992) pointed out, these studies do not show that low self-esteem participants prefer to make downward comparisons; they typically make upward comparisons, just less upward than high self-esteem participants make. Thus, these studies should be more properly interpreted as supporting the self-protection perspective than the self-enhancement perspective. Low self-worth people, especially those who are threatened in some way, appear to avoid highly unflattering comparisons rather than to choose flattering comparisons.

A study by Gibbons (1986, Experiment 1) also has been cited as supporting downward comparison theory, but it too may point to self-protection or even self-validation rather than self-enhancement. Gibbons's participants wrote personal statements about a positive or negative event and then had an opportunity to read a personal statement supposedly written by another participant. They could choose from a range of very negative to very positive personal statements. Dysphoric participants who had written about a negative experience chose statements that were more negative than those chosen by the other groups. As Wheeler and Miyake (1992) pointed out, however, it is unclear whether dysphoric participants were choosing to compare with others who were truly downward relative to themselves. Their Beck Depression Inventory scores were unusually high in this study (M = 21.6), so it is quite possible that they did not see themselves as superior to their comparison target. Although dysphoric participants may have intended to make self-enhancing downward comparisons in this study, then, it is also possible that they were seeking self-protection by avoiding an upward comparison or even seeking the consolation of a similar comparison target.

Research by Wood, Giordano-Beech, Taylor, Michela, and Gaus (1994) also points to self-protection on the part of low self-esteem participants. In two studies, they led participants to believe that they had failed or succeeded relative to another participant and then gave them an opportunity to seek further comparisons with that coparticipant. In each study, high self-esteem participants were especially likely to seek comparisons after they failed, and low self-esteem participants were especially likely to seek comparisons after they succeeded. Low self-esteem participants' relatively low interest in comparisons after they failed is self-protective, in that comparing themselves further with someone who had just performed much better than they had could invite further humiliation.

In that same light, high self-esteem participants' comparison seeking after failure may appear to be self-destructive. Wood et al. (1994) speculated, however, that highs sought comparisons after a failure in hopes of compensating for the failure. Their comparison measure involved selecting tests for the self and the coparticipant to take. By taking a new test, participants could hope to overturn the earlier failure. Wood et al. reasoned that only people with high self-esteem would have the motivation and confidence to attempt to compensate in this manner. Later studies support this interpretation (e.g., Wood, Giordano-Beech, & DuCharme, in press).

In summary, then, five laboratory studies of target selection suggest that low self-worth people are more self-protective than are high self-worth people in their comparison selections, perhaps especially when they feel threatened. In two of these studies, researchers either did not allow a clear distinction between self-protection and self-enhancement (Gibbons, 1986) or did not present a self-enhancing option that did not also carry considerable risk (because participants could choose only to compare with a coparticipant who had just outperformed them; Wood et al., 1994). However, in three of these studies (rank order studies), a self-enhancing comparison option was offered (i.e., downward target), but low self-worth participants did not tend to choose it. Hence, these studies suggest that low self-worth people seek self-protection rather than self-enhancement.

Countering this evidence of self-protection, however, are four laboratory target selection studies that suggest that low self-worth people are less self-protective than high self-worth people are. Two studies suggest that when they can expect comparisons to be unfavorable (e.g., because their own performance was poor), highs decrease their overall comparison seeking but lows do not (Northcraft & Ashford, 1990; Swallow & Kuiper, 1992).

Self-protectiveness also may take the form of preferring one type of comparison—namely, a favorable comparison—over another, and two studies suggest that highs are more self-enhancing or self-protective in this respect than are lows. Pinkley, Laprelle, Pyszczynski, and Greenberg (1988) showed that after they were led to believe that they had failed, nondysphoric participants sought more comparisons when they expected those comparisons to reveal that others received similarly low scores than when they expected them to reveal that others received high scores. Dysphoric participants who failed did not show this preference. Similarly, Swallow and Kuiper (1993, Study 1) showed that among participants who performed poorly, nondysphoric participants showed a preference for seeing the scores of others who had performed worse than they had, whereas dysphoric participants chose to see the scores of others who had performed similar to themselves.

Although these studies suggest that high self-worth people are more self-protective than low self-worth people, lows do appear to be somewhat self-protective in these studies. In the Northcroft and Ashford (1990) study, low self-esteem participants sought more comparisons than high self-esteem participants only after a poor performance when they could receive the comparison information privately. In the Swallow and Kuiper (1993) study, which also involved a very private situation, the selections of similar targets by dysphoric participants could have been self-protective or self-validating, even though they were less self-enhancing than the downward comparisons sought by nondysphoric participants.

But why would five studies point to more self-protectiveness on the part of low self-worth people and four studies point to more self-protectiveness on the part of high self-worth people? We have not been able to discern a pattern that accounts for all of these findings, but one factor worth pursuing concerns whether participants were forced to choose comparisons. In four of the five studies suggesting that lows are more self-protective, experimenters forced participants to choose comparisons, so lows' self-protectiveness was evidenced by target choices that were less upward than those chosen by highs (i.e., the rank order studies and the Gibbons, 1986, study). In three out of four studies that suggest more self-protectiveness among highs than lows, experimenters did not force participants to select comparisons. Highs' self-protectiveness was evidenced by avoiding comparisons after a poor performance. It appears, then, that high self-worth people are generally more likely than low self-worth people to avoid comparisons altogether as a self-protective strategy after failure, but when forced to choose comparisons, lows appear to be more self-protective in their comparison choices than are highs.

Why would this be so? First, it is important to note that in the studies suggesting more self-protectiveness in lows, highs may not have been as non-self-protective as their choices suggest. In the rank order studies, they may have construed an upward target to be less upward and as more similar to themselves overall than did lows (see Collins, 1996). In the Gibbons (1986) study, when nondysphoric participants chose to read other people's relatively positive personal statements, they may have been avoiding the potentially depressing nature of others' negative stories (which dysphoric participants, in contrast, may have experienced as validating). In the single "unforced" study that suggests lows were more self-protective than highs —namely, Wood et al.'s (1994)—highs' choices may not have represented self-depreciation but a desire to compensate, as argued earlier. Thus, when they are required to select comparisons, highs' comparison choices may not be as detrimental to their self-esteem as they appear.

In the studies suggesting more self-protectiveness in highs, highs appear to exercise the option of not comparing if they can. When they face comparisons that promise to be unfavorable, highs seem to know better than to seek comparisons, but lows do not. However, we do not interpret lows' failure to avoid comparisons after failure as supporting the self-depreciation perspective but as supporting the failure-to-self-protect perspective. Lows' interest in comparing after failure may not represent a desire for unfavorable comparisons; instead, it may stem from a greater need to socially compare, as suggested by the self-evaluation perspective, which simply does not diminish after they perform poorly. They even may be interested in self-improvement.

Finally, in two target selection studies, researchers found that low and high self-worth participants responded in the same way, but they pointed to opposite conclusions. Albright and Henderson (1995) found that a few days after they had written about a negative event that they had experienced, both dysphoric and nondysphoric participants preferred a downward comparison target—someone who was coping worse than they were. In contrast, Helgeson and Mickelson (1995, Study 2) found that both low and high self-esteem people chose to make upward comparisons with people who scored higher than themselves after they received negative feedback on a test of "relationship aptitude." Although this result may suggest that both groups are prone to self-depreciate, it seems quite possible that they both chose an upward target for self-improvement (Wood, 1989). Unlike most studies of target selection in which participants are permitted only to select another person's score for comparison, in Helgeson and Mickelson's study participants were permitted to see another person's responses on the test. Hence, participants may have hoped to learn how to improve their relationship aptitude. Several studies suggest that when the potential for improvement exists, responses to upward comparison are more likely to be favorable (see Aspinwall, 1997, for references).

In summary, the evidence concerning target selections is mixed. Most studies do show differences between high and low self-worth people, but some support the self-protection perspective and some support the failure-to-self-protect perspective. Clearly, however, little evidence suggests that lows truly self-depreciate or that they self-enhance by choosing targets who are truly inferior to themselves.

Surprisingly, there is evidence that low self-worth people self-enhance when they seem to need it least, namely, after success. Wood et al. (1994, Experiments 1 and 2) found that lows were interested in comparing after they succeeded with someone they had just outperformed, especially when they thought that the opportunity for comparison was "safe"—without risk of exposing their weaknesses (Experiment 3). Similarly, in Pinkley et al.'s (1988) study, dysphoric participants who succeeded sought more comparisons when they expected that those scores would be low rather than high. Swallow and Kuiper (1992) found that following good performances, dysphoric participants sought as many comparisons as did nondysphoric participants. These findings resemble those of Wood and Giordano's (1998) self-recording study mentioned earlier, in which low self-esteem participants reported that they sought downward comparisons for self-enhancement when they were happy rather than unhappy. Such results suggest that low self-worth people sometimes venture beyond their self-protectiveness to self-enhance, namely, when they can revel in their success or happiness (Wood et al., 1994).

Affiliation Studies

In several affiliation studies, researchers examined participants' choices of with whom they wish to interact. Such measures may reflect social comparison motives, in that a desire to compare may lead people to want the company of others. A desire to make an upward or downward comparison may lead them to want to be with a superior or inferior person. However, interest in affiliating also may reflect motives other than social comparison, such as attraction or social support seeking, and a desire to avoid others may reflect not a lack of interest in comparing but shame or embarrassment. Interest in particular affiliation partners may reflect not only social comparison motives but also an attraction to specific others, a wish to have a compatible discussion, a wish to avoid humiliation, and so forth. Thus, affiliation measures are especially vulnerable to alternative interpretations (Wood, 1996). However, the beauty of affiliation measures is that to the extent that they do reflect social comparison motives, they do so in ways that are richer and more consequential than the sometimes dry, comparatively impoverished contexts used in some target selection studies.

Although in three studies researchers have found no differences on affiliation choice measures between people who are high and low in self-esteem (Helgeson & Mickelson, 1995, Study 2; Helgeson & Taylor, 1993; Smith & Insko, 1987), other researchers have found some differences. In the Wilson and Benner (1971) rank order study described earlier, the public condition involved a choice of with whom participants wanted to discuss an issue. More high than low self-esteem people chose to have a discussion with the person who earned the highest score. Other researchers similarly found that low self-worth people chose to affiliate with people who were more downward than the people chosen by high self-worth people. Whereas nondysphoric people want to meet with nondysphoric people, the dysphoric ones want to meet with other dysphoric ones (Rosenblatt & Greenberg, 1988). Wenzlaff and Prohaska (1989) asked participants to read descriptions of life events supposedly written by other students and to rate how much they wanted to meet the author of the event description. Dysphoric participants most wanted to meet a person who was unhappy because of a misfortune, whereas nondysphoric participants wanted to meet someone who had experienced good fortune. Dysphoric people even seem to have best friends who are dysphoric (Rosenblatt & Greenberg, 1991, Study 1).

These results support downward comparison theory, in that the choices of low self-esteem or dysphoric people are more downward than the choices of their higher self-worth counterparts. However, again we encounter the two problems identified earlier with respect to target selection studies. In the Wilson and Benner (1971) study, low self-esteem participants still appeared to make upward comparison choices, just less upward than those made by high self-esteem participants. Second, it is not clear that participants perceive the downward targets as being truly downward relative to themselves. Thus, it is not clear that low self-worth people seek self-enhancement; they may be only protecting themselves from an embarrassing or painful comparison with a superior person. It is also plausible that low self-worth people are not avoiding upward comparisons as much as seeking validation by affiliating with similar others.

Not only do dysphoric people want to be in the company of others who are similarly miserable, they may even go so far as to create miserable discussion partners by focusing on negative topics (Kuiper & McCabe, 1985). This interest in negative topics appears especially pronounced when they interact with nondysphoric people (Locke & Horowitz, 1990). In a series of studies by Wenzlaff and Beevers (in press), participants were led to believe that they were going to interview someone who was happy or unhappy. They had a choice of questions to ask their coparticipant that varied in terms of their likelihood of evoking positive (e.g., "What are you most proud of?") or negative (e.g., "When are you the loneliest?") information. Participants themselves did not expect to have to answer the same questions. When they were faced with a happy partner for the upcoming interview, dysphoric participants chose questions that were especially negative. It appears that they either avoided the unflattering comparison that a cheerful coparticipant would bring or that they sought a similarly miserable comparison target.

Studies of the effects of affiliation support the idea that dysphoric people prefer to be with dysphoric people. In Locke and Horowitz's (1990) study, participants who were in homogeneous dyads were more satisfied with their interactions than were mixed dyads; nondysphoric people were happier with fellow nondysphoric people, and dysphoric people were happier with fellow dysphoric people. Similarly, Rosenblatt and Greenberg (1991, Study 2) found that dysphoric people felt more anxious and worse in their moods after interacting with a nondysphoric person than after interacting with a dysphoric person.

As we have said, such findings may reflect motives other than social comparison. However, it also seems quite plausible that the reason that dysphoric people feel worse about interacting with nondysphoric people is that the contrast with a cheerful person serves as a painful reminder of their own inadequacies (e.g., "Why can't I be that way?"). In contrast, fellow dysphoric people validate the negative feelings and attitudes of dysphoric people, which makes them feel more normal and justified in their reactions (cf. Rosenblatt & Greenberg, 1991).

In summary, to the extent that affiliation studies reflect social comparison motives, they suggest that people who are low in self-esteem or are dysphoric seek either self-protection or validation in their comparison choices. They either seek to avoid unflattering contrasts with their own moods or to validate their feelings through similar comparisons. Perhaps they also sometimes seek self-enhancement by being in the company of someone who is even more miserable than themselves, but the measures used do not show clearly that dysphoric people want to be in the company of people who are truly downward relative to themselves. Even the Locke and Horowitz (1990) and Wenzlaff and Beevers (in press) results argue against the self-enhancement view, in that dysphoric people did not seek especially negative conversation topics for fellow dysphoric people. Thus, they appeared to pass on an opportunity to create especially downward comparison targets. In any case, the affiliation studies argue that people who are low in self-worth are not self-defeating in their comparison choices; they do not seek out unflattering comparisons.

Studies of the Effects of Social Comparisons

The theoretical perspectives not only predict differences between low and high self-worth people in which comparisons they select, but they also predict different reactions to comparisons. Relative to people who are high in self-worth, the self-evaluation perspective predicts that people who are low in self-worth are more affected by social comparisons in general; the self-enhancement perspective predicts that lows benefit more from downward comparisons; the self-validation perspective predicts that lows are especially gratified by comparisons with similar others; and the failure to self-protect and self-depreciation views predict that low self-worth people respond more unfavorably to comparisons.

Although these predictions follow from the theoretical perspectives, one should keep in mind that the effects of comparison on an individual do not necessarily reflect the individual's motives for comparison. For example, one could select a downward comparison in the interests of self-enhancement but then not feel better after the comparison after all.

Global Self-Reported Effects of Comparison

In a few studies, researchers have examined self-reports of the effects of social comparisons. Interpretations of these findings should again be made cautiously, given the problems of global self-reports mentioned earlier. In any case, the self-evaluation perspective prediction that low self-worth people are especially affected by social comparisons was supported by Weary et al. (1987), who found that relative to nondysphoric people, dysphoric people reported that the social comparison information they received had more impact on them.

Other researchers have examined self-reported responses to specific comparison targets. Buunk et al. (1990, Study 1) asked people who had been diagnosed with cancer how often they felt lucky or grateful versus fearful or anxious when exposed to others who were worse off than they were and how often they felt frustrated or depressed versus inspired or comforted when they saw others who were better off than they were. Buunk et al. found that respondents with high self-esteem were less likely than those with low self-esteem to report feeling bad after both upward and downward comparisons. Similarly, Wayment and Taylor (1995) found that high self-esteem respondents were more likely than low self-esteem respondents to report social comparisons—whether upward, downward, or lateral—as self-enhancing, and Heidrich and Ryff (1993) found that among older women, the lower their psychological distress, the more they reported feeling good about their comparisons.

These findings contradict the self-enhancement perspective, in that low self-worth participants did not find downward comparisons to be more self-enhancing than high self-worth participants did. A problem in interpreting these results, however, is that people with low self-worth ordinarily feel worse than do those with high self-worth. Hence, it is not clear that these results reflect differences between highs' and lows' responses to social comparisons or merely preexisting differences in the affect of highs and lows. In addition, the results may reflect respondents' theories about social comparison effects rather than actual effects. People who are high in self-worth may believe that most events, social comparisons included, make them feel good, whereas low self-worth people may harbor the theory that comparisons do not make them feel good.

Self-Evaluations

Next, we review evidence that involves pre- and postcomparison self-evaluation and mood measures. Except where indicated, all of the studies described below are laboratory studies. Two studies of self-evaluation suggest that after receiving the same comparison information, low self-worth people draw more negative conclusions about the self than do high self-worth people. McFarland and Miller (1994) found that after being told that their performance on a bogus test of "social perceptiveness" was at the 30th percentile, participants classified as "negatively oriented" (based on a combination of the Beck Depression Inventory and a measure of optimism) rated their abilities as low (Study 1) and reported more negative affect (Study 2), whereas "positively oriented" participants reported higher ability levels (Study 1) and reported less negative affect (Study 2; these effects held only when they believed that the sample size was large rather than small). McFarland and Miller's second study suggested that negatively oriented people focus on how many people do better than they do whereas positively oriented people focus on how many people do worse than they do.

In a study by Ahrens (1991), participants were told that their performance on a test was either higher than a coparticipant's, lower than a coparticipant's, or higher than one coparticipant's and lower than another's. The subsequent self-judgments of nondysphoric and dysphoric participants were similarly affected by the favorable and unfavorable comparisons. However, following mixed feedback, dysphoric participants made judgments that matched those who had made unfavorable comparisons and nondysphoric participants made judgments that matched those who made favorable comparisons.

Similar results were obtained by Lyubomirsky and Ross (1997, Study 1), who found that unhappy people (as self-described in an earlier mass testing) lowered their self-assessments in the face of an unfavorable social comparison whereas happy people did not. Yet both happy and unhappy people enjoyed self-assessment benefits after downward comparisons. These effects were independent of dispositional self-esteem and optimism.

It appears, then, that low self-worth people respond less favorably than high self-worth people to the same social comparison information. In the failure-to-self-protect perspective, this finding would mean that highs are especially able to use comparison information in ways that benefit their self-esteem (cf. Lyubomirsky & Ross, 1997) whereas lows lack this capacity. In the self-depreciation perspective, this finding would mean that lows even seize on unfavorable comparison information. Clearly, however, these results may not mean that lows are actually motivated to self-depreciate; they simply may react to comparisons in ways that are consistent with their unfavorable self-views. Indeed, we believe that for social comparisons to boost a low's spirits, they would have to work against a low's natural tendency to put a negative spin on self-relevant information. It is encouraging, then, that Ahrens (1991) found that at least when the comparison information is unambiguous and salient, lows may benefit from downward comparisons.

Two studies even suggest that low self-worth people are more likely than high self-worth people to experience improvement in their self-esteem (T. J. Reis, Gerrard, & Gibbons, 1993) or self-evaluations (Aspinwall & Taylor, 1993, Study 2) after downward comparisons, and one of these suggests that low self-esteem people who were also threatened were especially likely to benefit. Specifically, Aspinwall and Taylor found that low self-esteem participants who had experienced a recent academic setback and who read about a fellow student who was doing poorly at school rated their adjustment to college more positively and had higher expectations of future success in college than did low self-esteem participants in the upward comparison or no-comparison conditions. Lows who had suffered no recent setback and highs did not experience the same benefits of downward comparisons.

These studies support the self-enhancement perspective prediction that people who are dysphoric or low in self-esteem are especially likely to improve their self-evaluations after downward comparisons. However, we should note that Lyubomirsky and Ross (1997, Study 1), who examined happy versus unhappy people with self-esteem controlled, found that happy people, like unhappy people, were responsive to downward comparisons. Why would lows be more likely than highs to benefit from downward comparisons in some studies but not in others? We examine the studies of mood before addressing this question.

Mood Measures

In some laboratory studies, researchers who obtained effects of social comparisons on mood did not obtain differences between high and low self-esteem people in their affective reactions to comparisons (Tesser, Millar, & Moore, 1988, Studies 1 & 2; Wood et al., 1994, Study 2). In studies that focus on downward comparisons specifically, both highs and lows appear to improve in mood after downward comparisons (Tesser et al., 1988, Study 1; Wood et al., 1994, Study 2; see also Lyubomirsky & Ross, 1997, Study 1, for evidence that both happy and unhappy people benefit from downward comparisons). Similarly, in studies of everyday social comparisons, Wheeler and Miyake (1992) and Giordano and Wood (1997) suggested that although downward comparisons improved mood, such comparisons were not more beneficial to low self-esteem people than high self-esteem people.

However, like some of the self-evaluation studies cited above, several studies suggest that low self-worth people benefit more in their moods from downward comparisons than do high self-worth people (Aspinwall & Taylor, 1993, Study 1; Gibbons, 1986, Study 2; Gibbons & Boney-McCoy, 1991, Studies 1 & 2; Gibbons & Gerrard, 1989; Wenzlaff & Prohaska, 1989; see also Lyubomirsky & Ross, 1997, Study 2, for similar results for happy vs. unhappy people). One study even suggests that nondysphoric people's moods worsen after downward comparisons (Wenzlaff & Prohaska, 1989). Why do some studies find that high and low self-worth people both benefit from downward comparisons (we cited five such studies if we count Lyubomirsky and Ross's study of happy vs. unhappy people), whereas other studies (seven) show that lows are especially likely to benefit from downward comparisons?

First, we examine in depth the studies that purport to show differences between highs and lows. Although these studies were very well conducted, in only one study did researchers use the perfect design for demonstrating definitively that lows are more likely than highs to benefit from downward comparisons: They crossed high versus low self-worth with upward, downward, and no-comparison conditions. However, they did not obtain mood effects (although they did obtain self-evaluation effects, as described earlier; Aspinwall & Taylor, 1993, Study 2). Some studies, by virtue of lacking either an upward or no-comparison condition, do not make it clear if downward comparisons in particular improve moods. It is reassuring, then, that two of the studies that do include both upward and downward comparison conditions clearly indicate that low self-worth people's moods do not improve in response to all comparisons. Specifically, they suggest that although after downward comparisons low self-worth people's moods are more likely than high self-worth people's to improve, after upward comparisons lows are less likely to show mood improvement (Gibbons & Gerrard, 1989) or lows' moods even worsen (Wenzlaff & Prohaska, 1989).

But could lows' moods have improved over time anyway, without the downward comparison? Perhaps the mood improvement of lows in the downward conditions was due to a "spontaneous remission." Upward–downward condition differences could still have been obtained; perhaps spontaneous remission was halted when lows encountered painful upward comparisons. Because the pre- and postcomparison mood assessments are just a few minutes apart, we regard this spontaneous remission possibility as implausible, except when there is reason to think that participants' moods were unusually low at precomparison, such as after a mood or threat induction. Such an induction did occur in some studies. Although studies with such an induction do not include the no-comparison condition that would most definitively rule out spontaneous remission, in three of these studies researchers included the next best thing, namely, an analysis of covariance controlling for precomparison mood (Gibbons & Boney-McCoy, 1991, Studies 1 & 2; Gibbons & Gerrard, 1989). In addition, Wenzlaff and Prohaska (1989) had no threat or negative mood induction prior to the comparison, and they obtained an upward–downward difference, which suggests that the downward comparison itself improved lows' moods.

Could the greater improvement of mood after downward comparisons in low self-worth people be due to a statistical artifact (Ladd Wheeler, personal communication, July, 1997)? In contrast to low self-worth people, high self-worth people may have little room to improve their moods. For example, in the Wenzlaff and Prohaska (1989) study, on a mood scale that ranged from 1.0 to 10.0, nondepressed people's average mood before comparison was 8.5, whereas depressed people's mood was 5.5. That may explain why nondepressed participants' moods never improved in response to comparisons but only worsened or stayed the same. We examined the ranges and mean mood scores in all of the studies cited above that provided that information. In virtually all of the studies, lows and highs differed significantly in their moods prior to comparison, as would be expected, but it appeared that highs did have room on the mood scales to show improvement (cf. Aspinwall & Taylor, 1993; Gibbons & Boney-McCoy, 1991).[2]

---

[2]In several of the articles cited in this section, authors addressed, perhaps in response to reviewers' criticisms, the possibility that "regression to the mean" accounts for the improvement in low self-worth participants' moods. We find this possibility implausible. Although it is true that typically participants were selected because they were at the extremes on dysphoria or self-esteem in a mass testing, any measurement error that contributed to these scores should have led to regression to the mean only for the precomparison scores in the laboratory a few weeks later, not from precomparison to postcomparison. Perhaps what is meant by regression to the mean in these cases is the spontaneous remission possibility we discussed in the text, which has nothing to do with measurement error but a true change in mood.

Although the mood scales do not seem to place a ceiling on highs' mood improvement, it does seem possible that the mutability of mood varies along the dimension of mood. That is, lightening a sad mood may be easier than making a happy person even happier. Recent research by Leary, Haupt, Strausser, and Chokel (1998) supports this possibility. In four studies, they found that positive evaluations improve state self-esteem and mood but only up to a point; once evaluations are moderately positive, self-esteem and mood do not improve further. If dispositional self-esteem operates as state self-esteem does, these results may suggest that downward comparisons would improve the moods and self-evaluations of low self-worth people but that high self-worth people's spirits may sometimes be too high for downward comparisons to noticeably change how they feel. If this is so, we would see it less as an artifact than as an interesting property of mood that places limits on high self-worth people's capacity to benefit from downward comparisons.

At the same time, this possibility raises an intriguing question: When highs do not benefit from downward comparisons, do their happy moods constrain them from benefiting? Or is it something about highs themselves—something that makes them fail to appreciate downward comparisons? In other words, would high self-worth people be especially likely to benefit from downward comparisons when their spirits are low?

A way to look at this question is to worsen the moods of people who are high in self-worth to see if they would then be more responsive to downward comparisons. Several of the studies that obtained high–low differences do include conditions in which participants' moods were probably dampened by a negative mood or threat induction. We say *probably* because there was either (a) no manipulation (only an induction) of negative mood or threat or (b) no neutral condition, thereby precluding a check on whether highs' moods were truly lower than usual in the negative mood or threat condition. (Aspinwall & Taylor, 1993, Study 2, did compare high and low threat groups [not manipulated experimentally] but found no mood effects.) Because of the absence of no-threat conditions, we do not know whether these threat or negative mood inductions lowered highs' moods to the level of that of lows' baseline moods. (In all of these studies, highs' moods in the negative mood or threat condition were still significantly better than those of lows' in the same conditions, which is to be expected.)

Although these studies do not address the question we raised in an ideal fashion and were not designed to, they are suggestive. Specifically, they suggest that when high self-worth people's moods should have been dampened, they did not improve in their moods in response to downward comparisons when lows' moods did improve (Aspinwall & Taylor, 1993, Study 1; Gibbons & Boney-McCoy, 1991, Studies 1 & 2; Gibbons & Gerrard, 1989). A possible exception is Lyubomirsky and Ross's (1997) Study 2, which again included happy versus unhappy people rather than low self-esteem or dysphoric people. They found that happy people who had received unfavorable performance feedback did appear to be comforted by the news that a coparticipant had performed even worse. Their moods did not decline, whereas the moods of happy people who did not receive the downward comparison information did decline. At the same time, this study agrees with the others involving self-esteem and dysphoria in showing that unhappy people who had been threatened were especially likely to benefit from downward comparisons; they actually improved in mood. Especially informative are threat studies that include an upward comparison condition; in these studies, researchers found that highs' moods did improve after an upward comparison but not after a downward one (Aspinwall & Taylor, 1993, Study 1; Gibbons & Gerrard, 1989). These studies indicate that highs' moods certainly were capable of improving, yet they did so only in response to upward comparisons.

A definitive answer to our question—Are highs sometimes unresponsive to downward comparisons due to something about their high self-worth or to their moods?—awaits further research. We can cautiously conclude, however, that at least under some conditions, highs do not respond as readily to downward comparisons as to upward comparisons and that they do not respond as readily to downward comparisons as do lows.

Gibbons and Boney-McCoy (1991) and Aspinwall and Taylor (1993) have offered a provocative interpretation of these studies involving negative mood or threat inductions, namely, that low self-worth must be coupled with a negative mood induction or a threat experience to trigger improvements in mood or self-evaluation after downward comparisons. However, the Gibbons (1986), T. J. Reis et al. (1993), and Wenzlaff and Prohaska (1989) studies indicate that lows may have favorable reactions to downward comparisons, even without a threat or mood induction.[3] In addition, several studies cited earlier indicate that high self-worth people sometimes do benefit from downward comparisons. Thus, clearly the "double whammy" (Aspinwall & Taylor, 1993) of low self-worth and a recent exacerbation of mood is not necessary for downward comparisons to be beneficial. But does the double whammy make those benefits more likely? Unfortunately, the role of threat cannot be determined definitively in these studies because most did not include a true no-threat condition. Participants who were not in the negative mood or threat condition were in either a positive mood condition (Aspinwall & Taylor, 1993, Study 1) or what appears to have been a "boost" condition (Gibbons & Boney-McCoy, 1991, Studies 1 and 2). Hence, it is not clear that the threat (or negative

[3]In the Gibbons study, all participants wrote a personal statement about an event of their choosing before they experienced a comparison. Although it seems plausible that dysphoric participants wrote about more negative events than did nondysphoric participants, raters' judgments of the affect in these statements revealed no such difference, which suggests that they were not in a threatened or especially negative state prior to the downward comparison.

mood) condition made downward comparisons especially beneficial; perhaps the boost (or positive mood) condition rendered downward comparisons, which usually may be helpful to low self-worth people, unnecessary (cf. Aspinwall & Taylor, 1993). In the sole study that has what appears to be a true no-threat condition, Aspinwall and Taylor (Study 2) did find self-evaluation effects for lows who were threatened but no mood effects. In addition, it is possible that the special benefits of downward comparisons for threatened, low self-worth people in these studies are restricted to the particular dimension of comparison used in these studies, as discussed shortly. Thus, more research is needed to be confident that the benefits of downward comparisons are especially likely to accrue to those who are low in self-worth and who are suffering an acute decrement in their moods.

Section Summary

Future research is required to resolve puzzling inconsistencies in this literature, such as when threat is important and why mood and self-evaluation effects sometimes fail to correspond with each other (Aspinwall & Taylor, 1993, Study 2; Gibbons & Gerrard, 1989; T. J. Reis et al., 1993; see also Lyubomirsky & Ross, 1997, Study 2). We can conclude, however, that at least under some conditions, low self-worth people are especially likely to benefit from downward comparisons and that high self-worth people are especially likely to benefit from upward comparisons. These results are consistent with the self-enhancement perspective.

Why do lows appear to benefit more than highs from downward comparisons in some studies but not others? One factor to consider is the nature of the comparison dimension, such as its self-relevance (Tesser et al., 1988). Giordano and Wood (1997), who did not find general differences between highs and lows in their affective responses to comparisons, did find that dysphoric people were especially vulnerable to upward comparisons in self-relevant domains. For example, *sociotropic* people, who are highly invested in close relationships, found comparisons involving others' successful interpersonal relationships especially painful. It is striking that virtually all of the studies in which researchers did obtain mood or self-evaluation differences between highs and lows involve comparisons with fellow university students who were either suffering or adjusting smoothly to university life, whereas the studies in which researchers found that highs also benefited from downward comparisons were more likely to involve other types of dimensions, such as performance (e.g., Wood et al., 1994).

It seems likely that performance and other dimensions are important to both highs and lows but that comparisons involving the coping of fellow students are most relevant to people who are themselves having difficulty adjusting. The people having such difficulty are probably especially likely to be dysphoric or to have low self-esteem. Comparisons involving others' coping also may be ideally suited to bring out different interpretations of downward and upward comparisons by lows and highs. People who are high in self-worth may identify with or assume similarity to the happy, successful upward target (Collins, 1996). They may infer that they, too, can maintain the target's level of adjustment, which would lead them to be inspired by an upward comparison (see Aspinwall, 1997). In contrast, as Ahrens and Alloy (1997) have suggested, the negative self-views and motivational deficits of dysphoric people may lead them to believe that the success of an upward target is unattainable. Low self-worth people instead may identify with the student who is homesick and anxious about academic progress.

Indeed, some authors have noted that the special benefit that lows draw from downward comparisons may stem in part from their similarity to the downward target (Aspinwall & Taylor, 1993; Gibbons & Gerrard, 1991). When one is under stress, the common bond that one shares with another person who is experiencing similar problems can be a great relief, validating one's own feelings and making one feel less abnormal (cf. Wills, 1981). Support for this idea was obtained by Gibbons and Boney-McCoy (1991), who found in two studies that high threat, low self-esteem participants—the ones who benefited most from downward comparisons —also perceived more similarity to the downward target than did any other group.

We may take this reasoning a step further and argue that if similarity is so important, perhaps the downward aspect of the comparison is unnecessary; perhaps what is most beneficial to low self-worth people is finding others in the same boat. There is no evidence in these studies to rule out the possibility that lateral comparisons are as effective as downward comparisons at improving lows' moods or self-evaluations. If future research suggests that similarity to the target is the key to making lows feel better, such a finding would shift the spotlight from the self-enhancement perspective to the self-validation perspective.

CONCLUSIONS

Which theoretical perspectives are supported in these studies of high and low self-worth people's social comparisons? Almost every perspective has at least some evidence to support it but evidence against it as well. It seems likely that both lows and highs harbor all of the motives for social comparison that we have identified and that the question, therefore, becomes what circumstances make each particular motive come to the forefront.

To see what light the studies shed on this issue, we first summarize the studies of comparison effects. There is suggestive evidence that low self-worth people are especially sensitive to social comparison information (cf. Lyubomirsky & Ross, 1997), which supports the self-evaluation perspective. Perhaps they are more sensitive to social comparisons because they are less clear and certain in their self-concepts (e.g., Campbell, 1990). Unfortunately, lows' sensitivity appears to be accompanied by a tendency to interpret social comparison information negatively or to focus on its unfavorable aspects. In that sense, lows seem to fail to self-protect when they interpret social comparison information, whereas highs may more selectively use comparison information to their advantage.

However, some evidence supports the self-enhancement perspective: At least under some circumstances, lows may be especially likely to benefit from downward comparisons, perhaps especially when they are threatened and the downward target shares a problem with them. Studies that point to special benefits for lows also involve instances when the downward comparison was quite salient and unambiguous. Given low self-worth people's tendency to interpret comparison information negatively, it seems likely that downward comparison information must be unambiguous and uniform to lift their spirits. Unfortunately, everyday life may typically present a mix of superior and inferior others rather than a sole salient inferior other.

As we have noted, comparison effects may not reflect people's motives behind comparisons. Lows may dearly want to self-enhance but have trouble interpreting social comparisons in flattering ways. Hence, we focus more on the studies of comparison selections. Studies involving self-report and selections of partners for discussions of opinions offer tantalizing evidence for the self-evaluation perspective; people who are low in self-worth may be generally more interested in social comparisons than people who are high in self-worth, especially comparisons that can help them to reduce uncertainty. More convincing evidence for the self-evaluation perspective is now needed. Especially useful would be selection studies that do not involve self-report or affiliation-type measures as well as studies of the effects of comparison that do include measures of uncertainty reduction.

At present, there is little support for the self-enhancement view that people who are low in self-worth seek truly downward comparisons. In part, this lack of evidence may be due to the measures used, which are sometimes unclear as to whether the comparison target is inferior to the participants themselves. However, several studies contradict the self-enhancement perspective by suggesting that low self-worth people seek upward comparisons (i.e., the rank order studies) or even that they are less likely than high self-worth people to make downward comparisons (i.e., the self-recording studies).

At the same time, we also found little evidence to support the self-depreciation view that lows actually seek unfavorable comparisons. There is evidence, however, that lows sometimes fail to self-protect. Namely, when they can choose not to compare at all after failure, they compare nonetheless, unlike highs. Further evidence of the failure-to-self-protect/

self-enhance perspective is offered by the self-recording studies, which suggest that highs are more likely than lows to compare downward.

The bulk of the experimental evidence, however, favors the view that low self-worth people select comparisons that are beneficial to their self-esteem. Target selection studies, which suggest that low self-worth people seek comparison targets who are less upward than those selected by high self-worth people, are consistent in spirit with Wills's (1981) downward comparison theory, even though they do not show that lows seek truly downward comparisons. We interpret them as supporting the self-protection perspective. The affiliation studies suggest that people who are low in self-esteem or are dysphoric seek either self-protection or self-validation in their comparison choices: They either seek to avoid unflattering contrasts with their own moods or to validate their feelings through similar comparisons. These findings, too, are consistent with Wills's theory, in that he argued that people sometimes seek comfort through comparisons with others who are similar rather than worse off.

In summary, it appears likely that low self-worth people are especially interested in social comparisons (supporting the self-evaluation perspective) but that their comparison choices are influenced by needs for self-protection and self-validation. They often self-protect by avoiding humiliating comparisons with others who are highly superior to themselves, and they seek the solace of others who are similar to themselves. As we have noted, even the benefits of downward comparisons may accrue from the similarities that lows share with the downward target rather than from their superiority to that target.

Clearly, much more research is needed to confirm that self-protection or self-validation is the primary motive guiding lows' choices for comparisons. Especially helpful would be studies that look at what participants expect from their comparisons and how they construe comparisons that they have received. At present, however, the evidence suggests that although lows' comparisons may not be the most self-enhancing ones possible, they seem to be chosen in the service of their self-esteem.

Why is it that low self-worth people enjoy the benefits of downward comparisons, sometimes even more than high self-worth people do, yet they do not seem to seek highly self-enhancing comparisons? It is possible that enhancing themselves does not have the same priority that it does for highs; lows are accustomed to feeling inferior. If their need to self-enhance is relatively weak, lows may be more likely than highs to allow other motives, such as self-evaluation or self-improvement, to lead them to make unfavorable comparisons at times. Another possibility is that lows want to self-enhance but are constrained by their negative expectations. They may fear that they will not find a target who is truly inferior to themselves or that they will worsen on the dimension and become like the downward target (Aspinwall, 1997; Wood & VanderZee, 1997). Given their self-protective natures, low self-worth people may well seek highly self-enhancing comparisons if a clear, safe opportunity presents itself—one that does not allow the possibility that they could be disappointed (Wood & Giordano, 1998; Wood et al., 1994).

Although we concluded that lows' social comparison choices are self-protective and self-validating, we are not saying they are necessarily adaptive; ultimately, they may be self-defeating. By taking the self-protective route, lows may forfeit opportunities to make favorable comparisons that could boost their self-esteem (Wood et al., 1994). Moreover, when dysphoric people choose to avoid reading upbeat stories written by fellow students (Gibbons, 1986) or to avoid affiliating with people who are happier, they may miss an opportunity to improve their own moods or to learn from someone else about how to cope better. Miserable company may be reassuring and comfortable in the short term but may not help to lift their misery (cf. Rosenblatt & Greenberg, 1991). Lows' seeming desire to create miserable comparison targets by focusing on unhappy topics also may bring about the social rejection that they often experience (Wenzlaff & Beever, in press, Experiment 4). Ultimately, then, self-protective and self-validation strategies may perpetuate the negative moods, feelings of inadequacy, and social isolation of low self-worth individuals.

REFERENCES

Abramson, L. Y., Seligman, M. E. P., & Teasdale, J. (1978). Learned helplessness in humans: Critique and reformulation. *Journal of Abnormal Psychology, 87*, 49–74.

Ahrens, A. H. (1991). Dysphoria and social comparison: Combining information regarding others' performances. *Journal of Social and Clinical Psychology, 10*, 190–205.

Ahrens, A. H., & Alloy, L. B. (1997). Social comparison processes in depression. In B. P. Buunk & F. X. Gibbons (Eds.), *Health, coping, and well-being: Perspectives from social comparison theory* (pp. 389–410). Mahwah, NJ: Erlbaum.

Albright, J. S., & Henderson, M. C. (1995). How real is depressive realism? A question of scales and standards. *Cognitive Therapy and Research, 19*, 589–609.

Alloy, L. B., Albright, J. S., & Clements, C. (1987). Depression, nondepression, and social comparison biases. In J. E. Maddux, C. D. Stoltenberg, & R. Rosenwein (Eds.), *Social processes in clinical and counseling psychology* (pp. 94–112). New York: Springer-Verlag.

Aspinwall, L. G. (1997). Future-oriented aspects of social comparisons: A framework for studying health-related comparison activity. In B. P. Buunk & F. X. Gibbons (Eds.), *Health, coping, and well-being: Perspectives from social comparison theory* (pp. 125–165). Mahwah, NJ: Erlbaum.

Aspinwall, L. G., & Taylor, S. E. (1993). Effects of social comparison direction, threat, and self-esteem on affect, self-evaluation, and expected success. *Journal of Personality and Social Psychology, 64,* 708–722.

Baumeister, R. F., Tice, D. M., & Hutton, D. G. (1989). Self-presentational motivation and personality differences in self-esteem. *Journal of Personality, 57,* 547–579.

Beck, A. T. (1976). *Cognitive therapy and the emotional disorders.* New York: International Universities Press.

Brickman, P., & Bulman, R. J. (1977). Pleasure and pain in social comparison. In J. M. Suls & R. Miller (Eds.), *Social comparison processes: Theoretical and empirical perspectives* (pp. 149–186). Washington, DC: Hemisphere.

Buunk, B. P., Collins, R. L., Taylor, S. E., VanYperen, N. W., & Dakof, G. A. (1990). The affective consequences of social comparison: Either direction has its ups and downs. *Journal of Personality and Social Psychology, 59,* 1238–1249.

Campbell, J. D. (1990). Self-esteem and clarity of the self-concept. *Journal of Personality and Social Psychology, 59,* 538–549.

Collins, R. (1996). For better or worse: The impact of upward social comparisons on self-evaluations. *Psychological Bulletin, 119,* 51–69.

Coyne, J. C. (1994). Self-reported distress: Analog or ersatz depression? *Psychological Bulletin, 116,* 29–45.

Crocker, J., Thompson, L. L., McGraw, K. M., & Ingerman, C. (1987). Downward comparison prejudice and evaluations of others: Effects of self-esteem and threat. *Journal of Personality and Social Psychology, 52,* 907–916.

DeVellis, R. F., Holt, K., Renner, B. R., Blalock, S. J., Blanchard, L. W., Cook, H. L., Klotz, M. L., Mikow, V., & Harring, K. (1990). The relationship of social comparison to rheumatoid arthritis symptoms and affect. *Basic and Applied Social Psychology, 11,* 1–18.

Diener, E., & Fujita, F. (1997). Social comparisons and subjective well-being. In B. P. Buunk & F. X. Gibbons (Eds.), *Health, coping, and well-being: Perspectives from social comparison theory* (pp. 329–357). Mahwah, NJ: Erlbaum.

Festinger, L. (1954). A theory of social comparison processes. *Human Relations, 7,* 117–140.

Flett, G. L., Vredenburg, K., Pliner, P., & Krames, L. (1987). Depression and social comparison information-seeking. *Journal of Social Behavior and Personality, 2,* 473–484.

Friend, R. M., & Gilbert, J. (1973). Threat and fear of negative evaluation as determinants of locus of social comparison. *Journal of Personality, 41,* 328–340.

Gibbons, F. X. (1986). Social comparison and depression: Company's effect on misery. *Journal of Personality and Social Psychology, 51,* 140–148.

Gibbons, F. X., & Boney-McCoy, S. (1991). Self-esteem, similarity, and reactions to active versus passive downward comparison. *Journal of Personality and Social Psychology, 60,* 414–424.

Gibbons, F. X., & Buunk, B. P. (in press). Individual differences in social comparison: The development of a scale of social comparison orientation. *Journal of Personality and Social Psychology.*

Gibbons, F. X., & Gerrard, M. (1989). Effects of upward and downward social comparison on mood states. *Journal of Social and Clinical Psychology, 8,* 14–31.

Gibbons, F. X., & Gerrard, M. (1991). Downward comparison and coping with threat. In J. Suls & T. A. Wills (Eds.), *Social comparison: Contemporary theory and research* (pp. 317–345). Hillsdale, NJ: Erlbaum.

Giordano, C., & Wood, J. V. (1997). *Social comparisons in everyday life: The roles of personality styles and dysphoria.* Manuscript in preparation, University of Waterloo.

Goethals, G. R. (1986). Fabricating and ignoring social reality: Self-serving estimates of consensus. In J. M. Olson, C. P. Herman, & M. P. Zanna (Eds.), *Relative deprivation and social comparison: The Ontario Symposium* (Vol. 4, pp. 135–158). Hillsdale, NJ: Erlbaum.

Goethals, G. R., & Darley, J. M. (1977). Social comparison theory: An attributional approach. In J. M. Suls & R. L. Miller (Eds.), *Social comparison processes: Theoretical and empirical perspectives* (pp. 259–278). Washington, DC: Hemisphere.

Heidrich, S. M., & Ryff, C. D. (1993). The role of social comparison processes in the psychological adaptation of elderly adults. *Journal of Gerontology: Psychological Sciences, 48,* 127–136.

Helgeson, V. S., & Mickelson, K. D. (1995). Motives for social comparison. *Personality and Social Psychology Bulletin, 21,* 1200–1209.

Helgeson, V. S., & Taylor, S. E. (1993). Social comparisons and adjustment among cardiac patients. *Journal of Applied Social Psychology, 23,* 1171–1195.

Kuiper, N. A., & McCabe, S. B. (1985). The appropriateness of social topics: Effects of depression and cognitive vulnerability on self and other judgments. *Cognitive Therapy and Research, 9,* 371–379.

Leary, M. R., Haupt, A. L., Strausser, K. S., & Chokel, J. L. (1998). Calibrating the sociometer: The relationship between interpersonal appraisals and state self-esteem. *Journal of Personality and Social Psychology, 74,* 1290–1299.

Locke, K. D., & Horowitz, L. M. (1990). Satisfaction in interpersonal interactions as a function of similarity in level of dysphoria. *Journal of Personality and Social Psychology, 58,* 823–831.

Lockwood, P., & Kunda, Z. (1997). Superstars and me: Predicting the impact of role models on the self. *Journal of Personality and Social Psychology, 73,* 91–103.

Lyubomirsky, S., & Ross, L. (1997). Hedonic consequences of social comparison: A contrast of happy and unhappy people. *Journal of Personality and Social Psychology, 73,* 1141–1157.

Major, B., Testa, M., & Bylsma, W. H. (1991). Responses to upward and downward social comparisons: The impact of esteem-relevance and perceived control.

In J. Suls & T. A. Wills (Eds.), *Social comparison: Contemporary theory and research* (pp. 237–260). Hillsdale, NJ: Erlbaum.

Marsh, H. W., & Parker, J. W. (1984). Determinants of student self-concept: Is it better to be a relatively large fish in a small pond even if you don't learn to swim as well? *Journal of Personality and Social Psychology, 47*, 213–231.

McFarland, C., & Miller, D. T. (1994). The framing of relative performance feedback: Seeing the glass as half empty or half full. *Journal of Personality and Social Psychology, 66*, 1061–1073.

Morse, S., & Gergen, K. J. (1970). Social comparison, self-consistency, and the concept of self. *Journal of Personality and Social Psychology, 16*, 148–156.

Northcraft, G. B., & Ashford, S. J. (1990). The preservation of self in everyday life: The effects of performance expectations and feedback context on feedback inquiry. *Organizational Behavior and Human Decision Processes, 47*, 42–64.

Paulhus, D. L. (1991). Measurement and control of response bias. In J. P. Robinson, P. R. Shaver, & L. S. Wrightsman (Eds.), *Measures of personality and social psychological attitudes* (pp. 17–59). New York: Academic Press.

Pelham, B. (1991). On the benefits of misery: Self-serving biases in the depressive self-concept. *Journal of Personality and Social Psychology, 61*, 670–681.

Pinkley, R. L., Laprelle, J., Pyszczynski, T., & Greenberg, J. (1988). Depression and the self-serving search for consensus after success and failure. *Journal of Social and Clinical Psychology, 6*, 235–244.

Reis, H. T., & Wheeler, L. (1991). Studying social interaction with the Rochester Interaction Record. In M. P. Zanna (Ed.), *Advances in experimental social psychology* (Vol. 24, pp. 270–312). San Diego, CA: Academic Press.

Reis, T. J., Gerrard, M., & Gibbons, F. X. (1993). Social comparison and the pill: Reactions to upward and downward comparison of contraceptive behavior. *Personality and Social Psychology Bulletin, 19*, 13–20.

Rosenblatt, A., & Greenberg, J. (1988). Depression and interpersonal attraction: The role of perceived similarity. *Journal of Personality and Social Psychology, 55*, 112–119.

Rosenblatt, A., & Greenberg, J. (1991). Examining the world of the depressed: Do depressed people prefer others who are depressed? *Journal of Personality and Social Psychology, 60*, 620–629.

Smith, R. H., & Insko, C. A. (1987). Social comparison choice during ability evaluation: The effects of comparison publicity, performance feedback, and self-esteem. *Personality and Social Psychology Bulletin, 13*, 111–122.

Swallow, S., & Kuiper, N. A. (1987). The effects of depression and cognitive vulnerability to depression on judgments of similarity between self and other. *Motivation and Emotion, 11*, 157–167.

Swallow, S., & Kuiper, N. A. (1988). Social comparison and negative self-evaluations: An application to depression. *Clinical Psychology Review, 8*, 55–76.

Swallow, S., & Kuiper, N. A. (1990). Mild depression, dysfunctional cognitions, and interest in social comparison information. *Journal of Social and Clinical Psychology, 9*, 289–302.

Swallow, S., & Kuiper, N. A. (1992). Mild depression and frequency of social comparison behavior. *Journal of Social and Clinical Psychology, 11*, 167–180.

Swallow, S., & Kuiper, N. A. (1993). Social comparison in dysphoria and non-dysphoria: Differences in target similarity and specificity. *Cognitive Therapy and Research, 17*, 103–122.

Swann, W. B., Jr. (1987). Identity negotiation: Where two roads meet. *Journal of Personality and Social Psychology, 53*, 1038–1051.

Tesser, A., Millar, M., & Moore, J. (1988). Some affective consequences of social comparison and reflection processes: The pain and pleasure of being close. *Journal of Personality and Social Psychology, 54*, 49–61.

VanderZee, K. I., Buunk, B. P., & Sanderman, R. (1996). The relationship between social comparison processes and personality. *Personality and Individual Differences, 22*, 551–565.

Vredenburg, K., Flett, G. L., & Krames, L. (1993). Analogue versus clinical depression: A critical reappraisal. *Psychological Bulletin, 113*, 327–344.

Wayment, H. A., & Taylor, S. E. (1995). Self-evaluation processes: Motives, information use, and self-esteem. *Journal of Personality, 63*, 729–757.

Weary, G., Elbin, S., & Hill, M. G. (1987). Attributional and social comparison processes in depression. *Journal of Personality and Social Psychology, 52*, 605–610.

Weary, G., Marsh, K. L., Gleicher, F., & Edwards, J. A. (1993). Depression, control motivation, and the processing of information about others. In G. Weary, F. Gleicher, & K. L. Marsh (Eds.), *Control motivation and social cognition* (pp. 255–287). New York: Springer-Verlag.

Weary, G., Marsh, K. L., & McCormick, L. (1994). Depression and social comparison motives. *European Journal of Social Psychology, 24*, 117–129.

Wenzlaff, R. M., & Beevers, C. G. (in press). Depression and interpersonal responses to others' moods: The solicitation of negative information about happy people. *Personality and Social Psychology Bulletin*.

Wenzlaff, R. M., & Prohaska, M. L. (1989). When misery loves company: Depression, attributions, and responses to others' moods. *Journal of Experimental Social Psychology, 25*, 220–233.

Wheeler, L., & Miyake, K. (1992). Social comparison and everyday life. *Journal of Personality and Social Psychology, 62*, 760–773.

Wills, T. A. (1981). Downward comparison principles. *Psychological Bulletin, 90*, 245–271.

Wills, T. A. (1991). Similarity and self-esteem in downward comparison. In J. Suls & T. A. Wills (Eds.), *Social comparison: Contemporary theory and research* (pp. 51–78). Hillsdale, NJ: Erlbaum.

Wilson, S. R., & Benner, L. A. (1971). The effects of self-esteem and situation upon comparison choices during ability evaluation. *Sociometry, 34*, 381–397.

Wood, J. V. (1989). Theory and research concerning social comparisons of personal attributes. *Psychological Bulletin, 106,* 231–248.

Wood, J. V. (1996). What is social comparison and how should we study it? *Personality and Social Psychology Bulletin, 22,* 520–537.

Wood, J. V., & Dodgson, P. G. (1996). When is self-focused attention an adaptive coping response? Rumination and overgeneralization versus compensation. In I. G. Sarason, B. R. Sarason, & G. R. Pierce (Eds.), *Cognitive interference: Theories, methods, and findings* (pp. 231–259). Hillsdale, NJ: Erlbaum.

Wood, J. V., & Giordano, C. (1998). *Downward comparison in everyday life: Self-enhancement models, the selective affect-cognition priming model, and the distinction between voluntary and involuntary comparisons.* Unpublished manuscript, University of Waterloo, Waterloo, Ontario, Canada.

Wood, J. V., Giordano-Beech, M., & DuCharme, M. (in press). Compensating for failure through social comparison. *Personality and Social Psychology Bulletin.*

Wood, J. V., Giordano-Beech, M., Taylor, K. L., Michela, J. L., & Gaus, V. (1994). Strategies of social comparison among people with low self-esteem: Self-protection and self-enhancement. *Journal of Personality and Social Psychology, 67,* 713–731.

Wood, J. V., & Taylor, K. L. (1991). Serving self-relevant goals through social comparison. In J. Suls & T. A. Wills (Eds.), *Social comparison: Contemporary theory and research* (pp. 23–49). Hillsdale, NJ: Erlbaum.

Wood, J. V., & VanderZee, K. I. (1997). Social comparisons among cancer patients: Under what conditions are comparisons upward and downward? In B. P. Buunk & F. X. Gibbons (Eds.), *Health, coping, and well-being: Perspectives from social comparison theory* (pp. 299–328). Hillsdale, NJ: Erlbaum.

II

THE SELF IN SOCIAL LIFE

5

SELF-REGULATION AND PSYCHOPATHOLOGY

KAREN L. DALE AND ROY F. BAUMEISTER

The term *self-regulation* refers to people's efforts to alter their own responses, such as overriding behavioral impulses, resisting temptation, controlling their thoughts, and altering (or artificially prolonging) their emotions. During the 1980s, social psychologists belatedly awoke to the importance of self-regulation for understanding human functioning. By necessity, clinical psychologists had gained some appreciation of self-regulation earlier (e.g., Kanfer & Karoly, 1972), but the full import of self-regulation for clinical phenomena could not be grasped until basic research established the major outlines of how it worked. Hence, it is only now that the implications of self-regulation for psychopathology can begin to be explained. In this chapter, we apply current self-regulation theory to clinical patterns and psychopathology.

The potential applications of self-regulation theory are extensive. In a review of the research literature on self-regulation failure, Baumeister, Heatherton, and Tice (1994) concluded that the majority of contemporary social and personal problems afflicting Western society contained some

Preparation of this chapter was facilitated by Research Grant MH-57039 from the National Institutes of Health.

significant element of self-regulation failure. These include alcohol and drug abuse, violence, teen pregnancy, school failure, addiction, unsafe sex, gambling, debt and overuse of credit cards, eating problems, failure to save money, child abuse, spouse abuse, elder abuse, divorce, and widespread deficiencies in exercise and physical fitness. If these problems of normal and supposedly healthy people involve deficiencies in self-regulation, it would be surprising if the problems of clinical populations were immune to self-regulation issues. Indeed, insofar as patterns of psychopathology reflect excesses or more extreme versions of the same problems that supposedly normal and healthy people suffer, one should expect self-regulation problems to prove central to many mental, emotional, and behavioral pathologies.

SELF-REGULATION THEORY: BACKGROUND

The concept of *self-regulation* is closely related to the colloquial term *self-control*, and here we use the two terms interchangeably. Self-regulation involves altering one's own responses. Thus, a given stimulus might elicit one typical or automatic reaction, but the person can respond differently by virtue of self-regulation. Dieting is a good example. A hungry person would respond to the presence of delicious food by eating it, but self-regulation allows the person to override that response and refrain from eating.

Self-regulation theory has its roots in the study of delay of gratification (e.g., Mischel, 1974). The standard paradigm for studying delay of gratification was to offer a child the choice between an immediate but small reward and a larger but delayed one. Optimal, rational choice would entail taking the larger reward, but this required the child to resist the impulse and temptation to take the immediate gratification. The capacity to delay gratification is essential to civilized life, and predictably recent evidence suggests that children who have a higher ability to delay gratification at age 4 grow up to be more successful both socially and academically (Mischel, Shoda, & Peake, 1988; Shoda, Mischel, & Peake, 1990).

An important advance in self-regulation theory was provided by using the concept of feedback loops to construct a system framework (Carver & Scheier, 1981; see also Powers, 1973). Using the analogy of a thermostat, these theorists explained self-regulation in terms of comparing the self's current status with a standard or goal and if the self fell short, making some change (as a thermostat turns on the furnace) to bring it up to the desired state. The acronym TOTE (i.e., test, operate, test, exit) was used to describe this sequence: One compares oneself with a standard (e.g., measures one's weight), operates to reduce discrepancies (i.e., undertakes a diet), and compares again, until the discrepancy is resolved and the self has matched the standard, whereon one exits the sequence.

Another decisive advance for self-regulation theory was the distinction between automatic and controlled processes (e.g., Bargh, 1982). Automatic processes are efficient and require few resources but are relatively rigid and inflexible. Controlled processes are inefficient and expensive (in terms of psychological resources) but are highly flexible. Pure automatic responses may be relatively immune to control, but there are many responses that proceed automatically unless they are overridden by a controlled process. Controlled processes are thus central to self-regulation. The inefficiency and resource requirements of controlled processes mean that only a small proportion of behavior can be regulated effectively. However, the flexibility of controlled processes entails that self-regulation is central to the diversity and adaptive variety of human behavior.

SELF-REGULATION FAILURE AND PROCESSES

On the basis of Carver and Scheier's (1981) analysis of the feedback loop, we can specify three main requirements of successful self-regulation: standards, monitoring, and strength. A deficiency in any of them can contribute to self-regulation failure (Baumeister et al., 1994). The first is having standards, which are norms, goals, ideals, or other values. These are cognitive representations of the way one ought ideally to be. If standards are lacking or are in conflict, self-regulation lacks direction and by definition cannot succeed.

The second requirement is monitoring. Carver and Scheier (1981) explained self-awareness as being essential to self-regulation because the person must attend to the self to ascertain how the self compares with the standard. More generally, people cannot alter their own behavior without being aware of it, and states that reduce self-awareness (e.g., alcohol intoxication; see Hull, 1981) tend to promote self-regulation failure. In contrast, elaborate and specific monitoring of target behaviors (e.g., weighing oneself and keeping track of caloric intake) is an important contributor to successful self-regulation.

The third ingredient is the application of a resource for altering the self. After all, self-regulation would hardly succeed without the capacity to override one's responses, even if one held clear standards and monitored the target behavior carefully. This corresponds to the "operate" phase in the TOTE model. Carver and Scheier (1981) did not clearly spell out how these operations occur, but the nature of these operations has been the focus of some recent efforts, including in our own laboratory. Because this work is relatively new, we summarize it briefly here.

We conclude that self-regulation operates like a muscle, in which strength or energy is used to override responses and alter behavior. In this analysis (Baumeister & Heatherton, 1996; Baumeister et al., 1994), the impulse contains some degree of strength; so for the person to resist that impulse, he or she must exert a greater amount of strength against it. There are individual and situational differences in self-regulatory strength, and so success at self-regulation will vary.

Evidence for the strength model of self-regulation has been found in studies of ego depletion. The strength model predicts that after an act of self-control, the resource will be temporarily depleted (akin to a muscle being tired after exertion) and subsequent efforts at self-control will be less successful. Contrary predictions can be made on the basis of other possible models of self-regulation. For example, if self-regulation operates like a cognitive schema, then an initial act of self-regulation would prime the schema and facilitate subsequent self-regulation. Alternatively, if self-regulation were primarily a skill, then there should be little or no change in consecutive acts of self-regulation, insofar as skill remains largely constant from one trial to the next (although over many acts it should improve through learning).

To test this model, Muraven, Tice, and Baumeister (1998) confronted people with two consecutive but seemingly unrelated demands for self-regulation. In a series of studies, they found that the effectiveness of self-regulation was diminished on the second task. In one study, for example, people first strove to regulate their thoughts (by suppressing thoughts about a white bear—a procedure borrowed from Wegner, Schneider, Carter, & White, 1987) and were then instructed to refrain from laughing or smiling in response to a humorous video. The thought suppression exercise impaired their ability to stifle their amusement. In another study, an initial act of controlling their emotional distress in response to an upsetting video reduced their performance on a physical endurance task.

Thus, the results of these studies indicate that initial acts of self-regulation consumed an important resource that was then unavailable to help them regulate their behavior on a subsequent task. The capacity for self-regulation appears to involve a common resource that is easily depleted. Like a muscle that becomes tired and loses its ability to perform, self-regulation can accomplish only a limited amount without having some time to recover.

Subsequent work suggests that the resource or strength involved in self-regulation is also used for other functions of the self. Baumeister, Bratslavsky, Muraven, and Tice (1998) concluded that all active responses by the self draw on that same volitional resource—hence, the choice of the term *ego depletion* rather than the narrower *self-regulatory depletion*. Using a procedure borrowed from cognitive dissonance research (Linder, Cooper, & Jones, 1967), they demonstrated that making a choice to perform a counterattitudinal behavior (specifically, a speech favoring a large tuition increase, which most tuition-paying students would oppose) depleted the resource and led to subsequent decrements in self-regulation. People who performed the same counterattitudinal behavior without free choice did not show the decrement. Moreover, people who chose to perform a pro-attitudinal behavior did show the drop in subsequent self-control. These findings indicate that it is the act of choice, not the behavior in question, that depleted the self and impaired subsequent self-regulation. In another study, Baumeister et al. linked self-regulatory exertion to greater passivity in choice behavior, suggesting that active responses draw on the same volitional resource required for self-regulation.

SELF-REGULATION THEORY: ADDITIONAL ASPECTS

Self-regulation failure can be divided into two types: underregulation and misregulation (Baumeister et al., 1994; Carver & Scheier, 1981). Underregulation is a failure to control one's behavior, and it is the more prevalent and important pattern of failure. Misregulation involves successfully altering one's responses but in a way that fails to bring about the desired result. An example of underregulation is the dieter who gives in to temptation and eats the forbidden, fattening food. An example of misregulation is the depressed person who consumes alcohol to cheer up but ends up feeling even worse.

Lack of strength is a common cause of underregulation, but the evidence is far from clear as to whether people are overwhelmed by powerful, uncontrollable impulses or instead simply neglect to use the strength they have. Baumeister et al. (1994; also see Baumeister & Heatherton, 1996, and commentaries in that issue) proposed a *mitigated acquiescence model*, by which people allow themselves to fail at self-regulation, although they do so under circumstances that allow them to think that self-regulation would be nearly impossible. They may feel overwhelmed for a moment to the point at which they cannot maintain self-control, but once they relax the self-control, they not only fail to restore it but also may even actively participate in thwarting it. For example, an abstaining drinker may feel overwhelmed by stress or emotion so that he or she is unable to avoid all drinking and therefore may break down and have one drink. At that point, however, he or she neglects to reinstate the abstinence and may even actively participate in obtaining and consuming more alcohol.

In any case, it is clear that success at self-regulation depends on both the strength of the impulse and the strength of the self-regulatory efforts that oppose it, and variations in either can tip the balance and affect the outcome. Stress and emotional upset are important causes of self-regulatory failure (Baumeister et al., 1994). Muraven and Baumeister (1997) explained these effects in terms of ego depletion. Stress makes demands on the self for active responses, and emotional distress consumes resources, when people try to avoid acting out negative or harmful impulses and try to extricate themselves from their distressed state. These are relevant to the present discussion because many forms of psychopathology involve stress or emotional upset, and so individuals may deplete their self-regulatory resources in that struggle. Hence, many of the side-effects or harmful consequences of mental illness could be mediated by ego depletion.

Many forms of self-regulation (including delay of gratification) involve a conflict between an immediate, short-term goal and a long-term one, and self-regulation succeeds when the person can resist the immediate impulse and pursue what is best in the long run. To accomplish this successfully, it is often necessary for the person to see beyond the immediate situation and its pressing stimuli. The capacity to do this has been termed *transcendence*. That is, the person must be mentally able to transcend the immediate situation and appreciate the long-term implications of the options and behaviors that are presently on offer. Factors that immerse the person in the immediate situation may therefore weaken self-regulation and contribute to impulsive, potentially regrettable acts.

The role of attention in self-regulation has been broadly recognized by both psychological theorists (e.g., Carver & Scheier, 1981, who titled their book *Attention and Self-Regulation*) and laypeople (e.g., the dieter who posts a photo of a pig on the refrigerator). Baumeister et al. (1994) concluded that the farther some response sequence has progressed, the more difficult it is to stop. Therefore, attention, which marks the beginning of most response sequences, is often the most effective and easiest way to control problem behaviors. Loss of control over attention is associated with many patterns of self-regulation failure.

Once self-regulation begins to fail, multiple additional factors come into play that can cause it to snowball into a major binge or breakdown. Marlatt (1985) coined the term *abstinence violation effects* to describe the way that once an addict or alcoholic begins to use the forbidden substance, the psychological consequences of crossing the line encourage him or her to continue using it and indeed to escalate to a problematic binge. Baumeister et al. (1994) used the more general term *lapse-activated patterns* to extend Marlatt's observation to forms of self-regulation failure other than substance abuse. Lapse-activated patterns may include rationalizing the initial misdeed, discovering that the anticipated bad consequences fail to materialize, enjoying the pleasure of the indulgence, losing control over attention (especially if abstinence depended on keeping one's attention off the forbidden stimulus), and cessing to monitor the target behavior.

The initial lapse of self-control is itself often trivial. For example, eating one cookie may technically violate one's diet, but the net effect on one's caloric intake is small. If the first cookie leads to a second and so on until the bag is empty, however, then the diet is thwarted. Thus, the factors that escalate a small lapse into a major binge are often important for understanding self-regulation failure.

SUMMARY OF SELF-REGULATION THEORY

Self-regulation involves the control of one's own behavior, normally by means of controlled (vs. automatic) processes and often accomplished by overriding a normal, habitual, or impulsive response. It typically involves a feedback loop in which the person compares the self against standards, operates to bring the self closer to these standards, and then compares again, until the goal is reached. The operate phase of self-regulation involves changing the self.

Underregulation, a form of self-regulation failure, can occur because standards are lacking or contradictory, because the person fails to monitor, or because the person cannot accomplish the desired change. Misregulation can occur when the person alters the self in nonoptimal ways.

Our work emphasizes that changing the self involves the use of a limited resource akin to strength. Strength is built up through exercise but temporarily depleted by exertion. Competing demands (e.g., emotional distress) and stresses thus impair the capacity to regulate a given behavior.

SELF-REGULATION, PSYCHOPATHOLOGY, AND TREATMENT

Besides being essential for optimal functioning, the capacity for self-regulation is an important component of adaptive functioning. Clinical and social psychologists alike have long recognized this importance (albeit sometimes implicitly). For instance, Maddux and Lewis (1995) referred to psychological dysfunction as "ineffective or maladaptive self-regulation in pursuit of goals" (p. 39). Self-regulation failures are symptomatic of psychopathology and are often listed among the diagnostic criteria for mental disorders. For example, criteria from the *Diagnostic and Statistical Manual of Mental Disorders* (4th ed. [DSM-IV]; American Psychiatric Association [APA], 1994) were recently modified to include difficulties controlling worry as a criterion for generalized anxiety disorder (Clark, Smith, Neighbors, Skerlec, & Randall, 1994). In addition to being symptomatic of "general" psychological dysfunction, the central role of regulatory failure has also been implied in a wide variety of specific psychological problems ranging from childhood disinhibition disorders to the paraphilias (see, e.g., DeWaele, 1996; Levine, Risen, & Althof, 1990; Newman & Wallace, 1993; Stein & Hollander, 1993; Strauman, 1995).

Successful treatment of psychopathology requires the ability to self-regulate. Indeed, much of the literature on regulatory failures and clinical psychology focuses on treatment implications. Gruber (1987) found that children with developmental disorders are deficient in their capacities for self-regulation, which reduces their ability to benefit from therapy. Seabaugh and Schumaker (1994) found that self-regulation training increased lesson completion in students with and without learning disabilities. A recent modification to behavioral couples therapy emphasized the change from partner- to self-defined behavioral change goals as an important factor in marital therapy (Halford, Sanders, & Behrens, 1994). The abilities to set goals and monitor progress toward one's goals—requirements of self-regulation—are important components of successful therapy.

The processes outlined in our model can be applied to psychopathology to elucidate the treatment implications of self-regulation failure. In the remainder of this section, we discuss the implications of *emotion regulation* for treatment in general. Specific disorders are discussed in the following sections.

Poor control over emotional experiences and expression is a central characteristic of many psychopathologies. Gross and Munoz (1995) suggested that "emotion regulation is an essential feature of mental health" (p. 151). They noted that successful emotion regulation helps to sustain attention in the workplace, is essential to healthy relationships requiring emotional reciprocity, and is an important component of feeling a sense of comfort within oneself. Unsuccessful emotion regulation can result in the development of problems such as mood disorders, substance use disorders, poor school performance, marital distress, and dysfunctional parenting (Gross & Munoz, 1995). The implications of unsuccessful attempts to escape a negative mood state are discussed in the section on mood disorders.

The capacity to generate, express, and sustain emotions also has implications for psychopathology. Indeed, allowing oneself to experience and express negative emotions may be a focus of treatment. Cole, Michel, and Teti (1994) noted that research is needed on how the amplification of emotions supports or interferes with behavior in specific contexts. Research based on the strength model of ego depletion may address this issue. According to the strength model, attempting to alter one's emotional responses could deplete regulatory resources and interfere with subsequent behaviors. Muraven et al. (1998) found that both the amplification and suppression of emotional responses require exertion and can decrease regulatory strength in subsequent tasks. Participants who altered their emotional responses to an upsetting movie exhibited poorer self-regulation on a subsequent physical stamina task. Furthermore, this effect was not attributable to the emotional state per se. Likewise, consistent with the strength model of ego depletion, suppressing emotional responses, whether happy or sad, resulted in lower performance on a cognitive task, Baumeister et al. (1998) found. Thus, although suppression of emotions (e.g., experiencing denial to survive an incest experience) can serve adaptive functions (Cole et al., 1994), suppression can have some harmful effects. Further research is needed to identify the conditions under which amplification or suppression of emotional responses is adaptive.

Our model suggests that attempting to regulate one's emotions will drain an already seemingly limited supply of resources and perhaps make regulatory failure in other spheres more likely. Recommendations for treatment based on such a model could perhaps include focusing on a limited number of changes at once. For instance, starting a new diet to boost one's confidence when depressed may be unwise. Attempting to regulate the depressed mood may deplete resources and increase the likelihood that the attempt to diet will fail. This failure may in term perpetuate the depressed mood and so on. Relevant treatment issues are noted later in the discussion of separate disorders.

ATTENTION DEFICIT HYPERACTIVITY DISORDER

One of the most fascinating areas of research integrating social and clinical perspectives on self-regulation is attention deficit hyperactivity disorder (ADHD). The primary symptoms of ADHD are impulsiveness, hyperactivity, and poor sustained attention (Barkley, 1997). Barkley reviewed the literature on neuropsychological functioning in those with ADHD and presented a model suggesting that deficiencies in behavioral inhibition are central to ADHD. Consideration of Barkley's model and the evidence he presented highlights the applicability of our model to ADHD. For example, consistent with our model, central factors in Barkley's model include conflict over immediate and delayed consequences, an inability to engage in successful goal-directed behavior, deficiencies in controlled processing, and deleterious effects of a drain on regulatory resources.

Barkley's (1997) review of the literature on ADHD showed extensive evidence of regulatory failure in those with ADHD. According to Barkley, these failures may arise from the toll that poor behavioral inhibition takes on self-regulation. The term *behavioral inhibition* refers to three processes: the inhibition of a response that will yield immediate reinforcement, the stopping of an ongoing response (to delay the decision to respond), and interference control. According to Barkley's model, behavioral inhibition is central to the successful functioning of working memory; internalization of speech; behavioral analysis and synthesis; and self-regulation of motivation, affect, and arousal. Each of these abilities affords control of goal-directed behavior. In children with ADHD, development of these abilities is impaired. That is, inhibitory deficits disrupt the successful execution of goal-directed behavior by its influence on the executive functions of the self, including self-regulation.

The need for successful behavioral inhibition may be strongest when there is a conflict between the immediate and distal consequences of an act. Given this conflict, inhibition permits a delay in the decision to respond, a delay that is necessary to determine one's further actions and monitor one's progress. Inhibition enables one to interrupt his or her ongoing behavior, to assess the situation, and to reengage in that behavior. This is consistent with our model of regulatory failure. To reiterate, the abilities to transcend the immediate situation and monitor progress toward one's future goals are essential components of effective self-regulation. Conceptualized in terms of Carver and Scheier's (1981) feedback loop, inhibition enables one to act in ways to reduce discrepancies between one's current standards and actual events.

Children with ADHD experience deficits in this necessary disengagement and reengagement. Schachar, Tannock, Marriott, and Logan (1995) examined response inhibition and response reengagement in boys with pervasive ADHD, boys with situational ADHD, and control boys and found that deficits were greatest in those with pervasive ADHD. Barkley's (1997) model illustrates how such deficits may arise. For instance, according to the model, children with ADHD should be largely influenced by the immediate context and be less able to recall information that may aid in planning for the future (and thus engaging in the appropriate behavioral responses). Indeed, children with ADHD exhibit poor performance on tasks that might reflect such a capacity for forethought and planning ahead, such as the Wisconsin Card Sorting Task.[1] Also important for the formulation of plans is the internalization of speech. This enables one to construct an organized method of behavioral change, which is necessary for effective self-regulation.

Consequently, tasks involving temporal delays and requiring inhibition should produce performance deficits in those with ADHD (e.g., Barkley, 1997). Poorer task performance may be attributed to boredom, distractibility, or lowered persistence. The deleterious effects of boredom and distractibility implicate the role of poor attention control in ADHD, which is also consistent with our model.

Barber, Milich, and Welsh (1996) noted the poorer effort exhibited by children with ADHD on repetitive tasks. Research showing performance deficits on controlled processing tasks across children with ADHD and control participants fails to show such differences in performance on *automatic processing tasks* (Borcherding et al., 1988). To reiterate, *controlled processes* are those that are central to self-regulation. Thus, the performance deficits exhibited by children with ADHD are found only on tasks requiring self-regulation. That is, relative to other children, children with ADHD exhibit deficits in self-regulation.

---

[1] Barkley reviewed studies on participants' performance on the Wisconsin Card Sorting Test, concluding that those with attention deficit exhibit poorer performance.

Other indications of regulatory failure are evident, such as problems deferring gratification and poor regulation of inappropriate verbal responses (Barkley, 1997). Children with ADHD are at risk for additional problems indicative of regulatory failure, such as impulse control disorders (Specker, Carlson, Christenson, & Marcotte, 1995). The depletion of regulatory strength could contribute to these additional problems. Furthermore, our model has implications for treating ADHD. Attempts to treat ADHD by instructing children to exert greater efforts at self-control could temporarily deplete resources and exacerbate immediate behavioral problems. Treatment programs that emphasize long-term outcomes and that educate parents and children about possible temporary "setbacks" could be beneficial. Research currently being conducted in our laboratory is examining the application of the strength model of ego depletion to children.

MOOD DISORDERS

Regulatory failure is both symptomatic and causal of the mood disorders. Symptoms of regulatory failure that are associated with the mood disorders are briefly described within the context of defining mood disorders. After this, we discuss the causal role of self-regulation failure.

The mood disorders section in the *DSM-IV* includes several conditions encompassing depressive disorders, bipolar disorders, and others. The predominant feature in all disorders is a disturbance in mood. That is, the individual experiences a particular emotional state such as a sad mood (in a major depressive episode) or an elevated, expansive, or irritable mood (in a manic episode). Although there are several diagnoses within the mood disorders, that section is largely restricted to a discussion of the disorders involving an unpleasant emotional state such as major depression. However, a brief description of the symptoms of manic episodes highlights the relevance of our model to other mood disorders.

Manic Episodes

Symptoms of manic episodes include distractibility; flight of ideas; increased goal-directed activity; and an abnormal and persistently elevated, expansive, or irritable mood (APA, 1994). Many of the components of regulatory failure outlined in our model are evident. For instance, the term *distractibility* refers to poor attention control. Increases in goal-directed behaviors are evident, but these behaviors are often self-defeating. That is, misregulation is evident in that individuals are able to alter their responses, but they do so in ways that yield negative outcomes. The combination of symptoms present in mania presents an interesting challenge for self-regulation theory. In mania, acts of volition are strengthened in some aspects (e.g., goal-directed activity) but are weakened in others (e.g., poor attention control). This is consistent with the strength model of ego depletion in that exertion of regulatory effort in one sphere has deleterious effects on another sphere.

Major Depressive Episodes

Many indications of self-regulation failure outlined in our model are also evident in major depressive episodes. Symptoms include poor attention control, underregulation of emotional states, and misregulation of emotional states. For example, a failure to control one's anger—an example of underregulation—can occur (APA, 1994). Misregulation is also evident. For instance, the inability to regulate one's depressed state often arises from the use of inappropriate or ineffective strategies. A discussion of the etiology of depression highlights how regulatory failure occurs in depression.

Strauman (1995) suggested that depression-related symptoms and emotions develop when events occur that are incongruent with self-standards. As noted, the monitoring and altering of one's behavior to reduce discrepancies between self-standards and one's current situation are important components of self-regulation. Pyszczynsksi and Greenberg's (1987) theory of depression described how these discrepancies can lead to depression. They proposed that a depressive self-focusing style is a maladaptive response to the inability to reduce discrepancies between actual and ideal standards. High levels of self-focus and negative affect produce a negative self-image and help maintain the depression.[2]

Although self-awareness in general is essential for effective monitoring, the failure to direct attention away from a negative focus on the self can lead to depressive episodes. Ruminating on the depressed state interferes with active problem solving and the execution of behaviors that bring pleasure and thus could lift one's mood. Furthermore, focusing on bad moods can result in risky behaviors that have negative outcomes that may perpetuate the bad mood (Baumeister et al., 1994). Thus, ruminating on the depressed state can be maladaptive in that attention may be drawn away from positive distractors that may lift one's mood. Furthermore, ineffective attempts at emotion regulation may deplete regulatory resources that could be used for more effective coping strategies.

Evidence for an attentional bias toward negative information in general in depression is mixed.[3] McCabe and Gotlib (1995) studied attentional deployment in individuals with and without clinical depression. They found that rather than showing an attentional bias toward negative infor-

---

[2]Specifically, Pyszczynski and Greenberg (1986) noted that self-focus among depressed people increases after failures and decreases after success.
[3]In an earlier review, Dalgleish and Watts (1990) found this bias to be weaker than that found in the anxiety disorders.

mation, participants with depression failed to demonstrate the positive bias exhibited by those without depression. Mathews, Ridgeway, and Williamson (1996) studied attentional deployment in participants with depression and anxiety and found that depressed participants (but not anxious participants) selectively attended to socially threatening words more so than neutral words. This is consistent with the hypothesis that depression involves a negative attentional focus on the self.

The negative attentional focus exhibited by individuals with depression can maintain and exacerbate the depression. Treatment for depression should focus on achieving attentional control of negative thoughts. However, simply trying to focus on external factors or trying to think of positive thoughts may not be successful. Wegner (1994) described how attempts at mental control can produce a resurgence of the very thoughts one is trying to control. Furthermore, people are less able to suppress thoughts when they are under stress or fatigued. This is consistent with the idea of ego depletion outlined earlier. When there are competing demands on resources, attempts at thought suppression may fail.

Wenzlaff, Wegner, and Roper (1988) examined the strategies of thought suppression in individuals with depression. Participants attempted to control their negative thoughts by focusing on unpleasant distractors. This pattern was found despite acknowledgment from participants that the use of positive distractors could aid the suppression of negative thoughts. These attempts represent misregulation in that depressed individuals use strategies that eventually backfire. These strategies can contribute to the maintenance of depression. Wenzlaff, Wegner, and Klein (1991) found that thought suppression attempts can produce a reinstatement of the prior mood state. They assessed participants' moods after the expression of thoughts that they had either previously expressed or suppressed. Those who had tried to suppress thoughts later experienced the same mood state that existed during this suppression period. Suppressing negative thoughts while one is depressed might seem to be an effective way of regulating one's mood, but this can produce a subsequent exacerbation of the depressed affect when this thought returns. Thus, a negative cycle may ensue that maintains the depression.

However, distraction can be an effective way of controlling a negative mood. To work, the distractor chosen must be positive and engrossing (Nolen-Hoeksema, 1993). Thus, finding positive distractors that are easily accessible could be an important component of therapy for depression. Wenzlaff et al. (1991) suggested that the use of positive distractors could be increased when these were made easily accessible to participants. Unfortunately, when one is depressed, it may be more difficult to conjure up positive distractors. Boden and Baumeister (1997) examined the use of distractors as a mood regulation strategy among repressors (i.e., those who habitually defend themselves against negative emotional stimuli) and nonrepressors. Boden and Baumeister demonstrated that among nonrepressors, experiencing negative affect can inhibit the accessibility of positive affective memories. Repressors, however, showed the opposite effect. Repressors coped by accessing pleasant thoughts. This research alluded to the possible automaticity of such an attentional control strategy—an important avenue for future research.

Achieving attentional control is important for reducing the symptoms of depression. Pyszczynski, Holt, and Greenberg (1987) found that inducing participants to focus their attention externally attenuated depressive individuals' pessimistic tendencies. That is, self-focused depressed participants were more pessimistic than control individuals, but externally focused depressed participants were not. Nix, Watson, Pyszczynski, and Greenberg (1995) manipulated the focus of attention in participants with and without depression and assessed their mood. They found that external focus reduced anxiety. Lowering the self-focus of depressed people reduced their depressive affect.

In summary, discrepancies between one's current situation and self-standards can contribute to the development of depression. Becoming immersed in one's mood and a negative self-focus can prevent the use of effective coping strategies, thus maintaining and exacerbating the depression.

OBSESSIVE–COMPULSIVE DISORDER

The predominant features of obsessive–compulsive disorder (OCD) are obsessions, compulsions, or both (APA, 1994). Obsessions are thoughts that are experienced as intrusive and senseless. These thoughts cause marked anxiety (APA, 1987, 1994). Compulsions are behaviors that are similar to obsessions in that the individual, although wishing to control them, cannot stop performing the behaviors. Compulsions represent an attempt to neutralize the anxiety caused by the obsessive thoughts. For example, an individual may be obsessed with thoughts of contamination. He or she may engage in repeated handwashing to ward off the anxiety associated with these thoughts.

The central self-regulatory deficit in OCD is one of self-stopping; that is, people are unable to stop themselves from having the forbidden thought or behavioral impulse (see Rachman & Hodgson, 1980; Reed, 1985). Several aspects of our theory can explain why individuals with OCD are unable to stop thinking obsessive thoughts or stop performing compulsive behaviors. Ineffective thought suppression attempts and lack of regulatory strength are particularly relevant.

When one wishes to control an intrusive thought, perhaps the most obvious solution is to suppress that thought. However, Wegner et al. (1987)

found that attempted suppression of thoughts can result in a *rebound effect*. Wegner et al. asked participants to suppress thoughts of a white bear and found that after attempted suppression, participants experienced more thoughts of a white bear.

Trinder and Salkovskis (1994) examined the effects of the long-term suppression of negative intrusive thoughts in an experiment designed to maximize the similarity of participants' experiences to those of obsessional patients. As Wegner did, they found that participants who tried to suppress their thoughts experienced more thoughts. Participants also found those thoughts to be more uncomfortable than did participants who did not suppress their thoughts. Trinder and Salkovskis suggested that suppression may be important in the development and maintenance of anxiety disorders such as posttraumatic stress disorder and OCD.

Wegner (1994; see also Smart & Wegner, 1996) developed the *ironic process theory* to explain the failure of thought suppression attempts. Wegner et al. proposed that successful self-regulation involves monitoring and operating processes. When attempting to regulate one's thoughts, an automatic monitoring process searches for signs of the thoughts and a controlled operating process overrides the thoughts. However, the operating process fails when one is tired. Thus, attention is directed to the unwanted thoughts, but the individual lacks the resources to override these thoughts. Specifically, the individual may lack regulatory strength.

Likewise, self-report data from compulsive patients suggest that rather than being at the mercy of some allegedly irresistible impulse of overwhelming strength, these individuals report that they lack the strength to override their compulsions. In other words, they acquiesce in relinquishing control (Reed, 1985).

Subsequent work on self-regulation has further elucidated this process. When resources are low, self-regulation may become more difficult. Indeed, OCD often begins under times of low resources, such as during stressful periods (Baumeister et al., 1994). Furthermore, the anxiety experienced by individuals with OCD can create a cognitive load that makes self-regulation more difficult. Attempts to regulate the negative affective state are a further drain on regulatory resources. That is, attempts to cope with OCD may render the individual unable to invoke the processes needed to control intrusive thoughts or compulsions. This inability may result in negative affect.

Indeed, OCD may be associated with depression and other anxiety disorders (APA, 1994). Our model can be applied to explain this relationship. As noted, poor resources result in regulatory failure. People with OCD who fail to control thoughts or compulsions may experience this failure as a threat to the self. Sommer and Baumeister (1996) found that vulnerability to ego threat is increased under conditions of ego depletion. Participants who were given a thought suppression task and exposed to an ego threat reported lower subsequent self-esteem scores than those who were not depleted by the thought suppression tasks. That is, when depleted, one is less able to invoke the resources needed to defend the self. Thus, the relationship between OCD and depression may be mediated by the harmful effect that ego depletion has on the ability to defend against ego threats.

Further evidence of lack of regulatory strength in individuals with OCD is provided by data on performance. According to the strength model of depletion, trying to suppress intrusive thoughts should produce regulatory failure in other spheres, such as performance and persistence. Consistent with this, Cooper (1996) found poor task performance to be one of the most frequently reported behavior problems associated with OCD. Likewise, in a study conducted in Spain examining the clinical records of children and adolescents with OCD, Toro, Cervera, Osejo, and Salamero (1992) found that poor school performance was a common feature.

Obsessive–compulsive behaviors in nonclinical populations are associated with poorer performance on some tasks requiring mental flexibility, such as the Wisconsin Card Sorting Test (Goodwin & Sher, 1992). Similar cognitive impairments were found in an Israeli sample exhibiting obsessive–compulsive symptoms (Zohar, LaBuda, & Moschel-Ravid, 1995). Participants with obsessive–compulsive symptoms exhibited mental rigidity that impaired performance on the Wisconsin Card Sorting Test. In the study by Goodwin and Sher, poorer performance could not be completely explained by affective variables. Thus, another explanation is needed to explain the results. It is possible that the poorer performance can be attributed to the effects of ego depletion. Both studies show that the impairment was not in the ability to maintain a set but in the ability to shift from an established set. Thus, it appears that once a behavioral set (e.g., repeated checking) is established, checkers adopt the passive response of maintaining that behavioral set and they can do this effectively. The deficits occur when active responding is needed. Recent research (Baumeister et al., 1998) indicates that ego depletion causes people to shift toward more passive responses because the active ones would consume more of the same resource that is already depleted. Attempting to control obsessions (from which compulsive behaviors arise) is such a condition. Hence, it seems plausible that some of the deficits associated with OCD may be attributable to chronic depletion, insofar as the person is frequently expending his or her ego resources in attempting to control the unwanted thought or impulse.

It is also possible that those with OCD are more susceptible than those in nonclinical populations to the effects of ego depletion. This susceptibility is perhaps evident in the nature of the symptoms experienced by OCD sufferers. Stein and Hollander (1993) found that there is a subset of people with OCD who have poor impulse control. These individuals also have learning problems and low frustration tolerance. Stein and Hollander suggested that the overlap of impulsive and compulsive symptoms in OCD is indicative of general regulatory failure.

EATING DISORDERS

Self-regulation theory provides a particularly interesting framework for examining the eating disorders anorexia nervosa and bulimia nervosa. Furthermore, research on the eating disorders offers valuable insights into the nature of self-regulation. In particular, the different manifestations of regulatory failure in the same class of clinical disorders may be particularly informative.

The central features of anorexia are a refusal to maintain a normal body weight, fear of gaining weight, and disturbed perceptions of one's body. The central features of bulimia are recurrent binge eating and engaging in inappropriate compensatory behaviors to prevent weight gain (APA, 1994). Both disorders are characterized by a "distorted attitude toward weight, eating and fatness" (Hsu, 1990, p. 1). This attitude is manifested in repeated ongoing attempts to regulate food intake. Thus, self-regulation is an essential component of even the most simplistic analysis of the eating disorders. A more complex analysis of the eating disorders elucidates the nature of the regulatory failure that occurs in them.

Several aspects of regulatory failure relevant to our model can be identified. Conflicting standards (e.g., healthy vs. tasty foods) and inappropriate standards (e.g., an unattainable body weight) set the stage for regulatory failure. The individual faced with the tempting foods yet desiring a thin body has to monitor his or her food intake to reconcile this conflict.

Bulimia

In bulimia, this process fails and the individual eats excessively. This failure may begin with a small lapse in one's diet such as eating an extra cookie and may escalate into a binge. The binge eating represents a lapse-activated pattern, described in the introduction. As noted, these patterns include loss of attentional control and cessation of monitoring.

Heatherton and Baumeister (1991) proposed a model outlining how this occurs. They suggested that falling short of one's standards elicits negative emotional responses and aversive self-awareness. To escape these negative responses, the individual directs attention away from meaningful thought (and toward the food and eating). Attention is drawn to the immediate stimuli and away from self-awareness. As noted, self-awareness is an important component of monitoring. If the individual escapes from the self-awareness, monitoring is impaired.[4]

Indeed, research shows that eating behavior can be influenced by experimentally manipulating the levels of self-awareness. Specifically, disinhibited eating occurs in conditions of low but not high self-awareness (Heatherton, Polivy, Herman, & Baumeister, 1993). Lowered self-awareness and a subsequent reduction in monitoring can also explain the relationship between alcohol and binge eating. Alcohol reduces self-awareness and thus the ability to monitor eating behavior. The prevalence of substance abuse in approximately one third of people with bulimia (APA, 1994) may be partially explained by this link. Furthermore, the narrow attentional focus on the immediate stimuli immerses bulimic individuals in the binge and contributes to their inability to consider the long-term implications of the binge. As noted, this failure to transcend the immediate situation weakens self-regulation.

While immersed in the binge, bulimic individuals experience a lack of control, as if they cannot stop the binge. However, bulimic individuals are able to stop eating during the binge. For instance, bingeing may stop when another individual enters the room (APA, 1994). This is consistent with the concept of mitigated acquiescence proposed by Baumeister et al. (1994). The eating is not uncontrollable but involves a failure by bulimic individuals to exert enough control to stop the binge.

Anorexia

Our model of self-regulation failure is also applicable to anorexia. Although anorexic individuals often monitor their food intake excessively and succeed in regulating food intake, this control over eating is an example of misregulation. Control is exerted but in a way that yields negative outcomes. Continuing progress toward one's goals is rarely perceived because anorexic individuals' (inappropriate) standards are revised upward when success is met (e.g., the desired weight continues to be lowered). As conceptualized in terms of the feedback loop described in the introduction, anorexic individuals proceed through the comparison of the self with the standards phase, act to reduce discrepancies, but do not exit the loop because standards are never reached.

Loss of attentional control is relevant to anorexia. The cognitions of individuals with anorexia may become entirely focused on weight and food as they become immersed in the goal of losing weight. Indeed, Bruch (1973; see also Vandereycken & Meerman, 1984) noted that self-starvation results in "narrowed consciousness."

---

[4]In bulimia, purging occurs as a means of coping with the negative emotions that emerge after the binge. Poor emotion regulation is discussed elsewhere in this chapter.

People with anorexia exhibit excessive control over eating. However, as noted, this is an example of misregulation. Regulatory failure in other spheres is also noted. There is often a loss of control over thoughts and fears of weight gain. Herman and Polivy (1993) found that chronic dieters and binge eaters were often preoccupied with thoughts of food and had difficulties suppressing those thoughts.

Ego depletion is also relevant to anorexia. The onset of anorexia often occurs after a stressful life event (APA, 1994). As noted, coping with stress or emotional stressors can tax regulatory resources and contribute to regulatory failures.

Ego Depletion and the Eating Disorders

The strength component of our model may be particularly relevant to eating disorders. To reiterate, attempts at self-regulation in one sphere may produce regulatory failures in other spheres. Resisting the temptation to eat a tempting food should produce deficits in persistence and performance. Indeed, Baumeister et al. (1998) found that participants who resisted eating cookies quit sooner on a cognitive task than did participants who did not have to resist eating cookies. This research was conducted with nonclinical populations, suggesting that the effects were caused by the exertion of regulatory effort rather than by other factors specific to the eating disorders. Furthermore, dieting and dietary restraint have been found to be related to deficits in cognitive performance (Green & Rogers, 1995; Green, Rogers, Elliman, & Gatenby, 1994; Rogers & Green, 1993).

Thus, attempts at resisting food produce a breakdown in subsequent self-control. This is consistent with recent research on the strength model of ego depletion. The distinctions between dieting, anorexia, and bulimia provide valuable insights into the nature of ego depletion and strength. Perhaps the most central factor distinguishing these related disorders is the difference in the nature of the misregulation evidenced by those who are affected by the disorders. Individuals with anorexia succeed in their attempts at self-starvation; people with bulimia frequently fail and engage in recurrent bingeing, which is accompanied by self-induced purging.

These apparent differences in regulatory strength are evident in other spheres, such as impulsivity and substance use. Self-report data suggest that individuals with bulimia are more impulsive than those with anorexia (Casper, Hedeker, & McClough, 1992; Fahy & Eisler, 1993; Pryor & Wiederman, 1996; Steiger, Puentes-Neuman, & Leung, 1991). Furthermore, bulimic individuals are more likely than anorexic individuals to engage in substance abuse (Wiederman & Pryor, 1996). Indeed, substance abuse or dependence occurs in approximately one third of bulimic individuals (APA, 1994). Holderness, Brooks-Gunn, and Warren (1994) reviewed the literature on eating disorders and substance abuse and found that substance abuse is more strongly associated with bulimia than with anorexia. This co-occurrence of bulimia and substance abuse may be partially explained by ego depletion. For instance, Bulik et al. (1992) analyzed the temporal patterns of substance use among bulimic, anorexic, and control participants and found that not only were bulimic behaviors and substance use related but that these behaviors were also more prevalent in the evening hours. This is consistent with our strength model of ego depletion. According to the model, regulatory failures are more likely to occur when one is tired and lacking in resources such as during the evening.

Other regulatory failures are evident in people with bulimia. For example, bulimic individuals often engage in risky sexual behavior. Irving, McClusky-Fawcett, and Thissen (1990) found that participants at a high risk for bulimia engaged in riskier contraceptive behavior than those at a lower risk for bulimia. Furthermore, bulimic individuals were more sexually active than controls (Coovert, Kinder, & Thompson, 1989) and less sexually inhibited than anorexic individuals (Haimes & Katz, 1988). These findings suggest that relative to other populations, bulimic individuals are more likely to engage in risky sexual behavior. This risky behavior may result from an inability to transcend the immediate situation and to consider the consequences of sexual intercourse without protection. Failure to consider the consequences of one's actions is also apparent in the increased incidence of stealing among bulimic individuals. McElroy, Hudson, Pope, and Keck (1991) noted that kleptomania is associated with the eating disorders. Consistent with this research, more than 42% of the bulimic participants studied reported stealing, Rowston and Lacey (1992) found. They concluded that stealing marked a greater severity in bulimia. Likewise, Christenson and Mitchell (1991) studied impulse control behaviors among bulimic and control individuals and found that bulimic individuals showed a greater trend toward compulsive stealing than did controls. In summary, these findings suggest that bulimic individuals exhibit regulatory failure in several spheres.

However, those with anorexia also exhibit self-regulation failure, such as failure to control a preoccupation with food and striving for inappropriate goals, such as attaining an unhealthy body weight. They are unable to engage in appropriate goal-directed behavior. However, the manifestations of regulatory failure differ across those with anorexia and bulimia. Further examination of these differences and similarities between anorexia and bulimia may prove useful in elucidating the role of self-regulation in the eating disorders. Muraven, Baumeister, and Tice (in press) proposed that repetitive exertions of regulatory strength may increase this strength over time. Anorexic individuals are often high achieving and perfectionistic. With a history of exerting considerable regulatory effort, perhaps regulatory strength develops in the way a dedicated athlete would develop muscle. In contrast, like athletes who do not succeed in pushing themselves to lift heavier and heavier weights and thus build muscle, perhaps bulimic individuals, succumbing to that initial morsel of food, have not yet exerted enough regulatory effort to build and develop strength over time. Factors contributing to these individual differences in regulatory success remain an important avenue for future research.

SUBSTANCE-RELATED DISORDERS

Regulatory failure is an essential component of substance-related disorders. Substance-related disorders include substance dependence and substance abuse (APA, 1994). Central to both disorders is continued substance use despite associated impairments in functioning. Several components of regulatory failure are relevant.

Different factors contributing to the escalation of substance use can be identified. Substance use may begin because it is reinforcing, bringing pleasure and perhaps reducing emotional suffering. The importance of the motivated need to reduce suffering implies that the adaptive regulation of negative affect states may reduce this motivation. Likewise, an ability to experience positive emotions is necessary if one is to avoid making "unhealthy" attempts to feel positive. The self-medicating effects of substance use have been well documented (e.g., Krueger, 1981; Pervin, 1988). Johnson and Gurin (1994) obtained interview data from more than 1,000 participants and found that expectancies moderated the relationship between negative affect and drinking. Co-occurrence was more likely when participants expected that alcohol would improve their mood. Consistent with current knowledge on the executive function, it appears that people actively choose to participate in self-defeating behavior to obtain immediate rewards. Currently our laboratory is examining the negative implications of such attempts to "feel better" on other areas of self-regulation.

One method of coping with negative emotions is to direct attention away from those emotions, perhaps toward lower level actions such as drinking. Like the bulimic individual who binges to escape from the aversiveness, the alcoholic individual may become immersed in drinking as a form of escape. Steele and Josephs (1990), however, found that alcohol is effective as an escape only when used in conjunction with a distraction. This is consistent with recent research that has demonstrated the importance of positive distractors for effective coping (see, e.g., Boden & Baumeister, 1997). Nevertheless, immersion in alcohol or drugs does promise the appeal of experiencing positive emotions and warding off negative emotions. Such immediate pleasures can contribute to the escalation of the drinking binge through the resultant narrow attentional focus and impairment of cognitive resources associated with drinking (Baumeister et al., 1994). This attentional focus contributes to the inability of alcoholic individuals to recognize the long-term consequences of their actions. In other words, they are unable to transcend the immediate situation and so regulatory failure ensues.

Substance abusers may completely break down and fail to resist temptation once they have started to use the substance. The likelihood of this giving in may be increased by attempts at restraint. Collins (1993) noted the increased attention in the literature to the role of attempts at restraint as a risk factor for substance abuse. The link between restraint and abuse can be explained by our model. An alcoholic individual attempting to refrain from drinking may be particularly attuned to drinking cues in the environment. However, when the person is stressed or depleted, the self-regulatory strength required to overcome these cues may be lacking and this attempt may fail.

The treatment implications of such a process are evident. Marlatt (1996) postulated a harm reduction model that acknowledges that although abstinence may be an ideal outcome of treatment programs, alternative goals may be more feasible. Such treatment implications are consistent with our data, which show that the self's regulatory resource is limited and that regulatory breakdowns occur readily and easily as a result (Muraven et al., 1998).

Treatment models that advocate complete abstinence may be based on the assumption that once the recovering substance abuser partakes in substance use, control failure has already occurred (Baumeister et al., 1994). Whether the initial lapse escalates into a binge is partially determined by interpretations of this lapse. If the alcoholic individual perceives that he or she is helpless in the face of this initial lapse, the binge may escalate.

The conceptualization of urges (e.g., to drink) as irresistible or beyond the individual's control has received considerable attention in the literature (e.g., Peele, 1989). According to the disease model of substance abuse, addiction is a disease affecting emotional and cognitive functioning (Stuart, 1995). Helplessness in the face of such a disease is implied by advocates of this model who suggest that the substance abuser is a "victim" whose recovery can be facilitated by a shift in treatment away from attempts to correct a weak character (Miller, 1991). Alternative views of alcoholism view substance abuse as a form of self-medication, motivated by the need to reduce emotional suffering (Goldsmith, 1993). This model implies that the substance abuser thus has some choice in exercising a lack of control. As noted, Baumeister and colleagues (Baumeister & Heatherton, 1996; Baumeister et al., 1994) concluded that self-control failure involves *mitigated acquiescence*. That is, rather than falling victim to irresistible impulses beyond his or her control, the substance abuser chooses at some point to relinquish control.

CONCLUSION

Self-regulation failures are central to many psychopathologies. Our discussion of specific childhood disorders, mood disorders, anxiety disorders, eating disorders, and substance use disorders has highlighted the applicability of a model of regulatory failure to psychopathology. These pathologies often arise from or are mediated by the use of ineffective, inappropriate strategies for reaching one's goals or for coping (e.g., with emotional distress). Conflicting standards and poor monitoring of behavior contribute to this misregulation. Furthermore, focusing and narrowing of attention on the immediate situation decreases the ability to monitor behavior effectively, increasing the likelihood that regulatory failure will occur. Our model also describes how this initial lapse may escalate into further regulatory failure, such as a drinking binge.

Perhaps one of the most promising applications of our model to clinical psychology arises from the concept of self-regulatory strength. Recent work suggests that self-regulation and other acts of volition all draw on a common, limited resource. In psychopathology, the constant struggle to manage one's emotional distress, control one's attention, and restrain unacceptable impulses may keep this resource constantly drained, which can contribute to some of the side-effects of the pathology. Conversely, stressful situations or heavy interpersonal demands may deplete the resource in the first place and make the person more vulnerable to the self-regulatory failures that form the essence of the psychopathology (e.g., eating disorders). If chronic ego depletion does indeed turn out to be a central factor in psychopathology, as seems plausible on the basis of the evidence we have reviewed, it may become possible to refine treatment strategies to benefit from this new understanding.

REFERENCES

American Psychiatric Association. (1987). *Diagnostic and statistical manual of mental disorders* (3rd ed. rev.). Washington, DC: Author.

American Psychiatric Association. (1994). *Diagnostic and statistical manual of mental disorders* (4th ed.). Washington, DC: Author.

Barber, M. A., Milich, R., & Welsh, R. (1996). Effects of reinforcement schedule and task difficulty on the performance of attention deficit hyperactivity disordered and control boys. *Journal of Clinical Child Psychology, 25,* 66–76.

Bargh, J. (1982). Attention and automaticity in the processing of self-relevant information. *Journal of Personality and Social Psychology, 43,* 425–436.

Barkley, R. A. (1997). Behavioral inhibition, sustained attention, and executive functions: Constructing a unifying theory of ADHD. *Psychological Bulletin, 121,* 65–94.

Baumeister, R. F., Bratslavsky, E., Muraven, M., & Tice, D. M. (1998). Ego depletion: Is the active self a limited resource? *Journal of Personality and Social Psychology, 74,* 1252–1265.

Baumeister, R. F., & Heatherton, T. F. (1996). Self-regulation failure: An overview. *Psychological Inquiry, 7,* 1–15.

Baumeister, R. F., Heatherton, T. F., & Tice, D. M. (1994). *Losing control: How and why people fail at self-regulation.* San Diego, CA: Academic Press.

Boden, J. M., & Baumeister, R. F. (1997). Repressive coping: Distraction using pleasant thoughts and memories. *Journal of Personality and Social Psychology, 73,* 45–62.

Borcherding, B., Thompson, K., Krusei, M., Bartko, J., Rapoport, J. L., & Weingartner, H. (1988). Automatic and effortful processing in attention deficit/hyperactivity disorder. *Journal of Abnormal Child Psychology, 16,* 333–345.

Bruch, H. (1973). Eating disorders: Obesity, anorexia nervosa, and the person within. In W. Vandereycken & R. Meerman (Eds.), *Anorexia nervosa: A clinician's guide to treatment* (p. 53). Berlin, West Germany: de Gruyter.

Bulik, C. M., Sullivan, P. F., Epstein, L. H., McKee, M., Kaye, W. H., & Dahl, R. E. (1992). Drug use in women with anorexia and bulimia nervosa. *International Journal of Eating Disorders, 11,* 213–225.

Carver, C. S., & Scheier, M. F. (1981). *Attention and self-regulation: A control theory approach to human behavior.* New York: Springer-Verlag.

Casper, R. C., Hedeker, D., & McClough, J. F. (1992). Personality dimensions in eating disorders and their relevance for subtyping. *Journal of the American Academy of Child and Adolescent Psychiatry, 31,* 830–840.

Christenson, G. A., & Mitchell, J. E. (1991). Trichotillomania and repetitive behavior in bulimia nervosa. *International Journal of Eating Disorders, 10,* 593–598.

Clark, D. B., Smith, M. G., Neighbors, B. D., Skerlec, L. M., & Randall, J. (1994). Anxiety disorders in adolescence: Characteristics, prevalence, and comorbidities. *Clinical Psychology Review, 14,* 113–137.

Cole, P. M., Michel, M. K., & Teti, L. O. (1994). The development of emotion regulation and dysregulation: A clinical perspective. In N. A. Fox (Ed.), *Monographs of the Society for Research in Child Development. Vol. 59: The development of emotion regulation: Biological and behavioral considerations* (pp. 73–100). Chicago, IL: University of Chicago Press.

Collins, R. L. (1993). Drinking restraint and risk for alcohol abuse [Special section]. *Experimental and Clinical Psychopharmacology, 1,* 44–54.

Cooper, M. (1996). Obsessive–compulsive disorder: Effects on family members. *American Journal of Orthopsychiatry, 66,* 296–304.

Coovert, D. L., Kinder, B. N., & Thompson, J. K. (1989). The psychosexual aspects of anorexia nervosa and bulimia nervosa. *Clinical Psychology Review, 9,* 169–180.

Dalgleish, T., & Watts, F. N. (1990). Biases of attention and memory in disorders of anxiety and depression. *Clinical Psychology Review, 10,* 589–604.

DeWaele, M. (1996). A process view of the self. *British Journal of Medical Psychology, 69*, 299–311.

Fahy, T. A., & Eisler, I. (1993). Impulsivity and eating disorders. *British Journal of Psychiatry, 162*, 193–197.

Goldsmith, R. J. (1993). An integrated psychology for the addictions: Beyond the self-medication hypothesis. *Journal of Addictive Diseases, 12*, 139–154.

Goodwin, A. H., & Sher, K. J. (1992). Deficits in set-shifting in nonclinical compulsive checkers. *Journal of Psychopathology and Behavioral Assessment, 14*, 81–92.

Green, M. W., & Rogers, P. J. (1995). Impaired cognitive functioning during spontaneous dieting. *Psychological Medicine, 25*, 1003–1010.

Green, M. W., Rogers, P. J., Elliman, N. A., & Gatenby, S. J. (1994). Impairment of cognitive performance associated with dieting and high levels of dietary restraint. *Physiology and Behavior, 55*, 447–452.

Gross, J. J., & Munoz, R. F. (1995). Emotion regulation and mental health. *Clinical Psychology: Science and Practice, 2*, 151–164.

Gruber, C. (1987). Repairing ego deficits in children with ego developmental disorders. *Child and Adolescent Social Work Journal, 4*, 50–63.

Haimes, A. L., & Katz, J. L. (1988). Sexual and social maturity versus social conformity in restricting anorectic, bulimic, and borderline women. *International Journal of Eating Disorders, 7*, 331–341.

Halford, W. K., Sanders, M. R., & Behrens, B. C. (1994). Self-regulation in behavioral couples' therapy. *Behavior Therapy, 25*, 431–452.

Heatherton, T. F., & Baumeister, R. F. (1991). Binge eating as escape from aversive self-awareness. *Psychological Bulletin, 110*, 86–108.

Heatherton, T. F., Polivy, J., Herman, C. P., & Baumeister, R. F. (1993). Self-awareness, task failure, and disinhibition: How attentional focus affects eating. *Journal of Personality, 61*, 49–61.

Herman, C. P., & Polivy, J. (1993). Mental control of eating: Excitatory and inhibitory food thoughts. In D. M. Wegner & J. W. Pennebaker (Eds.), *Handbook of mental control* (pp. 491–505). Englewood Cliffs, NJ: Prentice Hall.

Holderness, C. C., Brooks-Gunn, J., & Warren, M. P. (1994). Comorbidity of eating disorders and substance abuse: Review of the literature. *International Journal of Eating Disorders, 16*, 1–34.

Hsu, L. K. G. (1990). *Eating disorders*. New York: Guilford Press.

Hull, J. G. (1981). A self-awareness model of the causes and effects of alcohol consumption. *Journal of Abnormal Psychology, 90*, 586–600.

Irving, L. M., McClusky-Fawcett, K., & Thissen, D. (1990). Sexual attitudes and behavior of bulimic women: A preliminary investigation. *Journal of Youth and Adolescence, 19*, 395–411.

Johnson, P. B., & Gurin, G. (1994). Negative affect, alcohol expectancies and alcohol-related problems. *Addiction, 89*, 581–586.

Kanfer, F. H., & Karoly, P. (1972). Self-control: A behavioristic excursion into the lion's den. *Behavioral Therapy, 3,* 398–416.

Krueger, D. W. (1981). Stressful life events and the return to heroin use. *Journal of Human Stress, 7,* 3–8.

Levine, S. B., Risen, C. B., & Althof, S. E. (1990). Essay on the diagnosis and nature of paraphilia. *Journal of Sex and Marital Therapy, 16,* 89–102.

Linder, D. E., Cooper, J., & Jones, E. E. (1967). Decision freedom as a determinant of the role of incentive magnitude in attitude change. *Journal of Personality and Social Psychology, 6,* 245–254.

Maddux, J. E., & Lewis, J. (1995). Self-efficacy and adjustment: Basic principles and issues. In J. E. Maddux (Ed.), *Self-efficacy, adaptation, and adjustment: Theory, research, and application* (Plenum Series in Social/Clinical Psychology; pp. 37–68). New York: Plenum.

Marlatt, G. A. (1985). Relapse prevention: Theoretical rationale and overview of the model. In G. A. Marlatt & J. R. Gordon (Eds.), *Relapse prevention* (pp. 3–70). New York: Guilford Press.

Marlatt, G. A. (1996). Harm reduction: Come as you are. *Addictive Behaviors, 21,* 779–788.

Mathews, A., Ridgeway, V., & Williamson, D. A. (1996). Evidence for attention to threatening stimuli in depression. *Behavior Research and Therapy, 34,* 695–705.

McCabe, S. B., & Gotlib, I. H. (1995). Selective attention and clinical depression: Performance on a deployment-of-attention task. *Journal of Abnormal Psychology, 104,* 241–245.

McElroy, S. L., Hudson, J. I., Pope, H. G., & Keck, P. E. (1991). Kleptomania: Clinical characteristics and associated psychopathology. *Psychological Medicine, 21,* 93–108.

Miller, N. S. (1991). Drug and alcohol addiction as a disease. *Alcoholism Treatment Quarterly, 8,* 43–55.

Mischel, W. (1974). Processes in delay of gratification. *Advances in Experimental Social Psychology, 7,* 249–292.

Mischel, W., Shoda, Y., & Peake, P. K. (1988). The nature of adolescent competencies predicted by preschool delay of gratification. *Journal of Personality and Social Psychology, 54,* 687–696.

Muraven, M., & Baumeister, R. F. (1997). *Self-regulation and depletion of limited resources: Does self-control resemble a muscle?* Manuscript submitted for publication, Research Institute on Addictions, Buffalo, NY.

Muraven, M., Baumeister, R. F., & Tice, D. M. (in press). Longitudinal improvement of self-regulation through practice: Building self-control through repeated exercise. *Journal of Social Psychology.*

Muraven, M., Tice, D. M., & Baumeister, R. F. (1998). Self-control as a limited resource: Regulatory depletion patterns. *Journal of Personality and Social Psychology, 74,* 774–789.

Newman, J. P., & Wallace, J. F. (1993). Diverse pathways to deficient self-regulation: Implications for disinhibitory psychopathology in children [Special issue]. *Clinical Psychology Review, 13,* 699–720.

Nix, G., Watson, C., Pyszczynski, T., & Greenberg, J. (1995). Reducing depressive affect through external focus of attention. *Journal of Social and Clinical Psychology, 14,* 36–52.

Nolen-Hoeksema, S. (1993). Sex differences in control of depression. In D. Wegner & J. Pennebaker (Eds.), *Handbook of mental control* (pp. 306–324). Englewood Cliffs, NJ: Prentice Hall.

Peele, S. (1989). *The diseasing of America.* Boston: Houghton Mifflin.

Pervin, L. A. (1988). Affect and addiction. *Addictive Behaviors, 13,* 83–86.

Powers, W. T. (1973). *Behavior: The control of perception.* Chicago: Aldine.

Pryor, T., & Wiederman, M. W. (1996). Measurement of nonclinical personality characteristics of women with anorexia nervosa or bulimia nervosa. *Journal of Personality Assessment, 67,* 414–421.

Pyszczynski, T., & Greenberg, J. (1986). Evidence for a depressive self-focusing style. *Journal of Research in Personality, 20,* 95–106.

Pyszczynski, T., & Greenberg, J. (1987). Self-regulatory perseveration and the depressive self-focusing style: A self-awareness theory of reactive depression. *Psychological Bulletin, 102,* 122–138.

Pyszczynski, T., Holt, K., & Greenberg, J. (1987). Depression, self-focused attention, and expectancies for positive and negative future life events for self and others. *Journal of Personality and Social Psychology, 52,* 994–1001.

Rachman, S. J., & Hodgson, R. J. (1980). *Obsessions and compulsions.* Englewood Cliffs, NJ: Prentice Hall.

Reed, G. F. (1985). *Obsessional experience and compulsive behavior.* Orlando, FL: Academic Press.

Rogers, P. J., & Green, M. W. (1993). Dieting, dietary restraint and cognitive performance. *British Journal of Clinical Psychology, 32,* 113–116.

Rowston, W. M., & Lacey, J. H. (1992). Stealing in bulimia nervosa. *International Journal of Social Psychiatry, 38,* 309–313.

Schachar, R., Tannock, R., Marriott, M., & Logan, G. (1995). Deficient inhibitory control in attention deficit hyperactivity disorder. *Journal of Abnormal Child Psychology, 23,* 411–437.

Seabaugh, G. O., & Schumaker, J. B. (1994). The effects of self-regulation training on the academic productivity of secondary students with learning problems. *Journal of Behavioral Education, 4,* 109–133.

Shoda, Y., Mischel, W., & Peake, P. K. (1990). Predicting adolescent cognitive and self-regulatory competencies from preschool delay of gratification: Identifying diagnostic conditions. *Developmental Psychology, 26,* 978–986.

Smart, L., & Wegner, D. M. (1996). Strength of will. *Psychological Inquiry, 7,* 79–83.

Sommer, K., & Baumeister, R. F. (1996). *Ego depletion and defensive mobilization against self-esteem threat*. Unpublished manuscript, Case Western Reserve University.

Specker, S. M., Carlson, G. A., Christenson, G. A., & Marcotte, M. (1995). Impulse control disorders and attention deficit disorder in pathological gamblers. *Annals of Clinical Psychiatry, 7,* 175–179.

Steele, C. M., & Josephs, R. A. (1990). Alcohol myopia: Its prized and dangerous effects. *American Psychologist, 45,* 921–933.

Steiger, H., Puentes-Neuman, G., & Leung, F. Y. (1991). Personality and family features of adolescent girls with eating symptoms: Evidence for restricter/binger differences in a nonclinical population. *Addictive Behaviors, 16,* 303–314.

Stein, D. J., & Hollander, E. (1993). Impulsive aggression and obsessive–compulsive disorder. *Psychiatric Annals, 23,* 389–395.

Strauman, T. J. (1995). Psychopathology from a self-regulation perspective. *Journal of Psychotherapy Integration, 5,* 313–321.

Stuart, C. (1995). Control as a key concept in understanding addiction. *Issues in Psychoanalytic Psychology, 17,* 29–45.

Trinder, H., & Salkovskis, P. M. (1994). Personally relevant intrusions outside the laboratory: Long-term suppression increases intrusion. *Behavior Research and Therapy, 32,* 833–842.

Toro, J., Cervera, M., Osejo, E., & Salamero, M. (1992). Obsessive–compulsive disorder in childhood and adolescence: A clinical study. *Journal of Child Psychology and Psychiatry and Allied Disciplines, 33,* 1025–1037.

Vandereycken, W., & Meerman, R. (1984). *Anorexia nervosa: A clinician's guide to treatment.* Berlin, Germany: de Gruyter.

Wegner, D. M. (1994). Ironic processes of mental control. *Psychological Review, 101,* 34–52.

Wegner, D. M., Schneider, D. J., Carter, S. R., & White, T. L. (1987). Paradoxical effects of thought suppression. *Journal of Personality and Social Psychology, 53,* 5–13.

Wenzlaff, R. M., Wegner, D. M., & Klein, S. B. (1991). The role of thought suppression in the bonding of thought and mood. *Journal of Personality and Social Psychology, 60,* 500–508.

Wenzlaff, R. M., Wegner, D. M., & Roper, D. W. (1988). Depression and mental control: The resurgence of unwanted negative thoughts. *Journal of Personality and Social Psychology, 55,* 882–892.

Wiederman, M. W., & Pryor, T. (1996). Substance use among women with eating disorders. *International Journal of Eating Disorders, 20,* 163–168.

Zohar, A. H., LaBuda, M., & Moschel-Ravid, O. (1995). Obsessive–compulsive behaviors and cognitive functioning: A study of compulsivity, frame shifting and type A activity patterns in a normal population. *Neuropsychiatry, Neuropsychology, and Behavioral Neurology, 8,* 163–167.

6

PROBLEMATIC SOCIAL EMOTIONS: SHAME, GUILT, JEALOUSY, AND ENVY

JUNE PRICE TANGNEY AND PETER SALOVEY

Shame, guilt, jealousy, and envy are common human emotions that everyone experiences on occasion in the course of daily life. Although people may not welcome these feelings, they are quite normal and serve useful functions for individuals and their relationships. At the same time, these negatively valanced emotions can pose problems for social and emotional adjustment, particularly in cases of chronic or excessive experiences of shame, guilt, jealousy, or envy. In this chapter, we examine adaptive and maladaptive aspects of these potentially problematic emotions, drawing on current psychological theory and recent empirical work. We consider the implications of these emotions for both individual adjustment and interpersonal behavior.

DISTINGUISHING BETWEEN OFTEN-CONFUSED EMOTIONS: SHAME VERSUS GUILT AND JEALOUSY VERSUS ENVY

In everyday conversation—and in significant portions of the psychological literature too—people are somewhat imprecise in their use of emotion terms. It is not uncommon to see the terms *shame* and *guilt* used interchangeably. Similarly, the distinction between *jealousy* and *envy* is often unclear. But a growing body of emotions theory and research underscores important differences between these often-confused pairs of emotions.

What Is the Difference Between Shame and Guilt?

Historically, the terms *shame* and *guilt* have been used rather loosely by clinical, social, and developmental psychologists. Often, shame and guilt are mentioned in the same breath as "moral" emotions that inhibit socially undesirable behavior and foster moral conduct (e.g., Damon, 1988; Eisenberg, 1986; Harris, 1989; Schulman & Mekler, 1985). Other writers use guilt as a nonspecific term to refer to aspects of both emotions.

When people do make a distinction between shame and guilt, they often refer to differences in the content or structure of shame- and guilt-eliciting events. The notion is that certain kinds of situations lead to shame, whereas other kinds of situations lead to guilt. Most notably, it has long been suggested that shame is a more "public" emotion than guilt, arising from public exposure and disapproval whereas guilt represents a more "private" experience, arising from self-generated pangs of conscience (Ausubel, 1955; Benedict, 1946). Gehm and Scherer (1988), for example, recently asserted that

> shame is usually dependent on the public exposure of one's frailty or failing, whereas guilt may be something that remains a secret with us, no one else knowing of our breach of social norms or of our responsibility for an immoral act. (p. 74)

From this perspective, you would not feel guilty over "lashing out" at a romantic partner at home in private, but you would feel shame over doing so at a party with family or friends.

As it turns out, there is little empirical support for this public–private distinction. Tangney, Marschall, Rosenberg, Barlow, and Wagner (1994) took a close look at children's and adults' descriptions of personal shame and guilt experiences. Among both children and adults, there was no difference in the frequency with which shame and guilt experiences occurred when people were alone, namely, not in the presence of others. Shame and guilt were each most often experienced in the presence of others. Similarly, in an independent study of adults' narrative accounts of personal shame, guilt, and embarrassment experiences (Tangney, Miller, Flicker, & Barlow, 1996), there was no evidence that shame was the more public emotion. In fact, in this study shame was somewhat more likely (18.2%) than guilt (10.4%) to occur outside of the presence of an observing audience.

Shame and guilt do not differ substantially in the types of the transgressions or failures that elicit them either. Analyses of personal shame and guilt experiences described by both children and adults revealed very few, if any, "classic" shame-inducing or guilt-inducing situations (Tangney, 1992; Tangney et al., 1994). Most types of events (e.g., lying, cheating, stealing, failing to help another, disobeying parents) were cited by some people in connection with feelings of shame and by other people in connection with guilt. There was some evidence that nonmoral failures and shortcomings (e.g., socially inappropriate behavior or dress) may be more likely to elicit shame. Even so, failures in work, school, or sport settings and violations of social conventions were cited by a significant number of children and adults in connection with guilt.

So what is the difference between shame and guilt? The weight of evidence now appears to support Helen Block Lewis's (1971) influential distinction between shame and guilt. From Lewis's perspective, the crux of the difference between shame and guilt lies not in the type of transgression or circumstances of the situation that elicits these emotions but rather in the way in which these events are construed. Is one's focus on one's self or on one's behavior? According to Lewis, when one feels guilt, one's key concern is with a particular behavior. Feelings of guilt involve a negative evaluation of some specific behavior (or failure to act)—a feeling that "I did that horrible thing." With this focus on a specific behavior comes a sense of tension, remorse, and regret. People in the midst of a guilt experience often report a nagging focus or preoccupation with the specific transgression—thinking of it over and over, wishing they had behaved differently or could somehow undo the bad deed that was done.

When one feels shame, one's key concern is with one's self as a person. Feelings of shame involve a painful negative scrutiny of the entire self—a feeling that "I am an unworthy, incompetent, or bad person." People in the midst of a shame experience often report a sense of shrinking or of "being small." They feel worthless and powerless. They feel exposed. Although shame does not necessarily involve an actual observing audience present to witness one's shortcomings, there is often the imagery of how one's defective self would appear to others. As with guilt, feelings of shame can arise from a specific behavior or transgression, but the processes involved in shame extend beyond those involved with guilt. The bad behavior is taken not simply as a local transgression, requiring reparation or apology, but rather the offending or objectionable behavior is seen as a reflection, more generally, of a defective, objectionable self (Lewis, 1971; Tangney, 1995a).

In summary, what matters is not so much what was done (or not done). Instead, what matters is whether people focus on themselves (their character) or their behavior. In turn, this differential emphasis on self ("*I* did that horrible thing") versus behavior ("I *did* that horrible *thing*") is associated with very different phenomenological experiences that are called shame and guilt, respectively.

There is now an impressive body of research supporting Lewis's (1971) distinction between shame and guilt, including qualitative case study analyses (Lewis, 1971; Lindsay-Hartz, 1984; Lindsay-Hartz, de Rivera, & Mascolo, 1995), content analyses of shame and guilt narratives (Ferguson, Stegge, & Damhuis, 1990; Tangney, 1992; Tangney et al., 1994), participants' quantitative ratings of personal shame and guilt experiences (e.g., Ferguson, Stegge, & Damhuis, 1991; Tangney, 1993; Tangney, Miller, et al., 1996; Wallbott & Scherer, 1995; Wicker, Payne, & Morgan, 1983), and analyses of participants' counterfactual thinking (Niedenthal, Tangney, & Gavanski, 1994). Together, these studies underscore that shame and guilt are distinct emotional experiences, differing substantially along cognitive, affective, and motivational dimensions.

What Is the Difference Between Jealousy and Envy?

An important distinction can be made between jealousy and envy as well. The word *jealous* is derived from the same Greek root as that for *zealous*—a fervent devotion to the promotion of some person or object. *Jealousy* refers to the belief or suspicion that what has been promoted is in danger of being lost. *Envy* is derived from the Latin *invidere*—to look on another person with malice. Envy represents a discontent with and desire for the possessions of another (Salovey & Rodin, 1986, 1989).

When we perceive that a rival threatens the stability of a close relationship and subsequently feel a combination of anger, fear, and sorrow as a result, we usually say that we are jealous. Mere displeasure at the advantages of another and the desire to have those advantages for oneself result in envy (DeSteno & Salovey, 1995; Salovey, 1991). In examining situations that provoke envy or jealousy, we do not envy just anyone's random attributes that we have not attained ourselves. Nor are we invariably jealous when our lovers threaten to leave us for just any other person. Instead, envy is most likely experienced when comparisons are made in domains that are especially important and relevant to how we define ourselves (Salovey & Rodin, 1984). Likewise, jealousy is most likely experienced when an important relationship is threatened by a rival, and we worry that we do not measure up in domains that are especially important to us (DeSteno & Salovey, 1996; Salovey & Rodin, 1991).

Following Heider (1958), we can conceptualize differences among these terms as well by using the familiar triad of Persons P and O and Object or Person X (Bryson, 1977; Salovey & Rodin, 1989). The crucial factor discriminating among definitions of jealousy and envy is whether there is a previously established sentiment relationship between two elements in the triad. Jealousy is said to exist when Person P believes that his or her previously established unique relationship with X is threatened by real (or imagined) attempts between O and X to form an equivalent relationship. Envy is said to exist in Person P when Person O has a previously established relationship with X, and P attempts to supplant O in that relationship or tries to denigrate O, X, or the relationship between X and O.

Laypeople commonly use the words *jealousy* and *envy* synonymously but asymmetrically; they often use jealousy when they mean envy but rarely use envy to mean jealousy. The term *jealousy* is used generically in both romantic and social comparison situations whereas envy is not because there is generally a part–whole relationship between the two. When one compares oneself with another and does not measure up, one experiences envy. But when one's relationship with another person is threatened by a rival, one experiences jealousy as one imagines the loss of that relationship and envy when one reflects on the relatively superior attributes of the rival that have allowed him or her to threaten the relationship. Jealousy is thus used generically because jealousy often includes envy with the addition of other distressing elements. Jealousy is the whole, and envy is a part. Jealousy's power lies in the simultaneous threat to a valued relationship and threat to self-evaluation through negative social comparison (see Spinoza, 1675/1949).

SHAME, GUILT, JEALOUSY, AND ENVY: SOME COMMON THEMES

We group shame, guilt, jealousy, and envy under the common umbrella of "problematic" emotions. These negatively valanced emotions are well known to counselors and clinicians who frequently encounter clients distressed by them. At the same time, these emotions are part of people's normal "repertoire" of human affective experiences. Everyone experiences these feelings at times, and there is good reason to suspect that in the normal range, each of these emotions has adaptive functions. They are not, by their nature, necessarily pathological. In subsequent sections of this chapter, we discuss in greater detail the adaptive aspects of shame, guilt, jealousy and envy as well as the conditions under which these emotions are likely to go awry.

These emotions share several other notable features. First, each emotion arises from a comparison with some sort of standard—a comparison in which the individual comes up short. The nature of the comparison varies across these four emotions, but in each case, an aspect of the individual or his or her behavior is found wanting. Feelings of guilt arise from a negative evaluation of the behavior. One compares one's actions (or failure to act) with a guiding set of norms or moral standards and finds a significant discrepancy. These standards and norms may be solidly internalized (one's own code) or may be externally imposed (e.g., parents' rules of conduct); but in either case, the individual experiencing the guilt acknowledges the standards as worthy of regard. Having transgressed (or having failed to act when standards instead dictate action), the individual feels a sense of tension, remorse, and regret, which is the hallmark of guilt. In the case of shame, the comparison centers not on a specific behavior but on the self. A failure or transgression is seen as reflecting a bad or defective self which does not "measure up" to some ideal self. This negative comparison of the perceived actual with the ideal self leads to a sense of shrinking, of feeling small, which is the hallmark of shame. The comparisons involved in jealousy and envy are more explicitly interpersonal than those involved in shame and guilt. One's attributes or possessions are compared not with some internalized or socially prescribed standard but with the attributes or possessions of another person—someone specific. In the case of jealousy, the person with whom one compares oneself is perceived as a rival threatening an important established relationship.

Second, as a result of these negative comparisons, each emotion involves a threat to the self. The degree of ego threat may vary. For example, shame experiences typically involve the most profound threat to the self because the global self is painfully scrutinized and negatively evaluated. As discussed shortly, in the case of jealousy and envy, the degree of ego threat hinges greatly on the personal relevance of the dimensions involved in the comparison. Feelings of guilt, which involve a focus on a behavior somewhat apart from the global self, are likely to involve the mildest threat to the core self.

Third, shame, guilt, jealousy, and envy are each fundamentally interpersonal emotions. For example, Tangney et al. (1994) and Tangney, Miller, et al. (1996) observed that the vast majority of shame and guilt experiences reported by both children and adults occurred in social contexts. By their very nature, experiences of jealousy and envy arise in relation to others. Moreover, shame, guilt, jealousy, and envy each have significant implications for subsequent interpersonal behavior.

Although a considerable number of researchers have examined interpersonal aspects of these four emotions, the emphasis of studies on jealousy and envy differs considerably from the emphasis of studies on shame and guilt. In the case of jealousy and envy, much of the theory and research focuses on interpersonal factors contributing to the experience of these emotions. To what degree does the likelihood and intensity of jealous and envious feelings hinge on the nature of the interpersonal situation and the types of comparisons made? In the case of shame and guilt, considerable theory and research instead focus on the interpersonal outcomes or sequelae of these emotions. What kinds of interpersonal behaviors are motivated by these two moral emotions? How do individual differences in proneness to shame versus proneness to guilt relate to various aspects of social adjustment? We next summarize work conducted in these two important areas.

The Interpersonal Context of Jealousy and Envy: A Self-Evaluation Maintenance Perspective

In planning empirical work on jealousy and envy (e.g., DeSteno & Salovey, 1994, 1996; Salovey & Rodin, 1984, 1988, 1991), we generally find self-evaluation maintenance (SEM) theory (Tesser, 1986, 1988) a useful conceptual framework. The major premise of SEM theory is that individuals are motivated to maintain positive self-evaluation. Given a situation in which another has possessions that one desires or performs well on some task, two opposing processes are possible. In the first, called *reflection*, the good performance or possessions of another raise one's self-evaluation. That is, one basks in reflected glory (cf. Cialdini et al., 1976). In the second process, *comparison*, the superior performance or possessions of another lowers one's self-evaluation.

According to the theory of SEM, the relevance of the other's performance to self-definition determines whether comparison or reflection results. If the domain of the other person's performance is self-definitionally relevant, a comparison is likely. Reflection follows when the domain is irrelevant. Because, according to SEM theory, one is motivated to maintain (or raise) one's self-evaluation, one basks in reflected glory at one's friends' self-definitionally nonthreatening successes. When relevance is high, however, one maintains self-esteem by engaging in any of a number of coping strategies, such as changing one's self-definition to reduce the relevance of another's performance, reducing the closeness of the relationship with the comparison other, re-evaluating the quality of the other's performance, or actually maliciously preventing the other's good performance (e.g., Tesser, Millar, & Moore, 1988; Tesser, Pilkington, & McIntosh, 1989).

Supporting data on a SEM view of jealousy and envy has been generated in both survey and experimental research. For example, in a magazine survey some years ago, Salovey and Rodin (1991) asked respondents questions concerning what attributes were particularly important to them, how they would ideally like to be on these attributes, and how they actually perceived themselves. They measured self-esteem using a standard instrument and then obtained respondents' reports of their likelihood of engaging in a variety of jealous and envious behaviors as well as indications of the situations in which they would experience the most jealousy or envy. Feelings and behaviors associated with jealousy and envy were predicted by the importance of a domain to self-definition and by large discrepancies between actual self-descriptions and ideal self-descriptions on the relevant attributes, namely, wealth, fame, being well liked, or physical attractiveness. Domain importance and real–ideal discrepancies in each domain predicted jealousy and envy in that domain, even accounting for global self-esteem. Ideal–real self-discrepancies were most closely associated with experienced envy and jealousy in those domains rated as most important. A person with a large real–ideal discrepancy about personal wealth, for example, tended to report great jealousy if his or her spouse showed an interest in someone very wealthy, especially if the domain was rated as important. This pattern was particularly robust when the self-definitional area was physical attractiveness.

In another testing of the SEM model of jealousy, DeSteno and Salovey (1996) conducted two experiments to explore how the characteristics of the rival in a jealousy situation determine the amount of jealousy experienced. To the extent that a rival for a romantic relationship excels on some dimensions identified as especially self-relevant to an individual, that individual should experience greater jealousy as this represents an especially great threat to self-evaluation. They presented participants with hypothetical rivals excelling in various domains, such as athleticism, intelligence, and popularity. Participants were asked to imagine a situation in which they and their boyfriends or girlfriends were at a party and the rival and beloved flirted with each other. Which rivals elicited the most jealousy? According to the SEM model of jealousy, a match between the participant's self-relevant domain and the domain of achievement of the rival would maximize jealousy.

In a first study (DeSteno & Salovey, 1996, Experiment 1), participants were given a test that measured the importance of intelligence, athleticism, and popularity to them. Three groups were formed on the basis of their scores on this test. Participants were assigned to a group if they scored high on the importance of one domain but not the other two. They then imagined three different scenarios in which a rival flirted with their boyfriend or girlfriend at a party. Depending on the scenario, the rival was described as very popular, intelligent, or athletic. They completed a multi-item measure of jealousy to describe their feelings in these situations. Participants were most jealous when the rival was successful in their self-definitional domain for athleticism and popularity. When the experimenters created interaction scores and controlled for participant and rival domain main effects, the domain-matching hypothesis was confirmed in all three domains. This is not merely a social comparison effect—it is not simply that being compared with a relevant rival makes people feel bad. In fact, when they asked participants how much they liked the rivals in the absence of the flirtation incident, they actually liked the matching rivals the most.

A limitation of this experiment, however, is that DeSteno and Salovey (1996, Experiment 1) provided participants with descriptions of individuals that they felt were excellent in the specified domains. However, there was no way of knowing whether the participants conceived of them in the same way. So a second experiment was conducted in which a new set of scenarios was developed, and participants indicated who they believed to be most intelligent, athletic, and popular. In the second study, not enough of the participants indicated that popularity was the most important domain to them, so the experimenters only included participants for whom either intelligence or athleticism was their self-defining domain, and then participants were asked the following question: Would romantic rivals who excelled on a matching dimension elicit more jealousy? Once again, they did. Athletic students were jealous when an athlete honed in on their date. The ones who valued intelligence were threatened by smart rivals. The matching relationship seems to be *dose dependent*—the more important a domain, the greater the jealousy in the presence of a matching rival. However, in the absence of a threat to the relationship, these matching rivals were actually liked more than those who were dissimilar.

Taken together, results from each of these studies are consistent with a SEM perspective for understanding envy and jealousy. People appear especially vulnerable to experiences of envy and jealousy when the domain of comparison is self-definitionally relevant and when there are substantial real–ideal discrepancies in that domain. In other words, one's worst rival excels in highly valued areas, particularly those in which one feels inadequate.

The Interpersonal Context of Shame and Guilt: Contrasting Concerns, Motivations, and Behaviors

As we discussed earlier, the distinction between shame and guilt lies not so much with the nature of the eliciting event but more with a person's interpretation of that event. The situations that give rise to shame and guilt are objectively similar in terms of the types of failures and transgressions involved and of the degree to which others are aware of the event. Nonetheless, it appears that people's interpersonal concerns differ, depending on whether they are experiencing shame (about the self) or guilt (about a specific behavior).

In Tangney et al.'s (1994) qualitative analysis of children's and adults' autobiographical accounts of personal shame and guilt experiences, systematic differences were found in people's interpersonal focus as they described their personal failures, misdeeds, and transgressions. Among adults, especially, shame experiences were more likely to involve a concern with others' evaluations of the self, whereas guilt experiences were more likely to involve a concern with one's effect on others. This difference in *egocentric* versus *other-oriented* concerns is not that surprising in light of Lewis's (1971) observation that shame involves a focus on the self whereas guilt involves a focus on a specific behavior. A shamed person who focuses on negative self-evaluations would naturally be drawn to a concern over others' evaluations of the self as well. In contrast, a person experiencing guilt is already less self-absorbed (focusing on a negative behavior somewhat apart from the self) and, thus, is more likely to recognize (and become concerned with) the effects of that behavior on others.

Not surprisingly, when people describe guilt-inducing events, they convey more other-oriented empathy than when describing shame-inducing events (Leith & Baumeister, 1998; Tangney et al., 1994). In contrast, people induced to feel shame exhibit less empathy (Marschall, 1996). The acute self-focus of shame seems to interfere with an other-oriented empathic connection; in contrast, the processes involved in guilt appear congruent with perspective taking and sympathetic concern. This differential relationship of shame and guilt to empathy is evident not only when considering situation-specific episodes of shame and guilt but also when considering more general affective traits or dispositions. Across numerous studies of adults, a dispositional capacity for empathy was positively associated with proneness to guilt (Tangney, 1991, 1995a). That is, guilt-prone individuals are generally empathic individuals. In contrast, shame proneness has been repeatedly associated with an impaired capacity for other-oriented empathy and a propensity for self-oriented personal distress responses.

Not only do shame and guilt differ in the type of interpersonal concerns aroused and in the degree to which other-oriented empathy is facilitated, but also there is a good deal of evidence that shame and guilt give rise to very different motivations for subsequent behavior in interpersonal contexts (Ferguson et al., 1991; Lewis, 1971; Lindsay-Hartz, 1984; Lindsay-Hartz et al., 1995; Tangney, 1989, 1995a; Wicker et al., 1983). A consistent finding is that shame often motivates avoidance. Perhaps because shame is generally a more painful experience than guilt and because shame involves a sense of exposure before a real or imagined audience, people feeling shame often report a desire to flee from shame-inducing situations, to "sink into the floor and disappear." Thus, shame motivates behaviors that are likely to sever interpersonal contact. In contrast, guilt is more likely to keep people constructively engaged in the interpersonal situation at hand. Both qualitative and quantitative studies indicate that rather than motivating avoidance, guilt motivates corrective action. People feeling guilt often report a desire to confess or apologize for the offending behavior and to repair the damage that was done. This motivation for reparation may stem from the fact that guilt involves a focus on the offending behavior and, therefore, presumably on its harmful consequences to others. In addition, in guilt the self remains relatively intact, unimpaired as it is in the shame experience. Thus, the self remains mobile and ready to take reparative action.

These motivational differences between shame and guilt were highlighted in Tangney and colleagues' studies of people's narrative accounts of their personal shame and guilt experiences (Tangney, 1989, 1994; Tangney, Miller, et al., 1996). For example, an 18-year-old college student shared this shame experience: "I'm not allowed to date. One day my mom found me kissing this guy. I felt ashamed of myself. *I couldn't face my mom for months*" (emphasis added). This young woman, feeling shame, also felt moved to avoid subsequent interpersonal contact, namely, with her mother, someone with whom she was presumably close. Contrast this with the guilt experience related by another college student: "Well, there's this girl I really like. The other day at the hotel, I kind of messed around with another girl. . . . Now I feel sort of guilty and *maybe I should tell her*" (emphasis added). Rather than searching for a means of escape, this young man was actively debating whether to confess his misdeeds to his girlfriend.

In summary, across a range of studies, analyses of narrative accounts of shame and guilt and participant ratings of these experiences indicate that shame and guilt lead to contrasting motives relevant to interpersonal relationships. Whereas guilt tends to motivate reparative action, shame tends to motivate escapist responses. In fact, Barrett and colleagues (Barrett, 1995; Barrett, Zahn-Waxler, & Cole, 1993) used avoidant versus reparative patterns of behavior as early markers of shame-prone versus guilt-prone styles among toddlers—behavior patterns which were significantly related to independent parental reports of children's displays of shame and guilt in the home. In addition, as we discuss in a subsequent section, there is also considerable theoretical and empirical evidence that shame can motivate defensive, retaliative anger as well.

ADAPTIVE FUNCTIONS OF SHAME, GUILT, JEALOUSY, AND ENVY

How Are Shame and Guilt Useful?

The adaptive functions of guilt are perhaps most obvious. Humans are social beings. They spend much of their life involved in relationships of significance, interacting with people who matter to them. With all this social interaction, it is inevitable that they will make mistakes and transgress with some regularity. Tactless comments, unintended slights, flashes of irritation and anger, and betrayals large and small are part of the fabric of living relationships. In the wake of these inevitable rifts and transgressions, guilt appears to orient people in a constructive, proactive, future-oriented direction. A broad range of studies indicates that guilt typically motivates reparative action—confessing, apologizing, in some way undoing the harm that was done (Ferguson et al., 1991; Lewis, 1971; Lindsay-Hartz, 1984; Tangney, 1993; Tangney, Miller, et al., 1996; Wallbott & Scherer,

1995; Wicker et al., 1983). Unlike shame, feelings of guilt do not appear to interfere with feelings of empathy for others. In fact, if anything, guilt facilitates an other-oriented empathic connection (Leith & Baumeister, 1998; Tangney, 1991, 1995a). Thus, guilt encourages people to repair relationship rifts and other wrongs and change for the better.

In a recent review of the theoretical and empirical literature on guilt, Baumeister, Stillwell and Heatherton (1994) identified several other "relationship-enhancing" functions of guilt, beyond these explicitly corrective, reparative functions (see also Sommer & Baumeister, 1997). First, Baumeister et al. (1994) observed that in feeling guilty, people affirm their social bonds, signaling to one another that the relationship and each other's welfare are important. One feels guilty because one cares. Second, the authors pointed out that feelings of guilt can restore equity in a relationship. For example, usually it is the less powerful person in a relationship or situation who induces guilt; concessions or reallocations often follow. Third, there is the intriguing notion that guilt may serve to "redistribute" emotional distress. In instances of interpersonal harm, the victim is initially the distressed party. (In many instances, the perpetrator may experience significant benefits from the transgression.) Guilt can level the emotional playing field. Feeling guilty, perpetrators take on more negative affect, and there are some indications that victims, in response, feel better when their partners express guilt. So the upshot is that following an episode of guilt, the affective experiences of victim and perpetrator are closer in valence. Similarity breeds empathy and attraction. The relationship in the moment strengthens.

The adaptive functions of shame are less readily apparent. Much recent theory and research emphasizes the dark side of shame (e.g., Harder, 1995; Harder & Lewis, 1987; Lewis, 1971; Tangney, 1995a; Tangney, Burggraf, & Wagner, 1995; Tangney, Wagner, Barlow, Marschall, & Gramzow, 1996), underscoring negative consequences of this emotion for both psychological adjustment and interpersonal behavior. Two obvious questions then are Why do people have the capacity to experience this emotion? and What adaptive purpose might it serve?

Tomkins (1963) suggested that shame may play an important role in regulating experiences of excessive interest and excitement (see also Nathanson, 1987, and Schore, 1991). The notion is that especially at very early stages of development, a mechanism is needed to "put the brakes on" interest and excitement in social interactions (especially vis-à-vis one's mother). Feelings of shame ensue when a child's bid for attention is rebuffed or when a significant social exchange is interrupted (e.g., when a mother is distracted from focusing on her infant). According to this view, feelings of shame then help the child disengage when it is appropriate to do so.

Taking a sociobiological approach, Gilbert (1997) discussed the appeasement functions of shame and humiliation displays, noting continuities across human and nonhuman primates. Gilbert's approach in many ways echoes Leary's (1989; Leary, Britt, Cutlip, & Templeton, 1992; Leary, Landel, & Patton, 1996) analysis of the appeasement functions of blushing and embarrassment (see also Keltner, 1995). Both perspectives emphasize the communicative aspects of shame–embarrassment displays and their role in diffusing expressions of anger and aggression among conspecifics. In a related fashion, the motivation to withdraw—so often a component of the shame experience—may be a useful response, interrupting potentially threatening social interactions until the shamed individual has a chance to regroup.

Finally, there is the widely held assumption that because shame is such a painful emotion, feelings of shame help people avoid "doing wrong" (Barrett, 1995; Ferguson & Stegge, 1995; Zahn-Waxler & Robinson, 1995), decreasing the likelihood of transgression and impropriety. As it turns out, there is surprisingly little direct evidence of this inhibitory function of shame. But indirect evidence suggests that shame is not as effective as guilt in serving a moral, self-regulatory function. In one study, Tangney (1994) examined the relationship of shame proneness and guilt proneness to self-reported moral behavior (assessed by the Conventional Morality Scale; Tooke & Ickes, 1988). She found that self-reported moral behaviors were substantially positively correlated with proneness to guilt but unrelated to proneness to shame. Together with other results showing that guilt but not shame is associated with enhanced empathy (Leith & Baumeister, 1998; Tangney, 1991, 1994, 1995a; Tangney et al., 1994), a tendency to take responsibility (Tangney, 1990, 1994), and constructive responses to anger (Tangney, Wagner, et al., 1996), these findings really raise questions about the moral, self-regulatory functions of shame.

Although shame may not be as effective as guilt in motivating constructive change across most situations, there are possibly some circumstances in which this more global, self-focused emotion is especially useful. No doubt, there are instances when individuals are faced with fundamental shortcomings of the self (moral or otherwise) that would best be corrected. But as any clinician knows, changes to the core self do not come easily. The acute pain of shame and the corresponding directed self-focus can, in some cases, motivate productive soul searching and revisions to one's priorities and values. The challenge is to engage in such introspection and self-repair without becoming sidetracked by the defensive reactions so often engendered by shame. It seems likely that this positive function of shame would most likely ensue from private, self-generated experiences of shame as opposed to public, other-generated shame episodes. In particular, high "ego-strength" individuals with a solid sense of self may be especially able to circumvent "knee-jerk" defensive responses to make constructive use of shame in the privacy of their own thoughts.

How Are Jealousy and Envy Useful?

Regarding envy and jealousy, several intriguing adaptive functions have been suggested. A sociological perspective views envy as having adaptive significance in promoting economic development in (usually Western) societies (Schoeck, 1969). Envy is thought to motivate individuals to better their lot, improve their talents and abilities, and be more productive (Rorty, 1971). Although envy is an acknowledged motivator, admitting to it is still highly stigmatized, so most societies conceive of envy as a necessary evil. This conception of envy emphasizes what Foster (1972) termed the *competitive axis* of envy. The competitive axis of envy underscores wants and desires for the self rather than those things one wants to take from others. Envy expressed in this manner is expected to motivate self-improvement. The denigration of others and their possessions that embodies the dark side of envy is not featured in this formulation. Schoeck argued that Western nations promote envy specifically to motivate their citizens to improve themselves and advertising is an excellent window in which to view how societies attempt to motivate individuals to differentiate themselves from those around them.

We can consider this argument at the level of the individual as well. When of moderate intensity and limited duration, envy can be a motivator. One way individuals can become motivated to accomplish new goals is to harness their envy to energize goal-directed behavior. The social comparisons involved in envy can highlight areas in need of development. Perhaps at first, Salieri's envy of Mozart's obvious talents and productivity motivated his attempts to compose (Shaffer, 1981).

A second adaptive function of envy is its potential role in the formation and clarification of one's identity. Most individuals recognize that some situations are more likely to induce envy than others. This emotional feedback informs one about those dimensions of self that are especially crucial to one's unique identity. What does one learn when one's envy of a Nobel Prize-winning colleague involves rumination about how one would spend the prize money but little attention to his or her new-found fame? It would seem that a core part of one's identity includes a desire for material wealth but not necessarily for the admiration of others.

Jealousy too can have adaptive significance; perhaps that is why Freud (1922/1955) noted that it is "one of those affective states, like grief, that may be described as normal" (p. 232). For one, it is an early warning sign in relationships, signaling that attention needs to be paid to threats to the stability of that relationship, to the self-esteem of a relationship partner, or both. Only in the fantasy world of a Harlequin Romance is jealousy actually a sign of love itself. Nonetheless, jealousy is a signal that someone whom one cares very much about is in danger of being lost. If one never experiences jealousy, one must either be very sure that losing a loved one to another is simply impossible, or one must not care very much about this partner in the first place.

WHEN DO SHAME, GUILT, JEALOUSY, AND ENVY BECOME PROBLEMATIC?

Although shame, guilt, jealousy, and envy are normal emotions that can serve quite a range of adaptive functions for both individuals and groups, there are obviously darker sides to these emotions. When do these emotions become problematic? Intensity of affective reaction may seem the most obvious dimension of importance here. However, although brief flare-ups of intense jealousy, envy, shame, or guilt can represent unpleasantness for one's self and significant others, these experiences may be short lived and of relatively little consequence to on-going relationships and to the mental stability of the individual. Duration and pervasiveness, however, strike us as more significant warning signs of these emotions gone awry. It is not the intensity of one's guilt that drives one to seek therapy but rather the number of situations in which one finds oneself feeling guilt and the persistence with which these guilt experiences eat away at one's peace of mind. By the same token, a brief albeit intense flash of jealousy may simply reveal the depths of one's passion, but chronic obsessive jealousy can become all-consuming psychologically and can even land one in jail.

A closely related issue here concerns the appropriateness of the context eliciting these feelings. A person who is prone to pervasive feelings of shame across a multitude of situations is no doubt experiencing shame in situations that do not warrant such reactions—situations to which the typical individual would not respond with ugly feelings of shame. Thus, in assessing clinically relevant problems with these four emotions, one must attend more to their appropriateness, pervasiveness, and duration than the short-term intensity of these experiences per se.

A second set of issues concern people's ability to cope constructively with these feelings and resolve them satisfactorily. A person may experience guilt in an appropriate context, and the intensity of these feelings might be commensurate with the transgression. But that same person may lack the coping skills to express these feelings adaptively, to resolve these feelings, or both. For example, Tangney (1996) found that college students' reports of "useful" short-lived experiences of guilt were much more likely to involve active reparation of the harm done or a heart-felt resolution to change one's behavior for the better in the future. In contrast, nagging chronic experiences of guilt were not typically accompanied by constructive changes in one's behavior. It seems that some people are more adept at identifying avenues of reparation or change whereas others obsess unproductively ad infinitum. This may be a useful point of intervention with clients troubled by chronic unresolved feelings of guilt. Therapy may include helping distressed clients develop problem-solving skills aimed specifically at identifying proactive solutions or other constructive means of atoning for their transgressions.

Similarly, an effective method of coping with envy is to reframe the domain in which envy is elicited as not as important to one's sense of self. All life domains of the individual chronically smitten with envy are defined as equally significant in determining his or her self-worth. Perhaps it is for these reasons that therapists dealing with envious clients may ask them to fantasize about trading their life for that of the envied other. Salieri may have envied Mozart's profound musical talents, but would he really have wanted to be Mozart, including his psychological immaturity, physical infirmities, and abject poverty, along with his obvious musical gifts? Salieri might have benefited from this reframing (Shaffer, 1981). One can envy the specific attributes of another, but this envy may resolve when one must entertain the possibility of being that other person, part and parcel.

Links to Psychopathology

What kinds of psychological symptoms and disorders are likely to arise when tendencies to experience shame, guilt, envy, or jealousy take a turn for the worse? In her landmark book, *Shame and Guilt in Neurosis*, Lewis (1971) suggested that individual differences in cognitive style (i.e., field dependence vs. field independence) lead to contrasting modes of superego functioning (i.e., shame proneness and guilt proneness) and together these cognitive and affective styles set the stage for differential symptom formation. According to Lewis, the global, less differentiated self of the field-dependent individual should be particularly vulnerable to the global, less differentiated experience of shame—and ultimately then to affective disorders, including the global experience of depression. In contrast, the more clearly differentiated self of the field-independent individual should be particularly vulnerable to the experience of guilt (which requires a differentiation between self and behavior)—and to obsessive and paranoid symptoms involving a vigilance of the "field," separate from the self. As it turns out, there is very little support for this intriguing set of hypotheses.

Research consistently demonstrates a relationship between proneness to shame and a whole host of psychological symptoms, including depression, anxiety, obsessive patterns of thought, paranoid ideation, symptoms of eating disorders, subclinical sociopathy, and low self-esteem (Allan, Gilbert, & Goss, 1994; Brodie, 1995; Cook, 1988, 1991; Gramzow & Tangney, 1992; Harder, 1995; Harder, Cutler, & Rockart, 1992; Harder & Lewis, 1987; Hoblitzelle, 1987; Sanftner, Barlow, Marschall, & Tangney, 1995; Tangney, 1993; Tangney et al., 1995; Tangney, Wagner, Burggraf, Gramzow, & Fletcher, 1991; Tangney, Wagner, & Gramzow, 1992). These relationships appear robust across a range of measurement methods and across diverse age groups and populations. Moreover, the link between shame proneness and depression is robust, even after controlling for attributional style (Tangney, Wagner, & Gramzow, 1992). People who experience feelings of shame about the entire self frequently seem vulnerable to a range of psychological symptoms.

The research is more mixed regarding the relationship of guilt to psychopathology. In fact, two very different views of guilt are represented in the current literature. The traditional view, rooted in a long clinical tradition (e.g., Freud, 1909/1955, 1917/1957, 1924/1961), is that guilt contributes significantly to psychological distress and symptoms of psychopathology (Blatt, D'Afflitti, & Quinlin, 1976; Harder, 1995; Harder & Lewis, 1987; Rodin, Silberstein, & Striegel-Moore, 1985; Weiss, 1993; Zahn-Waxler, Kochanska, Krupnick, & McKnew, 1990). However, recent theory and research emphasize the adaptive functions of guilt, particularly for interpersonal behavior (Baumeister et al., 1994; Hoffman, 1982; Tangney, 1991, 1994, 1995a). Tangney and colleagues (Tangney et al., 1995; Tangney, Wagner, & Gramzow, 1992) have argued that once one makes the critical distinction between shame and guilt, there is no compelling theoretical reason to expect tendencies to experience guilt over specific behaviors to be associated with poor psychological adjustment.

Researchers using adjective checklist-type (and other globally worded) measures of shame and guilt have found that both shame-prone and guilt-prone styles are associated with psychological symptoms (Harder, 1995; Harder et al., 1992; Harder & Lewis, 1987; Kugler & Jones, 1992; Meehan et al., 1996). But a very different pattern of results emerges when measures are used that are sensitive to Lewis's (1971) self versus behavior distinction (e.g., scenario-based methods assessing shame proneness and guilt proneness with respect to specific situations). Across studies of both children and adults, the tendency to experience "shame-free" guilt is essentially unrelated to psychological symptoms, whereas people prone to experience shame appear vulnerable to a range of psychological problems (Burggraf & Tangney, 1990; Gramzow & Tangney, 1992; Tangney, 1994; Tangney et al., 1991, 1995; Tangney, Wagner, & Gramzow, 1992).

Jealousy and envy have also been linked to various psychological symptoms. Currently, the only disorder listed in the *Diagnostic and Statistical Manual of Mental Disorders* (4th ed. [DSM-IV]; American Psychiatric Association, 1994) in which jealousy or envy is the primary symptom is delusional disorder, jealous type. In this disorder, the individual is convinced, even in the absence of supporting data, that his or her spouse is unfaithful or likely to be unfaithful. Often trivial incidents—a partner's slip of the tongue, a slip of paper with a name written on it—are exaggerated and presented as evidence for the supposed infidelity. The delusionally jealous individual often confronts the partner with such evidence and may, in fact, take dramatic actions, such as to telephone presumed rivals, attempt to injure the partner, throw the partner out of the home, or even file for divorce. Such individuals may resort to stalking the partner or a presumed rival and attempt to curtail the freedom of the partner to associate with others or even leave the house.

Although delusional jealousy is the only mental disorder in which jealousy or envy are the primary symptoms, these emotions may feature in other psychological difficulties. For example, in paranoid personality disorder, the individual may ceaselessly question without justification the fidelity of a spouse or other sexual partner or may be focused excessively and resentfully on the attainments of others. Alternatively, the hypersensitivity to the evaluation of others that characterizes individuals with narcissistic personality disorder can sometimes involve extremes of envy. Such individuals generally feel that successful others do not deserve their success, despite chronically envying these successes, and may fantasize about injuring their rivals or in other ways interfering with their rivals' accomplishments. Because such people rarely experience the pleasurable accomplishment of their ambitions, envy of others is often chronic and unremitting. The *DSM-IV*, in fact, lists explicitly preoccupation with feelings of envy as one of the possible diagnostic symptoms of narcissistic personality disorder.

Links to Aggression

Research shows that three of these emotions—shame, jealousy, and envy—each can motivate aggressive behavior. (If anything, guilt appears to be inversely associated with overt acts of aggression.) In fact, the situations in which these emotions are most likely to come to the attention of clinicians are precisely those that involve aggression or threats of aggression.

Many legal scholars have argued that unbridled envy and jealousy are at the root of much criminal activity. Unfortunately, this issue has received little systematic attention by social scientists. Consideration of crimes of passion is fraught with political overtones. Many commentators (e.g., Jordan, 1985) have noted that the classic crime of passion, the murder of a lover and rival on discovering them in the midst of a sexual indiscretion, is a myth. Rather, such so-called crimes of passion are preceded by years of psychological abuse and physical battering and, in fact, very little passion at all.

Nonetheless, homicide committed in the alleged heat of passion is considered manslaughter rather than murder in many states (Dressler, 1982). The American Law Institute's Model Penal Code still lists *manslaughter* as any intentional killing committed under the influence of extreme mental or emotional disturbance for which there is a reasonable explanation or excuse. Yet confusion reigns in the courts' interpretation of the law in what are called "sight of adultery" cases. For example, a married person who kills on sight of adultery can be convicted of manslaughter, but an unmarried person who kills under similar circumstances has committed murder (Dressler, 1982). There is no real evidence that sight of adultery by a married person arouses any more intense and putatively cognitively disrupting "passion" than that in the unmarried person. As Dressler (1982) noted, "this rule is really a judgment by the courts that adultery is a form of injustice perpetrated upon the killer which merits a violent response, whereas 'mere' sexual unfaithfulness out of wedlock does not" (p. 438).

The psychiatric literature is the source of many case studies of jealous murderers, despite the legal confusion over the proper use and disposition of a heat of passion defense. Typically, many murderers experience intense jealousy immediately preceding the killing (Cuthbert, 1970; Lehrman, 1939). Psarska (1970) analyzed a string of homicide cases and found that in nearly one fourth, nondelusional jealousy was a causal factor. Among these 38 cases, 16 involved actual unfaithfulness and the remaining 22 cases comprised situations where long-standing marital conflicts developed into jealousy. Moreover, delusional jealousy has been reported as one of the leading motives of murderers judged insane (Mowat, 1966). Only a few social scientists have addressed these disturbing trends. Most have placed the blame on several interrelated factors: (a) societal sanctioning of aggression and battering (mostly by men) in the context of marital relationships, (b) an emphasis on exclusivity rather than permanence in what couples value in their marital relationships, (c) a lack of resolution of how couples should deal rationally with the availability of extramarital sexuality, and (d) unrealistic visions of what can be expected in a normal marital relationship (Whitehurst, 1971).

There is virtually no social scientific literature on envy as the motive for aggression against people or property, but one imagines such possibilities. Indeed, some have argued that hate crimes against ethnic or other minority group members are, at times, motivated by (often false) perceptions of the growing power of such individuals vis-à-vis the majority group and an envy of this power (or, perhaps, a jealous guarding of one's own power).

There also appears to be a special link between shame and anger. Lewis (1971) first noted the link between shame and anger (or humiliated fury) in her clinical case studies. Consistent with this notion, numerous empirical studies of both children and adults repeatedly find that individuals prone to the ugly feeling of shame are also prone to feelings of outwardly directed anger and hostility (Tangney, 1995a; Tangney, Wagner, et al., 1996; Tangney, Wagner, Fletcher, & Gramzow, 1992). For example, in a study of young adults, the tendency to experience shame was significantly positively correlated with measures of trait anger and indexes of indirect hostility, irritability, resentment, and suspicion. In contrast, proneness to shame-free guilt (i.e., independent of the variance shared with shame) was negatively or negligibly correlated with indexes of anger and hostility (Tangney, Wagner, Fletcher, & Gramzow, 1992). Similarly, in a study of 363 fifth-grade children (Tangney et al., 1991), shame proneness was positively correlated both with boys' self-reports of anger and teacher reports of aggression, whereas guilt was negatively correlated with boys' and girls' self-reports of anger. Among girls, proneness to shame was also positively correlated with self-reports of anger.

Not only are shame-prone individuals more prone to anger, in general, than their non-shame-prone peers, but once angered, they are also more likely to manage their anger in an unconstructive fashion. In a recent cross-sectional developmental study of 302 children (Grades 4–6), 427 adolescents (Grades 7–11), 176 college students, and 194 adult travelers passing through a large urban airport (Tangney, Wagner, et al., 1996), shame was clearly related to maladaptive and nonconstructive responses to anger, across individuals of all ages. Consistent with Scheff's (1987, 1995) and Retzinger's (1987) descriptions of the "shame–rage spiral," shame proneness was related to malevolent intentions; direct, indirect, and displaced aggression; self-directed hostility; and projected negative long-term consequences of everyday episodes of anger. In contrast, guilt was generally associated with constructive means of handling anger, including constructive intentions, attempts to take direct corrective action and to discuss the matter with the target of the anger in a nonhostile fashion, cognitive reappraisals of the target's role in the anger situation, and positive long-term consequences.

Similar findings have been observed at the situational level too. For example, Wicker et al. (1983) found that college students reported a greater desire to punish others involved in personal shame versus guilt experiences. In addition, in a study of specific real-life episodes of anger among romantically involved couples, shamed partners were significantly more angry, more likely to engage in aggressive behavior, and less likely to elicit conciliatory behavior from their significant other (Tangney, 1995b).

What accounts for this rather counterintuitive link between shame and anger? Shame is a painful, ugly feeling that involves a global negative evaluation of the entire self. When people feel shame, they feel devalued. Their sense of self—and self-efficacy—is impaired. Their awareness of others' negative evaluations (real or imagined) is highlighted. This is an extremely distressing experience that presses people to suppress or eliminate the pain associated with shame. At least two routes are open for shamed individuals to manage their feelings of shame. The more passive route involves interpersonal withdrawal—shrinking, withdrawing, hiding from the shame-eliciting situation. The more active route involves other-directed anger. When feeling shame, people initially direct hostility inward ("I'm such a bad person"). But this hostility can easily be redirected outward in a defensive attempt to protect the self, "turn the tables," and shift the blame elsewhere, for example, "oh what a horrible person I am, and damn it, how could you make me feel that way!" (Tangney, 1995a; Tangney, Wagner, Fletcher, & Gramzow, 1992).

In contrast, feelings of guilt are not as likely to invoke a defensive, retaliative sort of anger. Because guilt involves a negative evaluation of a specific behavior, somewhat apart from the global self, guilt experiences are less distressing and less likely to involve severe threats to the self. People experiencing guilt are not typically pressed toward anger in a desperate attempt to rescue a devalued self mired in shame. Because the experience of guilt is less likely to interfere with feelings of empathy for others, guilty individuals are more able to take the other person's perspective, even when angered, further contributing to their ability to find constructive solutions to events involving interpersonal conflict.

LINKS AMONG THESE PROBLEMATIC EMOTIONS

Surprisingly few empirical researchers have examined the links among shame, guilt, jealousy, and envy. But there is good reason to expect that these emotions frequently go hand in hand in human experience. Studies of people's real-life episodes of shame and guilt indicate that these two emotions often co-occur (Tangney, 1993; Tangney, Miller, et al., 1996). Correspondingly, there is a positive correlation between dispositional indexes of proneness to shame and proneness to guilt (Tangney, 1990, 1991). Most likely, people at times experience a cognitive-affective sequence running from guilt to shame. When faced with a failure or transgression, a person may initially experience feelings of guilt over a specific behavior but then generalize the implications of that behavior to a shameful evaluation of the self: "look what a horrible thing I did and aren't I a horrible person!" Nonetheless, this link between shame and guilt is by no means inevitable. People can experience a sense of guilt but still stop short of a full-blown shame reaction. Similarly, people can experience the shrinking sense of shame unaccompanied by the more articulated tension and remorse of guilt over a particular behavior.

To our knowledge, no one has examined the relationship of shame (or guilt) to feelings of jealousy and envy explicitly. But one can imagine a number of plausible scenarios. First, the experience of shame may render one vulnerable to subsequent experiences of envy or jealousy. Imagine a person who, having failed or transgressed, is faced with a shameful sense of shrinking, of being small, of being worthless and powerless. The self, in that moment, is diminished. That same person is still part of a social world that invites social comparisons. Feeling diminished, falling prey to global negative evaluations, that person seems particularly vulnerable to feelings of envy over others' positive attributes, self-relevant accomplishments, and superior abilities. To the extent that valued relationships may be seen as threatened, jealousy toward potential rivals is likely as well.

Not only may feelings of shame set the stage for subsequent experiences of envy and jealousy, but also people may feel shame or guilt over experiences of jealousy and envy themselves. Some theorists have gone so far as to characterize envy as a transgression of a moral order, in other words, a sin (Aquinas, 1270/1964; Sabini & Silver, 1982). LaRochefoucauld (circa 1665/1995) noted that envy is so shameful a passion that one can never dare to acknowledge it. Perhaps this connotation between envy and shame is why some societies often go to great lengths to organize social life, so as not to risk arousing the envy of others (Schoeck, 1969). In these cultures, envy is likely when a person deviates from highly valued social norms, such as the possession of food, the size of one's family, or the state of one's health. Because there is a fear of arousing envy in others, people try hard not to deviate from social norms. Women hide their pregnancies, farmers down play their bumper crops, and extremely successful people may even move out of their villages to avoid arousing envy. The fear of arousing envy in others is so great in these societies that people believe it will result in personal misfortune. This fear of misfortune is central to the notion of the "evil eye." The evil eye is an active expression of envy that can be found across a wide range of cultures (Foster, 1972; Schoeck, 1969). Individuals in many cultures hold that if one is looked on by the evil eye, one is cursed. Consequently, children, livestock, and other possessions of great value are shielded from the evil eye. Correspondingly, compliments related to these valued personal possessions as well as to personal successes are discouraged or rejected. As Friday (1985) has remarked, "envy is all about spoiling things. At the bottom it's a desire to destroy" (p. 159).

At present, we must rely on anecdotal reports of the interplay of shame, guilt, jealousy, and envy. But an exciting direction for future research would be to examine the dynamics of these social emotions in the relationships of daily life.

CONCLUSION

In this chapter, we described some of the antecedents and consequences involved in feelings of jealousy, envy, shame, and guilt. However, a theme that hovers over this chapter is the manner in which these four emotions can result from similar stimuli and can produce intertwined affective reactions. Investigators and clinicians who specialize in these emotions typically do not consider all four emotions in the same package. Shame and guilt experts do not typically collaborate with jealousy and envy experts along theoretical, empirical, or clinical lines. As our chapter emphasized, however, a richer understanding of the functions and adaptive significance of human emotions more generally may emerge from investigations of affective phenomena unconstrained by these traditional boundaries. Similarly, clinical interventions that attempt to draw on an integrated consideration of these maladaptive emotional patterns may be especially effective.

REFERENCES

Allan, S., Gilbert, P., & Goss, K. (1994). An exploration of shame measures. II: Psychopathology. *Personality and Individual Differences, 17,* 719–722.

American Psychiatric Association. (1994). *Diagnostic and statistical manual of mental disorders* (4th ed.). Washington, DC: Author.

Aquinas, T. (1964). *Treatise on happiness* (J. A. Desterle, Trans.). Englewood Cliffs, NJ: Prentice Hall. (Original work published 1270)

Ausubel, D. P. (1955). Relationships between shame and guilt in the socializing process. *Psychological Review, 62,* 378–390.

Barrett, K. C. (1995). A functionalist approach to shame and guilt. In J. P. Tangney & K. W. Fischer (Eds.), *Self-conscious emotions: Shame, guilt, embarrassment, and pride* (pp. 25–63). New York: Guilford Press.

Barrett, K. C., Zahn-Waxler, C., & Cole, P. M. (1993). Avoiders versus amenders: Implications for the investigation of shame and guilt during toddlerhood? *Cognition and Emotion, 7,* 481–505.

Baumeister, R. F., Stillwell, A. M., & Heatherton, T. F. (1994). Guilt: An interpersonal approach. *Psychological Bulletin, 115,* 243–267.

Benedict, R. (1946). *The chrysanthemum and the sword.* Boston: Houghton Mifflin.

Blatt, S. J., D'Afflitti, J. P., & Quinlin, D. M. (1976). Experiences of depression in normal young adults. *Journal of Abnormal Psychology, 86,* 203–223.

Brodie, P. (1995). *How sociopaths love: Sociopathy and interpersonal relationships.* Unpublished doctoral dissertation, George Mason University.

Bryson, J. B. (1977, September). *Situational determinants of the expression of jealousy.* Paper presented at the 85th Annual Convention of the American Psychological Association, San Francisco, CA.

Burggraf, S. A., & Tangney, J. P. (1990, June). *Shame-proneness, guilt-proneness, and attributional style related to children's depression.* Poster session presented at the meeting of the American Psychological Society, Dallas, TX.

Cialdini, R. B., Borden, R. J., Thorne, A., Walker, M. R., Freeman, S., & Sloane, L. T. (1976). Basking in reflected glory: Three (football) field studies. *Journal of Personality and Social Psychology, 34,* 366–375.

Cook, D. R. (1988, August). *The measurement of shame: The Internalized Shame Scale*. Paper presented at the 96th Annual Convention of the American Psychological Association, Atlanta, GA.

Cook, D. R. (1991). Shame, attachment, and addictions: Implications for family therapists. *Contemporary Family Therapy, 13*, 405–419.

Cuthbert, T. M. (1970). A portfolio of murders. *British Journal of Psychiatry, 116*, 1–10.

Damon, W. (1988). *The moral child: Nurturing children's natural moral growth*. New York: Free Press.

DeSteno, D., & Salovey, P. (1994). Jealousy in close relationships: Multiple perspectives on the green-ey'd monster. In A. L. Weber & J. H. Harvey (Eds.), *Perspectives on close relationships* (pp. 217–242). Boston, MA: Allyn & Bacon.

DeSteno, D., & Salovey, P. (1995). Jealousy and envy. In A. S. R. Manstead & M. Hewstone (Eds.), *The Blackwell encyclopedia of social psychology* (pp. 342–343). Oxford, England: Basil Blackwell.

DeSteno, D. A., & Salovey, P. (1996). Jealousy and the characteristics of one's rival: A self-evaluation maintenance perspective. *Personality and Social Psychology Bulletin, 22*, 920–932.

Dressler, J. (1982). Rethinking the heat of passion: A defense in search of a rationale. *Journal of Criminal Law and Criminology, 73*, 421–470.

Eisenberg, N. (1986). *Altruistic cognition, emotion, and behavior*. Hillsdale, NJ: Erlbaum.

Ferguson, T. J., & Stegge, H. (1995). Emotional states and traits in children: The case of guilt and shame. In J. P. Tangney & K. W. Fischer (Eds.), *Self-conscious emotions: Shame, guilt, embarrassment, and pride* (pp. 174–197). New York: Guilford Press.

Ferguson, T. J., Stegge, H., & Damhuis, I. (1990, March). *Spontaneous and elicited guilt and shame experiences in elementary school-age children*. Poster session presented at the Southwestern Society for Research in Human Development, Dallas, TX.

Ferguson, T. J., Stegge, H., & Damhuis, I. (1991). Children's understanding of guilt and shame. *Child Development, 62*, 827–839.

Foster, G. (1972). The anatomy of envy: A study in symbolic behavior. *Current Anthropology, 13*, 165–202.

Freud, S. (1955). Notes upon a case of obsessional neurosis. In J. Strachey (Ed. & Trans.), *The standard edition of the complete psychological works of Sigmund Freud* (Vol. 10, pp. 155–318). London: Hogarth Press. (Original work published 1909)

Freud, S. (1955). Some neurotic mechanisms in jealousy, paranoia, and homosexuality. In J. Strachey (Ed. & Trans.), *The standard edition of the complete psychological works of Sigmund Freud* (Vol. 18, pp. 221–232). London: Hogarth Press. (Original work published 1922)

Freud, S. (1957). Mourning and melancholia. In J. Strachey (Ed. & Trans.), *The *standard edition of the complete psychological works of Sigmund Freud* (Vol. 14, pp. 243–258). London: Hogarth Press. (Original work published 1917)

Freud, S. (1961). The dissolution of the Oedipus complex. In J. Strachey (Ed. & Trans.), *The standard edition of the complete psychological works of Sigmund Freud* (Vol. 19, pp. 173–182). London: Hogarth Press. (Original work published 1924)

Friday, N. (1985). *Jealousy*. New York: Morrow.

Gehm, T. L., & Scherer, K. R. (1988). Relating situation evaluation to emotion differentiation: Nonmetric analysis of cross-cultural questionnaire data. In K. R. Scherer (Ed.), *Facets of emotion: Recent research* (pp. 61–77). Hillsdale, NJ: Erlbaum.

Gilbert, P. (1997). The evolution of social attractiveness and its role in shame, humiliation, guilt, and therapy. *British Journal of Medical Psychology, 70*, 113–147.

Gramzow, R., & Tangney, J. P. (1992). Proneness to shame and the narcissistic personality. *Personality and Social Psychology Bulletin, 18*, 369–376.

Harder, D. W. (1995). Shame and guilt assessment and relationships of shame and guilt proneness to psychopathology. In J. P. Tangney & K. W. Fischer (Eds.), *Self-conscious emotions: Shame, guilt, embarrassment, and pride* (pp. 368–392). New York: Guilford Press.

Harder, D. W., Cutler, L., & Rockart, L. (1992). Assessment of shame and guilt and their relationship to psychopathology. *Journal of Personality Assessment, 59*, 584–604.

Harder, D. W., & Lewis, S. J. (1987). The assessment of shame and guilt. In J. N. Butcher & C. D. Spielberger (Eds.), *Advances in personality assessment* (Vol. 6, pp. 89–114). Hillsdale, NJ: Erlbaum.

Harris, P. L. (1989). *Children and emotion: The development of psychological understanding*. New York: Basil Blackwell.

Heider, F. (1958). *The psychology of interpersonal relations*. New York: Wiley.

Hoblitzelle, W. (1987). Attempts to measure and differentiate shame and guilt: The relation between shame and depression. In H. B. Lewis (Ed.), *The role of shame in symptom formation* (pp. 207–235). Hillsdale, NJ: Erlbaum.

Hoffman, M. L. (1982). Development of prosocial motivation: Empathy and guilt. In N. Eisenberg-Berg (Ed.), *Development of prosocial behavior* (pp. 281–313). New York: Academic Press.

Jordan, N. (1985). Till murder do us part. *Psychology Today, 19*(7), 7.

Keltner, D. (1995). Signs of appeasement: Evidence for the distinct displays of embarrassment, amusement, and shame. *Journal of Personality and Social Psychology, 68*, 441–454.

Kugler, K., & Jones, W. H. (1992). On conceptualizing and assessing guilt. *Journal of Personality and Social Psychology, 62*, 318–327.

LaRochefoucauld, F. (1995). *Maxims* (D. J. Culpin, Trans.). London: Grant & Cutter. (Original work published circa 1665)

Leary, M. R. (1989, August). Fear of exclusion and appeasement behaviors: The case of blushing. In R. F. Baumeister (Chair), *The need to belong*. Symposium presented at the 97th Annual Convention of the American Psychological Association, New Orleans, LA.

Leary, M. R., Britt, T. W., Cutlip, W. D., II., & Templeton, J. L. (1992). Social blushing. *Psychological Bulletin, 112*, 446–460.

Leary, M. R., Landel, J. L., & Patton, K. M. (1996). The motivated expression of embarrassment following a self-presentational predicament. *Journal of Personality, 64*, 619–637.

Lehrman, P. R. (1939). Some unconscious determinants in homicide. *Psychiatric Quarterly, 13*, 605–621.

Leith, K. P., & Baumeister, R. F. (1998). Empathy, shame, guilt, and narratives of interpersonal conflicts: Guilt-prone people are better at perspective taking. *Journal of Personality, 66*, 1–38.

Lewis, H. B. (1971). *Shame and guilt in neurosis*. New York: International Universities Press.

Lindsay-Hartz, J. (1984). Contrasting experiences of shame and guilt. *American Behavioral Scientist, 27*, 689–704.

Lindsay-Hartz, J., de Rivera, J., & Mascolo, M. (1995). Differentiating shame and guilt and their effects on motivation. In J. P. Tangney & K. W. Fischer (Eds.), *Self-conscious emotions: Shame, guilt, embarrassment, and pride* (pp. 274–300). New York: Guilford.

Marschall, D. E. (1996). *Effects of induced shame on subsequent empathy and altruistic behavior*. Unpublished master's thesis, George Mason University.

Meehan, M. A., O'Connor, L. E., Berry, J. W., Weiss, J., Morrison, A., & Acampora, A. (1996). Guilt, shame, and depression in clients in recovery from addiction. *Journal of Psychoactive Drugs, 28*, 125–134.

Mowat, R. R. (1966). *Morbid jealousy and murder: A psychiatric study of morbidly jealous murderers at Broadmoor*. London, England: Tavistock.

Nathanson, D. L. (1987). A timetable for shame. In D. L. Nathanson (Ed.), *The many faces of shame* (pp. 1–63). New York: Guilford Press.

Niedenthal, P. M., Tangney, J. P., & Gavanski, I. (1994). "If only I weren't" versus "if only I hadn't": Distinguishing shame and guilt in counterfactual thinking. *Journal of Personality and Social Psychology, 67*, 585–595.

Psarska, A. D. (1970). Jealousy factor in homicide in forensic psychiatric material. *Polish Medical Journal, 6*, 1504–1510.

Retzinger, S. R. (1987). Resentment and laughter: Video studies of the shame–rage spiral. In H. B. Lewis (Ed.), *The role of shame in symptom formation* (pp. 151–181). Hillsdale, NJ: Erlbaum.

Rodin, J., Silberstein, L., & Striegel-Moore, R. (1985). Women and weight: A normative discontent. In T. B. Sondregger (Ed.), *Psychology and gender: Nebraska Symposium on Motivation, 1984* (pp. 267–307). Lincoln: University of Nebraska Press.

Rorty, A. O. (1971). Some social uses of the forbidden. *Psychoanalytic Review, 58,* 497–510.

Sabini, J., & Silver, M. (1982). *Moralities of everyday life.* Oxford, England: Oxford University Press.

Salovey, P. (1991). Social comparison processes in envy and jealousy. In J. Suls & T. A. Wills (Eds.), *Social comparison theory: Contemporary theory and research* (pp. 261–285). Hillsdale, NJ: Erlbaum.

Salovey, P., & Rodin, J. (1984). Some antecedents and consequences of social-comparison jealousy. *Journal of Personality and Social Psychology, 47,* 780–792.

Salovey, P., & Rodin, J. (1986). The differentiation of romantic jealousy and social-comparison jealousy. *Journal of Personality and Social Psychology, 50,* 1100–1112.

Salovey, P., & Rodin, J. (1988). Coping with envy and jealousy. *Journal of Social and Clinical Psychology, 7,* 15–33.

Salovey, P., & Rodin, J. (1989). Envy and jealousy in close relationships. *Review of Personality and Social Psychology, 10,* 221–246.

Salovey, P., & Rodin, J. (1991). Provoking jealousy and envy: Domain relevance and self-esteem threat. *Journal of Social and Clinical Psychology, 10,* 395–413.

Sanftner, J. L., Barlow, D. H., Marschall, D. E., & Tangney, J. P. (1995). The relation of shame and guilt to eating disorders symptomotology. *Journal of Social and Clinical Psychology, 14,* 315–324.

Scheff, T. J. (1987). The shame–rage spiral: A case study of an interminable quarrel. In H. B. Lewis (Ed.), *The role of shame in symptom formation* (pp. 109–149). Hillsdale, NJ: Erlbaum.

Scheff, T. J. (1995). Conflict in family systems: The role of shame. In J. P. Tangney & K. W. Fischer (Eds.), *Self-conscious emotions: Shame, guilt, embarrassment, and pride* (pp. 393–412). New York: Guilford Press.

Schoeck, H. (1969). *Envy: A theory of social behavior.* New York: Harcourt, Brace & World.

Schore, A. N. (1991). Early superego development: The emergence of shame and narcissistic affect regulation in the practicing period. *Psychoanalysis and Contemporary Thought, 14,* 187–250.

Schulman, M., & Mekler, E. (1985). *Bringing up a moral child.* New York: Addison-Wesley.

Shaffer, P. (1981). *Amadeus* [Play]. New York: Harper & Row.

Sommer, K. L., & Baumeister, R. F. (1997). Making someone feel guilty: Causes, strategies, and consequences. In R. Kowalski (Ed.), *Aversive interpersonal behaviors* (pp. 31–55). New York: Plenum.

Spinoza, B. (1949). *Ethics* (J. Gutmann, Ed. & Trans.). New York: Hafner. (Original work published 1675)

Tangney, J. P. (1989, April). Shame-proneness, guilt-proneness, and interpersonal processes. In J. P. Tangney (Chair), *Self-conscious emotions and social behavior.*

Symposium conducted at the meeting of the Society for Research in Child Development, Kansas City, MO.

Tangney, J. P. (1990). Assessing individual differences in proneness to shame and guilt: Development of the Self-Conscious Affect and Attribution Inventory. *Journal of Personality and Social Psychology, 59*, 102–111.

Tangney, J. P. (1991). Moral affect: The good, the bad, and the ugly. *Journal of Personality and Social Psychology, 61*, 598–607.

Tangney, J. P. (1992). Situational determinants of shame and guilt in young adulthood. *Personality and Social Psychology Bulletin, 18*, 199–206.

Tangney, J. P. (1993). Shame and guilt. In C. G. Costello (Ed.), *Symptoms of depression* (pp. 161–180). New York: Wiley.

Tangney, J. P. (1994). The mixed legacy of the super ego: Adaptive and maladaptive aspects of shame and guilt. In J. M. Masling, & R. F. Bornstein (Eds.), *Empirical perspectives on object relations theory* (pp. 1–28). Washington, DC: American Psychological Association.

Tangney, J. P. (1995a). Shame and guilt in interpersonal relationships. In J. P. Tangney & K. W. Fischer (Eds.), *Self-conscious emotions: Shame, guilt, embarrassment, and pride* (pp. 114–139). New York: Guilford Press.

Tangney, J. P. (1995b, September). Tales from the dark side of shame: Further implications for interpersonal behavior and adjustment. In R. Baumeister & D. Wegner (Chairs), *From bad to worse: Problematic responses to negative affect*. Symposium conducted at the meeting of the Society for Experimental Social Psychology, Washington, DC.

Tangney, J. P. (1996, August). Functional and dysfunctional guilt. In J. Bybee & J. P. Tangney (Chairs), *Is guilt adaptive? Functions in interpersonal relationships and mental health*. Symposium presented at the 104th Annual Convention of the American Psychological Association, Toronto, Ontario, Canada.

Tangney, J. P., Burggraf, S. A., & Wagner, P. E. (1995). Shame-proneness, guilt-proneness, and psychological symptoms. In J. P. Tangney & K. W. Fischer (Eds.), *Self-conscious emotions: Shame, guilt, embarrassment, and pride* (pp. 343–367). New York: Guilford Press.

Tangney, J. P., Marschall, D. E., Rosenberg, K., Barlow, D. H., & Wagner, P. E. (1994). *Children's and adults' autobiographical accounts of shame, guilt, and pride experiences: An analysis of situational determinants and interpersonal concerns*. Manuscript under review, George Mason University.

Tangney, J. P., Miller, R. S., Flicker, L., & Barlow, D. H. (1996). Are shame, guilt, and embarrassment distinct emotions? *Journal of Personality and Social Psychology, 70*, 1256–1269.

Tangney, J. P., Wagner, P. E., Barlow, D. H., Marschall, D. E., & Gramzow, R. (1996). The relation of shame and guilt to constructive versus destructive responses to anger across the lifespan. *Journal of Personality and Social Psychology, 70*, 797–809.

Tangney, J. P., Wagner, P. E., Burggraf, S. A., Gramzow, R., & Fletcher, C. (1991, June). *Children's shame-proneness, but not guilt-proneness, is related to emotional and behavioral maladjustment.* Poster session presented at the meeting of the American Psychological Society, Washington DC.

Tangney, J. P., Wagner, P. E., Fletcher, C., & Gramzow, R. (1992). Shamed into anger? The relation of shame and guilt to anger and self-reported aggression. *Journal of Personality and Social Psychology, 62,* 669–675.

Tangney, J. P., Wagner, P. E., & Gramzow, R. (1992). Proneness to shame, proneness to guilt, and psychopathology. *Journal of Abnormal Psychology, 103,* 469–478.

Tesser, A. (1986). Some effects of self-evaluation maintenance on cognition and action. In R. M. Sorrentino & E. T. Higgins (Eds.), *Handbook of motivation and cognition: Foundations of social behavior* (Vol. 1, pp. 435–464). New York: Guilford Press.

Tesser, A. (1988). Toward a self-evaluation maintenance model of social behavior. In L. Berkowitz (Ed.), *Advances in experimental social psychology* (Vol. 21, pp. 181–227). New York: Academic Press.

Tesser, A., Millar, M., & Moore, J. (1988). Some affective consequences of social comparison and reflection processes. The pain and pleasure of being close. *Journal of Personality and Social Psychology, 54,* 49–61.

Tesser, A., Pilkington, C. J., & McIntosh, W. D. (1989). Self-evaluation maintenance and the mediational role of emotion: The perception of friends and strangers. *Journal of Personality and Social Psychology, 57,* 442–456.

Tooke, W. S., & Ickes, W. (1988). A measure of adherence to conventional morality. *Journal of Social and Clinical Psychology, 6,* 310–334.

Tomkins, S. (1963). *Affect, imagery, consciousness. Vol. 2: The negative affects.* New York: Springer.

Wallbott, H. G., & Scherer, K. R. (1995). Cultural determinants in experiencing shame and guilt. In J. P. Tangney & K. W. Fischer (Eds.), *Self-conscious emotions: Shame, guilt, embarrassment, and pride* (pp. 465–487). New York: Guilford Press.

Weiss, J. (1993). *How psychotherapy works.* New York: Guilford.

Whitehurst, R. N. (1971). Violence potential in extramarital sexual responses. *Journal of Marriage and the Family, 33,* 683–691.

Wicker, F. W., Payne, G. C., & Morgan, R. D. (1983). Participant descriptions of guilt and shame. *Motivation and Emotion, 7,* 25–39.

Zahn-Waxler, C., Kochanska, G., Krupnick, J., & McKnew, D. (1990). Patterns of guilt in children of depressed and well mothers. *Developmental Psychology, 26,* 51–59.

Zahn-Waxler, C., & Robinson, J. (1995). Empathy and guilt: Early origins of feelings of responsibility. In J. P. Tangney & K. W. Fischer (Eds.), *Self-conscious emotions: Shame, guilt, embarrassment, and pride* (pp. 143–173). New York: Guilford Press.

7

THE SOCIAL AND PSYCHOLOGICAL IMPORTANCE OF SELF-ESTEEM

MARK R. LEARY

Psychologists have been interested in the topic of self-esteem since the earliest days of the discipline. From the seminal writings of William James (1890) to contemporary social psychology and clinical practice, research on self-esteem can be found in virtually every area of human psychology. A recent scan of *PsycINFO* (American Psychological Association's literature database) using the keyword *self-esteem* yielded 13,585 articles published in the 30-year span between 1967 and 1996—an average of more than 450 articles per year. This does not include the 881 chapters and books published since 1987 or articles that may deal with self-esteem but do not have the term among their keywords or in their abstracts. The literature on self-esteem is truly voluminous.

Despite varying interests and orientations, most psychologists—both researchers and practitioners—share three fundamental assumptions regarding self-esteem on which virtually all of their work on the topic rests. These assumptions involve the motive to protect self-esteem, the benefits of high self-esteem, and the effects of raising self-esteem. Specifically, most psychologists—whatever their area of formal training—would likely endorse some version of the following three assumptions:

Assumption 1: Human beings are motivated to preserve, protect, and occasionally enhance their level of self-esteem.

Assumption 2: High self-esteem is typically more desirable than low self-esteem because it is associated with many psychological benefits.

Assumption 3: Raising low self-esteem improves psychological well-being and produces desirable changes in people's behavior.

On the surface, these three assumptions appear relatively noncontroversial. Most people, psychologists and laypersons alike, probably regard them as empirical facts. However, the validity of these assumptions is much less well established than is often believed. As seen later, many questions surround these assumptions, and there are reasons to suspect that they are in serious need of qualification.

My goal in this chapter is to critically examine these fundamental assumptions, primarily from the perspectives of social and clinical psychology. Although these assumptions have considerable research support, the case for each is not as airtight as it may first appear. I explore several issues that challenge these seemingly self-evident assumptions and then consider the utility of a reconceptualization of self-esteem—sociometer theory—for helping to resolve many of these questions and for integrating what is known about self-esteem. The chapter concludes with a look at the implications of sociometer theory for understanding and treating the emotional and behavioral problems that have traditionally been associated with low self-esteem.

THE ASSUMPTIONS

Assumption 1: The Self-Esteem Motive

Perhaps the most fundamental assumption that undergirds psychologists' understanding of self-esteem is that human beings are motivated to preserve, protect, and occasionally enhance their level of self-esteem. Virtually all of the major theorists have concurred with James's (1890) assumption that people want (or need) to feel good about themselves. For example, Allport (1937), who is often credited with founding the area of personality psychology, suggested that a person's "most coveted experience is the enhancement of his self-esteem" (p. 169). Greenwald (1980), a social psychologist, characterized the human ego as inherently "totalitarian." Just as a totalitarian regime controls information to maintain a particular, desired image of the government, people control information to maintain favorable images of themselves. Clinical and counseling psychologists of a variety of theoretical persuasions have embraced this theme as well. For example, Branden (1969, 1983), a clinician who helped to popularize the importance of self-esteem to the general public, argued that self-esteem is a fundamental human need; an inspection of the literature reveals dozens of other writers who echo this theme. As Markus (1980) observed, the "notion that we will go to great lengths to protect our ego or preserve our self-esteem is an old, respected, and when all is said and done, probably one of the great psychological truths" (p. 127).

Given differences in their scientific and professional goals, social and clinical psychologists have approached the self-esteem motive from slightly different angles. Social psychologists have been interested primarily in three issues: the kinds of events that heighten people's concerns with maintaining their self-esteem, the ways in which people deal with real and imagined assaults to their self-esteem, and personality variables that moderate people's reactions to self-esteem threats.

Experimental studies within social psychology typically induce threats to participants' self-esteem by leading them to expect or experience either failure (or other unflattering feedback about themselves) or social rejection. Research shows that these sorts of experiences do indeed "deal a blow" to self-esteem and heighten people's motivation to enhance the positivity of their feelings about themselves. For example, after failure, people tend to make self-serving attributions—explanations that reduce their apparent responsibility for negative events (Blaine & Crocker, 1993; Bradley, 1978). People who have experienced failure or rejection also behave in ways that make them feel good about themselves, for example, by associating with people who are successful (Cialdini et al., 1976) and distancing themselves from people who fail (Snyder, Lassegard, & Ford, 1986). In addition, they compensate for their shortcomings by presenting particularly favorable impressions of themselves on dimensions that are unrelated to the unflattering feedback they have received (Baumeister & Jones, 1978).

People do not always wait until their self-esteem has been damaged to take ego-defensive action. When they are concerned about a portending failure, people sometimes set up impediments to their performance—a self-created handicap that provides a plausible reason for failure that will minimize the impact of future failures on their self-esteem (Berglas & Jones, 1978)—or offer pre-emptive self-serving attributions, pointing out in advance that factors beyond their control will likely interfere with their performance (DeGree & Snyder, 1985; Pyszczynski & Greenberg, 1983).

Of course, people differ markedly in their motive to maintain self-esteem and in how they react to self-esteem threats, and social–personality psychologists are interested in individual difference variables that moderate their reactions. The most widely studied personality variable in this regard is trait self-esteem. People who score low on measures of trait self-esteem tend to respond differently to failure and rejection than people who score high on measures of trait self-esteem (Baumeister, Tice, & Hutton, 1989; Tice, 1991, 1993).

Clinical psychologists' interest in the self-esteem motive involves ways in which people's efforts to maintain their self-esteem underlie emotional problems and dysfunctional behavior. The self-esteem motive has often been discussed in the context of *ego defense*—people's inability or unwillingness to recognize and acknowledge undesired aspects of themselves. Allport (1961) wrote that "the mechanisms of ego-defense are sly devices by which we try to circumvent discomfort and anxiety. These self-protective strategies are common, but they do not by any means constitute the normal person's entire repertoire of adjustive reactions" (p. 29). The neurotic individual, Allport argued, overrelies on ego-defensive reactions, resulting in anxiety and inadequate coping. Clinical lore suggests that people who cannot sustain their self-esteem in socially acceptable ways sometimes turn to maladaptive means of doing so. Problems as diverse as domestic violence, prejudice, juvenile delinquency, and substance abuse have been attributed to dysfunctional efforts to protect or promote one's self-esteem (Mecca, Smelser, & Vasconcellos, 1989). Overall, then, considerable theory and research in social and clinical psychology suggest that the motive to maintain self-esteem is a pervasive and powerful influence on human behavior.

Assumption 2: The Desirability of High Self-Esteem

The second assumption is that high self-esteem is more desirable than low self-esteem. Most psychologists would agree that people who have high self-esteem are better off than people with low self-esteem and that "the absence of a healthy sense of self-appreciation seems to be one of the basic warning signs of a dysfunctional personality" (Bednar, Wells, & Peterson, 1989, p. 1). This notion also pervades the culture more generally; for example, parents and teachers appear to assume that children fare better if they have high self-esteem.

The strongest support for Assumption 2 comes from research showing that high self-esteem is associated with psychological well-being whereas low self-esteem tends to be associated with various psychological difficulties (for reviews, see Leary, Schreindorfer, & Haupt, 1995; Mecca et al., 1989; and Mruk, 1995). Low self-esteem is associated with greater depression (Hammen, 1988; Smart & Walsh, 1993) and anxiety (Coopersmith, 1967; Strauss, Frame, & Forehand, 1987) than is high self-esteem. People with low self-esteem tend to be more lonely than those with high self-esteem (Vaux, 1988) as well as more socially anxious and shy (Leary & Kowalski, 1993). They are also more prone to experience eating disorders (Katzman & Wolchik, 1984; Shisslak, Pazda, & Crago, 1990), to join deviant groups

(Tennant-Clark, Fritz, & Beauvais, 1989), and to abuse alcohol and other drugs (Cookson, 1994; Vega, Zimmerman, Warheit, & Apospori, 1993).

Clinical problems aside, social psychological research also shows that people with high self-esteem tend to behave in more socially skilled, adaptive, and prosocial ways than those with low self-esteem (Batson, Bolen, Cross, & Neuringer-Benefiel, 1986; Berkowitz, 1987). They are also less likely to conform to obviously incorrect opinions offered by other people and more likely to stand behind their principles (Coopersmith, 1967; Janis & Field, 1959). High self-esteem is also associated with more appropriate levels of self-disclosure, with leadership emergence in small groups, and with better social skills. In many cases, the correlations between self-esteem and these various measures of emotional and behavioral problems are small (see Dawes, 1994). Even so, given these findings, one can see why low self-esteem "is an assumed condition in virtually all contemporary models of disordered behavior" (Bednar et al., 1989, p. 1) and why most theories of mental health consider high self-esteem an essential aspect of a healthy ego (Taylor, 1989).

This assumption, buttressed by strong empirical support, has also gained widespread acceptance in the general American culture. In part, this has been because of a plethora of popular books touting the virtues of self-esteem. One popular author asserted that he could not "think of a single psychological problem—from anxiety and depression, to fear of intimacy or of success, to spouse battery or child molestation—that is not traceable to the problem of poor self-esteem" (Branden, 1984, p. 12). Along the same lines, a best-selling book on how parents can foster self-esteem in their children states that "the key to inner peace and happy living is high self-esteem" (Briggs, 1975, p. 26).

Assumption 3: The Consequences of Raising Self-Esteem

Following on the heels of the idea that high self-esteem is better than low self-esteem is the third assumption: Raising low self-esteem improves psychological well-being and produces desirable changes in people's behavior. This assumption pervades clinical practice, societal and educational interventions, and popular books on self-esteem. Regarding self-esteem as a causal agent is the basis of clinical and societal interventions that try to solve personal and social problems by elevating people's self-esteem. Within clinical psychology, several systemized approaches have been offered for raising clients' self-esteem in individual counseling, therapeutic groups, and psychoeducational workshops (e.g., Bednar et al., 1989; Burns, 1993; Frey & Carlock, 1989; Mruk, 1995; Pope, McHale, & Craighead, 1988). Within a broader societal context, efforts have been made to raise the public's self-esteem as a way to reduce such social problems as juvenile delinquency, drug abuse, and teenage pregnancy (Mecca et al., 1989). Furthermore, the self-help section of most bookstores is littered with books that offer to raise one's self-esteem (or the self-esteem of one's children, friends, or loved ones). The clear message is that high self-esteem is better than low self-esteem and that raising one's self-esteem will bring about improvements in one's life.

PARADOXES, CHALLENGES, AND QUESTIONS

Had I not cautioned the reader at the outset that there were good reasons to wonder about the validity of these assumptions, the chapter could have ended here with the resounding conclusion that the three assumptions are well supported by empirical research and that the efficacy of their clinical implications is indisputable. Yet lurking among these suppositions and their relevant findings are conceptual paradoxes, empirical challenges, and unanswered questions that call the assumptions into question and demonstrate gaping holes in psychologists' understanding of self-esteem. In this section, I examine several issues that pose difficulties for these assumptions and that should lead one to wonder how well self-esteem is understood after all.

Conceptual Paradoxes

According to the assumptions, people are motivated to preserve, protect, and occasionally enhance their self-esteem, presumably because high self-esteem confers a variety of benefits and adaptive advantages that low self-esteem does not. In support of this, studies clearly show that people think and behave in ways that protect their self-esteem from various onslaughts and that high self-esteem people appear to fare better than low self-esteem people.

However, if one accepts this assumption at face value, a paradox immediately arises: Many of the tactics that people use to protect their self-esteem involve distortions in their perceptions of reality. I can save my self-esteem in the face of failure or rejection, for example, only at the cost of concluding—perhaps erroneously—that I was not to blame. This conclusion is paradoxical because most models of psychological well-being assume that adjustment is associated with maintaining close contact with reality. People who distort reality are seen as more-or-less dysfunctional, depending on the degree of the discrepancy between their beliefs and reality. So if one accepts the assumptions, one must conclude that a fundamental psychological motive (to maintain self-esteem) leads people to misconstrue reality (presumably an undesirable, maladaptive response) in the service of promoting adjustment (as seen, high self-esteem is typically considered a keystone of mental health).

This paradox is the subject of a broader debate involving the relationship between "positive illusions" and psychological well-being (Colvin & Block, 1994; Taylor & Brown, 1988, 1994). Without entering the fray, let me mention a couple of points relevant to the present discussion. From the standpoint of adaptation and coping, it would seem that accurate perceptions—both of the world and of oneself—are most beneficial to a person's well-being. People are more likely to survive and to succeed when they perceive their abilities, characteristics, and worth accurately. It is difficult to identify any long-term benefits to feeling better about oneself than one "deserves" to feel; in fact, as seen in the next section, self-deception has several noteworthy drawbacks. Needless to say, it is difficult to understand how a motive that artificially reinforces flagging self-esteem in the absence of actual success or goal accomplishment is beneficial, either psychologically or pragmatically, except perhaps as a way of making the individual feel temporarily better. In the long run, self-deception works against the individual's best interests; narcissism is a prime, if extreme, example.

In an effort to resolve this paradox, Baumeister (1989) suggested that there may be an optimal margin of illusion; by seeing themselves as only slightly better than they really are, people can "reap the benefits of illusions while avoiding most of the negative consequences" (p. 182). Although the case can be made for the occasional benefits of self-deception, data suggest that either over- or underestimation sometimes may be beneficial (Baumeister, 1989; Baumeister & Scher, 1988). If this is so, slight distortions of reality may sometimes be beneficial, but negative illusions may be as helpful on occasion as positive ones. Little basis exists for assuming that positive self-illusions are more beneficial overall than negative self-illusions; as others have noted, the case for or against positive illusions must await further research (Tennen & Affleck, 1993). In any case, the self-esteem motive that promotes self-enhancement is not the unequivocal advantage to well-being that some have supposed.

Empirical Challenges

Contrary to Assumption 2, research shows that high trait self-esteem is not always good nor is low trait self-esteem always bad. I already discussed the extensive data showing that high self-esteem is correlated with more positive outcomes than low self-esteem. All of these are well-documented findings; although one can dispute the results of any particular study, the body of evidence demonstrates certain desirable correlates of high self-esteem.

The problem is that researchers and practitioners have been myopic when it comes to equally strong evidence showing that high self-esteem is sometimes associated with negative psychological outcomes as well. For example, people who hold excessively positive feelings about themselves are prone to take excessive risks, particularly when their ego is threatened (Baumeister, Heatherton, & Tice, 1993). This tendency is clearly dysfunctional; people who overestimate their ability and worth can present significant dangers to themselves and to others. (Do you want to ride in a car with a driver who overestimates his or her driving ability?)

People with high self-esteem also are inclined to engage in nonproductive persistence, beating their heads against the proverbial "brick wall" in the self-deluded belief that they will eventually succeed (McFarlin, Baumeister, & Blascovich, 1984; Shrauger & Sorman, 1977). They also tend to externalize their failures, which blinds them to opportunities for self-improvement (Dawes, 1994) and creates social difficulties when others become aware of their self-serving attributions (Forsyth, Berger, & Mitchell, 1981).

Baumeister, Smart, and Boden (1996) reviewed an extensive body of evidence showing that contrary to what is often supposed, high—not low—self-esteem is associated with excessive aggression and violence. Studies of violent offenders show that they are egotistical rather than self-deprecating. Research on childhood bullies leads to the same conclusion; contrary to popular conceptions, bullies do not have low self-esteem (Olweus, 1994). Many, although not all, rapists also have inflated views of themselves (Scully, 1990), as do violent members of youth and adult gangs (Jankowski, 1991). Among university students, people whose self-esteem is high but variable (showing considerable day-to-day fluctuations) are particularly angry and hostile (Kernis, Grannemann, & Barclay, 1989). Baumeister et al. pointed out that many of the most inhumane actions throughout history were perpetrated by people who, by virtue of their own sense of superiority, regarded themselves as entitled to manipulate, dominate, and harm others.

If one wants clear-cut evidence that high self-esteem can be dysfunctional, one need not look any further than the narcissistic personality. Despite narcissists' grandiose self-views and unmitigated arrogance, some theorists have suggested that narcissists actually have extremely low self-esteem and that their behavior is a defense against a painfully negative view of the self (Kohut, 1971). However, this psychological conceptualization of narcissism appears to arise, in part, from an implicit acceptance of Assumption 2. Given that high self-esteem is inherently beneficial, the argument goes, anyone who behaves as dysfunctionally as a narcissist must have very low self-esteem. However, the research evidence seems to refute this argument and shows narcissism to involve high self-esteem (Emmons, 1984; Raskin, Novacek, & Hogan, 1991a, 1991b). Narcissists appear to feel very good about themselves—far better than they deserve to feel—and their behavior is the consequence of believing that they are better than other people and, thus, duly entitled to dominate, manipulate, and exploit others (Leary, Bednarski, Hammon, & Duncan, 1997).

Finally, aside from the fact that self-esteem is not the unqualified blessing that it is often assumed to be, the empirical relationships between high self-esteem and psychological well-being (or, conversely, between low self-esteem and psychological difficulties) are generally weak (Dawes, 1994). Statistically speaking, these correlations may be reliably different from zero, yet they do not indicate a strong link between self-esteem and various emotional and behavioral problems. In commenting on the extensive report of the California Task Force to Promote Self-Esteem and Personal and Social Responsibility, Smelser (1989) concluded that "the news most consistently reported . . . is that the associations between self-esteem and its expected consequences are mixed, insignificant, or absent" (p. 15).

The Causal Error

Even so, enough connections have been documented between self-esteem and psychological difficulties to suggest that raising low self-esteem improves psychological well-being and produces desirable changes in people's behavior (Assumption 3). However, the problem with this conclusion is that it is based on the premise that self-esteem is causally related to behavior and emotion. It is said that low self-esteem "causes" avoidance or poor coping, that high self-esteem "leads to" positive changes, or that self-esteem "affects" happiness and well-being. However, to my knowledge, not one shred of scientific evidence exists to support the idea that self-esteem has any causal influence on behavior or emotion whatsoever.

Psychologists are taught at an early stage in their education and then repeatedly reminded that the fact that two variables are correlated with one another—even highly correlated—cannot be taken to mean that one causes the other. Yet in the case of self-esteem, many psychologists have disregarded this dictum. The data show that high self-esteem correlates with many indexes of psychological well-being (although, as seen, the data are neither as strong nor as consistent as often supposed). Yet these correlations do not tell anything about whether low self-esteem causes psychological difficulties or whether raising self-esteem causes positive psychological change. Given that virtually all of the research relevant to differences between low and high self-esteem people is correlational, no causal inferences can be drawn.

The Functional Question

No matter what might be said about particular conceptualizations, studies, and interpretations, theory and research convincingly portray self-esteem as an important psychological entity. Yet it is not at all clear from existing evidence what self-esteem does or why it is important to human functioning.

Few writers have addressed the question of self-esteem's function. Most theorists and researchers implicitly appear to assume either that people need self-esteem for its own sake or that people seek self-esteem simply because it creates positive feelings. The first perspective—that self-esteem is inherently important—is not an explanation at all because it begs the question of why do people need to feel good about themselves.

The second perspective—that people seek self-esteem because it is emotionally rewarding—likewise skirts the issue of function. Some have suggested that the positive feelings of high self-esteem promote well-being because people are more likely to take action and persevere in the face of obstacles when they feel confident, secure, and in control (Greenwald, 1980; Shrauger & Sorman, 1977; Taylor & Brown, 1988). This is undoubtedly true, yet the argument fails to account for the negative feelings of low self-esteem. Is it really beneficial to have a mechanism that deflates one's feelings of confidence, security, and control, particularly in response to events such as failure and rejection, where proactive, remedial action is often needed?

So one is left with the question of what purpose does self-esteem serve. Emotion theorists have insisted that emotions are functional—they warn, motivate, energize, reward, and punish a person—and their behavioral expressions serve important interpersonal functions by communicating that person's affective state to others (Frijda, 1986; Izard, 1977). Granted, people sometimes purposefully override the natural functions that emotions serve (by taking mood-altering drugs, e.g.), but at heart, emotions are functional. What then do the feelings associated with self-esteem do?

For readers who are drawn to evolutionary arguments, one can state the functional question even more strongly. The universality of the self-esteem motive suggests that it (whatever it really is) is an inherent aspect of human nature. All normal people beyond a certain age react emotionally to events that seem, at least on the surface, to threaten their self-esteem and engage in behaviors that maintain their self-esteem. Of course, cultural differences exist in the kinds of events that shake people's self-esteem and in the esteem-preserving tactics that people use, but clearly self-esteem is a potent psychological process worldwide. Such universality suggests that the self-esteem system is a basic aspect of human nature and likely a product of human evolution, but how and why would a mechanism for promoting self-esteem have evolved? Is there any adaptive advantage to seeing oneself more positively than one ought? Would not a general motive for self-accuracy be more adaptive than one for self-enhancement? Without denying the occasional benefits of self-deception discussed earlier, organisms undoubtedly fare best in the evolutionary game when they accurately perceive their own personal resources and challenges.

One of the few explicit efforts to address the function of self-esteem comes from the proponents of terror management theory. According to the theory, self-esteem serves to buffer people against the existential terror they experience at the thought of their own death and annihilation (Solomon, Greenberg, & Pyszczynski, 1991). Thus, people are motivated to maintain their self-esteem because it helps them avoid the paralyzing terror they would otherwise experience. Considerable experimental evidence supports aspects of terror management theory. For example, making mortality salient appears to heighten people's concerns with self-esteem, and high self-esteem does, in fact, lower people's anxiety about death (to name one of many threatening things; Greenberg et al., 1992). Yet the data do not yet support the strong argument that the function of the self-esteem system is to buffer existential anxiety, and at least a few studies fail to support aspects of the theory (Sowards, Moniz, & Harris, 1991). Even so, terror management theory must be credited for providing an account, albeit a controversial one, of what self-esteem does.[1]

Bednar et al. (1989) also offered a functional explanation of self-esteem; they suggested that self-evaluative processes provide "a basis for continuous affective feedback from the self about the adequacy of the self" (p. 112). This affective feedback—self-esteem—varies as a function of whether the individual is coping with or avoiding a psychological threat. Coping leads to high self-esteem; avoidance leads to low self-esteem. In turn, the level of self-esteem affects the probability of subsequent coping versus avoiding responses; high self-esteem increases coping, and low self-esteem increases avoidance. The difficulty with this perspective, however, is that the feedback loop is dysfunctional when people are already coping poorly. Decreasing self-esteem would signal inadequacy, thereby leading to further avoidance, followed by even lower self-esteem, greater avoidance, and so on. As Bednar et al. (1989) noted, "the psychologically weak will become weaker with the passage of time" (p. 133). Such a feedback system might be functional if changes in self-esteem reflected a person's true resources for effective coping because a poorly coping individual might be better off avoiding than engaging the threat. But given that self-esteem is only weakly tied to one's "true" ability to deal with one's environment, such a system would have questionable benefit.

---

[1]Terror management theory does not appear to fare well when considered from an evolutionary perspective. Although freeing people from paralyzing existential terror might promote survival and reproduction, evolutionary processes would seem unlikely to produce a system that lowers a conscious organism's concerns about death. An evolutionary perspective predicts that people who worry about possible misfortunes, including death, will more likely survive and reproduce than those whose existential anxiety is mitigated by high self-esteem (Leary & Schreindorfer, 1997).

Section Summary

Readers who were formerly unacquainted with the complexities of the existing literature on self-esteem may be surprised by the "mess" this last section revealed. Given the vast volume of theory and research that invokes the construct of self-esteem, one might have imagined that most of the fundamental issues would have long been resolved and the central questions answered. I think that the current state of the area itself is attributable, in part, to psychologist's noncritical acceptance of fundamental assumptions that are on surprisingly shaky logical and empirical ground. It all seemed so plausible—so conceptually tidy—that most psychologists (myself included) did not stop to question the basic premises. Once one wades into the quagmire of paradoxical claims, empirical challenges, and unanswered questions, one cannot escape the conclusion that the assumptions under which one is operating are, at worst, wrong headed or, at best, in need of qualification or revision.

SOCIOMETER THEORY

My own interest in self-esteem began with the question, Why are people motivated to maintain their self-esteem? My sense was that if one could concoct a viable, functional explanation of the self-esteem motive, one might begin to make sense of the paradoxes, challenges, and questions that plague the literature. The outcome of this work is what is called *sociometer theory*.[2] The details of sociometer theory are available elsewhere (Leary & Baumeister, in press; Leary & Downs, 1995; Leary, Tambor, Terdal, & Downs, 1995), so I confine my discussion to points that are most relevant to the issues raised above and that have implications for understanding the social and psychological importance of self-esteem.

Basic Premises

The basic premise of sociometer theory is that the self-esteem system is essentially a subjective indicator or gauge that monitors the quality of one's relationships with other people. Upward changes in state self-esteem signal an improvement in the degree to which one is socially included or accepted by other people, whereas downward changes in state self-esteem signal a deterioration in the degree to which one is included or accepted.

Human beings evolved as social animals because they could not survive and reproduce without the support and protection of other human beings. Because brain systems that promoted social living conferred a dis-

---

[2]*Sociometer* is pronounced *soc'-e-ahm-a-ter* (not *socio-meter*).

tinct adaptive advantage (How long would you last alone on the Seren-ghetti Plains of Africa armed with only a spear?), motivational systems evolved that prompted people to seek out the company of other people, to live in social groups, and to form social bonds (Barash, 1977; Baumeister & Leary, 1995). Maintaining these vital relationships depended not only on the individual being motivated toward sociality but also on the assur-ance that one would be accepted by other people in one's social group. Failure to be accepted and socially included by at least a few other people would leave the individual isolated and without the protective affordances of group living. Given that social acceptance by the clan was vital and that rejection was tantamount to death, a system evolved to monitor the degree to which others responded to the individual in an accepting or rejecting fashion.

This system, which operates more or less continuously at a preatten-tive level (because a person cannot consciously think about other people's reactions all of the time), monitors others' reactions for cues indicating disinterest, disapproval, avoidance, or outright rejection—any signal that the person is not adequately valued and accepted as a member of the group. When such cues are detected, the individual is alerted through the induc-tion of negative feelings—just as many other systems induce negative affect when threats to well-being are detected. Furthermore, the system induces a motive to restore one's acceptance through whatever behaviors seem appropriate to the social context.

Thus, according to sociometer theory, the self-esteem system is a so-ciometer that monitors the social environment for threats to one's social inclusion, induces negative self-relevant affect—a loss of self-esteem—when such threats are detected, and motivates the individual to attend to his or her interpersonal relationships. Subjective feelings of self-esteem function in this process as a psychological readout of one's inclusionary status. Having sketched the basics of sociometer theory, I now consider how the theory makes sense of the three assumptions described earlier.

Assumption 1: The Self-Esteem Motive

Sociometer theory casts the self-esteem motive in a considerably dif-ferent light from previous conceptualizations. In fact, the phrase "self-esteem motive" becomes somewhat of a misnomer because, strictly speak-ing, people are not motivated to maintain their self-esteem at all. Instead, their goal is to sustain an acceptable degree of social acceptance and to avoid social rejection. Subjective self-esteem is the internal, psychological indicator that guides their efforts to promote acceptance and ward off re-jection.

According to the theory, the kinds of events that threaten self-esteem and induce people to protect and restore their self-esteem are best understood as events that affect a person's perceived acceptance and inclusion by other people (inclusionary status). Events that threaten a person's self-esteem are precisely those things that if known by others, would likely lead them to devalue their relationship with the person. As seen earlier, the events that are most likely to lower self-esteem (and which experimental social psychologists use precisely for that purpose) involve rejection (which, by definition, indicates social exclusion) and failure (which is often associated with relational devaluation and possible rejection because other people do not like "losers"). However, events that raise self-esteem are those that increase a person's perceptions of being accepted and included —achievement, recognition, compliments, admiration, and the like.

Empirical support for this notion comes from a series of studies (Leary, Tambor, et al., 1995). In one study, participants indicated how they thought other people would react if the participants performed each of several behaviors and then rated how their own self-esteem would be affected if they performed each behavior. As sociometer theory predicts, participants' ratings of their self-esteem closely mirrored their expectations regarding how others would respond vis-à-vis acceptance and rejection. In a second study, participants described a past interpersonal encounter and then rated how included or excluded they felt in the situation as well as how they felt about themselves at the time. Again, perceived inclusion–exclusion correlated very highly with self-feelings, as sociometer theory predicts. The strong link between social inclusion–exclusion and state self-esteem was replicated in two laboratory experiments as well. Participants who believed that other participants had decided to exclude them from a laboratory group demonstrated sharp decreases in state self-esteem.

Furthermore, when one looks at the behaviors that researchers have interpreted as ways of preserving self-esteem, these behaviors are actions that one would expect to halt the slide of relational devaluation, if not actually increase social acceptance. When people make self-serving attributions, offer excuses, "scapegoat," self-handicap, and engage in other ego-defensive behaviors, they not trying to preserve self-esteem per se but are trying to protect their inclusionary status.

Assumption 2: The Benefits and Liabilities of Self-Esteem

Within sociometer theory, individual differences in trait self-esteem can be reconceptualized as individual differences in perceived inclusionary status. People with relatively high self-esteem tend to believe that they are generally acceptable individuals and that other people value their relationships with them. People with relatively low self-esteem walk through life assuming that they are less acceptable and that other people value their relationships less if not expressly devalue them (Leary, Tambor, et al., 1995, Study 5).

Viewed in this way, the correlates of low versus high trait self-esteem reflect the impact of feeling generally rejected versus accepted, respectively. Because being accepted and valued results in more positive psychological outcomes than being rejected and devalued, one generally finds positive relationships between high self-esteem and well-being and negative relationships between high self-esteem and several psychological difficulties (Leary, Schreindorfer, et al., 1995). However, from the standpoint of sociometer theory, self-esteem has no causal impact on the link between self-esteem and psychological well-being. Self-esteem and psychological well-being are coeffects of the degree to which people perceive they are included, accepted, and valued. Thus, the causal agent in these relationships is not self-esteem but perceived social acceptance or rejection.

Sociometer theory also can help one understand those instances in which high self-esteem is associated with negative outcomes. For example, in the case of the link between high self-esteem and aggression (Baumeister et al., 1996), people who already feel highly included may not worry about the interpersonal implications of behaving in a socially inappropriate or undesirable fashion. Similarly, the egocentric, exploitive behavior of narcissists is what one would expect of people who believe their superiority entitles them to exploit others with no fear of serious interpersonal consequences. Indeed, narcissists often seem genuinely surprised when others react negatively to their egocentric behavior; they seem to take others' acceptance of them for granted.

Assumption 3: The Consequences of Enhancing Self-Esteem

Sociometer theory does not dispute that interventions designed to enhance self-esteem often produce measurable psychological benefits, as the advocates of self-esteem programs maintain. However, the theory suggests that the mediating processes are different from what are typically assumed. Specifically, improvements in well-being that accompany enhanced self-esteem are mediated by changes in people's perceptions of the degree to which they are accepted, included, and valued by other people rather than by heightened self-esteem per se. A large body of research attests to the psychological benefits of being accepted and valued. People who experience deficits in their sense of belongingness suffer a wide range of emotional and behavioral problems (for a review, see Baumeister & Leary, 1995).

An examination of programs designed to enhance self-esteem reveals that these interventions typically include features that would be expected to increase real or perceived social acceptance. For example, Frey and Carlock's (1989) model stresses that the facilitator should consistently offer sincere positive feedback to the participant. Among other things, participants learn to affirm the positive qualities they see in themselves and others. Clearly, such an approach not only makes one's own desirable attributes salient, but it also changes one's behavior toward others in ways that increase the likelihood of social acceptance.

Pope et al.'s (1988) program, designed specifically for children, takes a more behavioral approach, but it too would be expected to increase social acceptance. After a careful analysis of the participants' self-esteem in several domains, exercises are undertaken to improve "performance" in deficient domains (e.g., social relationships, academics, or physical appearance). Among other things, the participants learn to solve social problems, develop social and communication skills, and increase self-control. From the perspective of sociometer theory, Pope et al. are helping children improve their chances of social acceptance, thereby producing changes in how acceptable they feel.

Many clinical interventions and much popular advice explicitly or implicitly stress the importance of interpersonal acceptance and positive social relationships in raising self-esteem. Considerable research supports the speculations of early symbolic interactionists (Cooley, 1902; Mead, 1932) that people's self-concepts, as well as their self-esteem, are related to their perceptions of how they are perceived by other people—what are often called *reflected appraisals* (Felson, 1993; Shrauger & Schoeneman, 1979). For example, participants who learn that other people hold negative impressions of them or that others do not want to interact with them show drops in their state self-esteem (Leary, Haupt, Strausser, & Chokel, 1998; Leary, Tambor, et al., 1995). Likewise, research in developmental psychology clearly shows that children incorporate the reflected appraisals of their parents and peers into their self-concepts (Harter, 1993) and that self-esteem is strongly related to the quality of the relationships that exist between children and significant others in their lives (Coopersmith, 1967). Not surprisingly then, accepted children have higher self-esteem than rejected children.[3]

Sociometer theory helps to explain why self-esteem is an inherently social phenomenon. People's self-esteem is based on how they think others evaluate them because that is precisely how the system was "designed" to operate. Furthermore, the theory explains why self-esteem correlates more highly with how people believe they are viewed by others than with others' true perceptions of them (Felson, 1993; Shrauger & Schoeneman, 1979) and why self-esteem is correlated highly with people's performance in domains that they think are important to other people (Harter & Marold,

---

[3]Cooley (1902), who championed the idea that self-esteem is based largely on reflected appraisals, nonetheless puzzled over the question of why self-esteem is so closely tied to others' opinions. In discussing people's reactions to events that cast undesirable aspersions on them, he wrote that "we find with a chill of terror that . . . our self-esteem, self-confidence, and hope, being chiefly founded upon opinions, attributed to others, go down in the crash. Our reason may tell us that we are no less worthy than we were before, but dread and doubt do not permit us to believe it" (p. 216).

1991). Contrary to theories that conceptualize self-esteem as a purely personal evaluation of one's own characteristics, research suggests that people's self-esteem is far more sensitive to others' reactions to them than to how they see themselves.[4]

Private Threats to Self-Esteem

On the surface, sociometer theory may seem to suggest that all threats to self-esteem reflect interpersonal events that have implications for the individual's social acceptance and that people's efforts to deal with such threats always involve behaviors that are directed toward other people. However, such an extreme interpretation flies in the face of evidence suggesting that purely private events can affect self-esteem and that people sometimes deal with such threats in cognitive rather than behavioral ways. How does sociometer theory account for these "private" threats to self-esteem?

First, events do not need to occur in public for them to affect one's relationships with others (and, thus, involve the sociometer). All individuals have done things in private that if found out by others, would undermine their relationships. To protect people against such indiscretions, the sociometer must alert people to the possible interpersonal repercussions of private behaviors, so that they will refrain from doing them, conceal them more carefully, or take anticipatory measures to minimize the interpersonal damage that will occur if others should learn about them.

Second, some writers have suggested that private self-deception does serve an interpersonal function (Neese & Lloyd, 1992; Trivers, 1985). One is more likely to succeed in convincing others of one's ability, virtue, and worth if one believes in them oneself. In this view, private self-esteem maintenance helps people behave in ways that enhance their social desirability and acceptance by others.

Third, sociometer theory does not deny that people may engage in purely cognitive self-deceptions that serve no purpose other than to make them feel good. These positive illusions may contribute to a transitory sense of well-being by reducing anxiety, depression, and a sense of helplessness when more direct means of improving one's lot are not readily available (Taylor & Brown, 1988). The fact that people may do this does not argue against sociometer theory as much as it suggests that people can "bypass"

---

[4]Rollo May (1983) expressly denied that healthy self-esteem was found in reflected appraisals: "The sense of being gives the person a basis for self-esteem which is not merely the reflection of others' views about him. For if your self-esteem must rest in the long run on social validation, you have not self-esteem, but a more sophisticated form of social conformity" (p. 102). Along similar lines, Bednar et al. (1989) offered a model of self-esteem that largely disengages it from others' reactions. But theories that disengage self-esteem from interpersonal processes have great difficulty accounting for the strength of the connections among reflected appraisals, social rejection, and self-esteem.

the sociometer system if they desire. Just as the fact that people sometimes eat when they are not hungry does not indicate that they lack a system to regulate food intake, the fact that people sometimes engage in cognitive strategies simply to improve their mood and feelings about themselves does not imply that the self-esteem system is not, at heart, a mechanism for maintaining a minimum degree of social inclusion.[5]

Section Summary

Sociometer theory provides an alternative perspective on the social and psychological importance of self-esteem. Self-esteem is important socially because it is involved in the maintenance of interpersonal relationships. The self-esteem system helps people to avoid rejection by alerting them to potential exclusion and motivating behaviors that promote acceptance, thereby enhancing the quality of their interpersonal lives and increasing the chances of them obtaining a variety of social affordances. Psychologically, self-esteem is important because social acceptance promotes psychological well-being.

IMPLICATIONS FOR CLINICAL AND COUNSELING PSYCHOLOGY

In this final section, I briefly explore some implications of sociometer theory for understanding and treating emotional and behavioral problems that implicate self-esteem. The most important point is that whatever a client's presenting difficulty, low self-esteem should rarely be regarded as the underlying problem. Low self-esteem may signal the nature of the problem—a sense of relational devaluation or rejection—but low self-esteem itself is not the cause of the client's emotional distress or dysfunctional behavior.

---

[5]The evidence regarding purely cognitive tactics for maintaining self-esteem is rather meager, and very little is known about the pervasiveness or nature of cognitive esteem maintenance. Studies that examine how people react when their self-esteem is in jeopardy typically use esteem threats that were known not only by the research participants but by the researcher or others. Furthermore, participants' responses to the threat—their reports of what they were ostensibly thinking—are typically seen by the researcher as well. Thus, the experimental context of research on self-esteem is typically an interpersonal one, often despite the researcher's best efforts to render participants' responses as private and anonymous as possible. In light of this, researchers have found it very difficult to determine whether participants' responses reflect an internal, cognitive response to a threat to self-esteem or a public, behavioral response that has implications (at least in the participant's mind) for how he or she might be accepted or rejected by other people. (For discussions of this methodological problem, see Leary, 1993; and Tetlock & Manstead, 1985.) However, researchers who have used ingenious experimental designs to do so have typically found that the prevalence and strength of ego-defensive behaviors are strongly affected by the publicness of either the threat to esteem or participants' responses and, in fact, often occur only when the situation is an interpersonal one.

Given that self-esteem is not the problem, raising self-esteem is rarely the solution. Sociometer theory suggests that the focus should be on helping clients to cope—through either behavioral or cognitive means—with their feelings of relational devaluation. This point may seem to fly in the face of the documented efficacy of clinical interventions that include efforts to raise self-esteem. However, as suggested earlier, the effectiveness of such approaches is not mediated by enhanced self-esteem. Instead, the clinical strategies that practitioners use to raise self-esteem often involve procedures that increase real or perceived social inclusion.

From the standpoint of sociometer theory, raising self-esteem artificially—that is, without a corresponding increase in perceived inclusion—is particularly ill informed. As callous (and possibly elitist) as it may sound, sociometer theory suggests that some people ought to have low self-esteem. People who consistently behave in destructive and inappropriate ways that lead others to ignore, avoid, or reject them have low self-esteem because their sociometer has accurately detected a low degree of inclusion. To try to convince these individuals that they are in fact valuable, worthy, wonderful people may dissuade them from taking action to deal with the real problem (Dawes, 1994) as well as lead to confusion and anger. ("If I'm so wonderful, why does everybody avoid me?") Such an approach tries to override the sociometer's natural signals that the person's social acceptance is in jeopardy—somewhat akin to trying to convince a driver to ignore the fact that the fuel gauge of the car is on empty.

A more complex situation arises when a normal and socially acceptable client receives undue rejection from important people in his or her life. Such an individual might well have low self-esteem not because of any personal shortcomings but because others do not sufficiently value their relationships with him or her. Critical or uncaring parents, abusive spouses, and egocentric friends may induce low self-esteem in people who do not deserve it.

The clinical approach in such cases would be to help unfairly rejected clients understand that the self-esteem system is, by design, an indicator of others' reactions to them and, thus, their low self-esteem is nothing more than an accurate reflection of how others have treated them. At the same time, they must see that their self-esteem is not, as they likely assume, an index of their true worth as an individual. If they can view their low self-esteem as a product of other people's weaknesses and shortcomings rather than their own deficiencies, they may feel badly about how they have been devalued by significant others yet learn not to make the unwarranted leap to self-deprecation. At the same time, they may be encouraged to pursue new relationships in which they are valued.

Some practitioners have denied that clinical interventions should focus on helping clients to obtain more positive responses from others to

raise self-esteem. Bednar et al. (1989), for example, reflected this sentiment:

> If individuals must depend upon the affirmation of others in order to
> overcome low self-esteem, then part of a clinician's job is to teach the
> client to be a consummate performer, sensitive to the demands of the
> audience in order to win plaudits and "atta boys" from others. In our
> opinion, such a task is as impossible as it is undesirable. (p. 11)

However, sociometer theory does not suggest that people should simply
seek pats on the back or pursue social acceptance disgenuinely. In fact, obtaining social approval through conscious deception will do little to placate
the sociometer because the person knows that no matter how positively
other people respond, he or she is in reality not acceptable. High trait self-
esteem is associated with perceiving that one is a socially acceptable person
who will likely be valued as a relational partner in the future (Leary &
Baumeister, in press), and momentary kudos do little to promote this perception. Everyone needs relationships, and everyone needs to feel that they
are accepted by the important people in their lives. To help clients pursue
ways of promoting social acceptance seems a valid clinical goal.

CONCLUSIONS

I return one last time to the three assumptions about self-esteem that
provided the framework for this chapter. Sociometer theory suggests that
these assumptions—regarding the self-esteem motive, the benefits of high
self-esteem, and the effects of enhancing self-esteem—should be revised
in the following manner:

Revised Assumption 1: Human beings are motivated to preserve, protect, and occasionally enhance the degree to
which they are accepted, included, and valued
by other people. The self-esteem system is involved in the process of monitoring and regulating people's social acceptance.

Revised Assumption 2: The psychological benefits of low and high self-
esteem derive from the fact that both self-
esteem and psychological benefits are associated with perceived social acceptance.

Revised Assumption 3: Raising low self-esteem improves psychological
well-being and produces desirable changes in
people's behavior because interventions that
raise self-esteem promote a sense of social inclusion. It is this sense of being accepted—not
self-esteem per se—that produces the desirable
effects.

REFERENCES

Allport, G. W. (1937). *Personality: A psychological interpretation*. New York: Holt.

Allport, G. W. (1961). *Pattern and growth in personality*. New York: Holt, Rinehart & Winston.

Barash, D. P. (1977). *Sociobiology and behavior*. New York: Elsevier.

Batson, C. D., Bolen, J. G., Cross, J. A., & Neuringer-Benefiel, H. E. (1986). Where is the altruism in the altruistic personality? *Journal of Personality and Social Psychology, 50*, 212–220.

Baumeister, R. F. (1989). The optimal margin of illusion. *Journal of Social and Clinical Psychology, 8*, 176–189.

Baumeister, R. F., Heatherton, T. F., & Tice, D. M. (1993). When ego threats lead to self-regulation failure: The negative consequences of high self-esteem. *Journal of Personality and Social Psychology, 64*, 141–156.

Baumeister, R. F., & Jones, E. E. (1978). When self-presentation is constrained by the target's knowledge: Consistency and compensation. *Journal of Personality and Social Psychology, 36*, 608–618.

Baumeister, R. F., & Leary, M. R. (1995). The need to belong: Desire for interpersonal attachments as a fundamental human motivation. *Psychological Bulletin, 117*, 497–529.

Baumeister, R. F., & Scher, S. J. (1988). Self-defeating behavior patterns among normal individuals: Review and analysis of common self-destructive tendencies. *Psychological Bulletin, 104*, 3–22.

Baumeister, R. F., Smart, L., & Boden, J. M. (1996). Relation of threatened egotism to violence and aggression: The dark side of high self-esteem. *Psychological Review, 103*, 5–33.

Baumeister, R. F., Tice, D. M., & Hutton, D. G. (1989). Self-presentational motivations and personality differences in self-esteem. *Journal of Personality, 57*, 547–579.

Bednar, R. L., Wells, M. G., & Peterson, S. R. (1989). *Self-esteem: Paradoxes and innovations in clinical theory and practice*. Washington, DC: American Psychological Association.

Berglas, S., & Jones, E. E. (1978). Drug choice as a self-handicapping strategy in response to noncontingent success. *Journal of Personality and Social Psychology, 36*, 405–417.

Berkowitz, L. (1987). Mood, self-awareness, and willingness to help. *Journal of Personality and Social Psychology, 52*, 721–729.

Blaine, B., & Crocker, J. (1993). Self-esteem and self-serving biases in reactions to positive and negative events. In R. F. Baumeister (Ed.), *Self-esteem: The puzzle of low self-regard* (p. 55–85). New York: Plenum.

Bradley, G. W. (1978). Self-serving biases in the attribution process: A reexamination of the fact or fiction question. *Journal of Personality and Social Psychology, 36*, 56–71.

Branden, N. (1969). *The psychology of self-esteem*. New York: Bantam.

Branden, N. (1983). *Honoring the self*. Los Angeles, CA: Teacher.

Branden, N. (1984, August–September). In defense of self. *Association for Humanistic Psychology Perspectives*, pp. 12–13.

Briggs, D. C. (1975). *Your child's self-esteem*. Garden City, NY: Doubleday.

Burns, D. (1993). *Ten days to self-esteem*. New York: Quill.

Cialdini, R. B., Borden, R. J., Thorne, A., Walker, M., Freeman, S., & Sloane, L. T. (1976). Basking in reflected glory: Three (football) field studies. *Journal of Personality and Social Psychology, 34*, 366–375.

Colvin, C. R., & Block, J. (1994). Do positive illusions foster mental health? An examination of the Taylor and Brown formulation. *Psychological Bulletin, 116*, 3–20.

Cookson, H. (1994). Personality variables associated with alcohol use in young offenders. *Personality and Individual Differences, 16*, 179–182.

Cooley, C. H. (1902). *Human nature and the social order*. New York: Scribner.

Coopersmith, S. (1967). *The antecedents of self-esteem*. San Francisco: Freeman.

Dawes, R. M. (1994). *House of cards: Psychology and psychotherapy built on myth*. New York: Free Press.

DeGree, C. E., & Snyder, C. R. (1985). Adler's psychology (of use) today: Personal history of traumatic life events as a self-handicapping strategy. *Journal of Personality and Social Psychology, 48*, 1512–1519.

Emmons, R. A. (1984). Factor analysis and construct validity of the Narcissistic Personality Inventory. *Journal of Personality Assessment, 48*, 291–300.

Felson, R. B. (1993). The (somewhat) social self: How others affect self-appraisals. In J. Suls (Ed.), *Psychological perspectives on the self* (Vol. 4, pp. 1–26). Hillsdale, NJ: Erlbaum.

Forsyth, D. R., Berger, R. E., & Mitchell, T. (1981). The effects of self-serving vs. other-serving claims of responsibility on attraction in groups. *Social Psychology Quarterly, 44*, 59–64.

Frey, D., & Carlock, C. J. (1989). *Enhancing self-esteem*. Muncie, IN: Accelerated Development.

Frijda, N. (1986). *The emotions*. Cambridge, England: Cambridge University Press.

Greenberg, J., Pyszczynski, T., Solomon, S., Rosenblatt, A., Burling, J., Lyon, D., Simon, L., & Pinel, E. (1992). Why do people need self-esteem? Converging evidence that self-esteem serves an anxiety-buffering function. *Journal of Personality and Social Psychology, 63*, 913–922.

Greenwald, A. G. (1980). The totalitarian ego: Fabrication and revision of personal history. *American Psychologist, 35*, 603–618.

Hammen, C. (1988). Self-cognitions, stressful events, and the prediction of depression in children of depressed mothers. *Journal of Abnormal Child Psychology, 16*, 347–360.

Harter, S. (1993). Causes and consequences of low self-esteem in children and adolescents. In R. F. Baumeister (Ed.), *Self-esteem: The puzzle of low self-regard* (pp. 87–116). New York: Plenum.

Harter, S., & Marold, D. B. (1991). A model of the determinants and mediational role of self-worth: Implications for adolescent depression and suicidal ideation. In G. Goethals & J. Strauss (Eds.), *The self: An interdisciplinary approach* (pp. 117–136). New York: Springer-Verlag.

Izard, C. E. (1977). *Human emotions*. New York: Plenum.

James, W. (1890). *The principles of psychology* (Vol. 1). New York: Holt.

Janis, I. L., & Field, P. B. (1959). Sex differences and personality factors related to persuasibility. In I. L. Janis & C. I. Hovland (Eds.), *Personality and persuasibility* (pp. 55–101). New Haven, CT: Yale University Press.

Jankowski, M. S. (1991). *Islands in the streets: Gangs and American urban society*. Berkeley: University of California Press.

Katzman, M. A., & Wolchik, S. A. (1984). Bulimia and binge eating in college women: A comparison of personality and behavioral characteristics. *Journal of Consulting and Clinical Psychology, 52*, 423–428.

Kernis, M. H., Grannemann, B. D., & Barclay, L. C. (1989). Stability and level of self-esteem as predictors of anger arousal and hostility. *Journal of Personality and Social Psychology, 56*, 1013–1023.

Kohut, H. (1971). *The analysis of the self*. New York: International Universities Press.

Leary, M. R. (1993). The interplay of private self-processes and interpersonal factors in self-presentation. In J. Suls (Ed.), *Psychological perspectives on the self* (Vol. 4, pp. 127–155). Hillsdale, NJ: Erlbaum.

Leary, M. R., & Baumeister, R. F. (in press). The nature and function of self-esteem: Sociometer theory. *Advances in Experimental Social Psychology*.

Leary, M. R., Bednarski, R., Hammon, D., & Duncan, T. (1997). Blowhards, snobs, and narcissists: Interpersonal reactions to excessive egotism. In R. M. Kowalski (Ed.), *Aversive interpersonal behaviors* (pp. 111–131). New York: Plenum.

Leary, M. R., & Downs, D. L. (1995). Interpersonal functions of the self-esteem motive: The self-esteem system as a sociometer. In M. H. Kernis (Ed.), *Efficacy, agency, and self-esteem* (pp. 123–144). New York: Plenum.

Leary, M. R., Haupt, A. L., Strausser, K. S., & Chokel, J. L. (1998). Calibrating the sociometer: The relationship between interpersonal appraisals and state self-esteem. *Journal of Personality and Social Psychology, 74*, 1290–1299.

Leary, M. R., & Kowalski, R. M. (1993). The Interaction Anxiousness Scale: Construct and criterion-related validity. *Journal of Personality Assessment, 61*, 136–146.

Leary, M. R., & Schreindorfer, L. S. (1997). Unresolved issues with terror management theory. *Psychological Inquiry, 8*, 26–29.

Leary, M. R., Schreindorfer, L. S., & Haupt, A. L. (1995). The role of self-esteem in emotional and behavioral problems: Why is low self-esteem dysfunctional? *Journal of Social and Clinical Psychology, 14*, 297–314.

Leary, M. R., Tambor, E. S., Terdal, S. J., & Downs, D. L. (1995). Self-esteem as an interpersonal monitor: The sociometer hypothesis. *Journal of Personality and Social Psychology, 68,* 518–530.

Markus, H. (1980). The self in thought and memory. In D. M. Wegner & R. R. Vallacher (Eds.), *The self in social psychology* (pp. 102–130). New York: Oxford University Press.

May, R. (1983). *The discovery of being.* New York: Norton.

McFarlin, D. B., Baumeister, R. F., & Blascovich, J. (1984). On knowing when to quit: Task failure, self-esteem, advice, and nonproductive persistence. *Journal of Personality, 52,* 138–155.

Mead, G. H. (1932). *Mind, self, and society.* Chicago: University of Chicago Press.

Mecca, A. M., Smelser, N. J., & Vasconcellos, J. (Eds.). (1989). *The social importance of self-esteem.* Berkeley: University of California Press.

Mruk, C. (1995). *Self-esteem: Research, theory, and practice.* New York: Springer.

Neese, R. M., & Lloyd, A. T. (1992). The evolution of psychodynamic mechanisms. In J. H. Barkow, L. Cosmides, & J. Tooby (Eds.), *The adapted mind* (pp. 601–626). New York: Oxford University Press.

Olweus, D. (1994). Bullying at school: Long-term outcomes for the victims and an affective school-based intervention program. In R. Huesmann (Ed.), *Aggressive behavior: Current perspectives* (pp. 97–130). New York: Plenum.

Pope, A., McHale, S., & Craighead, E. (1988). *Self-esteem enhancement with children and adolescents.* New York: Pergamon.

Pyszczynski, T., & Greenberg, J. (1983). Determinants of reduction in intended effort as a strategy for coping with anticipated failure. *Journal of Research in Personality, 17,* 412–422.

Raskin, R., Novacek, J., & Hogan, R. (1991a). Narcissism, self-esteem, and defensive self-enhancement. *Journal of Personality, 59,* 19–38.

Raskin, R., Novacek, J., & Hogan, R. (1991b). Narcissistic self-esteem management. *Journal of Personality and Social Psychology, 60,* 911–918.

Scully, D. (1990). *Understanding sexual violence: A study of convicted rapists.* New York: HarperCollins.

Shisslak, C. M., Pazda, S., & Crago, M. (1990). Body weight and bulimia as discriminators of psychological characteristics among anorexic, bulimic, and obese women. *Journal of Abnormal Psychology, 99,* 380–384.

Shrauger, J. S., & Schoeneman, T. J. (1979). Symbolic interactionist view of self-concept: Through the looking glass darkly. *Psychological Bulletin, 86,* 549–573.

Shrauger, J. S., & Sorman, P. B. (1977). Self-evaluations, initial success and failure, and improvement as determinants of persistence. *Journal of Consulting and Clinical Psychology, 45,* 784–795.

Smart, R. G., & Walsh, G. W. (1993). Predictors of depression in street youth. *Adolescence, 28,* 41–53.

Smelser, N. J. (1989). Self-esteem and social problems: An introduction. In A. M.

Mecca, N. J. Smelser, & J. Vasconcellos (Eds.), *The social importance of self-esteem* (pp. 1–23). Berkeley: University of California Press.

Snyder, C. R., Lassegard, M., & Ford, C. E. (1986). Distancing after group success and failure: Basking in reflected glory and cutting off reflected failure. *Journal of Personality and Social Psychology, 51,* 382–388.

Solomon, S., Greenberg, J., & Pyszczynski, T. (1991). A terror management theory of social behavior: The psychological functions of self-esteem and cultural worldviews. *Advances in Experimental Social Psychology, 24,* 93–159.

Sowards, B. A., Moniz, A. J., & Harris, M. J. (1991). Self-esteem and bolstering: Testing major assumptions of terror management theory. *Representative Research in Social Psychology, 19,* 95–106.

Strauss, C., Frame, C., & Forehand, R. (1987). Psychosocial impairment associated with anxiety in children. *Journal of Clinical Child Psychology, 16,* 235–239.

Taylor, S. E. (1989). *Positive illusions: Creative self-deception and the healthy mind.* New York: Basic Books.

Taylor, S. E., & Brown, J. D. (1988). Illusion and well-being: A social psychological perspective on mental health. *Psychological Bulletin, 103,* 193–210.

Taylor, S. E., & Brown, J. D. (1994). Positive illusions and well-being revisited: Separating fact from fiction. *Psychological Bulletin, 116,* 21–27.

Tennant-Clark, C. M., Fritz, J. J., & Beauvais, F. (1989). Occult participation: Its impact on adolescent development. *Adolescence, 24,* 757–772.

Tennen, H., & Affleck, G. (1993). The puzzles of self-esteem: A clinical perspective. In R. F. Baumeister (Ed.), *Self-esteem: The puzzle of low self-regard* (pp. 241–262). New York: Plenum.

Tetlock, P. E., & Manstead, A. S. R. (1985). Impression management versus intrapsychic explanations in social psychology: A useful dichotomy? *Psychological Review, 92,* 59–77.

Tice, D. M. (1991). Esteem protection or enhancement? Self-handicapping motives and attributions differ by trait self-esteem. *Journal of Personality and Social Psychology, 60,* 711–725.

Tice, D. M. (1993). The social motivations of people with low self-esteem. In R. F. Baumeister (Ed.), *Self-esteem: The puzzle of low self-regard* (pp. 37–53). New York: Plenum.

Trivers, R. (1985). *Social evolution.* Menlo Park, CA: Benjamin/Cummings.

Vaux, A. (1988). Social and emotional loneliness: The role of social and personal characteristics. *Personality and Social Psychology Bulletin, 14,* 722–734.

Vega, W. A., Zimmerman, R. S., Warheit, G. J., & Apospori, E. (1993). Risk factors for early adolescent drug use in four ethnic and racial groups. *American Journal of Public Health, 83,* 185–189.

III

INTERPERSONAL PROCESSES

8

SPEAKING THE UNSPEAKABLE: SELF-DISCLOSURE AND MENTAL HEALTH

ROBIN M. KOWALSKI

Secrets are a burden. That's the reason we are so anxious to have somebody help us carry them. (McKenzie, 1980, p. 462)

Recall for a moment some of the most bizarre, most fearful, and most disturbing thoughts you have ever had. Some of these thoughts may have involved killing someone or running down people on the highway. Others may have focused on sexual fantasies or unusual sexual practices (Roberts, 1995). Think also about some of the most embarrassing or the most troubling events that you have experienced. These may range from mildly discomforting occurrences, such as giving a presentation with one's zipper down, to truly traumatic experiences, such as being molested by a family member. Most people are so appalled by such thoughts or events that they would never dream of sharing them with others. Indeed, most people perceive these thoughts and behaviors as "unspeakable acts." But should they be regarded as truly unspeakable? In spite of the risks associated with revealing heinous thoughts or actions to others, are there any benefits to be gained from such revelations? Are there costs associated with the failure to reveal these thoughts or behaviors to others? What are the interpersonal implications of such disclosures?

The purpose of this chapter is to examine some of the positive and

225

negative consequences of self-disclosure as well as the variables that influence decisions to self-disclose. Although self-disclosures can cover a range of topics, this chapter focuses primarily on disclosures of personally distressing information. These types of self-disclosures are most likely to have both positive and negative consequences associated with them, and decisions surrounding their disclosure are typically the most difficult.

Self-disclosure is a topic important to both social psychologists and clinicians. From the perspective of social psychology, self-disclosure is a fundamental interpersonal process. According to Yalom (1985),

> self-disclosure is always an interpersonal act. What is important is not that one discloses oneself but that one discloses something important in the context of a relationship to others. . . . [E]ven more important than the actual unburdening of oneself is the fact that disclosure results in a deeper, richer, and more complex relationship with others. (p. 129)

From the perspective of clinical and counseling psychology, self-disclosure is important because it is related to well-being, therapy and counseling are essentially exercises in self-disclosure, and many clients seek psychotherapy because of problems relating to self-disclosure in their relationships (Berg & Derlega, 1987).

OVERVIEW OF SELF-DISCLOSURE

Self-disclosure involves revealing personal information about oneself to others (Jourard, 1971). People self-disclose for both interpersonal and intrapsychic reasons—to establish intimacy and relationships with others, to achieve catharsis, and to gain social comparison information, to name a few (Stiles, 1995). People disclose about a large variety of personally relevant topics, ranging from the mundane and superficial to the highly intimate and personal. Whereas some people freely reveal intimate details about themselves, others are more inclined to conceal such information (Larson & Chastain, 1990). Some individuals seem indiscriminate in selecting an audience for their self-disclosures, whereas others are very selective in choosing the people to whom they self-disclose.

According to Carpenter (1987), the likelihood of self-disclosure increases when three conditions are met: (a) The person is motivated to self-disclose, (b) there is an opportunity to self-disclose, and (c) the discloser has the skill or "relational competence" to self-disclose. Thus, people who have experienced traumatic events that they want to discuss with another person and who find a willing and supportive listener to whom they can communicate in an effective and socially skilled manner will likely self-disclose. In addition to clarifying when people are likely to self-disclose, however, this model highlights those instances in which self-disclosure is unlikely to occur. Some people (i.e., inhibitors or repressors; Baldwin, 1974; Carroll, 1972) are not motivated to self-disclose. Thus, even with the requisite skills and opportunities, they are unlikely to self-disclose. Other people are very motivated to discuss personal information about themselves, but they have insufficient opportunities to do so. For example, people in the armed services may believe that they should always project a stoic image and, thus, refrain from disclosing their fears, weaknesses, or personal problems. Or people may simply lack a social support network, leaving them no one with whom to discuss troubling or upsetting thoughts or events. Finally, people may be motivated to disclose and have the opportunity to disclose, but they perceive that they lack the skills needed for effective self-disclosure. This would include people who are unassertive or socially anxious (Leary & Kowalski, 1995).

Thus, according to Carpenter (1987), an individual who is motivated to self-disclose, has the opportunity to do so, and possesses the requisite social skills is prone to self-disclose. However, this model does not completely address some of the paradoxical interactive effects of the three precursors to self-disclosure. For example, the greater the distress an individual experiences, the higher his or her self-reported need to self-disclose (Pennebaker, 1993; Rimé, 1995; Stiles, 1987). However, the higher the person's need to self-disclose, the fewer opportunities he or she may have to self-disclose because potential confidants may avoid or even reject people who disclose traumatic or upsetting events.

An individual who is motivated to self-disclose, sees a potential opportunity for disclosure, and feels that he or she has the skills to self-disclose does so only after an assessment of the positive and negative consequences associated with such a disclosure. As seen later in this chapter, revealing traumatic events to others can lead to improved physical and psychological health for the discloser. Through self-disclosure, people can establish relationships with others, develop trust, acquire social comparison information, and develop their own identity (Fishbein & Laird, 1979; Hymer, 1982, 1988). However, disclosing personal problems to others can have negative consequences as well, perhaps the most serious of which is rejection. The fear of being rejected may be so strong that some individuals avoid revealing anything negative to other people (Coates & Winston, 1987).

POSITIVE CONSEQUENCES OF SELF-DISCLOSURE

Few people have failed to experience the cathartic release associated with self-disclosure, particularly disclosures of troubling thoughts or events. As discussed later, the catharsis associated with self-disclosures can have beneficial physical and psychological consequences. In addition, self-disclosure allows people to gain insight into events, to receive validation for their thoughts and feelings, and to establish meaningful relationships with others.

Physical and Psychological Well-Being

The idea that confession is good for the soul has a long history (Ellenberger, 1966; Georges, 1995). In the Bible (New International Version, 1978), Proverbs 28:13 states that "he who conceals his sin does not prosper but whoever confesses and renounces them finds mercy." Publilius Syrus (cited in Bartlett, 1901) stated that "confession of our faults is the next thing to innocence" (p. 625).

Research over the past decade shows that confession is not only good for the soul but also for a person's physical and psychological health (Hymer, 1988; Jourard, 1971; Kelly & McKillop, 1996; Larson & Chastain, 1990; Pennebaker, 1990, 1995; Pennebaker & Beall, 1986; Pennebaker & O'Heeron, 1984). For example, university students who disclosed distressing or traumatic experiences in a laboratory setting subsequently visited the university health center less frequently in the 6 months following the disclosure than those who did not disclose such experiences (Pennebaker & Beall, 1986). Similarly, the disclosure of negatively valenced information in psychosocial support groups is related to longer survival rates among women with advanced-stage breast cancer (Spiegel, Bloom, Kraemer, & Gottheil, 1989; Spiegel & Kato, 1996). Likewise, rheumatoid arthritis patients who talked about stressful life events demonstrated improved psychological health, relative to those in a control group (Kelley, Lumley, & Leisen, 1997). Such effects may be due, in part, to the fact that disclosure enhances immunological functioning (Pennebaker, Kiecolt-Glaser, & Glaser, 1988; Petrie, Booth, Pennebaker, Davison, & Thomas, 1995).

The disclosure of troubling or upsetting thoughts or events has also been linked to increases in positive affect and decreases in negative affect (Pennebaker, Colder, & Sharp, 1990), stemming in some instances from a reduction in the experience of negative emotions such as shame and guilt (Kelly & McKillop, 1996). Confession has also been shown to result in better autonomic functioning immediately following the disclosure (Pennebaker, Hughes, & O'Heeron, 1987). This relationship between disclosure and a person's physical and psychological health is so strong that one of the leading researchers in this area, James Pennebaker (1985), stated that "the act of not disclosing or confiding the event with another may be even more damaging than having experienced the event per se" (p. 82).

People's attempts to inhibit distressing thoughts or feelings require physiological work. The more traumatic or distressing the event, the greater the need to talk about the event and, thus, the greater work required to inhibit revealing or discussing it with others (Pennebaker, 1993; Rimé, 1995; Stiles, 1987, 1995; Stiles, Shuster, & Harrigan, 1992). These effortful attempts to actively suppress one's thoughts can, over time, result in impaired immune functioning (Petrie, Booth, & Davison, 1995).

Other researchers have suggested, however, that it is not the act of inhibition per se that leads to negative physical and psychological effects. Instead, these negative health effects follow from an individual's inability to avoid thinking about a traumatic event. Specifically, inhibitors who continued to perseverate over traumatic events experienced more adverse health effects than both disclosers and inhibitors who did not ruminate about the trauma (Ogden & Von Sturmer, 1984).

Unfortunately, inhibition and rumination frequently are directly linked, so that the more an individual attempts to inhibit thoughts about the distressing event, the more salient those thoughts become—a phenomenon referred to as the *hyperaccessibility of suppressed information* (Erber & Wegner, 1996; Wegner & Erber, 1992). For people to be sure that they do not reveal the distressing information, they must remember the very information that they are trying to suppress: "The secret must be remembered, or it might be told. And the secret cannot be thought about or it might be leaked" (Wegner, Lane, & Dimitri, 1994, p. 288; see also Wegner & Lane, 1995). As a result, efforts at thought suppression increase the cognitive availability of the undesired thought.

The degree to which suppressed thoughts become hyperaccessible depends on the emotion attached to the thoughts. Emotionally charged events exhibit this effect more than less emotionally charged events (Wegner, Shortt, Blake, & Page, 1990). The greater the distress or emotion experienced, the higher the likelihood of intrusive thoughts (Rimé, 1995). Rimé, Mesquita, Philippot, and Boca (1991) found that the intensity of emotional distress correlated positively ($r = .44$) with the frequency of intrusive thoughts. They also found a correlation of .49 between the intensity of the emotional experience and the amount of social sharing. Thus, people who have experienced traumatic events are likely to ruminate about the events, resulting in adverse health effects unless the traumas are disclosed to others.

In discussing the health consequences of self-disclosure, four qualifications are in order. First, the most significant physical and psychological benefits of self-disclosure are experienced not immediately but rather after the individual has experienced heightened negative affect from the disclosure itself (Kelley et al., 1997; Kowalski, Cantrell, & VanHout, 1995; Pennebaker & Beall, 1986). One would expect that in the recollection and disclosure of traumatic events, negatively valenced memories would be resurrected and the accompanying negative affect experienced. However, by talking about the feelings and emotions surrounding the experience, the negative affectivity subsides over time and the longer term health benefits of the disclosure become evident.

Second, the health benefits of self-disclosure are most evident following revelations of negatively valenced personal information that one has not previously disclosed. People who regularly self-disclose or who disclose about neutral or positive topics do not show significant changes in physical or psychological health.

Third, more disclosure is not necessarily better. Jourard (1971) noted that there was a curvilinear relationship between self-disclosure and mental health. Too little or too much disclosure compromises psychological adjustment. Too little self-disclosure deprives an individual of potentially validating social comparison information (Yalom, 1985). Withholding information from others also compromises an individual's ability to form enduring, long-term relationships. Excessive disclosure, however, is equally maladaptive. People who disclose too much information induce anxiety and apprehension in others, leading them to reject the discloser (Yalom, 1985).

Fourth, the affective and health consequences associated with self-disclosure appear to vary as a function of the nature of the disclosure as opposed to simply the act of disclosing (Rimé, 1995). Simply disclosing the facts surrounding a traumatic event does little for an individual's psychological health. Instead, the important element appears to be disclosing the emotions that accompany recollections of the event (Pennebaker, 1988). Pennebaker and Beall (1986) had university students write about either a traumatic life event or a trivial event for 4 consecutive days. Among students assigned to write about a traumatic event, a third were assigned to write about only the facts surrounding the event, a third to write about their feelings regarding the event, and a third to write about both the facts and emotions surrounding the trauma. Students who wrote about the emotions or about the emotions and the facts surrounding the trauma experienced fewer illnesses and reported better overall health than the students in the other experimental condition.

Finding Meaning and Insight

People often find that simply talking aloud about an issue helps them come to terms with that issue and to find a meaningful resolution to something that is troubling or upsetting (Kelly & McKillop, 1996). Pennebaker (1988) referred to this process as finding meaning and assimilation. By disclosing intimate information to others, people can gain insight into and meaning for the events that have transpired. Once people begin translating their experiences into words, either verbal or written, they often come to realize that the event was not as traumatic, shameful, or distressing as they originally thought. Conversely, the awareness that one is intentionally withholding information from others may lead one to perceive the content of the information more negatively than one did previously (Derlega, Metts, Petronio, & Margulis, 1993; Fishbein & Laird, 1979; Kelly, Mc-Killop, & Neimeyer, 1991; McKillop, Berzonsky, & Schlenker, 1992; Schlenker & Trudeau, 1990).

Validation

"Many patients enter therapy with the disquieting thought that they are unique in their wretchedness, that they alone have certain frightening or unacceptable problems, thoughts, impulses, and fantasies" (Yalom, 1985, p. 7). In light of this, one benefit of speaking the unspeakable is that people may find that others have thought similar things or experienced similar events (Derlega & Grzelak, 1979; Roberts, 1995). Frequently responses to self-disclosures provide the discloser with validation for his or her feelings. "The sharing of personal thoughts and feelings is a form of social comparison that fosters self-exploration, self-clarification, and open communication in relationships" (Leaper, Carson, Baker, Holliday, & Myers, 1995, p. 387). By the same token, the failure to disclose or active concealment deprives people of social comparison information that may prove validating and, thus, have effects on the individual's self-esteem (Larson & Chastain, 1990; Yalom, 1985).

Development of Personal Relationships

When used in moderation, self-disclosure is instrumental in the development of close relationships (Goodstein & Reinecker, 1974; Last & Aharoni-Etzioni, 1995). Following a fairly predictable sequence, one individual discloses to another. The listener then responds to the self-disclosure, followed by a disclosure of his or her own (Yalom, 1985). Through this process of social penetration (Altman & Taylor, 1973), the individuals level the intimacy playing field and a relationship between the two people develops. Indeed, the act of disclosure conveys something about the nature of the relationship between two people. People confide in those whom they like, and they come to like those in whom they confide (Collins & Miller, 1994; Pennebaker, 1988).

Through the development of these personal relationships and the ability to freely disclose to others, people gain access to social support. An abundance of evidence supports the idea that social support helps people cope with stressful life events (see Rhodes & Lakey, this volume, chapter 10). However, according to Derlega (1988),

> the effects of talking about one's feelings may depend on its timing— whether it occurs before or after the stressful event. Subjects who talk

with their friend about their feelings before the stressful event may magnify their negative feelings whereas those who talk about their feelings after the stressful event may undergo a cathartic experience represented by ventilating and dissipating their negative feelings. (p. 29)

Thus, self-disclosure may be beneficial after but not before a stressful event.

Cultural norms dictate the frequency and content of self-disclosures in developing relationships. Typically, cultural norms related to self-disclosure are tied to sex roles, such that it is more socially acceptable for women than men to self-disclose (Fitzpatrick, 1987). However, once relationships and friendships have developed, these norms may change. For example, men who seldom disclose intimate details to other men or women outside the context of their primary relationship may be very expressive with their intimate partner (Reis, Senchak, & Soloman, 1985). With established relationships, the important issue may not be self-disclosure per se but rather knowing that one could self-disclose to one's friend or romantic partner if needed. Thus, it is the potential for self-disclosure that may be important to relational quality and well-being.

NEGATIVE CONSEQUENCES OF SELF-DISCLOSURE

In spite of its many positive consequences, self-disclosure has risks associated with it. Revelations of personal information can result in negative effects for both the discloser and the listener.

Interpersonal Costs

Typically, the thoughts or feelings that people are most reluctant to disclose—the thoughts or feelings that seem to be truly unspeakable—are those that are negative (Regan & Hill, 1992), are perceived to be humiliating or embarrassing, or have serious implications, such as legal consequences. Self-disclosures of negative, traumatic, or embarrassing thoughts or events are most likely to result in rejection or ostracism (Coates, Wortman, & Abbey, 1979; Harber & Pennebaker, 1992). Studies of gay men (Weinberg, 1983) and lesbians (Moses, 1978) show that one of the primary reasons these people have not disclosed their sexual orientation is due to their concerns with the reactions of others and, consequently, the fear of rejection (Franke & Leary, 1991). Such concerns as these are reinforced by mandates such as the military's "don't ask, don't tell" policy, which actively discourages any personal revelations of homosexuality and imposes severe penalties for such disclosures.

Depending on the content of the disclosure, people's concerns of being rejected because of those disclosures are often well founded. For example, depressed individuals frequently find themselves rejected or distanced from others (Gurtman, 1986). Similarly, victims of serious illness, such as cancer, often find that members of their social network are suddenly too busy to visit them in the hospital (Dunkel-Schetter, 1984). Even if the disclosers do not experience outright rejection, they may perceive a more indirect rejection in the form of a dismissal by a listener who is a little too quick to offer unsolicited advice or to change the subject to something less threatening (Kelly & McKillop, 1996; Pennebaker, 1993). After all, people typically are far more interested in talking about their own problems or issues than in hearing someone else discuss his or hers. The discloser subsequently perceives that others are really not that interested in the events that have happened.

An additional factor that accounts for people's reluctance to disclose negative information is that they are concerned that disclosing troubling or negatively valenced information may be burdensome to the listener. In their study of Holocaust survivors, Pennebaker, Barger, and Tiebout (1989) found that one of the primary reasons few of the survivors had disclosed their experiences was because they did not want to upset other people. Apparently, these expectations were well grounded. In a subsequent study, Shortt and Pennebaker (1992) had college students watch videotapes of Holocaust survivors as they disclosed their experiences. Although disclosure reduced the skin conductance levels of the disclosers, the skin conductance levels of the student listeners increased. Hearing about another's traumas may jeopardize listeners' illusions of invulnerability and leave them feeling helpless in their attempts to respond to the individual in crisis (Silver, Wortman, & Crofton, 1990). Thus, because of the physical and psychological distress levied on the listener, people who have experienced traumatic events "find that their urge to confide is not matched by confidants' willingness to listen. As bearers of disturbing thoughts and negative emotions, victims themselves become the objects of suppression" (Harber & Pennebaker, 1992, p. 366).

This "dilemma of distress disclosure" is a cruel irony of self-disclosure (Coates & Winston, 1987; Silver et al., 1990). To reveal their distress is to risk alienating others and, thus, to experience rejection. Yet to act as if one is coping well is to fail to let others know of one's need for social support. The best resolution is to reveal one's distress to others but to give the appearance that one is taking action to cope with the problem (Silver et al., 1990).

Given the concerns of being rejected or of having one's listeners experience negative physical and psychological effects, a psychotherapist should be a "godsend" for people who have experienced traumatic or otherwise negative events. They can pay money to a professional who is unlikely to reject them and trained to adopt a detached emotional stance, so they are unlikely to be adversely affected by information others reveal to them. However, clients oftentimes do not see the therapist as quite the "savior" that one might expect. Having been rejected by others for revealing certain personal facts, clients may fear similar rejection by their therapists (C. E. Hill, Thompson, Cogar, & Denman, 1993; Kelly & McKillop, 1996; Regan & Hill, 1992).

In addition to their concerns with interpersonal rejection, people may also wonder what others will do with the information that they disclosed. Most people have experienced apprehension after disclosing some intimate detail about their life to another person. As soon as certain revelations are made, people may wonder who else will find out, whether the listener will use the information against them, or use the information to negatively influence others' perceptions of them. Kelvin (1977) noted that "the disclosure of areas of privacy reveals the underlying causes and motives of the individual's behavior; this potentially gives those to whom they are disclosed power over him; and in doing so, disclosures make him vulnerable to exploitation" (p. 355).

Creating Undesired Impressions

People may also be reluctant to disclose personal information because they are uncertain of how the disclosure will affect other people's impressions of them (Fishbein & Laird, 1979). The magnitude of these impression-relevant concerns was demonstrated in a study of the content of people's secrets. Twelve percent of the secrets (and the fourth most common type of secret) involved *masking*, projecting a public image that differed from one's private reality (Norton, Feldman, & Tafoya, 1974). For example, an individual with a history of mental or physical illness may be reluctant to disclose such information because of concerns with the impressions that others may form of him or her. Few would doubt that others' impressions of the individual would be changed in some way.

Should the individual choose not to disclose, however, a self-presentational predicament may arise. If others find out that the individual has withheld information, they may view the individual negatively. Either he or she must have done something terrible (if he or she is so reluctant to reveal it) or else the person was simply deceitful. In this sense, the failure to disclose potentially creates a more negative impression than the content of the disclosure itself (Fishbein & Laird, 1979).

Changes in Self-Perception

The literature is replete with examples of how one's self-presentations can produce corresponding changes in one's self-view (Kelly et al., 1991; Kowalski & Leary, 1990; Leary, 1995; Schlenker & Trudeau, 1990). To the degree that this is true, the self-presentations that accompany a person's self-disclosures could exert considerable impact on his or her self-perceptions. Thus, in an attempt to elicit social support from others, if people disclose their distress and the fact that they are not coping well with the situation, they may come to see themselves as, in fact, coping more poorly than they really are.

Affect Regulation

The affective benefits that follow from most self-disclosures were discussed above, and few people would question the feeling of relief that follows from the disclosure of distressing information. Criminals who had confessed their crimes while connected to polygraph machines showed relaxed physiological responses, even though they would assuredly be sent to prison (Pennebaker, 1990). People who had revealed their infidelity to their partners also reported feeling relieved (Kelly & McKillop, 1996).

Part of this relief follows from simply making the disclosure. People's fear that their secret may be "leaked out" is obviously eliminated after the secret is revealed. In addition, the mental anguish people experience as they struggle with the pros and cons of revealing certain information is reduced.

However, in spite of the affective benefits, dealing with the consequences of the disclosure may be very costly, particularly in terms of feelings of regret that may be experienced. Especially when the implications of the disclosure are serious, such as a marriage break up, the sense of relief may be followed by uncertainty over whether revealing the secret was the correct thing to do.

Boundary Regulation

Recently, my 2-year-old niece was asked not to tell her grandmother about a surprise birthday cake. Of course, as soon as she saw her grandmother, she told her about the cake. To her credit, however, she whispered the information to her grandmother, perhaps to maintain the secret from everyone else. Like all other children, my niece is learning personal boundaries. As the old saying "out of the mouths of babes" suggests, most children tell it like it is and disclose exactly what they are thinking or feeling at the moment, even when that information might best be left untold. Of course, some adults, particularly when they are told particularly juicy gossip, seem unable to contain themselves any better than my niece. Typically, with maturation, children learn when to keep secrets and when they may tell them. They also learn that not disclosing allows people to maintain their personal boundaries (Altman, 1975; Derlega et al., 1993; Kelly & McKillop, 1996). This process of boundary regulation is one reason why therapists reveal little about themselves during sessions. Although there is some evidence that self-disclosure on the part of the therapist is beneficial in eliciting client self-disclosure (Beutler, Crago, & Arizmendi, 1986; May & Thompson, 1973), not revealing intimate details about themselves allows therapists to maintain a professional boundary between themselves and their clients.

On a related note, keeping at least some information secret from others allows for individuation (Last & Aharoni-Etzioni, 1995) and for feelings of uniqueness from others. If someone knows everything about you, there is no mystery or intrigue surrounding your interactions. To the degree that people know something that others do not, they might also feel a sense of power over the other person.

Ethical Dilemmas in Self-Disclosure

In deciding whether to disclose intimate information about themselves or about others, people frequently confront ethical dilemmas. For individuals such as psychotherapists, who may be confronted with breaching the confidentiality of their clients, the resolution to the ethical dilemma is clear in most cases. In talking about their cases with supervisors or other mental health professionals, therapists are trained not to disclose any information that would reveal the identity of their client. Of course, in instances in which the client reveals participation in illegal activities, such as child abuse, the therapist is legally obligated to report the information to the appropriate authorities.

In group therapy settings, group members are instructed to maintain the confidentiality of other group members. However, they have no professional obligation to do so, hence the participants cannot be sure that what they disclose in group therapy will not find its way outside the therapy setting. A study of confidentiality dilemmas in group therapy involving chemically dependent physicians revealed that some group members did break the confidences of other group members (Roback, Moore, Waterhouse, & Martin, 1996). When these breaches of confidentiality were uncovered, the physicians whose identities had been revealed outside of the group therapy setting reported a need for litigation to deal with such infractions.

Perhaps even more problematic are situations in which information about a patient is disclosed to a physician or therapist by a family member who requests that the information remain confidential (Burnam, 1991; Newman, 1993). To whom is the practitioner obligated? If the information would be instrumental in the treatment of the patient, what obligation does the practitioner have to maintain the confidences of the family member? Are practitioners obligated to make full disclosures to their patients?

Outside the therapeutic setting, how and when to ethically self-disclose is equally unclear. In choosing to disclose personal information about themselves, people often find themselves in a position of unwittingly disclosing information about others that those individuals might have chosen not to reveal (Bok, 1982). Imagine the difficulty of discussing your frustration regarding your partner's sexual difficulties with a mutual friend who will have subsequent interactions with your partner. The discloser in such a situation finds himself or herself caught between the potential benefits to be gained from personal revelation and the costs associated with betraying the confidences of another. To not disclose, he or she sacrifices personal gains to be obtained from the disclosure. To disclose, however, places the individual in a state of cognitive dissonance associated with the promise not to break confidentiality and a subsequent betrayal. For example, imagine a child who has a family member arrested for perpetrating incest (Saffer, Sansone, & Gentry, 1979). By opening up about the experience of sexual abuse, he or she implicated a family member who almost certainly has threatened the child if he or she breaks the confidence.

Another ethical dilemma concerns when and how to disclose to another person information that he or she may find personally troubling. For example, when do you tell family members that you have a terminal illness? The timing of such revelations may have a substantial impact on the reactions of those to whom one discloses and, subsequently, on oneself. If one discloses information at an inopportune time, others are likely to react negatively. These negative reactions may then increase the likelihood that the discloser will subsequently withhold similar revelations.

VARIABLES INFLUENCING SELF-DISCLOSURE

A number of situational and dispositional variables influence an individual's willingness to self-disclose and the positive and negative consequences of that self-disclosure. Among these are the content of the disclosure, the target of the disclosure, the nature of the situation, cultural influences, and individual differences in self-disclosure.

Content of the Disclosure

People's self-disclosures can range from revelations of mundane, superficial aspects of themselves to much more significant, highly intimate details. The self-disclosures can also range from revelations of pleasant feelings one experienced or positive events that occurred to disclosures of unspeakable acts or topics that are socially undesirable. Of course, the nature of the information disclosed determines not only the person's willingness to disclose but also the rewards and costs associated with the disclosure. Disclosures of one's deepest and most troubling secrets, although perhaps psychologically beneficial to the discloser, carry significant risks in terms of jeopardizing one's interpersonal relationships.

Derlega et al. (1993) distinguished between private information and secrets (see also Karpel, 1980; Schwartz, 1984); private information

> refers to material that others do not normally know about us (e.g., opinions, beliefs, and feelings about ourselves, social issues, or relationships with others) but that we might be willing to disclose based on others' need to know. . . . Secrets, however, refer to content that we actively withhold and conceal from others. "Secret" information might be disclosed under unusual conditions, but it often is concealed because the material is considered to be too threatening or shameful to divulge . . . or the disclosure of the secret would cause pain to oneself or others. (p. 74)

This distinction between private information and secrets raises the question of whether there is a psychological difference between disclosing something you are motivated to conceal and disclosing something that you are not motivated to hide but simply have not mentioned. The literature suggests that there is a difference. Someone who is motivated to hide information is more likely to ruminate about the secret and would be more concerned about the secret leaking out than someone who simply has not thought to mention some personal fact about himself or herself. There is also a difference in the costs associated with revealing secrets that one is motivated to inhibit versus those one just has not revealed. Information that one has actively inhibited almost certainly has a more negative valence than information that one has simply omitted revealing to others. Thus, it is more likely to place a burden on the listener or to cause the listener to form negative impressions of the discloser. So qualitatively different kinds of information likely produce qualitatively different reactions in the person to whom the information is revealed.

It is interesting to note that interpretations and evaluations of the content of a disclosure may vary between the discloser and the listener. What may appear objectively to a listener as a fairly superficial self-disclosure may subjectively be of significant import to the individual who has never disclosed this information before (Yalom, 1985). For example, someone who finally opens up about the anxiety he or she experiences when speaking in public may be met with only a cursory acknowledgement by a listener who fails to appreciate the enormity of the problem to the discloser.

Target of the Disclosure

Most people are not indiscriminately self-disclosing (Goodstein & Reinecker, 1974). Instead, people tend to select as confidants people who are discrete (able to be trusted not to reveal the secret to others), nonjudgmental, and have the ability to offer new insights into the problem (Kelly & McKillop, 1996). People are also more likely to disclose to those whom they like (Collins & Miller, 1994; Goodstein & Reinecker, 1974) and who have provided them with favorable reactions to disclosures in the past. Thus, people self-disclose to individuals who have not punished their disclosures in the past or who have little power to punish the discloser. Perhaps this is why people so readily self-disclose to mental health professionals. According to Towbin (1978, as cited in Larson & Chastain, 1990), "the therapist's role as confidant—someone to whom clients can disclose their most private thoughts, feelings, and behaviors—is a hallmark of the therapeutic relationship" (pp. 441–442).

People's perceptions of another's suitability as a confidant and the confidant's reactions to their self-disclosures are determined in part by the nature of the relationship between the discloser and the confidant. People typically disclose to those with whom they are more intimate, although some people are more comfortable revealing intimate details about themselves to total strangers—the "stranger on the bus" phenomenon (Goodstein & Reinecker, 1974). As people's perception of the psychological closeness to another person waxes and wanes, so too should the nature of their self-disclosures to that other person.

Not surprisingly, gender of both the self-discloser and the confidant is also an important determinant of the nature and type of self-disclosure. In a meta-analysis of 205 research studies, women tended to disclose more frequently than men, although the effect size was small ($d = .18$; Dindia & Allen, 1992). However, situational factors, such as the gender of the listener and the content of the disclosure, influence these gender effects (C. T. Hill & Stull, 1987). For example, in the Dindia and Allen meta-analysis, the effect size was stronger if the listener was female ($d = .35$) than if the listener was male ($d = .00$). Gender stereotypes suggest that women are better listeners than men and, thus, more consistently elicit self-disclosures from others (Pegalis, Shaffer, Bazzini, & Greenier, 1994). Similarly, social norms suggest that intimate self-disclosures from women are more acceptable than similar self-disclosures from men (Collins & Miller, 1994; Pegalis et al., 1994).

However, situational variables may interact with the gender of the discloser to determine when men or women disclose about themselves. Specifically, on the one hand, when expressivity is emphasized, women would be expected to disclose more than men to same-sex others. On the other hand, when instrumentality is emphasized, men may disclose more than women to same-sex others. It is interesting to note that men and women may differ in the focus of their self-disclosure selectivity. Whereas men tend to be more vigilant in the content of their self-disclosures, women more closely monitor their target (West, 1970). Last and Aharoni-Etzioni (1995), in their analysis of the secrets of third, fifth, and seventh graders, found that boys more than girls disclosed secrets relating to possessions and moral transgressions. Girls disclosed more than boys about secrets relating to their family.

Nature of the Situation

Some situations, such as psychotherapy, lend themselves to open self-disclosure from one person to another. However, this same situation forces an effective therapist to inhibit reciprocally self-disclosing and to maintain some psychological distance from the client. Furthermore, as already discussed, the nature of the therapeutic setting requires that mental health professionals maintain the confidentiality of their clients. But what do therapists do when they learn horrifying information about their clients, which they feel the need to disclose to others? Of course the answer to that question is that they can discuss the nature of the information while still maintaining the confidentiality of the client. Nevertheless, only certain situations are conducive to the disclosure of such information. In a study of hospital complaint representatives, the way in which the majority of the representatives handled the burden of listening to patient complaints all day was to discuss the patients' problematic situations with family members or friends (Kowalski & Brendle, 1996).

Normative constraints in particular social settings also regulate the nature of self-disclosures in such situations. For example, therapists and other professionals who feel that someone should just "get a grip" can hardly disclose that feeling to their client. Similarly, in everyday interactions, one occasionally withholds self-disclosures that one believes would hurt a person's feelings.

Cultural Influences

My discussion thus far focused primarily on Westernized views of the relationship between self-disclosure and mental health. To adopt a strictly Westernized perspective, however, is to ignore important cultural elements that may moderate the relationship between disclosure and mental health. Just as there are individual differences in willingness to disclose and in the effects of disclosure on physical and psychological health, similarly cross-cultural variations would be expected. Indeed, Simmel (1950) stated that "secrets are the sociological expression of what is conceived of as moral badness" (p. 334). In an analysis of culture and self-disclosure, Wellenkamp (1995) suggested that there are cross-cultural variations in "the need for self-disclosure, and in the forms and effectiveness of disclosure" (p. 306). Specifically, she stated that some cultures provide outlets other than self-disclosure that allow people to cognitively assign meaning to emotionally laden events. As an example, she cited the Toraja, who in the event of a death in which the body is not recovered, create a substitute body, which is then treated as if it were the actual body.

On a related note, privacy regulation is not a universal phenomenon (Wellenkamp, 1995). Because of cultural practices and the nature of housing in some cultures, attempts to maintain privacy are futile. Thus, people in these cultures are less likely to experience the ill effects associated with cognitive inhibition and rumination because they have few secrets from others.

In addition, in cultures characterized by traditional values and strong family loyalty, concerns with hurting family members or being rejected by those individuals may inhibit people from revealing intimate or distressing information about themselves. For example, among Hispanics, the happiness and cohesiveness of the family is of central importance. Thus, Hispanic gay men are less inclined to reveal their HIV status to family members, perhaps to the detriment of their own mental health (Szapocznik, 1995; see also Mason, Marks, Simoni, Ruiz, & Richardson, 1995). This suggests that cultural attitudes toward self-disclosure are likely to influence the effectiveness of the disclosure on physical and psychological health (Wellenkamp, 1995).

Individual Differences in Self-Disclosure

A number of different individual difference variables moderate the frequency of and the effects of self-disclosure. To discuss all of these personality variables is beyond the scope of this chapter. However, a couple of exemplars are mentioned. For example, people high in *private self-consciousness* (i.e., people who think a great deal about private aspects of themselves) are expected to disclose more both because they are more attuned to their internal states and because they may have a higher need to self-disclose relative to people low in private self-consciousness (Davis & Franzoi, 1987).

Similarly, relative to low self-monitors, *high self-monitors* (i.e., people who are sensitive to the ways in which they are perceived by others and, thus, carefully regulate their public behaviors) appear more effective in resolving the dilemma of distress disclosure. Because of their sensitivity to the reactions of other people, high self-monitors are more strategic in selecting an audience for their self-disclosures and are more attuned to the reactions of those audience members to disclosures, particularly revelations of negatively valenced information (Coates & Winston, 1987).

CONCLUSION

Lying at the heart of both social and clinical psychology, self-disclosure pervades both everyday and therapeutic interactions. It is the means through which people develop relationships with friends, romantic partners, and in some instances counselors and psychotherapists. Through one's self-disclosures, one may experience psychological and physical well-being, find meaning in negative or traumatic events, and gain social comparison information. However, the self-disclosure picture is not entirely positive. Negative consequences, such as interpersonal rejection, may follow from disclosures that are burdensome to the listener.

Inappropriate or poorly timed self-disclosures may lead to the creation of undesired impressions and, subsequently, changes in how the discloser views himself or herself. In addition, depending on the nature of the situation, including the relationship among the participants, ethical dilemmas may be involved in self-disclosures. Most of these dilemmas center around the questions of when, to whom, about whom, and how often to disclose. Answers to these questions reveal the complexity of self-disclosure as a process on which every social interaction hinges.

REFERENCES

Altman, I. (1975). *The environment and social behavior: Privacy, personal space, territory, and crowding.* Monterey, CA: Brooks/Cole.

Altman, I., & Taylor, D. A. (1973). *Social penetration.* New York: Holt, Rinehart, & Winston.

Baldwin, B. A. (1974). Self-disclosure and expectations for psychotherapy in repressors and sensitizers. *Journal of Counseling Psychology, 21,* 455–456.

Bartlett, J. (1901). *Familiar quotations* (9th ed.). Boston: Little, Brown.

Berg, J. H., & Derlega, V. J. (1987). Themes in the study of self-disclosure. In V. J. Derlega & J. H. Berg (Eds.), *Self-disclosure: Theory, research, and therapy* (pp. 1–8). New York: Plenum.

Beutler, L. E., Crago, M., & Arizmendi, T. G. (1986). Therapist variables in psychotherapy process and outcome. In S. L. Garfield & A. E. Bergin (Eds.), *Handbook of psychotherapy and behavior change* (3rd ed., pp. 257–310). New York: Wiley.

Bok, S. (1982). *Secrets: On the ethics of concealment and revelation.* New York: Pantheon Books.

Burnam, J. F. (1991). Sounding board: Secrets about patients. *New England Journal of Medicine, 324,* 1130–1133.

Carpenter, B. N. (1987). The relationship between psychopathology and self-disclosure: An interference/competence model. In V. J. Derlega & J. H. Berg (Eds.), *Self-disclosure: Theory, research, and therapy* (pp. 203–228). New York: Plenum.

Carroll, D. (1972). Repression–sensitization and the verbal elaboration of experience. *Journal of Consulting and Clinical Psychology, 38,* 147.

Coates, D., & Winston, T. (1987). The dilemma of distress disclosure. In V. J. Derlega & J. H. Berg (Eds.), *Self-disclosure: Theory, research, and therapy* (pp. 229–256). New York: Plenum.

Coates, D., Wortman, C. B., & Abbey, A. (1979). Reactions to victims. In I. H. Frieze, D. Bar-Tal, & J. S. Carroll (Eds.), *New approaches to social problems* (pp. 21–52). San Francisco: Jossey-Bass.

Collins, N. L., & Miller, L. C. (1994). Self-disclosure and liking: A meta-analytic review. *Psychological Bulletin, 116,* 457–475.

Davis, M. H., & Franzoi, S. L. (1987). Private self-consciousness and self-disclosure. In V. J. Derlega & J. H. Berg (Eds.), *Self-disclosure: Theory, research, and therapy* (pp. 59–80). New York: Plenum.

Derlega, V. J. (1988). Self-disclosure: Inside or outside the mainstream of social psychological research? *Journal of Social Behavior and Personality, 3,* 27–34.

Derlega, V. J., & Grzelak, J. (1979). Appropriateness of self-disclosure. In G. Cherlune (Ed.), *Self-disclosure: Origins, patterns, and implications of openness in interpersonal relationships* (pp. 151–176). San Francisco: Jossey-Bass.

Derlega, V. J., Metts, S., Petronio, S., & Margulis, S. T. (1993). *Self-disclosure.* Newbury Park, CA: Sage.

Dindia, K., & Allen, M. (1992). Sex differences in self-disclosure: A meta-analysis. *Psychological Bulletin, 112,* 106–124.

Dunkel-Schetter, C. (1984). Social support and cancer: Findings based on patient interviews and their implications. *Journal of Social Issues, 40,* 77–98.

Ellenberger, H. F. (1966). The pathogenic secret and its therapeutics. *Journal of the History of the Behavioral Sciences, 2,* 29–42.

Erber, R., & Wegner, D. M. (1996). Ruminations on the rebound. In R. S. Wyer (Ed.), *Advances in social cognition* (Vol. 9, pp. 73–80). Mahwah, NJ: Erlbaum.

Fishbein, M. J., & Laird, J. D. (1979). Concealment and disclosure: Some effects of information control on the person who controls. *Journal of Experimental Social Psychology, 15,* 114–121.

Fitzpatrick, M. A. (1987). Marriage and verbal intimacy. In V. J. Derlega & J. H. Berg (Eds.), *Self-disclosure: Theory, research, and therapy* (pp. 131–154). New York: Plenum.

Franke, R., & Leary, M. R. (1991). Disclosure of sexual orientation by lesbians and gay men: A comparison of private and public processes. *Journal of Social and Clinical Psychology, 10,* 262–269.

Georges, E. (1995). A cultural and historical perspective on confession. In J. W. Pennebaker (Ed.), *Emotion, disclosure, and health* (pp. 11–22). Washington, DC: American Psychological Association.

Goodstein, L. D., & Reinecker, V. M. (1974). Factors influencing self-disclosure: A review of the literature. In B. A. Maher (Ed.), *Progress in experimental personality research* (pp. 49–77). New York: Academic Press.

Gurtman, M. B. (1986). Depression and the response of others: Re-evaluating the re-evaluation. *Journal of Abnormal Psychology, 95,* 99–101.

Harber, K. D., & Pennebaker, J. W. (1992). Overcoming traumatic memories. In S. A. Christianson (Ed.), *The handbook of emotion and memory* (pp. 359–387). Hillsdale, NJ: Erlbaum.

Hill, C. E., Thompson, B. J., Cogar, M. C., & Denman, D. W. (1993). Beneath the surface of long-term therapy: Therapist and client report of their own and each other's covert processes. *Journal of Counseling Psychology, 40,* 278–287.

Hill, C. T., & Stull, D. E. (1987). Gender and self-disclosure: Strategies for exploring the issues. In V. J. Derlega & J. H. Berg (Eds.), *Self-disclosure: Theory, research, and therapy* (pp. 81–100). New York: Plenum.

Hymer, S. M. (1982). The therapeutic nature of confessions. *Journal of Contemporary Psychotherapy, 13,* 129–143.

Hymer, S. M. (1988). *Confessions in psychotherapy.* New York: Gardner Press.

Jourard, S. M. (1971). *Self-disclosure: An experimental analysis of the transparent self.* New York: Wiley Interscience.

Karpel, M. A. (1980). Family secrets. *Family Process, 19,* 295–306.

Kelley, J. E., Lumley, M. A., & Leisen, J. C. C. (1997). Health effects of emotional disclosure in rheumatoid arthritis patients. *Health Psychology, 16,* 331–340.

Kelly, A. E., & McKillop, K. J. (1996). Consequences of revealing personal secrets. *Psychological Bulletin, 120,* 450–465.

Kelly, A. E., McKillop, K. J., & Neimeyer, G. J. (1991). Effects of counselor as audience on internalization of depressed and nondepressed self-presentations. *Journal of Counseling Psychology, 38,* 126–132.

Kelvin, P. A. (1977). Predictability, power, and vulnerability in interpersonal attraction. In S. Duck (Ed.), *Theory and practice in interpersonal attraction* (pp. 355–378). New York: Academic Press.

Kowalski, R. M., & Brendle, M. (1996). *Profiles of a patient representative.* Unpublished manuscript, Western Carolina University.

Kowalski, R. M., Cantrell, C. C., & VanHout, M. (1995). *Interpersonal and affective consequences of complaints and complaint responses.* Unpublished manuscript, Western Carolina University.

Kowalski, R. M., & Leary, M. R. (1990). Strategic self-presentation and the avoidance of aversive events: Antecedents and consequences of self-enhancement and self-depreciation. *Journal of Experimental Social Psychology, 26,* 322–336.

Larson, D. G., & Chastain, R. L. (1990). Self-concealment: Conceptualization, measurement, and health implications. *Journal of Social and Clinical Psychology, 9,* 439–455.

Last, U., & Aharoni-Etzioni, A. (1995). Secrets and reasons for secrecy among school-aged children: Developmental trends and gender differences. *Journal of Genetic Psychology, 156,* 191–203.

Leaper, C., Carson, M., Baker, C., Holliday, H., & Myers, S. (1995). Self-disclosure and listener verbal support in same-gender and cross-gender friends' conversations. *Sex Roles, 33,* 387–406.

Leary, M. R. (1995). *Self-presentation: Impression management and interpersonal behavior.* Dubuque, IA: Brown & Benchmark.

Leary, M. R., & Kowalski, R. M. (1995). *Social anxiety.* New York: Guilford.

Mason, H. R. C., Marks, G., Simoni, J. M., Ruiz, M. S., & Richardson, J. L. (1995). Culturally sanctioned secrets? Latino men's nondisclosure of HIV infection to family, friends, and lovers. *Health Psychology, 14,* 6–12.

May, O. P., & Thompson, C. L. (1973). Perceived levels of self-disclosure, mental health, and helpfulness of group leaders. *Journal of Counseling Psychology, 20,* 349–352.

McKenzie, E. C. (1980). *14,000 quips and quotes.* New York: Wings Books.

McKillop, K. J., Berzonsky, M. D., & Schlenker, B. R. (1992). The impact of self-presentations on self-beliefs: Effects of social identity and self-presentational context. *Journal of Personality, 60,* 789–808.

Moses, A. E. (1978). *Identity management in lesbian women.* New York: Praeger.

Newman, N. K. (1993). Family secrets: A challenge for family physicians. *Journal of Family Practice, 36,* 494–496.

Norton, R., Feldman, C., & Tafoya, D. (1974). Risk parameters across types of secrets. *Journal of Counseling Psychology, 21,* 450–454.

Ogden, J. A., & Von Sturmer, G. (1984). Emotional strategies and their relationship to complaints of psychosomatic and neurotic symptoms. *Journal of Clinical Psychology, 40,* 772–779.

Pegalis, L. J., Shaffer, D. R., Bazzini, D. G., & Greenier, K. (1994). On the ability to elicit self-disclosure: Are there gender-based and contextual limitations on the opener effect? *Personality and Social Psychology Bulletin, 20,* 412–420.

Pennebaker, J. W. (1985). Traumatic experience and psychosomatic disease: Exploring the roles of behavioral inhibition, obsession, and confiding. *Canadian Psychology, 26,* 82–95.

Pennebaker, J. W. (1988). Confiding traumatic experiences and health. In S. Fisher & J. Reason (Eds.), *Handbook of life stress, social cognition, and health* (pp. 669–682). New York: Wiley.

Pennebaker, J. W. (1990). *Opening up.* New York: Avon.

Pennebaker, J. W. (1993). Social mechanisms of constraint. In D. Wegner & J. W. Pennebaker (Eds.), *Handbook of mental control* (pp. 200–219). Englewood Cliffs, NJ: Prentice Hall.

Pennebaker, J. W. (Ed.). (1995). *Emotion, disclosure, and health.* Washington, DC: American Psychological Association.

Pennebaker, J. W., Barger, S. D., & Tiebout, J. (1989). Disclosure of traumas and health among Holocaust survivors. *Psychosomatic Medicine, 51,* 577–589.

Pennebaker, J. W., & Beall, S. K. (1986). Confronting a traumatic event: Toward an understanding of inhibition and disease. *Journal of Abnormal Psychology, 95,* 274–281.

Pennebaker, J. W., Colder, M., & Sharp, L. K. (1990). Accelerating the coping process. *Journal of Personality and Social Psychology, 58,* 528–537.

Pennebaker, J. W., Hughes, C. F., & O'Heeron, R. C. (1987). The psychophysiology of confession: Linking inhibitory and psychosomatic processes. *Journal of Personality and Social Psychology, 52*, 781–793.

Pennebaker, J. W., Kiecolt-Glaser, J. K., & Glaser, R. (1988). Disclosure of traumas and immune function: Health implications for psychotherapy. *Journal of Consulting and Clinical Psychology, 56*, 239–245.

Pennebaker, J. W., & O'Heeron, R. C. (1984). Confiding in others and illness rate among spouses of suicide and accidental-death victims. *Journal of Abnormal Psychology, 93*, 473–476.

Petrie, K. J., Booth, R. J., & Davison, K. P. (1995). Repression, disclosure, and immune function: Recent findings and methodological issues. In J. W. Pennebaker (Ed.), *Emotion, disclosure, and health* (pp. 223–237). Washington, DC: American Psychological Association.

Petrie, K. J., Booth, R. J., Pennebaker, J. W., Davison, K. P., & Thomas, M. G. (1995). Disclosure of trauma and immune response to a hepatitis B vaccination program. *Journal of Consulting and Clinical Psychology, 63*, 787–792.

Regan, A. M., & Hill, C. E. (1992). Investigation of what clients and counselors do not say in brief therapy. *Journal of Counseling Psychology, 39*, 168–174.

Reis, H., Senchak, M., & Soloman, B. (1985). Sex differences in interaction meaningfulness. *Journal of Personality and Social Psychology, 48*, 1204–1217.

Rimé, B. (1995). Mental rumination, social sharing, and the recovery from emotional exposure. In J. W. Pennebaker (Ed.), *Emotion, disclosure, and health* (pp. 271–291). Washington, DC: American Psychological Association.

Rimé, B., Mesquita, B., Philippot, P., & Boca, S. (1991). Beyond the emotional event: Six studies on the social sharing of emotion. *Cognition and Emotion, 5*, 435–465.

Roback, H. B., Moore, R. F., Waterhouse, G. J., & Martin, P. R. (1996). Confidentiality dilemmas in group psychotherapy with substance-dependent physicians. *American Journal of Psychiatry, 153*, 1250–1260.

Roberts, P. (1995, May–June). Forbidden thinking. *Psychology Today,* 34–40, 62, 64, 66.

Saffer, J. B., Sansone, P., & Gentry, J. (1979). The awesome burden upon the child who must keep a family secret. *Child Psychiatry and Human Development, 10*, 35–40.

Schlenker, B. R., & Trudeau, J. T. (1990). The impact of self-presentations on private self-beliefs: Effects of prior self-beliefs and misattribution. *Journal of Personality and Social Psychology, 58*, 22–32.

Schwartz, R. S. (1984). Confidentiality and secret-keeping on an inpatient unit. *Psychiatry, 47*, 279–284.

Shortt, J. W., & Pennebaker, J. W. (1992). Talking versus hearing about Holocaust experiences. *Basic and Applied Social Psychology, 13*, 165–179.

Silver, R. C., Wortman, C. B., & Crofton, C. (1990). The role of coping in support provision: The self-presentational dilemma of victims of life crises. In B. R.

Sarason, I. G. Sarason, & G. R. Pierce (Eds.), *Social support: An interactional view* (pp. 397–426). New York: Wiley.

Simmel, G. (1950). The secret and the secret society. In K. H. Wolff (Ed.), *The sociology of George Simmel* (pp. 307–376). New York: Free Press.

Spiegel, D., Bloom, J. H., Kraemer, H. C., & Gottheil, E. (1989). Effects of psychosocial treatment of patients with metastatic breast cancer. *Lancet, 2,* 888–891.

Spiegel, D., & Kato, P. M. (1996). Psychosocial influences on cancer incidence and progression. *Harvard Review of Psychiatry, 4,* 10–26.

Stiles, W. B. (1987). "I have to talk to somebody": A fever model of disclosure. In V. J. Derlega & J. H. Berg (Eds.), *Self-disclosure: Theory, research, and therapy* (pp. 257–282). New York: Plenum.

Stiles, W. B. (1995). Disclosure as a speech act. In J. W. Pennebaker (Ed.), *Emotion, disclosure, and health* (pp. 71–91). Washington, DC: American Psychological Association.

Stiles, W. B., Shuster, P. L., & Harrigan, J. A. (1992). Disclosure and anxiety: A test of the fever model. *Journal of Personality and Social Psychology, 63,* 980–988.

Szapocznik, J. (1995). Research on disclosure of HIV status: Cultural evolution finds an ally in science. *Health Psychology, 14,* 4–5.

Wegner, D. M., & Erber, R. (1992). The hyperaccessibility of suppressed thoughts. *Journal of Personality and Social Psychology, 63,* 903–912.

Wegner, D. M., & Lane, J. D. (1995). From secrecy to psychopathology. In J. W. Pennebaker (Ed.), *Emotion, disclosure, and health* (pp. 71–91). Washington, DC: American Psychological Association.

Wegner, D. M., Lane, J. D., & Dimitri, S. (1994). The allure of secret relationships. *Journal of Personality and Social Psychology, 66,* 287–300.

Wegner, D. M., Shortt, J. W., Blake, A. W., & Page, M. S. (1990). The suppression of exciting thoughts. *Journal of Personality and Social Psychology, 58,* 409–418.

Weinberg, T. S. (1983). *Gay men, gay selves: The social construction of homosexual identities.* New York: Irvington.

Wellenkamp, J. (1995). Cultural similarities and differences regarding emotional disclosure: Some examples from Indonesia and the Pacific. In J. W. Pennebaker (Ed.), *Emotion, disclosure, and health* (pp. 293–311). Washington, DC: American Psychological Association.

West, L. W. (1970). Sex differences in the exercise of circumspection in self-disclosure among adolescents. *Psychological Reports, 26,* 226.

Yalom, I. D. (1985). *The theory and practice of group psychotherapy* (3rd ed.). New York: Basic Books.

9

MALADAPTIVE IMAGE MAINTENANCE

JAMES A. SHEPPERD AND KIMBERLEY D. KWAVNICK

How a person is perceived by others has a substantial impact on how he or she is treated. A person who is perceived by others to be honest and responsible is trusted more and given greater responsibility than a person who is perceived to be dishonest and irresponsible. A woman who is perceived as sexually promiscuous receives more sexual advances from men than a woman who is perceived as prudish. Given that the way people are perceived affects how they are treated, it is no surprise that people are concerned with the image they project and how these images are perceived by others. The term *impression management* refers to the process of controlling the impressions that others form (Goffman, 1959; Leary, 1995; Schlenker, 1980). People carefully control and cultivate the image they convey to others. By controlling the image they project, people can exercise some influence over how they are perceived by others and the way others respond to them.

In this chapter, we examine how attempts to procure or maintain certain images, although perhaps well intended, can be maladaptive, having negative consequences for the person presenting the image. Although people can often benefit by projecting a particular image, their attempts to create that image occasionally can be harmful to them. Our central thesis is that a variety of emotional, behavioral, and interpersonal problems can arise as a result of people's efforts to convey particular impressions of themselves to others.

We organize our discussion of maladaptive image maintenance around two broad image goals: competence and likability. Although not exhaustive, the goals of competence and likability capture much of the behavior directed at image maintenance and provide excellent forums for discussing the pitfalls of pursuing desired images. Within the topic of competence, we discuss the goal of appearing competent and avoiding appearing incompetent. We also note that people occasionally may convey an image of weakness and incompetence. Within the topic of likability, we discuss two avenues to likability—conformity and physical attractiveness—and describe how pursuit of each of these goals can be problematic. Although we occasionally note some of the ways in which people's efforts to appear competent and likable may backfire, creating something other than the intended image, our primary focus is on how pursuing the goals of competence and likability can give rise to emotional, behavioral, and interpersonal problems.

COMPETENCE

Competence and skill are associated with innumerable rewards. Those who are competent are more likely to score high on college and graduate school achievement examinations and thus are more likely to get into better schools. People who are regarded as competent are also more likely to acquire better jobs and to get promotions. Competent people are also more likely to realize the American dream of economic success (Herrnstein & Murray, 1994). Perhaps just as important as being competent is *appearing* competent. The job applicant who appears the most competent on the phone, at the interview, or on the résumé is more likely to get the job, regardless of his or her actual competence. Indeed, given the numerous rewards associated with competence, it is not surprising that people are motivated to appear skilled and capable.

People can create or sustain an image of competence or high ability in several ways. One way is through performance on diagnostic tests of ability. Whether it is a test of athletic ability, typing speed, or intellectual acumen, people who score well are perceived to be more competent, skilled, and able than are people who score poorly. Indeed, concern with scores on diagnostic tests such as the college board has created a thriving business for companies providing instruction on how test takers can raise their scores. A second way people can create or sustain an image of competence is by describing personal accomplishments or abilities to others.

The résumé or curriculum vita serves as a formal and accepted vehicle for displaying competence by describing personal accomplishments, awards, skills, and abilities. However, people also show competence informally by simply describing their accomplishments, skills, and associations to others. A young man may attempt to impress a date with his high school athletic and academic achievements. No doubt, it is a concern with appearing competent that leads students occasionally to exaggerate their reports of their college board scores (Shepperd, 1993).

A third way people can appear competent is through association. The people one associates with can often be thought of as extensions of the self (Schlenker & Britt, in press). This is frequently the case with friends but even more so with family. As such, people can garner an image of competence when close others perform well or display competence. This "halo effect" of competence is partly grounded in an awareness by others that people associate with similar others (i.e., birds of a feather flock together; Byrne, 1971). Audiences often assume (generally correctly) that the friends and family of smart people are also smart. However, among biological relatives, the halo effect of competency may be due in large part to the fact that many competence-related attributes are genetically determined. Intelligent parents tend to have intelligent children, athletic parents tend to have athletic children, and musically adept parents tend to have musically adept children. Thus, when people judge that a person is competent, they also are inclined to infer that the person's parents and siblings are also competent.

AVOIDING IMAGES OF LOW COMPETENCE

What happens when people stumble or fail, when performance falls below expectation, or when a poor performance seems inevitable? The dilemma that people often face is not one of how to appear competent but one of avoiding appearing incompetent. Two broad strategies can be used to avoid appearing incompetent. The first strategy is *excuse making* and addresses displays of poor performance that have already occurred. The second strategy is *self-handicapping* and addresses anticipated displays of low competence.

Excuse Making

The Function of Excuses

A former golfing partner of one of us once made the following astute observation: The amount of verbalizing made by a golfer after a golf stroke or shot is inversely related to the quality of the shot. Lousy shots are followed by an outpour of excuses for why the ball dribbled a few feet or veered wildly out of bounds ("I looked up"; "the sun caught my eye during the back swing"; "my clubs need new grips"; "the other golfers distracted me"). Excellent shots that sail down the fairway are followed by silence, implying that such shots are commonplace and deserve no comment.

Excuses represent attempts to reduce personal responsibility for an event (Schlenker, 1980; C. R. Snyder & Higgins, 1988; C. R. Snyder, Higgins, & Stucky, 1983). People make excuses for all sorts of events including wild golf shots, poor test performance ("I didn't study"), missed appointments ("I overslept"), failures at love ("I don't drive a nice enough car for her"), and transgressions and other misdeeds ("I was abused as a child"). One framework for conceptualizing excuse making is the "triangle model of responsibility" (Schlenker, Britt, Pennington, Murphy, & Doherty, 1994). The triangle model of responsibility proposes that people are held responsible for an event to the extent that (a) there are clear prescriptions for the event that explain how a person is to behave in the situation (the prescription–event link); (b) the prescriptions are applicable to the actor by virtue of his or her role, conviction, or characteristics (the prescription–identity link); and (c) the actor is associated with the event by having control over it (identity–event link). To the extent that one or more of these links is weak, then a person's responsibility for an event is diluted.

Excuses function to reduce responsibility for an event by weakening one or more of the links in the triangle model. For example, a woman fired from a job might claim that the job requirements were unclear or contradictory, thereby weakening the prescription–event link. Alternatively, she might claim that she should not be judged by her performance because she was not properly trained or because family problems or obligations kept her from doing her work, thereby weakening the prescription–identity link. Finally, the woman might weaken the identity–event link by claiming that some external factor such as an alcohol or drug problem kept her from doing her work or that an unprincipled boss evaluated her unfairly. Although each of these explanations may excuse responsibility, they may undermine improvement and steps to avoid a similar situation in the future.

The Maladaptive Side of Excuse Making

Of course, not all excuses are disingenuous. Sometimes work expectations truly are unclear, training is incomplete, family problems require attention, one drinks too much, or bosses or teachers evaluate the person unfairly. Moreover, excuses often successfully serve their purpose of excusing the person from transgressions and failures at tasks. Nevertheless, excuses can produce problems that make them maladaptive.

One problem with excuses is that they may lead the excuse makers to persist toward goals they cannot achieve. An aspiring yet talent-challenged actress may believe that she can break into movies if she just finds the right agent or meets the right people, when in fact she lacks the skills to star on the "silver screen" and her efforts would be better spent pursuing another career. Some inner-city youths neglect or abandon their education in favor of playing sports with the excuse that being a basketball or football star is the path to fame and fortune. They ignore the fact that precious few athletes have the skills to become professionals. Ultimately, pursuing unobtainable goals can lead to time wasted as well as to frustration, disappointment, and regret over opportunities lost from not pursuing more fruitful domains. In the case of the inner-city youths, ignoring their education can result in losing the one certain avenue for escaping the poverty of the inner city.

A second problem with excuses is that they may keep the excuse maker from changing or improving. That is, often the excuse distracts the excuse maker's attention from the real cause of the outcome to some pseudocause; they often provide an external explanation for a problem that may be internally caused. For example, a worker may attribute being passed over for a promotion to an external cause such as racism (or reverse racism), when in fact the real problem is internal, such as a lack of skill or an attitude problem. Likewise, a victim of spousal abuse may make excuses for the spouse's abusive behavior rather than attempt to seek help or escape the situation. In addition, alcoholic individuals are notorious for making excuses for their problems. These excuses often delay or interfere with seeking help (C. R. Snyder et al., 1983). When change or improvement is needed, an excuse serves to feed a harmful and destructive situation. For the chronic excuse maker, excuses can lead to never taking responsibility for undesired outcomes.

A third problem with excuses is that they can give the person tacit permission to engage in deviant or dangerous behavior, behavior the person later regrets. Two examples illustrate this maladaptive aspect of excuses. The first example comes from a study of wife beating by Gelles (1972), who noted that incidents of wife beatings are often preceded by the husband drinking alcohol. The wife typically blamed her husband's actions on the alcohol, suggesting that things would be okay if it were not for the alcohol. The husbands readily agree. However, Gelles (1972) went as far as to say that in some cases, the husbands "drink in order to provide an excuse for becoming violent" (p. 116). It would appear that these husbands have learned that they can rely on alcohol to excuse bad behavior.

The second example comes from an informal study of Catholic students at a small New England college where one of us once taught. Given their age, the students naturally had a strong interest in having sexual intercourse. However, premarital intercourse is strictly and explicitly forbidden by the teachings of the Catholic Church. What resulted was striking: The students would drink excessively and then give in to their desires to have sexual intercourse. The alcohol served to reduce self-awareness, thereby decreasing the immediate guilt associated with violating their religious rules. It also provided an excuse that partially absolved them from their sin—they could be forgiven because the alcohol made them too drunk to resist temptation. The students nevertheless expressed considerable guilt afterward about their behavior. Moreover, the students played a dangerous game, one that placed them at risk for unwanted pregnancies and STDs. The students rarely took precautions such as using condoms or other effective birth control methods because such birth control methods were forbidden by the Catholic Church. Just as important, using or having such devices implied that sexual intercourse was planned, something that students were unwilling to acknowledge even to themselves.

In both examples, the excuse was used to externalize and thus partially pardon a destructive, dangerous, or taboo behavior. It allowed the wife-beating husbands and sexually active students to act out in ways that were harmful or forbidden.

Self-Handicapping

Sometimes people suspect in advance that they may perform poorly on a task diagnostic of ability or competence. Before a race, a runner may be uncertain that he or she has the speed or stamina to defeat his or her opponents. The night before taking the Graduate Record Examinations, a student may doubt that he or she has the ability to achieve a score that will secure admission into graduate school. In both cases, a poor performance is regarded as highly likely and the person faces the prospect of appearing incompetent.

A strategy people can use to avoid inferences of low ability in the face of impending poor performance is self-handicapping. Self-handicapping involves setting up or claiming barriers to performance. More formally, it is the preemptive claim or creation of a performance impediment that decreases the likelihood of success yet provides a nonability attribution for failure should it occur (Berglas & Jones, 1978; Higgins, Snyder, & Berglas, 1990). Although self-handicapping can be a tactic for maintaining self-esteem, research suggests that its primary function is to manage the attributions made by others (Kolditz & Arkin, 1982). Self-handicapping is illustrated by the student who gets drunk the night before an important examination or the speaker who does not prepare adequately before a speech. In both cases, the handicapper does something that decreases the likelihood of a good performance. Should a poor performance occur, the handicapper can attribute it to the handicap rather than to personal lack of ability. Thus, should the student perform poorly on the examination, he or she can blame it on being hungover or still drunk from the previous night's drinking binge. Should the speaker give a poor speech, he or she can attribute it to lack of adequate preparation. In both cases, the handicapper deflects low-ability explanations for a poor performance. As such, the handicapper can maintain an image, albeit perhaps more illusory than real, of skill, competence, or ability.

Although researchers have identified a variety of factors that lead to self-handicapping (Self, 1990), the two most important preconditions appear to be the importance of task performance to identity and the perceived likelihood of success. The consistent finding is that people are more likely to self-handicap when task performance is central to identity and when a good performance is deemed unlikely by the handicapper. Regarding task importance, if the performance is not important to identity, then a poor performance is not threatening and people are less concerned with the attributions made for a poor performance. Consequently, people are less likely to self-handicap on unimportant tasks. Regarding the perceived likelihood of success, when the performance outcome is uncertain, people face the possibility that a rosy picture of themselves will be disconfirmed. The self-handicap, however, provides an alternate, nonability explanation for a poor performance, thereby preserving the rosy self-view.

Types of Self-Handicaps

Researchers have distinguished between two types of self-handicaps: self-reported handicaps and behavioral handicaps (Leary & Shepperd, 1986; see also Arkin & Baumgardner, 1985, for a similar distinction). Reported handicaps involve claims or reports of impediments to performance. A student, for example, may claim excessive test anxiety before an examination (see T. W. Smith, Snyder, & Handelsman, 1982). Test anxiety serves as a reasonable excuse should the student perform poorly. Other examples include claims of shyness (C. R. Snyder, Smith, Augelli, & Ingram, 1985) and traumatic childhood events (DeGree & Snyder, 1985). Unlike excuses, which typically follow a failure, self-reported handicaps are preemptive, occurring before performance. Nevertheless, self-reported handicaps are similar to excuses in that both are verbal claims and both carry the same disadvantages and consequences.

Behavioral handicaps involve acquiring or setting up barriers to performance either by embracing a performance impediment (e.g., drinking alcohol) or failing to take actions to eliminate or minimize existing barriers (e.g., failing to prepare for an examination or performance). Drug addiction, for example, is a serious problem. However, it can provide the addict with a ready-made excuse for shortcomings and failings in a variety of domains. The addict can always blame the addiction for why he or she failed or performed poorly. With behavioral handicaps, the handicapper, either by acting or failing to act, creates conditions that interfere with performance and diminish the likelihood of success. Examples of behavioral self-handicaps include ingesting drugs or alcohol (Berglas & Jones, 1978; Kolditz & Arkin, 1982), withholding effort (Harris & Snyder, 1986; Pysz-czynski & Greenberg, 1983; M. L. Snyder, Smoller, Strenta, & Frankel, 1991), and not practicing for an important task (Rhodewalt, Saltzman, & Wittmer, 1984; Tice & Baumeister, 1990).

The Maladaptive Side of Self-Handicapping

Although self-handicapping provides a nonability explanation for a poor performance, it does so at a cost. That is, self-handicapping has several liabilities that can make it a maladaptive strategy. One liability of self-handicapping is that it may produce a long-term undesirable image. That is, many self-handicaps, although excusing a poor performance in the short run, are stigmatizing. Although alcohol and drugs can serve as convincing excuses for a poor performance, they reflect poorly on the handicapper, portraying him or her as alcoholic or drug abusing.

A second and perhaps greater liability of self-handicapping, particularly behavioral self-handicapping, is that the handicap actually decreases the likelihood of success in most cases, producing an unwanted consequence. With a handicap in place, the student is in a weaker position to pass the examination, the speaker is less likely to persuade or impress the audience, the interviewee has a lower probability of getting the job, and the athlete is less likely to defeat his or her opponent. To the extent that self-handicapping is used repeatedly, it can lead to life-long problems. Jones and Berglas (1978) have argued that the underachiever may best be thought of as a chronic self-handicapper. By not preparing adequately or by not applying himself or herself when being tested, the underachiever may succeed less often. However, the underachiever can maintain an image of unrealized potential—as someone who could have been so much more if only he or she applied himself or herself more. In short, by undermining his or her own performance, the handicapper may rarely enjoy the thrills and benefits of success. Peers will pass the handicapper by climbing the corporate ladder and garnering other successes, whereas the handicapper stagnates with only his or her excuses for comfort. Although it feels good to avoid the pain of failure, it is unwise to do so at the expense of progress.

Finally, using handicaps such as alcohol and drugs to provide a preemptive excuse can exact a heavy toll on the handicapper. The addictive and debilitating effects of these controlled substances speak to their dangers. Moreover, handicaps may produce regret to the extent that a resulting poor performance produces permanent consequences. People who fail to prepare adequately for a job interview or for a professional school entrance examination, and perform poorly as a consequence, may forever regret their actions, wondering "If only I had prepared more, my life would be so much different."

Other-Enhancement

Another strategy that is similar to self-handicapping is *other-enhancement* (Shepperd & Arkin, 1991). Other-enhancement occurs in competitive settings and involves supplying an opponent with a performance advantage. It is similar to self-handicapping in that it provides a ready-made explanation for a poor performance. By supplying an opponent with resources, tools, and other advantages that improve performance, the person can attribute a relatively poor performance to the opponent's advantage. Other-enhancement has two advantages not found in self-handicapping. First, with self-handicapping, the person does something that diminishes his or her own performance. With other-enhancement, the person does nothing to hurt his or her own performance; instead, he or she supplies an opponent with an advantage. As such, we suspect that other-enhancement would be preferred in settings such as rigorous graduate programs, where relative comparisons are inevitable and interfering with one's own performance through self-handicapping could prove disastrous. Second, by providing an opponent with an advantage, the person is seen as selfless, even altruistic. After all, who but the most altruistic person would help out an opponent? Of course, the time and energy devoted to helping others could be channeled into one's own achievements. By neglecting his or her performance in the interest of the performances of others, the person using this strategy may diminish his or her progress.

Yet other-enhancement has two additional liabilities. First, it can create dependency in others and may even lead the recipient of the advantage to question his or her abilities (e.g., "Could I have done well on my own?"). For example, a father who competes with his son in a game may provide his son with an advantage to "level the playing field." However, the son may question whether he can win without the advantage (see Gilbert & Silvera, 1996). Second, it can lead to resentment on the part of the recipient, who may feel deprived of the opportunity to show that he or she could succeed on his or her own. The resentment can lead to a strained relationship with the recipient and may even lead to anger or bitterness on the part of the enhancer because the recipient appears ungrateful for the assistance he or she received.

CLAIMING A NEGATIVE IMAGE

Thus far, our focus has been on how people seek to appear competent and how the pursuit of this goal, or at least the complimentary goal of avoiding appearing incompetent, can be maladaptive. It is important to note that people do not always want to appear competent and may occasionally attempt to create or embrace a negative image of low ability or incompetence. Although claiming a negative identity may seem counterintuitive, the responses elicited from others may make a negative image an attractive goal in some situations. People respond with sympathy to someone who appears sick. People demand less effort or work from another who appears incapable or disabled. Furthermore, people exert less energy against an opponent who appears weak or ill equipped. We focus on three broad categories of situations in which people present themselves negatively.

Appearing Weak or Helpless: Supplication and Strategic Failure

In many ways, appearing competent is a double-edged sword. Demonstrations of achievement and competence can lead to respect, admiration, and other material and interpersonal rewards. However, people assign more responsibility to and exact higher standards of performance from people who are more competent than people who are less competent.

One reason people may underplay their skills, abilities, and apparent competence is to avoid challenging tasks or to get out of things they do not want to do. A strategy used occasionally by some college students facing foreign language requirements is to perform poorly intentionally on language placement examinations. By so doing, the students appear to be less capable than they really are and thus are assigned to language classes that are less demanding and that thus promise a higher grade. In a similar vein, a spouse may claim ignorance of how to sort clothes, run the washing machine, or iron to get out of doing laundry. These strategic failures and displays of low ability are undertaken either to reduce audience expectations to create lower, more easily attainable goals (Baumgardner & Brownlee, 1987; Weary & Williams, 1990) or to get out of a job or avoid some onerous task (Kowalski & Leary, 1990; Stires & Jones, 1969).

Alternatively, sometimes people present themselves as weak or incapable to solicit aid, nurturance, protection, or assistance from others. Jones and Pittman (1982) called these types of displays of weakness "supplication" (see also Schlenker, 1980). For example, a person may exaggerate his or her feelings of depression to receive emotional support from others. Similarly, an elderly person might display helplessness in doing menial chores such as changing a lightbulb or setting a digital clock to elicit attention from or contact with a family member.

Supplication and strategic failure and other similar displays pose certain liabilities for the person using these strategies. One liability is that the target of the displays may perceive the person negatively—as weak, incompetent, and insecure. For example, the person who attempts to solicit emotional support by revealing feelings of depression may receive the support or nurturance that he or she seeks, but that person may also be regarded negatively. Although people will support and help a person who supplicates, they nevertheless view the supplicator less favorably (Powers & Zuroff, 1988). A second risk that arises from these displays of weakness and helplessness is that they may provoke feelings of resentment from targets. A spouse may resent the fact that she or he has to do the laundry because his or her mate seems incapable. Beginner students in language classes are no doubt annoyed by the presence of other students in the class who clearly have had prior exposure to the language, perhaps in high school, but who purposely performed poorly on the placement examination to secure an easy class.

Finally, people who use the self-presentational strategies of supplication and strategic failure often forfeit an opportunity for growth and advancement that comes with undertaking challenging tasks and risking failure. The students who perform poorly on language placement tests get an easy class as a reward, but they may rob themselves of the opportunity to improve their language skills. Similarly, those who never learn to drive, do laundry, or program a VCR may condemn themselves to a life of dependence on others (or at least a flashing 12:00 on the VCR).

Sandbagging: Undermining an Opponent's Effort

Sometimes portrayals of relatively low ability are not designed to solicit help or get out of an aversive situation but are intended to "sandbag" the audience. Sandbagging means to display oneself as an unworthy foe to undermine another's effort or to induce another to let down his or her guard (Shepperd & Soucherman, 1997). The sandbagger's goal is to persuade an opponent that victory is inevitable or complete. The sprinter who feigns a limp on his or her way to the starting blocks in the hope of tricking an opponent into responding less quickly to the starter's gun is attempting to sandbag an opponent. So too is the momentary loser among wrestling playmates who feigns injury or pain or cries "uncle" in an attempt to lull the other playmate into letting down his or her guard. Moreover, there is evidence that sandbagging works. People report that they match their efforts to the efforts of their opponents, reducing their efforts when they perceive that an opponent is disadvantaged (Shepperd & Soucherman, 1997). Note that the sandbagger does not need to display a blatantly negative self-image. Rather, he or she simply needs to look weaker or less able than he or she really is. Thus, sandbagging is often a display of less competence rather than incompetence.

Sandbagging occurs when people are competing for an important outcome and the outcome of the competition is uncertain. Yet sandbagging is not appropriate for every type of competition. Although a tennis player might attempt to catch an opponent off guard by claiming that he or she is a beginner, the claim is promptly dismissed by the opponent the moment the first serve whizzes by. The sandbagger may fool the opponent into letting down his or her guard for one serve but no more. Thus, sandbagging is a useful one-time strategy that is best suited for undermining an opponent's preparation for a competition or for contests in which the outcome can be determined by a single move or play.

Aside from sandbagging, people in competition might present themselves as weak, incompetent, or low in ability to an opponent for reasons other than to influence the opponent's effort. For instance, a dishonest country club golfer may purposely perform poorly or lose in the weeks before a tournament to get a higher handicap. Here the motivation is to obtain an unfair advantage. Another example involves coaches who downplay the strengths of their team, highlight their own team's weaknesses, or praise the skills of the opposing team. The underlying motivation is either to generate fan interest in what would likely be a one-sided game or to provide a preemptive excuse should the game be closer than expected.

Finally, *hustling* represents another instance in which people portray themselves as weak for reasons other than undermining an opponent's effort. The goal of the hustler is to acquire money or resources and is illustrated by poolsharks and cardsharks who lose initial games until the "mark" wagers serious money, at which point the hustlers display their true ability. Hustling has been chronicled is several popular movies, including *The Color of Money* (Scorsese, 1986), *White Men Can't Jump* (Shelter, Miller, & Lester, 1992), and, of course, *The Hustler* (Rossen, 1961). Hustling and sandbagging are similar in that both involve displays of relative weakness or low ability and both can be regarded as attempts to persuade another to let down his or her guard. However, hustling is distinct from sandbagging in the prerequisite conditions. With hustling, the hustler's ability is superior to that of the opponent and the ultimate outcome of the competition is known (at least to the hustler).

Portraying oneself as weak, unskilled, or incompetent, however, is not always a wise strategy and can be maladaptive in several ways. First, if the opponent is unconvinced by the display, then the sandbagger may acquire an unwanted image or reputation of being deceitful, as someone not to be trusted. This is particularly problematic if the reputation is generalized beyond the competition to other interpersonal settings. Second, if the sandbagger loses after a false display of low ability, then the sandbagger is left with a public image of being less competent or able than he or she really is. To the extent that social and financial rewards are tied to a public image of competence independent of the outcome of the competition, the sandbagger may fare worse from displaying weakness than from displaying strength. Third, self-verification theory suggests that the sandbagger may suffer personal discomfort from having his or her ability perceived inaccurately (see Swann & Read, 1981). That is, people generally want to be perceived accurately and are distressed when they are not. Fourth, should the opponent reduce effort in response to the sandbagging display and still defeat the sandbagger, then the sandbagger suffers doubly. Not only does the sandbagger lose, but he or she loses to an opponent who was not trying hard. From an attributional standpoint, a low-ability attribution is virtually unavoidable (Heider, 1958; Jones & Davis, 1965; Kelley, 1967).

Fifth, to some extent people are influenced by their own self-presentations. People induced, for example, to present themselves as extraverted come to see themselves as extraverted, whereas people who are induced to present themselves as introverted come to see themselves as introverted (Fazio, Effrein, & Falender, 1981; Tice, 1992). The same may be true of sandbagging, such that people who present themselves as weak or incompetent may come to question their abilities and suffer losses in self-esteem as a result of their doubts (Jones, Berglas, Rhodewalt, & Skelton, 1981).

Finally, some attempts to portray oneself as weak or nonthreatening can produce an image that leads to social avoidance by others. For example, a therapist friend of one of us once described a male patient who was desperate for female companionship. His strategy for getting women to date him was to portray himself as someone who was safe and nonthreatening. To this end, he would describe himself to new female acquaintances as impotent, a tactic that likely succeeded in conveying an image of nonthreat, along with the accompanying image of undesirable.

Displays of Mental Illness

In Shakespeare's play *Hamlet*, the character Hamlet at various times displays symptoms of mental illness in his behavior and speech. It is not clear in the play whether Hamlet's displays are authentic or are merely a ruse intended to cover Hamlet's investigation of his father's death and mother's betrayal (Shakespeare, 1964). Nevertheless, there are some instances in which people present themselves as mentally ill to avoid obligations or responsibilities for their actions. As a result, some instances of the insanity plea are viewed as thinly veiled attempts to avoid prison.

Of course, many if not most displays of psychiatric symptoms are authentic and reflect real underlying disorders. Many people do suffer from delusions, hallucinations, problems with impulse control, and depression. However, there is some evidence that the degree to which people display psychiatric symptoms is determined in part by impression management concerns. For example, in one study, 30 long-term schizophrenia patients on an open ward in a mental hospital were interviewed individually by a psychiatrist. Some patients were told that the interview would determine whether they should be transferred from an open ward to a closed ward. A closed ward is considerably less pleasant than an open ward because it is populated by more disturbed patients, offers fewer privileges, and provides less freedom of movement and behavior. Other patients were told that the interview would determine whether they should be discharged from the hospital. A final group of patients was in the control condition and was told that the interview was to assess how they were feeling. In all cases, the psychiatrist was unaware of the experimental condition to which the patients were assigned. Patients who believed they were being evaluated for transfer to a closed ward displayed considerably fewer symptoms of schizophrenia during the interview than did the patients in the control condition. In contrast, patients who believed that they were being evaluated for their suitability for release from the hospital displayed considerably more symptoms of schizophrenia during the interview than did the patients in the control condition (Braginsky & Braginsky, 1967).

Although this latter finding may seem surprising, one must remember that these were long-term psychiatric patients who had been hospitalized for years. Having been in the hospital for so long, many of the patients likely harbored doubts about their ability to function outside the hospital. Release from the safe, familiar surroundings of the hospital likely presented an unknown, frightening future. Furthermore, some patients were indigent and had nowhere to go should they be discharged from the hospital. Finally, some researchers have suggested that the mental hospital for some patients is somewhat like a "resort"—a place where they could rest and be cared for (Braginsky, Braginsky, & Ring, 1969). Of course, although constant care may be comfortable, in the case of the mental hospital it comes at the expense of respect and life experiences offered by the outside world. Real life can be frightening, but when nothing is ventured, nothing can ever be gained.

Summary

Most people want to appear competent and will go to great lengths to create an image of skill and ability. When their image of competence is threatened, people will use a variety of excuses and self-handicaps to externalize responsibility for their missteps and failures. However, attempts to conceal dubious competence through excuses or self-handicapping can be problematic, leading to emotional, behavioral, and interpersonal difficulties. People may become bitter and regretful over missed opportunities resulting from expending too much time and energy pursuing unobtainable goals or from sabotaging performance in important domains. Others may regard the excuse maker or handicapper as foolish or deceitful and choose to avoid him or her. Finally, excusing destructive, dangerous, and taboo behaviors can be harmful to oneself and to others, whereas self-handicaps not only are harmful in that they sabotage success but in instances such as alcohol and drug abuse, they can also be dangerous to the handicapper. Some people have abandoned the goal of appearing competent in favor of appearing incompetent to secure assistance from others, dupe opponents, or avoid responsibilities. Displays of incompetence, however, carry their own costs (e.g., stigmas, distrust from others, dependence, social exclusion) that often make them maladaptive in the long run.

LIKABILITY

Imagine a group of adolescents preparing to go to the mall; they carefully select outfits that will appear perfectly effortless and casual and request that their fathers drop them off a block from the mall entrance. Next, imagine a young woman nervously preparing for a date; she styles her hair, applies tasteful makeup, and irons her favorite skirt. Several miles away, her date spends an hour lifting weights before showering, shaving, and splashing on his best cologne. What do all these individuals have in common? They are all aspiring to be liked.

People of all ages want to be liked—by their peers, families, teachers, bosses, and romantic partners. Their efforts are understandable: Likability brings a variety of rewards. First, being liked can contribute to survival. When people encounter danger or distress, it is helpful to have the support and assistance of their friends. Second, having friends is enjoyable; friends contribute to people's sense of belonging (Baumeister & Leary, 1995) and provide entertainment and conversation. Third, people who are liked are more likely to receive privileges and rewards such as invitations to parties and other social gatherings. Because of the benefits associated with being liked, people will go to great lengths to be likable or to appear likable.

People attempt to gain liking from others in at least two ways. First, because others often like people who are similar to themselves, many people conform to the behavior of others in an effort to be liked by them. The teenagers just described seek social approval by following unwritten but widely known prescriptions for "coolness." Second, as the young man and woman are aware, people often like others who are physically attractive. Because of the many benefits, people will go to great lengths to be or appear likable. However, creating or maintaining an image of someone who is "one of the gang" or of someone who is physically attractive can be problematic if taken too far.

MALADAPTIVE CONFORMING

For children and adolescents, popularity and liking often require conveying an image of someone who is "cool," someone who fits in. The child who is distinctive because of different clothing or an accent may be the target of torment and social exclusion. Thus, children learn quickly that to be liked and accepted, they must conform to social standards. Kids who adhere to the prevailing standard of dress and behavior are cool. Those who do not are called "nerds," "dweebs," and other uncharitable names. In many ways, conforming is beneficial—if nobody observed society's mores or unwritten rules of conduct, there would be chaos and disorder. However, when taken to extremes, conforming to fit in or appear cool can have dangerous consequences.

For example, sexual activity can be safe and free of consequences. However, the loss of one's virginity is often expedited by a desire to foster an image of someone who is mature or by a desire to "join the club." The decision to become sexually active, especially when made too soon, can lead to remorse and sorrow. Of course, sexual intercourse carries risks beyond hurt feelings and regret. One million unplanned pregnancies each year (Fielding & Williams, 1991) and prevalent STDs are the tangible results of irresponsible sex. Although adolescents are often knowledgeable about protected sex, many are swayed more by the perceived behavior of their friends. A. M. A. Smith and Rosenthal (1995) reported that risky behavior, such as engaging in unprotected sex, is partly influenced by peer approval.

One might expect members of the gay male community, individuals who are at particular risk for HIV and AIDS, to be more conscientious about their protection. However, some continue to shun condoms and engage in unsafe sexual activities. Among the strongest predictors of unsafe sex in homosexuals is the fear of making a negative impression (Gold, Skinner, Grant, & Plummer, 1991). In addition, embarrassment about buying or carrying condoms can also discourage safe sex (Zabin, Stark, & Emerson, 1991). It would appear that many people are more concerned with managing their partners' impressions than with preserving their health. Ironically, the STDs that may result can be the greatest obstacle of all to romance.

A desire to fit in and foster an image of someone who is cool also plays a role in the decision to use controlled substances (alcohol, cigarettes, illicit drugs). Researchers have documented that peer approval and a fear of being rejected by friends should they refuse is a primary motivator for youths who try cigarette smoking (Friedman, Lichtenstein, & Biglan, 1985; Sussman, 1989), illicit drugs (A. M. A. Smith & Rosenthal, 1995), and alcohol (Hunter, Vizelberg, & Berenson, 1991). By accepting the offered substance, youths may create a desired image of being cool, reckless, or brave. However, they also place themselves at risk to experience the negative consequences of these substances.

Failure to Seek or Accept Treatment

People like others who are healthy and tend to fear and avoid people who are unhealthy or otherwise suffering. This may be due to discomfort with the appearance or behavior of ill people. Some illnesses are disfiguring.

Other illnesses such as mental illness often produce unpredictable or inappropriate behavior. The avoidance of people who are ill or suffering may also arise from a fear that the illness is contagious. Finally, the prevailing Western view places much blame on the victims of illness, often holding them responsible for the onset and outcome of their diseases (Finerman & Bennett, 1995). Indeed, research on the "just-world phenomenon" (Lerner & Miller, 1978) reveals a tendency to regard people who are suffering as somehow deserving the condition, perhaps because they are bad people. Because they are blamed and avoided, unhealthy people are often motivated to hide their illness. Although this may help them preserve an image of normalcy, it often precludes necessary treatment to alleviate the problem.

Childhood Incest and Abuse

Abused or molested children are blameless victims, yet they often feel responsible, ashamed, and embarrassed about their abuse (Pipe & Goodman, 1991). Indeed, although it is estimated that 22.3% of women and 8.5% of men experience sexual abuse as children (Gorey & Leslie, 1997), the exact incidence is unknown because virtually all cases involve some element of secrecy (Sgroi, Porter, & Blick, 1982). In some cases, the children may receive threats from their abusers that frighten them into silence; 75% of incestuous relationships may be described as a parent–child secret (Bander, Fein, & Bishop, 1982). However, young victims of abuse often remain secretive because they fear a possible negative response and public disapproval (Lowery, 1987), and this fear is not unfounded. Research on the just-world phenomenon suggests that some people may judge incest victims as responsible or inferior and therefore dislike or reject them. In short, victims who admit to their incest and abuse may not be liked or accepted.

By remaining silent, victims maintain a public image of normalcy yet deprive themselves of treatment. By disclosing their experience, they could learn that they are not alone in their suffering and work toward absolving themselves of responsibility. Left untreated, victims of childhood sexual abuse can suffer devastating manifestations well into adulthood. These results can include sexual dysfunction, difficulty with intimate relationships, depression, low self-esteem, feelings of powerlessness, lack of trust, compulsive disorders, impulsivity, self-destructive behaviors, and difficulties in parenting their own children (Lowery, 1987). Although people may be motivated to convey an image of normalcy to their friends, their silence and avoidance of treatment may produce problems that haunt them for years to come.

Drug or Alcohol Abuse

As discussed earlier, many individuals begin using drugs or alcohol in attempts to fit in and impress friends. Ironically, these activities can develop into harmful habits that then bring social disapproval and stigma. Addicts or their families may be ashamed of the problem and thus attempt to conceal it from friends and acquaintances. In so doing, they fail to seek treatment for the addiction, often allowing it to progress to a deeper level.

Many drug addicts are capable of hiding their problem if they are motivated to do so. In one study, in which drug addicts were instructed to hide their habit, 52% succeeded in deceiving the interviewer and avoiding detection (Craig, Kuncei, & Olson, 1994). In addition to the addicts themselves, family members may feel ashamed of the addicts and assist in concealing the substance abuse (Naiditch, 1987), hoping to portray a public image of a happy, well-adjusted family. By failing to address the problem at hand, these families create future difficulties for both themselves and the addict: The addict remains untreated, and the family members can experience emotional difficulties. Children of alcoholic parents are especially prone to future problems, such as developmental delays and difficulties with trust and security (Naiditch, 1987). Furthermore, children of nonalcoholic parents function better behaviorally, cognitively, and emotionally than children raised in the family of an alcoholic parent (Bennett, 1995). If children of alcoholic parents could overcome their shame and reveal the problem to a teacher or trusted adult, the children could then receive intervention to avoid these developmental difficulties.

Addicts and their families generally conceal the addiction to appear normal and likable. Thus, it may seem that the greatest obstacle to treatment is failure to reveal that a problem exists. However, in some cases, admitting to the addiction does not ensure a smooth road to recovery. Some addicts may resist treatment even after their problem is acknowledged. Because drinking and drug use are admired in some social circles, some individuals may not want to be "cured." Many adolescents drop out of drug treatment programs because they are embarrassed to be receiving treatment or because they are suspicious that "the establishment" will try to infuse them with more conventional values (Raniseki & Sigelman, 1992). Indeed, refusing drug or alcohol treatment may help teens appear cool to their peers; however, those friends may mature and outgrow their respect for recklessness, leaving the untreated addict alone.

Mental or Physical Illness

Many illnesses, such as mental illness or STDs, carry a powerful stigma that is difficult to overcome (Link, Mirotznik, & Cullen, 1991). As a result, victims and their families may be afraid to reveal that they or a relative suffers from such an ailment. Because of this secrecy, victims may fail to seek treatment or to find appropriate support to cope with the situation.

In some cases, it is not the illness that is stigmatizing but the treatment. For example, although some children may not be ashamed of a particular disorder, they may refuse vital medication if it causes unattractive side-effects, like bloating or hairiness (Korsch, Fine, & Negrete, 1978). Furthermore, some children may avoid medication even without side-effects because the frequent doses force them to take medication at school and during social activities, setting them apart from their friends. This effect applies not only to medication but also to a variety of mental and physical problems that could otherwise be easily treated. Although many schools employ staff psychologists, speech therapists, and remedial tutors, students may reject their assistance to avoid an embarrassing summons from class.

In some cases an ailment may be hidden or denied, not because it is stigmatizing but because it is inconvenient. A child who suffers the misfortune of a sore throat on the day of a party may feign good health to avoid being kept at home. Likewise, an injured athlete may hide the injury to avoid missing an important game (Leary, 1995). These individuals often gain social approval for their behavior: The party goer remains part of the cool scene, and the athlete basks in the glory of a major sporting event. However, these rewards are not without a cost: By hiding their ailments, these individuals avoid treatment, perhaps allowing the condition to worsen and posing a serious threat to their physical well-being.

Rites of Passage

In some cultures, adolescents engage in rites of passage, activities that earn the respect of their peers and distinguish them from cowards or the uninitiated. Although these rituals may be dangerous or painful, youths consider them a necessary price for approval and acceptance. Portuguese boys construct an elaborate series of activities designed to demarcate the onset of manhood. These rites of passage are mandatory for any boy who wishes to achieve status or power; those who refuse are considered cowards or "girls." For these boys, the rite of passage consists of a frightening rampage, during which they confront a variety of dangerous situations. The 9- and 10-year-old participants report that the experience is frightening, but any boy who desires respect and acceptance takes part in the ritual (Alves, 1993).

In the United States, many Americans are subject to a variety of hazardous rites of passage. Fraternity hazing, the rigorous initiation faced by new fraternity pledges, has led to critical injuries and deaths. Although hazing is banned at virtually all universities and by all national fraternities, occasional news reports of accidents and other mishaps involving fraternity men and initiation reveal that hazing still occurs secretly. Sports teams also may impose dangerous initiation rites on players, as illustrated in the 1993 film *The Program* (Ward & Goldwyn, 1993), in which football players were required to lie on the yellow line of a busy street to prove their mental strength and fearlessness. Although the movie characters emerged un-scathed, some movie viewers later tried the stunt and suffered paralysis and death ("Disney plans," 1993). In their attempts to earn respect by proving themselves as courageous and brave, these young individuals sadly sacrificed their lives.

Sexual Interest

In some societies, women are discouraged from expressing interest in sex before marriage. Instead, they are expected to remain celibate until the night of their wedding. In many cases, women who hope to be liked and admired conform to this image of chastity in efforts to create a desirable image. Indeed, throughout history, virgin women have been prized and respected. In contrast, women who are sexually active before marriage are shunned. For adolescent girls, there is perhaps nothing worse than being called "easy" or labeled a "slut." It is noteworthy that there is no compa-rable pejorative term for promiscuous males, suggesting a double standard: Chastity is important for women but not men. Of course, an interest in sex is natural. For many women this presents a dilemma. How can women communicate an interest in sex without being disrespected?

A strategy used by some women is to express less interest in sex than they really feel. That is, some women may occasionally feign resistance to initial sexual advances solely to avoid appearing easy. In one study, 39% of college women surveyed reported saying no to male sexual advances when they really meant yes (Muehlenhard & Hollabaugh, 1988). Many of the women reported that they played "hard to get" for self-presentational reasons: to avoid appearing easy or promiscuous. The danger in the token resistance is that sometimes "no" does mean "no." However, some males may perceive a female's rejection as token resistance. No doubt, many instances of date rape occur because the male falsely interprets a refusal as a veiled acceptance. By attempting to appear pure or chaste, players of the hard-to-get game set a dangerous precedent that could haunt them—or others—later.

PHYSICAL ATTRACTIVENESS

People are often told that "beauty is only skin deep" and that "you can't judge a book by its cover." There is little doubt, however, that society places a high value on physical appearance. People tend to assume that attractive people have positive qualities (Feingold, 1992). The success of the fashion and cosmetic industries is a testament to people's desire to look their best. Because of the benefits of a presentable appearance, attention to one's grooming is wise. However, an extreme preoccupation with physical appearance can be dangerous or deadly.

Nutrition and Weight

Diet and exercise are often motivated by health concerns and can therefore have a positive impact on one's fitness. However, many people, especially females, aspire to achieve a weight that is actually below the average weight for healthy individuals (Brownell, 1991a), and twice as many people diet as those who medically need to do so (Brownell, 1991b). Excessive diet and preoccupation with food can have a variety of negative results, including malnutrition, lowered resistance to illness, and reduced energy. Some people may turn to drugs or diet pills to control their weight (Leary, Tchividjian, & Kraxberger, 1994) or resort to using laxatives and vomiting to purge excess eating.

Eating disorders, such as anorexia nervosa and bulimia, can produce severe physical damage. Victims may suffer hair loss, erosion of tooth enamel, heart disease, and even death. Sadly, many individuals who develop such disorders are motivated by beauty and popularity. Interviews with women with bulimia reveal that they believe weight loss will increase their popularity (Sacker & Zimmer, 1987) or will enable them to wear more stylish clothes (Hampshire, 1988). This effect can be especially pronounced in dating situations. Pliner and Chaiken (1990) found that women ate less when accompanied by an attractive male confederate than when accompanied by a less attractive male or a female confederate; other research reveals that women ate less if they were trying to convey an image of femininity (Mori, Chaiken, & Pliner, 1987). Unfortunately, some women are willing to starve or purge their way to a feminine image, damaging their health along the way.

A small appetite and narrow waist are considered feminine traits; in contrast, many males feel pressure to be muscular and strong. Males often turn to weight lifting and exercise to achieve a desirable physique, sometimes resorting to steroids to enhance this effect. These males believe that a muscular body will win them respect and attention from females (Leary et al., 1994). However, steroids can also bring acne, balding, reproductive difficulties, increased aggression, and depression—symptoms that are unappealing to many females. Thus, in their attempt to appear masculine and attractive in the short run, steroid users risk both their health and their attractiveness in the long run.

Suntanning

A hallmark of attractiveness is a "healthy" tan. Sun worshippers everywhere spend hours on beaches, by swimming pools, and, if necessary, in tanning salons in pursuit of the perfect bronze hue. Ironically, however, the healthy tan is anything but healthy. The dangers of ultraviolet exposure have been widely publicized and the incidence of skin cancer is growing: Recent estimates suggest that 40%–50% of Americans who live to age 65 will have skin cancer at least once (Hanley, Pierce, & Gayton, 1996). However, many people continue to equate a suntan with beauty and with an appearance of good health (Hanley et al., 1996). One survey revealed that 80% of college students spent most summer weekends in the sun and one third of female college students frequented tanning salons (Banks, Silverman, Schwartz, & Tunnessen, 1992).

Individuals who persist in tanning are typically aware of the risks (Hanley et al., 1996). However, they are motivated to create a good impression and to be seen as physically attractive (Leary & Jones, 1993). Indeed, the strongest predictors for people who expose themselves to ultraviolet radiation are an interest in personal appearance and a belief that a tan will enhance that appearance (Leary & Jones, 1993). Although a tan may temporarily increase attractiveness, the long-term skin damage and wrinkling is decidedly unattractive.

Tattoos and Body Piercing

More conservative individuals often view a tattoo as a stigma, a contemptible symbol of rebellion or recklessness. Thus, it may seem that people get tattoos to indicate defiance and individuality. However, in certain social circles, tattoos are admired as attractive statements of personality and expression, and people usually get tattoos to create a desired impression. Most commonly, people get tattoos to arouse their sexual partners, to increase affiliation with friends, to prove loyalty to their partners, or to shock the public (Myers, 1992).

Despite the social benefits they may bring, tattoos are not without risks. Acquiring a tattoo can cause pain, infection, viral transmission, tissue damage, venereal diseases, tuberculosis, skin diseases, allergic reactions, and warts (Houghton, Durkin, & Carroll, 1995; Myers, 1992). In addition to the health risks, people who choose to get a tattoo risk possible rejection from family or social groups, discrimination from employers, stigmatization, and possible regret (Myers, 1992).

Although body piercing is not as permanent as tattooing, it does carry many of the same health risks such as pain, infection, allergic reactions, and tissue damage (Myers, 1992). Nonetheless, people pierce a variety of body parts often to arouse or please their sexual partner or to create a desired impression among friends (Myers, 1992).

Summary

People generally aspire to be likable and will often go to great lengths to be liked by their peers, families, and others. One way people seek liking is by conforming to the behaviors and habits of others. Although this can win friends, it can be extremely dangerous when it interferes with precautionary behaviors (e.g., responsible sex, medical or psychological treatment) or when it leads to hazardous behaviors (e.g., substance abuse, dangerous rites of passage). A second way people attempt to be liked is by enhancing their physical beauty. However, although enhancing one's appearance is beneficial in a variety of ways, it can be extremely harmful when taken to extremes. Dieting, suntanning, tattoos, and body piercing can all injure—or even kill. In summary, although likability has a variety of rewards, an overzealous quest for liking can be one's downfall.

CONCLUSION

Much of human behavior is in the service of maintaining, either consciously or unconsciously, a particular self or social image. Two of the most common images that people seek to create or maintain are competence and likability. Many, if not most, efforts to appear competent or likable are beneficial (or at least harmless). As we noted, however, in some cases these efforts can be maladaptive and harmful to oneself or others. Our central thesis is that efforts to convey particular self-images can lead to a variety of emotional, behavioral, and interpersonal problems. If readers still feel that the negative consequences of image maintenance are minor, we offer a tragic anecdote of image maintenance gone terribly wrong. In 1995, the nationally televised *Jenny Jones Show* taped a program about secret admirers. One young man was shocked and humiliated to learn that his secret admirer was not a woman, as he had expected, but a long-time male acquaintance. During the taping, he laughed the surprise off. However, on his return home, he purchased a gun and killed his male admirer, apparently in a desperate attempt to regain face and quell any suspicion that he might be homosexual ("Talk show," 1995).

A modicum of efforts directed at image maintenance is reasonable and desirable. However, when the efforts become excessive, threatening the very image the person wishes to create or, worse yet, the health or well-being of oneself or others, then some intervention is necessary.

REFERENCES

Alves, J. (1991). Transgressions and transformations: Initiation rites among urban Portuguese boys. *American Anthropologist, 94,* 894–928.

Arkin, R. M., & Baumgardner, A. H. (1985). Self-handicapping. In J. H. Harvey & G. W. Weary (Eds.), *Attribution: Basic issues and applications* (pp. 169–202). New York: Academic Press.

Bander, K. W., Fein, E., & Bishop, G. (1982). Evaluation of child sexual abuse programs. In S. M. Sgroi (Ed.), *Handbook of clinical intervention in child sexual abuse* (pp. 345–376). Lexington, MA: Lexington Books.

Banks, B. A., Silverman, R. A., Schwartz, R. H., & Tunnessen, W. W. (1992). Attitudes of teenagers toward sun exposure and sunscreen use. *Pediatrics, 89,* 40–42.

Baumeister, R. F., & Leary, M. R. (1995). The need to belong: Desire for interpersonal attachment as a fundamental human motive. *Psychological Bulletin, 117,* 497–529.

Baumgardner, A. H., & Brownlee, E. A. (1987). Strategic failure in social interaction: Evidence for expectancy disconfirmation processes. *Journal of Personality and Social Psychology, 52,* 525–535.

Bennett, L. A. (1995). Accountability for alcoholism in American families. *Social Science and Medicine, 40,* 15–25.

Berglas, S., & Jones, E. E. (1978). Drug choice as a self-handicapping strategy in response to noncontingent success. *Journal of Personality and Social Psychology, 36,* 405–417.

Braginsky, B. M., & Braginsky, D. D. (1967). Schizophrenic patients in the psychiatric interview: An experimental study of their effectiveness at manipulation. *Journal of Consulting Psychology, 31,* 543–547.

Braginsky, B. M., Braginsky, D. D., & Ring, K. (1969). *Methods of madness: The mental hospital as a last resort.* New York: Holt, Rinehart & Winston.

Brownell, K. D. (1991a). Dieting and the search for the perfect body: Where physiology and culture collide. *Behavior Therapy, 22,* 1–12.

Brownell, K. D. (1991b). Personal responsibility and control over our bodies: When expectation exceeds reality. *Health Psychology, 10,* 303–310.

Byrne, D. (1971). *The attraction paradigm.* New York: Academic Press.

Craig, R. J., Kuncei, R., & Olson, R. E. (1994). Ability of a drug abuser to avoid detection of substance abuse on the MCMI-II. *Journal of Social Behavior and Personality, 9,* 95–106.

DeGree, C. E., & Snyder, C. R. (1985). Adler's psychology (of use) today: Personal history of traumatic life events as a self-handicapping strategy. *Journal of Personality and Social Psychology, 48,* 1512–1519.

Disney plans to omit film scene after teenager dies imitating it. (1993, October 20). *New York Times,* p. A21.

Fazio, R. H., Effrein, E. A., & Falender, V. J. (1981). Self-perceptions following social interactions. *Journal of Personality and Social Psychology, 41,* 232–242.

Feingold, A. (1992). Good-looking people are not what we think. *Psychological Bulletin, 111,* 304–341.

Fielding, J. E., & Williams, C. A. (1991). Adolescent pregnancy in the United States: A review and recommendations for clinicians and research needs. *American Journal of Preventive Medicine, 7,* 47–52.

Finerman, R., & Bennett, L. A. (1995). Guilt, blame, and shame: Responsibility in health and sickness. *Social Science and Medicine, 40,* 1–3.

Friedman, L. S., Lichtenstein, E., & Biglan, A. (1985). Smoking onset among teens: An empirical analysis of initial situations. *Addictive Behaviors, 10,* 1–13.

Gelles, R. J. (1972). *The violent home.* Beverly Hills, CA: Sage.

Gilbert, D. T., & Silvera, D. H. (1996). Overhelping. *Journal of Personality and Social Psychology, 70,* 678–690.

Goffman, E. (1959). *The presentation of self in everyday life* (rev. ed.). New York: Doubleday.

Gold, R. S., Skinner, M. J., Grant, P. J., & Plummer, D. C. (1991). Situational factors and thought processes associated with unprotected intercourse in gay men. *Psychology and Health, 5,* 259–278.

Gorey, K. M., & Leslie, D. R. (1997). The prevalence of child sexual abuse: Integrative review adjustment for potential response and measurement biases. *Child Abuse and Neglect, 21,* 391–398.

Hampshire, E. (1988). *Freedom from food.* Park Ridge, IL: Parkside.

Hanley, J. M., Pierce, J. L., & Gayton, W. F. (1996). Positive attitudes towards sun tanning and reported tendency to engage in lifestyle behaviors that increase risk to skin cancer. *Psychological Reports, 79,* 417–418.

Harris, R. N., & Snyder, C. R. (1986). The role of uncertain self-esteem in self-handicapping. *Journal of Personality and Social Psychology, 51,* 451–458.

Heider, F. (1958). *The psychology of interpersonal relations.* New York: Wiley.

Herrnstein, R. J., & Murray, C. A. (1994). *The bell curve: Intelligence and class structure in American life.* New York: Free Press.

Higgins, R. L., Snyder, C. R., & Berglas, S. (1990). *Self-handicapping: The paradox that isn't.* New York: Plenum.

Houghton, S., Durkin, K., & Carroll, A. (1995). Children's and adolescents' awareness of the physical and mental health risks associated with tattooing: A focus group study. *Adolescence, 30,* 971–988.

Hunter, S. D., Vizelberg, I. A., & Berenson, G. S. (1991). Identifying mechanisms of adoption of tobacco and alcohol use among youth: The Bogalusa Heart Study. *Social Networks, 13,* 91–104.

Jones, E. E., & Berglas, S. (1978). Control of attributions about the self through self-handicapping strategies: The appeal of alcohol and the role of underachievement. *Personality and Social Psychology Bulletin, 4,* 200–206.

Jones, E. E., Berglas, S., Rhodewalt, F., & Skelton, J. R. (1981). Effects of strategic self-presentation on subsequent self-esteem. *Journal of Personality and Social Psychology, 41*, 407–421.

Jones, E. E., & Davis, K. E. (1965). From acts to dispositions: The attribution process in person perception. In L. Berkowitz (Ed.), *Advances in experimental social psychology* (Vol. 2, pp. 219–266). New York: Academic Press.

Jones, E. E., & Pittman, T. S. (1982). Toward a general theory of strategic self-presentation. In J. Suls (Eds.), *Psychological perspectives on the self* (pp. 231–262). Hillsdale, NJ: Erlbaum.

Kelley, H. H. (1967). Attribution theory in social psychology. In D. Levine (Ed.), *Nebraska Symposium on Motivation* (Vol. 15, pp. 192–238). Lincoln: University of Nebraska Press.

Kolditz, T. A., & Arkin, R. M. (1982). An impression management interpretation of the self-handicapping strategy. *Journal of Personality and Social Psychology, 43*, 492–502.

Korsch, B. M., Fine, R. N., & Negrete, V. F. (1978). Noncompliance in children with renal transplants. *Pediatrics, 61*, 872–876.

Kowalski, R. M., & Leary, M. R. (1990). Strategic self-presentation and the avoidance of aversive events: Antecedents and consequences of self-enhancement and self-depreciation. *Journal of Experimental Social Psychology, 26*, 322–336.

Leary, M. R. (1995). *Self-presentation: Impression management and interpersonal behavior.* Boulder, CO: Westview Press.

Leary, M. R., & Jones, J. L. (1993). The social psychology of tanning and sunscreen use: Self-presentational motives as a predictor of health risk. *Journal of Applied Social Psychology, 23*, 1390–1406.

Leary, M. R., & Shepperd, J. A. (1986). Behavioral self-handicaps versus self-reported handicaps: A conceptual note. *Journal of Personality and Social Psychology, 51*, 1265–1268.

Leary, M. R., Tchividjian, L. R., & Kraxberger, B. E. (1994). Self-presentation can be hazardous to your health: Impression management and health risk. *Health Psychology, 13*, 461–470.

Lerner, M. J., & Miller, D. T. (1978). Just-world research and the attribution process: Looking back and ahead. *Psychological Bulletin, 85*, 1030–1051.

Link, B. G., Mirotznik, J., & Cullen, F. T. (1991). The effectiveness of stigma coping orientations: Can negative consequences of mental illness labeling be avoided? *Journal of Health and Social Behavior, 32*, 302–320.

Lowery, M. (1987). Adult survivors of childhood incest. *Journal of Psychosocial Nursing and Mental Health Services, 25*, 27–31.

Mori, D., Chaiken, S., & Pliner, P. (1987). "Eating lightly" and the self-presentation of femininity. *Journal of Personality and Social Psychology, 53*, 693–702.

Muehlenhard, C. L., & Hollabaugh, L. C. (1988). Do women sometimes say no when they mean yes? The prevalence and correlates of women's token resistance to sex. *Journal of Personality and Social Psychology, 54*, 872–879.

Myers, J. (1992). Nonmainstream body modification: Genital piercing, branding, burning, and cutting. *Journal of Contemporary Ethnography, 21,* 267–306.

Naiditch, B. (1987). Rekindled spirit of a child: Intervention strategies for shame with elementary age children of alcoholics. *Alcoholism Treatment Quarterly, 4,* 57–69.

Pipe, M., & Goodman, G. S. (1991). Elements of secrecy: Implications for children's testimony. *Behavioral Sciences and the Law, 9,* 33–41.

Pliner, P., & Chaiken, S. (1990). Eating, social motives, and self-presentation in women and men. *Journal of Experimental Social Psychology, 26,* 240–254.

Powers, T. A., & Zuroff, D. C. (1988). Interpersonal consequences of overt self-criticism: A comparison with neutral and self-enhancing presentations of self. *Journal of Personality and Social Psychology, 54,* 1054–1062.

Pyszczynski, T., & Greenberg, J. (1983). Determinants of reduction in intended effort as a strategy for coping with anticipated failure. *Journal of Research in Personality, 17,* 412–422.

Raniseki, J. M., & Sigelman, C. K. (1992). Conformity, peer pressure, and adolescent receptivity to treatment for substance abuse: A research note. *Journal of Drug Education, 22,* 185–194.

Rhodewalt, F., Saltzman, A. T., & Wittmer, J. (1984). Self-handicapping among competitive athletes: The role of practice in self-esteem protection. *Basic and Applied Social Psychology, 5,* 197–209.

Rossen, R. (Producer and Director). (1961). *The hustler* [Film]. (Available from CBS/Fox Video, 1211 Avenue of the Americas, New York, NY 10036)

Sacker, I. M., & Zimmer, M. A. (1987). *Support for weight loss: Dying to be thin.* New York: Warner Books.

Schlenker, B. R. (1980). *Impression management: The self-concept, social identity, and interpersonal relations.* Monterey, CA: Brooks/Cole.

Schlenker, B. R., & Britt, T. W. (in press). Beneficial impression management: Strategically controlling information to help friends. *Journal of Personality and Social Psychology.*

Schlenker, B. R., Britt, T. W., Pennington, J., Murphy, R., & Doherty, K. (1994). The triangle model of responsibility. *Psychological Review, 101,* 632–652.

Scorsese, M. (Producer and Director). (1986). *The color of money* [Film]. (Available from Touchstone Home Video, 500 South Buena Vista Street, Burbank, CA 91521-7145)

Self, E. A. (1990). Situational influences on self-handicapping. In R. L. Higgins, C. R. Snyder, & S. Berglas (Eds.), *Self-handicapping: The paradox that isn't* (pp. 37–68). New York: Plenum.

Sgroi, S. M., Porter, F. S., & Blick, L. C. (1982). Validation of child sexual abuse. In S. M. Sgroi (Ed.), *Handbook of clinical intervention in child sexual abuse* (pp. 39–79). Lexington, MA: Lexington Books.

Shakespeare, W. (1964). *Hamlet* [Play]. New York: St. Martin's Press.

Shelter, R. (Writer and Director), Miller, D., & Lester, D. (Producers). (1992).

White men can't jump [Film]. (Available from Fox Video Inc., P.O. Box 900, Beverly Hills, CA 90213)

Shepperd, J. A. (1993). Student derogation of the SAT: Biases in perceptions and presentations of college board scores. *Basic and Applied Social Psychology, 14,* 455–473.

Shepperd, J. A., & Arkin, R. M. (1991). Behavioral other-enhancement: Strategically obscuring the link between performance and evaluation. *Journal of Personality and Social Psychology, 60,* 79–88.

Shepperd, J. A., & Soucherman, R. (1997). On the manipulative behavior of low Machiavellians: Feigning incompetence to "sandbag" an opponent's effort. *Journal of Personality and Social Psychology, 72,* 1448–1459.

Smith, A. M. A., & Rosenthal, D. A. (1995). Adolescents' perceptions of their risk environment. *Journal of Adolescence, 18,* 229–245.

Smith, T. W., Snyder, C. R., & Handelsman, M. M. (1982). On the self-serving function of an academic wooden leg: Test anxiety as a self-handicapping strategy. *Journal of Personality and Social Psychology, 42,* 314–321.

Snyder, C. R., & Higgins, R. L. (1988). Excuses: Their effective role in the negotiation of reality. *Psychological Bulletin, 104,* 23–35.

Snyder, C. R., Higgins, R. L., & Stucky, R. J. (1983). *Excuses: Masquerades in search of grace.* New York: Wiley Interscience.

Snyder, C. R., Smith, T. W., Augelli, R. W., & Ingram, R. E. (1985). On the self-serving function of social anxiety: Shyness as a self-handicapping strategy. *Journal of Personality and Social Psychology, 48,* 970–980.

Snyder, M. L., Smoller, B., Strenta, A., & Frankel, A. (1991). A comparison of egotism, negativity, and learned helplessness as explanations for poor performance after unsolvable problems. *Journal of Personality and Social Psychology, 40,* 24–30.

Stires, L. D., & Jones, E. E. (1969). Modesty versus self-enhancement as alternative forms of ingratiation. *Journal of Experimental Social Psychology, 5,* 172–188.

Sussman, S. (1989). Two social influence perspectives of tobacco use development and prevention. *Health Education Research, 4,* 213–223.

Swann, W. B., Jr., & Read, S. J. (1981). Self-verification processes: How we sustain our self-conceptions. *Journal of Experimental Social Psychology, 17,* 351–372.

Talk show sparks murder. (1995, March 11). *Rocky Mountain News,* p. A3.

Tice, D. M. (1992). Self-concept change and self-presentation: The looking glass self is also a magnifying glass. *Journal of Personality and Social Psychology, 63,* 435–451.

Tice, D. M., & Baumeister, R. F. (1990). Self-esteem, self-handicapping, and self-presentation: The strategy of inadequate practice. *Journal of Personality, 58,* 443–464.

Ward, D. S. (Director), & Goldwyn, S., Jr. (Producer). (1993). *The program* [Film]. (Available from Buena Vista Home Video, Dept. CS, Burbank, CA 91521)

Weary, G., & Williams, J. P. (1990). Depressive self-presentation: Beyond self-handicapping. *Journal of Personality and Social Psychology, 58,* 892–898.

Zabin, L. S., Stark, H. A., & Emerson, M. R. (1991). Reasons for the delay in contraceptive clinic utilization. *Journal of Adolescent Health, 12,* 225–232.

IV

PERSONAL RELATIONSHIPS

10

SOCIAL SUPPORT AND PSYCHOLOGICAL DISORDER: INSIGHTS FROM SOCIAL PSYCHOLOGY

GARY L. RHODES AND BRIAN LAKEY

Social support research has always been multidisciplinary, and important contributions have come from the fields of epidemiology, medicine, sociology, psychology, and public health. Within psychology, important contributions have come from diverse areas such as clinical, community, health, social, personality, and developmental psychology, and, most recently, social cognition. Social support research has played an important role in helping to reintroduce the study of social relationships to psychopathology and medicine and holds great promise for promoting the integration of clinical and social psychology. The results of clinical research make it abundantly clear that social relations are integral to mental and physical health, a fact that underscores the legitimacy of basic research on social processes and social cognition. At the same time, insights from basic

The preparation of this chapter was supported by a pilot research grant from the Alzheimer's Association, New York City chapter. Kathy Adams made valuable comments on an earlier draft of this chapter.

research in social psychology can inform applied questions about support and well-being (Lakey & Drew, 1997; G. R. Pierce, Lakey, Sarason, Sarason & Joseph, 1997).

Our basic premise in this chapter is that social support phenomena are so diverse and complex that researchers in the field need a wide range of theoretical perspectives to understand them. In fact, one of the most important advances in social support research has been the discovery that different components of social support are only weakly related and reflect different processes. For example, the belief that others would help (i.e., perceived support) is distinct from others' actual helping behaviors (i.e., enacted support), which is distinct from social network characteristics (e.g., size, density). Moreover, perceived support itself appears to reflect at least three distinct classes of processes, and these different processes appear to have different relations to outcomes. Despite this complexity, social support theory focuses on only a few potential mechanisms. To advance, social support research needs to import a wide range of explanatory mechanisms from other areas of scholarship, especially social and personality psychology.

Social support research exists because of the well-documented relation between low social support and emotional disorder. This effect has been observed in hundreds, if not thousands, of studies (Barrera, 1986; Cohen & Wills, 1985; G. R. Pierce, Sarason, & Sarason, 1996; Vaux, 1988). Moreover, many studies show that low social support predicts future deterioration in mental health, even when initial levels of mental health are controlled statistically (Compas, Wagner, Slavin, & Vannatta, 1986; Hays, Turner, & Coates, 1992; Holahan, Moos, Holahan, & Brennan, 1995; Lepore, Evans, & Schneider, 1991; Phifer & Murrell, 1986; Swindle, Cronkite, & Moos, 1989; Valentiner, Holahan, & Moos, 1994). Results of these studies provide evidence that low support may precede the development of symptoms and cast doubt on the alternative hypothesis that low support is merely a result of chronic emotional disorder. Other research shows that low support and emotional distress are not merely a result of chronically low levels of social competence (Cohen, Sherrod, & Clark, 1986; Lakey, 1989). Thus, although a causal relation between social support and emotion cannot be established with correlational designs, a few of the most obvious alternative hypotheses have not fared well.

In contrast to emotional disorder, the relation between low social support and physical illness is somewhat less clear (Smith, Fernengel, Holcroft, Gerald, & Marien, 1994). However, individuals with poor support are at greater risk for specific disease-related processes (e.g., Uchino, Cacioppo, & Kiecolt-Glaser, 1996). Moreover, several studies show that low-support individuals are more likely to die than their high-support counterparts. The relation between low support and mortality is especially impressive because the effect is not due to obvious risk factors (e.g., physical health) nor is it limited to death by suicide (Berkman & Syme, 1979;

Blazer, 1982; House, Landis, & Umberson, 1988). Thus, there is little doubt that social support is an important part of emotional and physical health.

Nonetheless, important questions remain unanswered. First, because research on social support and health is primarily correlational in nature, researchers do not know whether social support has a causal relation to mental and physical health. Second, the exact mechanisms by which support is related to health remain unknown. There is even substantial uncertainty about how social support is represented cognitively and how such representations are related to what actually happens in the social world. Before psychologists can use their knowledge of social support to improve treatment and preventive interventions, they must have a better understanding of the basic psychology of social support. Research from social psychology is especially helpful in understanding these basic mechanisms.

HISTORICAL DEVELOPMENT OF SOCIAL SUPPORT RESEARCH

Most social support research focuses on the role that social support plays in psychological and physical health. To a large extent, research in social support and health is an outgrowth of research on life stress (Holmes & Rahe, 1967; Selye, 1956) and social networks (Durkheim, 1895/1957).

Social network approaches, derived from sociology and anthropology, had a strong influence on early social support research (Berkman & Syme, 1979; Durkheim, 1895/1957; Lowenthal & Haven, 1968; Mitchel, 1969). In this tradition, social support was conceptualized and measured as the number of interpersonal relationships, number of social contacts, or the interrelation among network members (e.g., density or the extent to which network members have relationships with other network members). This tradition can trace its roots to Durkeim's (1895/1957) classic study relating social integration to suicide.

Several early studies fueled interest in network approaches. Lowenthal (1964, 1965; Lowenthal & Haven, 1968) found that measures of social isolation and confidant relationships were related to morale and psychological disorder in community samples of older people. Berkman and Syme (1979) found that social networks prospectively predicted mortality in a large, randomly selected community sample. Brown and Harris (1978) found that the presence of a confidant appeared to protect women from developing clinical depression and anxiety after experiencing severe life events. Hirsch (1979, 1980) found that network density was linked to receiving more enacted support but less satisfaction with the support received.

Although the studies on network characteristics and physical and mental health were impressive and influential, social support research grad-

ually deemphasized network approaches in the 1980s. This deemphasis occurred for both theoretical and empirical reasons. Empirically, network
measures came to be viewed as inferior predictors of mental health, especially compared with the newly developed measures of perceived support
(Barrera, 1986; Cohen & Wills, 1985; Sandler & Barrera, 1984). Theoretically, network measures were criticized for not providing information
about the psychological and interpersonal processes that linked social support to emotional well-being (Barrera, 1986; Cohen & Wills, 1985).

Another important impetus to the study of social support was research
on stressful life events. Life events research (Holmes & Rahe, 1967) established an intriguing relation between events and subsequent health
problems. However, scholars were disappointed in the strength of this effect
($r = .30$) and began an earnest search for factors that might moderate the
events–health relation (Rabkin & Streuning, 1976). The assumption underlying this search was that if scholars could identify groups of people who
were especially vulnerable to events, then at least among these people the
strength of the relation between events and disorder might be strong. Researchers focused on two basic vulnerability factors: the characteristics of
the person (e.g., locus of control; Cohen & Edwards, 1989) and the characteristics of the environment (e.g., social support). The environmental
side of the equation has expanded beyond a mere subcomponent of the
stress process and has evolved into social support research—a literature
that is at least as rich and vast as stress research itself.

Perhaps the single most important influence in the development of
social support research was the publication of several highly influential
reviews that describe research linking social relations to mental and physical health (Caplan, 1974; Cassel, 1973; Cobb, 1976; Dean & Lin, 1977;
Kaplan, Cassel, & Gore, 1977). Although research on social relations and
health had been gradually emerging before this time, these reviews
prompted an avalanche of new work. These reviews emphasize the stress-
buffering effects of social ties (i.e., the ability of an aspect of social relations
to reduce the effects of stress on mental and physical health).

The early emphasis on stress buffering led to a widely influential
model of social support throughout the 1980s and 1990s. This traditional
view of social support has been the driving force behind most social support
studies. According to this view, social support protects people from stressful
events by enhancing their coping ability. According to Caplan (1974),

> significant others help the individual mobilize his psychological re-
> sources and master his emotional burdens; they share his tasks; and
> they provide him with extra supplies of money, materials, tools, skills,
> and cognitive guidance to improve his handling of his situation. (p. 6)

This conceptualization of social support was reflected in the development of new measures of the construct. Social support research in the

1970s was limited by the absence of good support measures with known psychometric qualities (Dean & Lin, 1977). During the early 1980s, several social support measures were developed, including those by Barrera, Sandler, and Ramsay (1981), Cohen and Hoberman (1983), Procidano and Heller (1983), and I. G. Sarason, Levine, Basham, and Sarason (1983). By and large, these scales include items that reflect the provision of aid similar to those outlined by Caplan (1974). These scales were extremely important in the evolution of social support research. Not only did they provide psychometrically sound means for measuring support in subsequent studies, but the content of the items also described the kinds of behaviors and beliefs that made up the social support construct.

Although social support researchers later increasingly emphasized the role of support perceptions, perceived support was seen as important because of its link to actual supportive behaviors during times of stress (i.e., enacted support). For example, Procidano and Heller (1983) and Heller and Swindle (1983) saw perceived support as being derived from enacted support and as serving to stimulate the seeking and receiving of subsequent enacted support. Similarly, although Cohen and Hoberman (1983) and Cohen and McKay (1984) hypothesized that perceived support acted by influencing appraisal processes (Lazarus & Folkman, 1984), they believed perceived support was based directly on enacted support.

THE ASCENDANCY OF THE STRESS-BUFFERING PERSPECTIVE

Although social support came to be viewed almost universally in terms of stress buffering acting through enacted support, this conception was only one of several perspectives identified in the early theoretical work of Caplan, Cassel, Cobb, Kaplan, and Gore. In our opinion, stress buffering through enacted support emerged as the dominant model because of a variety of historical factors rather than because other conceptions were thoroughly explored and rejected empirically.

Caplan (1974), Cobb (1976), and Kaplan et al. (1977) explicitly stated that social support meets basic human needs. Caplan (1974), in particular, seemed to take a broad view of social support:

> People have a variety of specific needs that demand satisfaction through enduring interpersonal relationships, such as for love and affection, for intimacy that provides the freedom to express feelings easily and unself-consciously, for validation of personal identity and worth, for satisfaction of nurturance and dependency, for help with tasks, and for support in handling emotion and controlling impulses. Most people develop and maintain a sense of well-being by involving themselves in a range of relationships in their lives that in toto satisfy these specific needs. (p. 5)

Similarly, Kaplan et al. (1977) cited Murray (1938) in stating that social support may meet basic psychological needs. Murray conducted an intensive study of personality and derived a list of 20 basic psychogenic human needs. Among them were the "need for succorance" and the "need for affiliation." The need for succorance corresponds closely to the modern concept of social support because it involves being "nursed, supported, advised, guided and consoled" (Murray, 1938, p. 182). Murray hypothesized several distinct emotions and behavior patterns associated with these needs and cited specific environmental factors that produce strong needs for affiliation and succorance.

Lowenthal and Haven (1968) appeared to have been somewhat less influential in their theoretical development of social support research. However, their 1968 article is theoretically rich. Lowenthal and Haven argued that research on social relations and mental health has not focused sufficiently on the subjective and psychological aspects of relationships. They cited a wide range of research from psychology and sociology, suggesting that intimacy in itself is important for mental health. In building their thesis, Lowenthal and Haven cited research by Harlow and Zimmerman (1959), Bowlby (1958), and Erikson (1959).

Although Cobb (1976) and Caplan (1974) clearly emphasized stress buffering, their conception of buffering was much broader than the interpretation that subsequently dominated the field. The stress construct in most stress-buffering research came to be conceptualized and measured in terms of major, discrete life events (e.g., divorce or bereavement). However, the conception of stress that guided Cobb, Caplan, Cassel, and Kaplan placed a greater emphasis on what might be called "social disorganization" (Caplan, 1974, p. 10). Caplan (1974) began his chapter on social systems with Cassel's (1973) concept of stress that involved "individuals . . . not receiving any evidence (feedback) that their actions are leading to desirable and/or anticipated consequences" (p. 1). Family support acts to protect individuals from "inadequate feedback in the outside world" (Caplan, 1974, p. 10). If stress is the lack of consistent and meaningful information and support is the provision of that information (Cobb, 1976), then support operates through the same principles as stress rather than representing a different process. Stress buffering in this sense is an additive model rather than a multiplicative one. Stress is a lack of clear information; support provides that information. Thus, the amount of social disorganization reflects the amount of stress minus the amount of support. This is a different conception of stress buffering than the one that emerged in the early 1980s. Subsequent scholars worked to ensure that stress and support were distinct processes (Cohen & Hoberman, 1983; Heller, 1979; Heller & Swindle, 1983).

Although not explicitly identified as such by Caplan, Cassel, Cobb, and Kaplan, viewing stress and support in terms of inadequate information about social performance is essentially a symbolic interactionist view (Stry-ker, 1980). Somewhat later, the sociologist Thoits (1985) developed an explicitly symbolic interactionist conception of social support. She hy-pothesized that social support leads directly to emotional well-being (re-gardless of stress level) by providing a sense of identity and belonging, self-esteem, and comparative mastery. Thoits (1985) wrote that

> aspects of regularized social interaction, and not emotional support dimensions per se, are responsible for maintaining well-being. What we recognize as dimensions of emotional support and main effects of sup-port are simply byproducts of these more abstract social-psychological processes. (pp. 57–58)

In revisiting the work of early social support theorists, one can see that a wide range of potential perspectives were offered. Each of these perspectives suggests that social support plays a much broader role than merely enhancing coping with stress. From the symbolic interactionist, at-tachment, and need perspectives, social support promotes well-being in and of itself. There is no need to link support effects to stress and coping theory. However, as social support research developed in the 1980s, a single per-spective achieved hegemony. However, this dominance was not a result of a scientific process in which a wide range of models were articulated and tested. In our opinion, stress buffering achieved dominance because of sev-eral historical factors.

Social support research largely was introduced to psychology by schol-ars with a strong connection to community psychology (e.g., Barrera, Gott-lieb, Heller, Hirsch, Moos, Sandler), and the *American Journal of Com-munity Psychology* was one of the main outlets for this new research. At that time, community psychology emphasized prevention through under-standing risk factors for psychological disorder. Community psychology was heavily influenced by community psychiatry, public health, and epidemi-ology. Thus, scholars were looking for ways to increase the support available in the community from diverse sources such as barbers and bartenders as well as mutual-aid groups (Caplan, 1974; Heller & Monahan, 1977). Re-search on social support offered the promise of showing how support could be provided to individuals who had been marginalized.

Research on stressful life events was a primary area of empirical in-vestigation by community psychologists, and one of the main conceptual tools was Lazarus's (1966; Lazarus & Folkman, 1984) stress and coping theory. Thus, conceptualizing social support as an adjunct to coping fit nicely within an important conceptual model of community psychology. Thus, even though social support could have been conceptualized in terms of need, attachment, symbolic interactionist, or cognitive theory, the psy-chologists who began work in social support were less influenced by these models than they were by stress and coping theory. Moreover, the late

1970s represented one of the low ebbs of personality approaches. Personality psychology had not yet recovered from Mischel's (1968) near-annihilating critique of trait approaches, and many empirically oriented psychologists avoided personality perspectives. Similarly, cognitive approaches (e.g., Beck, 1967) had not yet achieved the ascendancy that they have enjoyed in recent years, and many social support scholars saw it as a virtue to avoid respondents' subjective judgments about their social networks (e.g., Barrera et al., 1981; Brown & Harris, 1978).

In our view, the stress-buffering perspective achieved hegemony because of the particular interests and backgrounds of the scholars who introduced social support research to psychology. If these same scholars had been interested primarily in research on psychological needs, attachment, or symbolic interactionism, social support research would have developed much differently. Of course, if these scholars had been primarily interested in such factors, they probably would not have been reading epidemiology journals and may have missed social support research altogether. Our point is not that stress buffering is unimportant but that it is not the only, or even the most important, perspective from which to understand social support. As we discuss in the following pages, social support phenomena are extremely complex and diverse. To adequately capture the wide range of social support phenomena, those in the field must cultivate a wide range of perspectives.

THE DISAGGREGATION OF SOCIAL SUPPORT PROCESSES

One of the first major advances in social support research was the recognition that many social support measures actually reflected different processes. There are several different types of support measures. Perceived support measures ask for subjective judgments of the availability or quality of social support. Measures of enacted support refer to the receipt of specific supportive behaviors, such as advice or reassurance. Network measures assess more structural aspects of the social network, such as the size of a social network or the extent to which network members know each other (i.e., density). Measures of support seeking assess individual differences in the tendency to seek out support for a range of problems. Heller and Swindle (1983) were among the first to provide a model of social support and coping that distinguished among social networks, perceived support, support seeking, and enacted support.[1] Heller and Lakey (1985) reviewed studies conducted at Indiana University in the early 1980s that show that measures of social networks, enacted support, perceived support, and sup-

---

[1]Mitchel (1969) made a similar observation regarding social networks. However, Mitchel's primary audience appeared to be anthropologists and sociologists, thus his work did not appear to have a great influence on the development of social support research within psychology.

port seeking were only weakly related and had different relations to other constructs. In 1986, Barrera reviewed a number of studies and concluded that perceived support, enacted support, and network characteristics were only weakly related and that only perceived support appeared to have strong, consistent relations to emotional well-being. Similarly, Wethington and Kessler (1986) found in a large community study that perceived support, but not enacted support, was related to emotional well-being. Approaching social support from a different perspective, Rook showed that negative social interactions (Rook, 1984) and companionship (Rook, 1987) were distinct from social support and were related to emotion independently of social support.

The importance of distinguishing among the different social support processes was not widely understood in the early days of social support research. In the late 1970s and early 1980s, researchers used many different support measures that reflected different processes. These disparate measures all were referred to as "social support," even though the measures reflected different things. This led to a contradictory and confusing literature because different studies produced different outcomes depending on the measures used. As a result, the social support construct was widely viewed as vague (Dean & Lin, 1977; Heller, 1979; Rabkin & Struening, 1976).

Theoretically, the absence of a strong link between perceived and enacted support is of fundamental importance because the dominant stress-buffering model assumes a strong link between perceived and enacted support. The literature on the relation between perceived and enacted support has been reviewed in more detail elsewhere (Lakey & Drew, 1997; Lakey, McCabe, Fisicaro, & Drew, 1996), so we provide only a brief summary here. Self-report measures of perceived and enacted support generally are no more highly correlated than $r = .30$, with many correlations approaching zero (Barrera, 1986; Dunkel-Schetter & Bennett, 1990; Newcomb, 1990; Sandler & Barrera, 1984; B. R. Sarason, Sarason, & Pierce, 1990; B. R. Sarason, Shearin, Pierce, & Sarason, 1987). Moreover, this relation may be an overestimate because of shared methods variance and a tendency of high-perceived-support people to have better memory for support-relevant behavior than low-support individuals (Lakey & Cassady, 1990; Lakey, Moineau, & Drew, 1992; Rudolph, Hammen, & Burge, 1995). Observational laboratory studies also failed to show strong relationships between enacted and perceived support (Belsher & Costello, 1991; Gurung, Sarason, & Sarason, 1994; Heller & Lakey, 1985; Kirmeyer & Lin, 1987; Lakey & Heller, 1988). Stronger effects have been found by researchers who have examined supportive behavior during specific interactions and participants' judgments of those same interactions (Burleson & Samter, 1985, Study 1; Cutrona & Suhr, 1994; Winstead, Derlega, Lewis, Sanchez-Hucles, & Clarke, 1992), but it is unclear to what extent judgments of specific interactions are generalized to an enduring sense of perceived support. In addition to the weak link between perceived and enacted support, perceived and enacted support show different relations to mental health. Low perceived support is consistently related to poor mental health, whereas enacted support is either unrelated or positively related to emotional distress (Barrera, 1986; Dunkel-Schetter & Bennett, 1990; B. R. Sarason et al., 1990).

Thus, at best, enacted support accounts for 10% of the variance in perceived support. When phenomena are assumed to be multiply determined, effect sizes of this magnitude are perfectly reasonable (Ahadi & Diener, 1989). Thus, the size of the perceived–enacted support relation suggests that both constructs are multiply determined. Although perceived support may be based partly on enacted support, enacted support is only one of its many determinants.

Disaggregating Perceived Support

Perceived support itself appears to result from at least three distinct classes of processes. Lakey, McCabe, et al. (1996) recently applied generalizability theory (Cronbach, Gleser, Nanda, & Rajaratnam, 1972; Shavelson & Webb, 1991) to the study of perceived support. Generalizability theory provides a powerful set of conceptual and methodological tools for determining the sources of variation for a set of scores. When perceivers rate the same supporters on supportiveness, generalizability theory can be used to estimate the extent to which support judgments are based on perceivers, supporters, or the Perceiver × Supporter interaction. Lakey, McCabe, et al. conducted three generalizability studies and concluded that the Perceiver × Supporter interaction was the largest single determinant of support judgments, accounting for an average of 41% of the variance. The effects of perceivers and supporters were important but were comparatively smaller (8% and 20%, respectively).

The Perceiver × Supporter interaction reflects processes by which perceivers disagree on which targets are most supportive, even though perceivers are rating the same targets. In this way, judging support is similar to judging beauty or art appreciation. One should not expect high levels of agreement about what is beautiful or what is good art. For example, in the 1996 presidential election, voters were asked to consider who was more concerned about voters' problems: Bob Dole or Bill Clinton. Voters disagreed substantially about whom they viewed as more sympathetic, even when they had access to similar information about the candidates. Such effects are conceptually identical to relationship effects in person perception research (Kenny, 1994). Kenny and his colleagues (e.g., Kenny, Albright, Malloy, & Kashy, 1994) have conducted extensive analyses of person perception using the social relations model (a variation on generalizability theory) and found that a large portion of personality judgments reflected the unique relationship between the perceiver and the target. In fact, Kenny's (1994) estimate of the size of the relationship effect in liking judgments (38%) was nearly identical to the Lakey, McCabe, et al. (1996) estimate for support judgments (41%).

The Perceiver × Supporter interaction most likely is a result of a wide range of both cognitive and behavioral processes. Thus, the Perceiver × Supporter interaction does not reflect a single entity or construct. As an example of a behavioral process, certain perceivers may elicit different behaviors from some targets but not others. One target may be cool and aloof to almost everyone but may be especially sympathetic to a few people who have shared an important personal experience (e.g., the death of a parent). For an example of cognitive processes, Lakey, Ross, Butler, and Bentley (1996) found that support judgments are based partly on the similarity between perceivers' and targets' attitudes and values. This effect reflects the Perceiver × Supporter interaction because the same attitudes and values that make one perceiver similar to a supporter make that perceiver dissimilar to another supporter. In addition, people may differ in the types of information they use to infer supportiveness and the relative weights they assign to that information.

Lutz (1997; Lutz & Lakey, 1997) conducted a series of studies designed to examine individual differences in how people use personality information to infer supportiveness. Respondents rated several hypothetical targets that varied systematically on each of the Big Five personality dimensions. Regression equations were constructed for each respondent to explain her or his use of the Big Five in making support judgments. The results revealed substantial individual differences in the traits used to infer supportiveness, although the large majority of respondents relied on the trait of agreeableness to some extent. Many respondents' regression models were complex and required nonlinear and configural terms.

Lutz (1997; Lutz & Lakey, 1997) also found that respondents' personalities predicted how they used trait information to make support judgments: People used a given personality dimension insofar as they believed that they possessed the trait themselves. Thus, respondents saw similar others as supportive. In another study, Lutz extended these findings to perceptions of actual network members. Again, respondents saw network members as supportive insofar as network members' personality characteristics were similar to respondents' own. In Lutz's third study, respondents rated the supportiveness and personality of a group of TV characters from a popular situation comedy. Again, the traits that were used to make support judgments were the same traits that respondents believed they possessed. Thus, Lutz's research indicates that part of the Perceiver × Supporter interaction reflects a process by which different people use different decision rules to infer supportiveness. These decision rules would lead two people to perceive the same targets differently, even if they were exposed to the same information about targets.

Beyond the Perceiver × Supporter interaction, perceiver effects also account for a significant portion of support judgments (Lakey, McCabe, et al., 1996). Perceiver effects represent the tendency for some perceivers to see the same targets as more or less supportive than other perceivers, apart from actual differences in targets' "true" supportiveness. Perceiver effects can result from both behavioral and cognitive processes. Behaviorally, perceivers may act in a way to elicit consistently supportive or nonsupportive behaviors across all targets. Such a process may be similar to the tendency of depressed people to elicit negative responses in others (Coyne, 1976). Cognitive mechanisms would involve perceivers seeing targets as consistently supportive or unsupportive regardless of targets' actual characteristics. Several studies show that people with low perceived support view the same targets as less supportive than do high-support people, even when respondents are supplied with identical information about the targets (Anan & Barnett, 1997; Lakey & Cassady, 1990; Lakey & Dickinson, 1994; Lakey et al., 1992; Mallinckrodt, 1991; G. R. Pierce, Sarason, & Sarason, 1992; Rudolph et al., 1995; B. R. Sarason, Pierce, Sarason, Waltz, & Poppe, 1991). Similarly, low- versus high-support people also make more negative attributions for the times when they did not get the social support they needed (Ross, Lutz, & Lakey, in press). These effects have been replicated in several different laboratories, using a range of different methods, in studies of college students, psychotherapy patients, poor inner-city African American children, and middle-class children. Similar findings have been obtained by Andersen and her colleagues (Andersen & Cole, 1990; Andersen, Reznik, & Manzella, 1996; Hinkley & Andersen, 1996). They have shown that people transfer the features of significant others onto novel targets who resemble those significant others. Furthermore, such transference is associated with evaluations, expectancies, and affect similar to that elicited by significant others. Similarly, N. L. Collins (1996) found that individuals who differ in attachment style differ in how they interpret ambiguously negative partner behavior.

Supporter effects reflect the part of supportiveness that resides in the "actual" characteristics of targets. In this sense, the word *actual* refers to an agreement among a group of perceivers that a target is more or less supportive. This is the component of supportiveness emphasized by traditional social support research. Lakey, Ross, et al. (1996) estimated the size of the supporter effect at 20%. This is similar to Repetti's (1987) earlier estimate of 23%, which was based on a similar methodology. These estimates of targets' supportiveness are also highly similar to the level of judges' agreement on targets' personality characteristics (Kenny, 1994).

The "objectively supportive" aspect of support probably is related to the quality and amount of enacted support that targets provide. However, target effects likely have multiple determinants. For example, perceivers base support judgments partly on the personality characteristics of targets (Lakey, Ross, et al., 1996; Lutz, 1997; Lutz & Lakey, 1997). Thus, although support judgments are partly based on the actual characteristics of targets, the enacted support provided by targets appears to be only one of several potential determinants of such judgments.

Subcomponents of Perceived Support May Have Different Relations to Outcomes

As we discussed, rather than reflecting a single entity, perceived support is composed of at least three distinct classes of processes. Furthermore, these three classes of processes may have different relations to outcomes. At first, it may seem counterintuitive that a single score on a perceived support scale may reflect a range of distinct processes. Whenever one assigns a single score to represent a given construct, the singularity of the score is frequently interpreted as indicating that the score reflects a unified psychological entity. This implicit assumption is reflected in how psychologists describe their constructs. Psychologists talk about anxiety rather than the component processes that make up anxiety. They talk about self-concepts rather than the concepts of self as lover or self as child.

Yet there are several reasons why psychologists should doubt this apparent unity of psychological constructs. First, consider the internal consistency of a perceived support measure. Although psychologists sum across items to produce a single score and obtain high estimates of internal consistency,[2] the correlations among the items themselves are usually only moderate (rs typically range from .30 to .40). Thus, the different items must reflect a range of different influences, or they would be nearly perfectly correlated. Psychologists tend to assume that error in measurement is the only reason the items are not more highly correlated. Yet meaningful processes that are not explicitly represented in a reliability study are represented statistically as error (Cronbach et al., 1972). However, it is only error in the sense that psychologists do not understand it. Second, it is widely assumed in social–cognitive research that people have several different concepts of the self and the social world (Higgins, 1996). Thus, the total score on a social support measure probably reflects some combination

---

[2] It is worthwhile to reflect on what estimates of internal consistency mean. Although Cronbach's alpha usually is interpreted as the proportion of variance attributable to reliable differences between individuals, it must be remembered that situational influences are typically not assessed and, when present, are averaged out. Second, the standard formula used by software packages, such as SPSS, exclude variance attributable to items when estimating effects attributable to individual differences (see Wiggins, 1973). When the researcher is interested only in comparing the relative ranking of individuals, differences produced by items are unimportant. However, researchers should remember that such alphas are typically high, not so much because all items in a scale reflect the same construct primarily but because other sources of variance (e.g., situations and items) typically are not modeled and are averaged out.

of different concepts of supportiveness corresponding to different targets. Furthermore, the items themselves may reflect different processes. Consider two items from Procidano and Heller's (1983) perceived support scale: "My family gives me the moral support I need," and "Members of my family seek me out for companionship." Responses to these items may reflect different transactions with different family members and may be represented by different constructs in the minds of respondents. Furthermore, the processes tapped by these items may have different relations to outcomes. For example, moral support may be strongly influenced by religiosity, whereas companionship may be strongly influenced by extraversion.

We believe that these rational arguments and the data by Lakey, McCabe, et al. (1996) provide reasons to believe that the different components of perceived support may have different relations to outcomes. Moreover, two recent studies provide evidence that different components of perceived support have different relations to emotion and that the component that is related to emotion may differ according to which social construct is under study.

Lakey, Drew, and Sirl (in press) examined whether differences in support judgments between clinically depressed patients and controls followed the pattern of perceiver effects or Perceiver × Supporter interaction. Inpatients and nondisordered controls rated the likely supportiveness of four videotaped targets. Because each participant rated the same four targets, Lakey et al. analyzed this design as a generalizability study. If differences between patients and controls followed the pattern of perceiver effects, then patients should have seen targets as less supportive than controls and there should have been a stronger perceiver effect than a Perceiver × Supporter interaction. However, if differences between patients and controls followed the pattern of the Perceiver × Supporter interaction, then patients and controls should have had different opinions of which targets were more or less supportive and the Perceiver × Supporter interaction should have been larger than the perceiver effect.

Lakey et al. (in press) found that the support judgments of patients and controls followed the pattern of the Perceiver × Supporter interaction rather than perceiver effects. Clinically depressed patients did not see targets, as a group, as less supportive than did controls. Furthermore, even though the patients made up almost half the sample, the size of the perceiver effect remained comparatively small, similar to that observed by Lakey, McCabe, et al. (1996) and when only controls were analyzed. Like the results of the Lakey, McCabe, et al. study, the strongest influence on support judgments was the Perceiver × Supporter interaction. In other words, controls and patients had different perceptions about who were the most and least supportive targets. Thus, the results of that study suggest that the differences in the support judgments of patients with clinical de-

pression and controls more closely follows the pattern of the Perceiver ×
Supporter interaction than perceiver effects.

McCaskill and Lakey (in press) also examined the question of Which
component of perceived support is related to emotion? However, they distinguished between the components in a different way than did Lakey
et al. (in press). One limitation of Lakey et al.'s study was that because
they used videotaped targets, they could not meaningfully examine whether
supporter effects were related to depression. It was unreasonable to expect
that videotaped supporters would have an effect on clinical depression.
However, McCaskill and Lakey's design enabled them to examine the extent to which the supporter effect was related to emotion for both perceived support and perceived conflict.

Young adolescents in outpatient treatment and their family members
completed measures of perceived family support and family conflict. Adolescents also completed measures of positive and negative affect. Because
the perspectives of both adolescents and family members were available,
McCaskill and Lakey (in press) were able to estimate the extent to which
affect was related to (a) the shared perspective of the family held by adolescents and family members and (b) adolescents' idiosyncratic perceptions (i.e., not shared with other family members). Within families, the
shared family perspective corresponds to supporter effects because it reflects
a consensus across several people regarding the supportiveness of others.
Adolescents' idiosyncratic perceptions represent both perceiver effects and
the Perceiver × Supporter interaction. Both the Perceiver × Supporter
interaction and perceiver effects make adolescents' perceptions discrepant
from the shared family perspective, so both contribute to adolescents' idiosyncratic perceptions. However, because McCaskill and Lakey (in press)
did not use a full generalizability design, they could not distinguish between
perceiver effects and the Perceiver × Supporter interaction.

For family conflict, both the shared family perspective and the idiosyncratic perceptions of adolescents predicted emotion. However, for family
support, only adolescents' idiosyncratic perspectives predicted emotion.
Thus, not only were different components of perceived support related
differently to emotion but the component related to emotion also differed
as a function of support versus conflict.

In summary, just as social support was found to be composed of distinct components, perceived support itself is not a single entity but is composed of at least three distinct groups of processes. Furthermore, these processes may have different relations to outcomes. Figure 10.1 is a graphic
representation of how the three components of perceived support may be
related to different constructs. In this figure, the three components of perceived support are represented by different ovals within the perceived support oval. Each component has different relations to outcomes. For example, perceiver effects are hypothesized to be related to interpretive biases

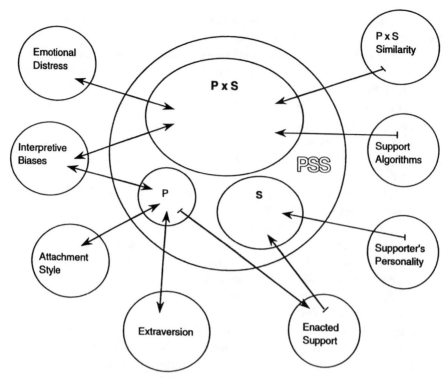

Figure 10.1. A hypothesized model depicting relations among different components of perceived support and outcomes. P = perceiver; S = supporter; PSS = perceived social support.

and attachment style, whereas supporter effects are hypothesized to be related to enacted support and supporters' personality (e.g., agreeableness); the Perceiver × Supporter interaction is hypothesized to be related to similarity between perceivers and supporters and emotional distress. Moreover, the exact components that are related to outcomes may differ depending on whether perceived support or social undermining is the object of investigation. Of course, many of these links are speculative, although we have just reviewed evidence for some of the hypothesized relations.

Given that perceived support is composed of distinct processes, researchers need to develop methods that provide separate estimates of each component's relation to other constructs. The time is approaching when generic measures of perceived support will need to be discarded for most research purposes. Finding a relation between perceived support and an outcome tells researchers nothing about which component is linked to that outcome. Such specific knowledge is essential for effective treatment and prevention programs. Interventions will need to be targeted to the aspect of social relations that are linked to disorders. For example, modifying the perceiver effect should have only small effects on symptoms because the perceiver effect is not the strongest determinant of support perceptions and does not appear to be the component linked to disorder (cf. Brand, Lakey, & Berman, 1995).

A SOCIAL–COGNITIVE MECHANISM LINKING PERCEIVED SOCIAL SUPPORT AND PSYCHOLOGICAL DISORDER

We argued that psychologists must draw on a wide range of explanatory mechanisms to explain diverse social support phenomena. In this section, we review one mechanism by which thoughts about social support may lead to emotional disturbance. Many more perspectives are worthy of review (e.g., attachment, symbolic interactionism, Murrian need theory, evolutionary social psychology), but because of space limitations, we limit our discussion to a social–cognitive mechanism (Baldwin, 1992; Lakey & Drew, 1997; Mankowski & Wyer, 1997; T. Pierce, Baldwin, & Lydon, 1997). The social–cognitive perspective described here differs from stress buffering partly because the occurrence of stressful life events is not necessary for perceived support's relation to symptoms. According to the stress-buffering model, perceived support should be related to symptoms only in the presence of stressful events. From the social–cognitive perspective, perceived support can be related to emotion regardless of stress level. In the language of Cohen and Wills (1985), this social–cognitive model focuses on main effects. That is, negative thoughts about social support should lead to emotional disturbance regardless of stress level. This model also differs from many traditional social support perspectives in that it is more deeply rooted in experimental social psychology than epidemiology and stressful life events research. This model hypothesizes that negative thoughts about social support overlap with and make more accessible negative thoughts about the self. Negative thoughts about the self overlap with and make more accessible negative emotional states.

As discussed earlier, social support theory has always made reference to the self. Symbolic interactionism appears to have been an early influence on social support theory, and symbolic interactionism is largely a proto-cognitive theory of the relation between self and the social world. For example, an important goal of symbolic interactionism is to understand how social relations provide for identity and self-regulation. Cobb (1976) hypothesized that one of the chief roles of social support was to provide "information leading the subject to believe that he is esteemed and valued" (p. 300). Caplan (1974) hypothesized that social support helps to fulfill a basic need for the "validation of personal identity and worth" (p. 5). Throughout the years, many investigators have posited that social support and self-esteem are related in important ways (Cohen & Wills, 1985; Cutrona & Russell, 1990; Heller & Swindle, 1983). Self-esteem support is strongly correlated with other aspects of perceived support (Cohen, Mermelstein, Kamark, & Hoberman, 1985; Newcomb, 1990), and several studies show links between perceived support and self-regard (e.g., Barrera & Li, 1996; Lakey & Cassady, 1990; Maton, 1990; Rowlison & Felner, 1988).

This social–cognitive perspective of social support is based largely on research and theory of concept accessibility (Carlston & Smith, 1996; Higgins, 1996; Wyer & Carlston, 1994). This perspective assumes that people have multiple representations of the self and multiple representations of others. For example, a given person may have concepts of the self as both "brilliant" and "stupid" available in memory simultaneously. Similarly, most people probably have the person concepts of both "kind" and "cruel" available to understand the actions of others. People may even have separate representations of the same person that involve both kind and cruel. Whether any given concept will be used in judging the self or interpreting experience depends on the construct's accessibility. Accessibility essentially is the probability of use in a given context.

The accessibility of a construct is thought to be determined by two basic types of processes: momentary influences and chronic accessibility. Momentary influences arise when a situation activates the use of a given construct. For example, viewing photos of Albert Einstein probably calls to mind the concept of *intelligent* for many people. The recent use of intelligent then increases the odds that this construct will be used again if it can be appropriately applied to a situation. Of course, the increased accessibility resulting from recent use will decay over time. In addition to momentary influences on accessibility, there are also individual differences in the chronic accessibility of certain constructs. For example, some people habitually use certain constructs to interpret experience. Lutz's (1997; Lutz & Lakey, 1997) research on how people use different trait concepts to infer support is an example of this process.

Constructs can also be linked to each other, such that activating some constructs makes other constructs more accessible. For example, accessing the construct of intelligent may also activate the construct "beautiful" or "strong" depending on a person's previous joint use of these constructs (Carlston & Smith, 1996). Similarly, representations of others and representations of the self can be linked. That is, thinking of a significant other as "hostile" may make more accessible the self-referent construct of *guilty*. Thinking of another as "loving" may make more accessible the concept of *accepted*. In fact, a growing body of research suggests that increasing the accessibility of specific-other concepts increases the accessibility of self-evaluations and self-concepts.

Baldwin and his colleagues have conducted a series of groundbreaking studies that provide evidence that activating thought about specific others influences self-evaluations. This is important research because it shows how methodologies can be borrowed from cognitive psychology to explore relations between concepts of self and others. In each of the studies, representations of others were primed by requiring respondents to think about significant others. The effects of priming on self-evaluation and emotion were then examined.

Baldwin, Carrell, and Lopez (1990, Study 1) exposed graduate students to photographs of a neutral face; the scowling, disapproving face of their department chair; or the approving face of another person. Exposure was brief (2 ms) and below the participants' level of awareness. Participants' rated the quality of their research ideas more negatively after exposure to the disapproving face versus the approving face. In Study 2, Catholic women read mildly erotic prose and then were briefly exposed to a photograph of either the pope or a scowling unfamiliar person or a blank card. Participants' rated themselves more negatively after exposure to the pope than the blank card, and women exposed to the pope also reported more anxiety. The scowling unfamiliar other did not produce differences in self-evaluation compared with the blank card. As expected, this effect was stronger among women who were practicing Catholics.

Baldwin (1994, Study 1) exposed participants to brief exposures (16-ms exposure with masks) to the name of either an accepting or critical person from the respondents' social networks. Exposure to the critical primes led to more negative self-evaluations but not more negative mood. In Study 2, participants visualized a wide range of objects, situations, and persons, including either an accepting or critical other. Visualizing a critical, versus accepting, other led to more negative self-evaluations among those who had been made more self-aware by the presence of a mirror. Similarly, primes had an effect on mood only for the more self-aware participants. Similar effects on self-evaluation and mood were obtained by Baldwin and Holmes (1987, Study 2).

Baldwin and Sinclair (1996) used a lexical-decision task to test the hypothesis that people with low self-esteem had relationship schemas that described social acceptance as contingent on performance. The lexical-decision task is commonly used in cognitive psychology to test hypotheses about associations among concepts. Respondents identify whether a given letter string is a real word as quickly as possible. Performance on this task can be facilitated by presenting a thematically related word immediately before the target word. For example, respondents identify the word *nurse* more quickly when the word has been preceded by *doctor* than when *nurse* is preceded by an unrelated word. Such data are typically interpreted to mean that certain concepts are more closely associated with others (A. M. Collins & Loftus, 1975; Meyer & Schvaneveldt, 1971). Baldwin and Sinclair (1966) hypothesized that if low self-esteem individuals have relationship schemas in which self-regard is contingent on acceptance, they should identify words that connote rejection faster (e.g., *ridiculed*) when preceded by failure prime words (e.g., *lose*) than when preceded by success primes (e.g., *win*). Consistent with predictions, low-esteem participants recognized rejection words faster when preceded by failure primes than when preceded by success primes. High self-esteem participants did not show a relation between primes and responses to target words.

Baldwin and Sinclair's (1996) Study 3 primed representations of contingent and accepting relationships. An accepting relationship is with a person who "accepts you for who you are" (Baldwin & Sinclair, 1996, p. 1136), and a contingent relationship is with a person who "seems to accept you only if you live up to certain standards of performance" (p. 1136). Participants visualized either an accepting or contingent significant other. Respondents then completed a similar lexical-decision task as in Study 1. For participants who imagined a contingent relationship, rejection words were recognized more quickly when preceded by failure primes than when preceded by success primes. Thus, the results of these studies by Baldwin and Sinclair suggest that the link between failure and rejection is made more accessible by chronically low self-esteem and by priming critical relationships.

Hinkley and Andersen (1966) also provided evidence that activating representations of others influences the accessibility of specific representations of the self. In their study, participants read a description of a novel other who shared some features of the participants' significant others. Participants' self-descriptions changed when presented with novel others who shared features with significant others, compared with control conditions. Self-descriptions changed to become more similar to how participants viewed themselves when they were with the significant other. In a similar experiment, Andersen et al. (1996) found that participants' moods could be influenced by presenting them with novel others who shared features with positive and negative significant others. Novel others who shared features with yoked controls did not elicit change in emotion. However, the effect on emotion was complex and increases in positive facial affect occurred in some conditions, contrary to predictions.

The research of Andersen, Baldwin, and colleagues provides intriguing evidence that activating representations of critical versus accepting others activates negative self-evaluations and produces negative emotion. We believe this work is important for several reasons. It provides a model of how methods from experimental social psychology (especially social cognition) can provide new perspectives on social support. With methods such as these, more precise hypotheses can be tested about how social support cognition may influence the self and psychological symptoms. In our opinion, these methods offer a higher level of precision than can be obtained by the typical field study. The typical survey respondent simply is unable to report on momentary changes in self-referent thought as a result of nonconscious priming of support-relevant categories. Moreover, because relationship cognition can be experimentally manipulated, such methodologies may provide causal evidence that support cognition influences emotion and self-representations. In our view, although field studies are essential, their correlational design prevents researchers from ever obtaining strong evidence for a causal role for social support. No amount of sophisticated statistics can rescue a correlational design from itself.

It is important to remember that it is not well established why negative thought about the self should lead to distress. Although a direct causal link between such cognition and distress has great intuitive appeal and is assumed by several major theoretical perspectives on emotion (e.g., Abramson, Metalsky, & Alloy, 1989; Beck, 1967; Lazarus & Folkman, 1984), we know of no completely satisfactory account of why and how negative thought leads to emotional disturbance. Thus, appealing to cognitive models of emotion to explain the link between perceived support and distress will not be fully satisfactory until the links between cognition and emotion are better understood. Baumeister and Leary (1995) have moved such theory in the right direction by focusing on the evolutionary advantages of social connectedness and self-esteem, but additional work still needs to be done in this area.

CONCLUSION

In this chapters, we described the historical development of social support research, focusing on two major developments: the dominance of the stress-buffering paradigm and breaking down social support constructs into smaller subcomponents. We believe that the stress-buffering paradigm alone cannot account for the wide range of different social support constructs and effects. In reviewing the development of social support research, we argued that the stress-buffering perspective achieved dominance primarily because of the interests and goals of the scholars who introduced social support research to psychology. Early social support theorists (e.g., Caplan, Cassel, Cobb, Kaplan) drew from a much wider palette of perspectives, including attachment theory, Murrian need theory, and symbolic interactionism. We believe that social support phenomena are so diverse and complex that a similarly wide range of perspectives are needed. A consistent theme in social support research is that measures and constructs, initially assumed to reflect singular constructs, ultimately are broken down into a number of distinct constructs and processes. This theme can be seen in the early to mid-1980s, when scholars recognized that perceived support, enacted support, and network characteristics were distinct. This theme emerges again in more recent research indicating that perceived support itself is composed of at least three different classes of processes. Because of this complexity, no single model or perspective will be able to explain the range of social support effects. As a small contribution to this diversification, we described a social–cognitive perspective on the link between perceived support and emotion.

REFERENCES

Abramson, L. Y., Metalsky, G. I., & Alloy, L. B. (1989). Hopelessness depression: A theory-based subtype of depression. *Psychological Review, 96,* 358–372.

Ahadi, S., & Diener, E. (1989). Multiple determinants and effect size. *Journal of Personality and Social Psychology, 56,* 398–406.

Anan, R. M., & Barnett, D. (1997). *Children's perception of social support: Links with attachment and social information processing.* Unpublished manuscript, Wayne State University.

Andersen, S. M., & Cole, S. W. (1990). "Do I know you?": The role of significant others in general social perception. *Journal of Personality and Social Psychology, 59,* 384–399.

Andersen, S. M., Reznik, I., & Manzella, L. M. (1996). Eliciting facial affect, motivation, and expectancies in transference: Significant other representations in social relations. *Journal of Personality and Social Psychology, 71,* 1108–1129.

Baldwin, M. W. (1992). Relational schemas and the processing of social information. *Psychological Bulletin, 112,* 461–484.

Baldwin, M. W. (1994). Primed relational-schemas as a source of self-evaluative reactions. *Journal of Social and Clinical Psychology, 13,* 380–403.

Baldwin, M. W., Carrell, S. E., & Lopez, D. F. (1990). Priming relationship schemas: My advisor and the pope are watching me from the back of my mind. *Journal of Experimental Social Psychology, 26,* 435–454.

Baldwin, M. W., & Holmes, J. G. (1987). Salient private audiences and awareness of the self. *Journal of Personality and Social Psychology, 52,* 1087–1098.

Baldwin, M. W., & Sinclair, L. (1996). Self-esteem and "if . . . then" contingencies of interpersonal acceptance. *Journal of Personality and Social Psychology, 71,* 1130–1141.

Barrera, M., Jr. (1986). Distinctions between social support concepts, measures, and models. *American Journal of Community Psychology, 14,* 413–445.

Barrera, M., Jr., & Li, S. A. (1996). The relation of family support to adolescents' psychological distress and behavior problems. In G. R. Pierce, B. R. Sarason, & I. G. Sarason (Eds.), *Handbook of social support and the family* (pp. 313–343). New York: Plenum.

Barrera, M., Jr., Sandler, I. N., & Ramsay, T. B. (1981). Preliminary development of a scale of social support: Studies on college students. *American Journal of Community Psychology, 9,* 435–447.

Baumeister, R. F., & Leary, M. R. (1995). The need to belong: Desire for interpersonal attachments as a fundamental human motivation. *Psychological Bulletin, 117,* 497–529.

Beck, A. T. (1967). *Depression: Clinical, experimental, and theoretical aspects*. New York: Harper & Row.

Belsher, G., & Costello, C. G. (1991). Do confidants of depressed women provide less social support than confidants of nondepressed women? *Journal of Abnormal Psychology, 100*, 516–525.

Berkman, L. F., & Syme, S. L. (1979). Social networks, host resistance, and mortality. *American Journal of Epidemiology, 109*, 186–204.

Blazer, D. (1982). Social support and mortality in an elderly community population. *American Journal of Epidemiology, 115*, 684–694.

Bowlby, J. (1958). The nature of the child's tie to his mother. *International Journal of Psychoanalysis, 24*, 190–194.

Brand, E., Lakey, B., & Berman, S. (1995). A preventive, psychoeducational approach to increase perceived support. *American Journal of Community Psychology, 23*, 117–136.

Brown, G. W., & Harris, T. (1978). *Social origins of depression: A study of psychiatric disorder in women*. New York: Free Press.

Burleson, B. R., & Samter, W. (1985). Consistencies in theoretical and naive evaluations of comforting messages. *Communication Monographs, 52*, 103–123.

Caplan, G. (1974). *Support systems and community mental health: Lectures on concept development*. New York: Behavioral.

Carlston, D. E., & Smith, E. R. (1966). Principles of mental representation. In E. T. Higgins & A. W. Kruglanski (Eds.), *Social psychology: Handbook of basic principles* (pp. 184–210). New York: Guilford Press.

Cassel, J. (1973). Psychiatric epidemiology. In G. Caplan (Ed.), *American handbook of psychiatry* (Vol. 2, pp. 401–410). New York: Basic Books.

Cobb, S. (1976). Social support as a moderator of life stress. *Psychosomatic Medicine, 38*, 300–314.

Cohen, S., & Edwards, J. R. (1989). Personality characteristics as moderators of the relationship between stress and disorder. In R. W. J. Neufeld (Ed.), *Advances in the investigation of psychological stress* (pp. 235–283). New York: Wiley.

Cohen, S., & Hoberman, H. M. (1983). Positive events and social supports as buffers of life change stress. *Journal of Applied Social Psychology, 13*, 99–125.

Cohen, S., & McKay, G. (1984). Social support, stress, and the buffering hypothesis: A theoretical analysis. In A. Baum, S. E. Taylor, & J. E. Singer (Eds.), *Handbook of psychology and health* (Vol. 4, pp. 253–267). Hillsdale, NJ: Erlbaum.

Cohen, S., Mermelstein, R., Kamarck, T., & Hoberman, H. (1985). Measuring the functional components of social support. In I. G. Sarason & B. R. Sarason (Eds.), *Social support: Theory research and applications* (pp. 73–94). Dordrecht, The Netherlands: Martinus Nijhoff.

Cohen, S., Sherrod, D. R., & Clark, M. S. (1986). Social skills and the stress-protective role of social support. *Journal of Personality and Social Psychology*, 50, 963–973.

Cohen, S., & Wills, T. A. (1985). Stress, social support, and the buffering hypothesis. *Psychological Bulletin, 98*, 310–357.

Collins, A. M., & Loftus, E. F. (1975). A spreading activation theory of semantic processing. *Psychological Review, 82*, 407–428.

Collins, N. L. (1996). Working models of attachment: Implication for explanation, emotion, and behavior. *Journal of Personality and Social Psychology, 71*, 810–832.

Compas, B. E., Wagner, B. M., Slavin, L. A., & Vannatta, K. (1986). A prospective study of life events, social support, and psychological symptomatology during the transition from high school to college. *American Journal of Community Psychology, 14*, 241–257.

Coyne, J. C. (1976). Depression and the response of others. *Journal of Abnormal Psychology, 85*, 186–193.

Cronbach, L. J., Gleser, G. C., Nanda, H., & Rajaratnam, N. (1972). *The dependability of behavioral measurements: Theory of generalizability of scores and profiles.* New York: Wiley.

Cutrona, C. E., & Russell, D. W. (1990). Type of social support and specific stress: Toward a theory of optimal matching. In B. R. Sarason, I. G. Sarason, & G. R. Pierce (Eds.), *Social support: An interactional view* (pp. 319–366). New York: Wiley.

Cutrona, C. E., & Suhr, J. A. (1994). Social support communication in the context of marriage: An analysis of couples' supportive behavior. In B. Burleson, T. L. Albrecht, & I. G. Sarason (Eds.), *Communication of social support: Messages, interactions, relationships, and community* (pp. 113–135). Thousand Oaks, CA: Sage.

Dean, A., & Lin, N. (1977). The stress-buffering role of social support: Problems and prospects for systematic investigation. *Journal of Nervous and Mental Disease, 165*, 403–417.

Dunkel-Schetter, C., & Bennett, T. L. (1990). Differentiating the cognitive and behavioral aspects of social support. In B. R. Sarason, I. G. Sarason, & G. R. Pierce (Eds.), *Social support: An interactional view* (pp. 267–296). New York: Wiley.

Durkheim, E. (1957). *Suicide.* New York: Free Press of Glencoe. (Original work published 1895)

Erikson, E. H. (1959). Identity and the life cycle: Selected papers. *Psychological Issues, 1*, 1–171.

Gurung, R. A. R., Sarason, B. R., & Sarason, I. G. (1994, August). *Observing conflict and support: Global vs. behavioral-specific approaches.* Paper presented at the 102nd Annual Convention of the American Psychological Association, Los Angeles, CA.

Harlow, H. F., & Zimmerman, R. R. (1959). Affectional responses in the infant monkey. *Science, 130*, 421–432.

Hays, R. B., Turner, H., & Coates, T. J. (1992). Social support, AIDS-related symptoms, and depression among gay men. *Journal of Consulting and Clinical Psychology, 60,* 463–469.

Heller, K. (1979). The effects of social support: Prevention and treatment implications. In A. P. Goldstein & F. H. Kanfer (Eds.), *Maximizing treatment gains: Transfer enhancement in psychotherapy* (pp. 353–382). New York: Academic Press.

Heller, K., & Lakey, B. (1985). Perceived support and social interaction among friends and confidants. In I. G. Sarason & B. R. Sarason (Eds.), *Social support: Theory research and applications* (pp. 287–302). Dordrecht, The Netherlands: Martinus Nijhoff.

Heller, K., & Monahan, J. (1977). *Psychology and community change.* Homewood, IL: Dorsey Press.

Heller, K., & Swindle, R. W. (1983). Social networks, perceived social support, and coping with stress. In R. D. Felner, L. A. Jason, J. N. Moritsugu, & S. S. Farber (Eds.), *Preventive psychology: Theory, research and practice* (pp. 87–103). Elmsford, NY: Pergamon Press.

Higgins, E. T. (1996). Knowledge activation: Accessibility, applicability and salience. In E. T. Higgins & A. W. Kruglanski (Eds.), *Social psychology: Handbook of basic principles* (pp. 133–168). New York: Guilford Press.

Hinkley, K., & Andersen, S. M. (1996). The working self-concept in transference: Significant-other activation and self-change. *Journal of Personality and Social Psychology, 71,* 1279–1295.

Hirsch, B. (1979). Psychological dimensions of social networks: A multimethod analysis. *American Journal of Community Psychology, 7,* 263–277.

Hirsch, B. (1980). Natural support systems and coping with major life changes. *American Journal of Community Psychology, 8,* 159–172.

Holahan, C. J., Moos, R. H., Holahan, C. K., & Brennan, P. L. (1995). Social support, coping, and depressive symptoms in a late-middle-aged sample of patients reporting cardiac illness. *Health Psychology, 14,* 152–163.

Holmes, T. H., & Rahe, R. H. (1967). The Social Readjustment Rating Scale. *Journal of Psychosomatic Research, 11,* 213–218.

House, J. S., Landis, K. R., & Umberson, D. (1988). Social relationships and health. *Science, 241,* 540–545.

Kaplan, B. H., Cassel, J. C., & Gore, S. (1977). Social support and health. *Medical Care, 15,* 47–58.

Kenny, D. (1994). *Interpersonal perception: A social relations analysis.* New York: Guilford Press.

Kenny, D., Albright, L., Malloy, T., & Kashy, D. A. (1994). Consensus in interpersonal perception: Acquaintance and the Big Five. *Psychological Bulletin, 116,* 245–258.

Kirmeyer, S. L., & Lin T. (1987). Social support: Its relationship to observed communication with peers and superiors. *Academy of Management Journal, 30,* 138–151.

Lakey, B. (1989). Personal and environmental antecedents of perceived social support. *American Journal of Community Psychology, 17,* 503–519.

Lakey, B., & Cassady, P. B. (1990). Cognitive processes in perceived social support. *Journal of Personality and Social Psychology, 59,* 337–343.

Lakey, B., & Dickinson, L. G. (1994). Antecedents of perceived support: Is perceived family environment generalized to new social relationships? *Cognitive Therapy and Research, 18,* 39–54.

Lakey, B., & Drew, J. B. (1997). A social–cognitive perspective on social support. In G. R. Pierce, B. Lakey, I. B. Sarason, & B. R. Sarason (Eds.), *Sourcebook of social support and personality* (pp. 107–140). New York: Plenum.

Lakey, B., Drew, J. B., & Sirl, K. (in press). Clinical depression and perceptions of supportive others: A generalizability analysis. *Cognitive Therapy and Research.*

Lakey, B., & Heller, K. (1988). Social support from a friend, perceived support, and social problem solving. *American Journal of Community Psychology, 16,* 811–824.

Lakey, B., McCabe, K. M., Fisicaro, S., & Drew, J. B. (1996). Environmental and personal determinants of support systems: Three generalizability studies. *Journal of Personality and Social Psychology, 70,* 1270–1280.

Lakey, B., Moineau, S., & Drew, J. B. (1992). Perceived social support and individual differences in the interpretation and recall of supportive behavior. *Journal of Social and Clinical Psychology, 11,* 336–348.

Lakey, B., Ross, L., Butler, C., & Bentley, K. (1996). Making social support judgments: The role of perceived similarity and conscientiousness. *Journal of Social and Clinical Psychology, 15,* 283–304.

Lazarus, R. S. (1966). *Psychological stress and the coping process.* New York: McGraw-Hill.

Lazarus, R. S., & Folkman, S. (1984). *Stress, appraisal and coping.* New York: Springer.

Lepore, S. J., Evans, G. W., & Schneider, M. L. (1991). Dynamic role of social support in the link between chronic stress and psychological distress. *Journal of Personality and Social Psychology, 61,* 899–909.

Lowenthal, M. F. (1964). Social isolation and mental illness in old age. *American Sociological Review, 29,* 54–70.

Lowenthal, M. F. (1965). Antecedents of isolation and mental illness in old age. *Archives of General Psychiatry, 12,* 245–254.

Lowenthal, M. F., & Haven, C. (1968). Interaction and adaptation: Intimacy as a critical variable. *American Sociological Review, 33,* 20–29.

Lutz, C. J. (1997). *An idiographic approach to the Person × Environment interaction in support judgments.* Unpublished doctoral dissertation, Wayne State University.

Lutz, C. J., & Lakey, B. (1997, August). *Individual differences in the cognitive representation of social support.* Paper presented at the 105th Annual Convention of the American Psychological Association, Chicago.

Mallinckrodt, B. (1991). Client's representations of childhood emotional bonds with parents, social support, and the formation of a working alliance. *Journal of Counseling Psychology, 38,* 401–409.

Mankowski, E. S., & Wyer, R. S., Jr. (1997). Cognitive causes and consequences of perceived social support. In G. R. Pierce, B. Lakey, I. G. Sarason, & B. R. Sarason (Eds.), *Sourcebook of social support and personality* (pp. 141–165). New York: Plenum.

Maton, K. I. (1990). Meaningful involvement in instrumental activity and well-being: Studies of older adolescents and at-risk urban teen-agers. *American Journal of Community Psychology, 18,* 297–320.

McCaskill, J., & Lakey, B. (in press). Perceived support, social undermining and emotion: Idiosyncratic and shared perspectives of adolescents and their families. *Personality and Social Psychology Bulletin.*

Meyer, D., & Schvaneveldt, R. W. (1971). Facilitation in recognizing pairs of words: Evidence of a dependence between retrieval operations. *Journal of Experimental Psychology, 90,* 227–234.

Mischel, W. (1968). *Personality and assessment.* New York: Wiley.

Mitchel, J. C. (1969). *Social networks and urban situations.* Manchester, England: Manchester University Press.

Murray, H. A. (1938). *Explorations in personality.* New York: Oxford University Press.

Newcomb, M. D. (1990). What structural equation modeling can tell us about social support. In B. R. Sarason, I. G. Sarason, & G. R. Pierce (Eds.), *Social support: An interactional view* (pp. 26–63). New York: Wiley.

Phifer, J. F., & Murrell, S. A. (1986). Etiological factors in the onset of depressive symptoms in older adults. *Journal of Abnormal Psychology, 95,* 282–291.

Pierce, G. R., Lakey, B., Sarason, I. G., Sarason, B. R., & Joseph, H. J. (1997). Personality and social support processes: A conceptual overview. In G. R. Pierce, B. Lakey, I. G. Sarason, & B. R. Sarason (Eds.), *Sourcebook of social support and personality* (pp. 3–18). New York: Plenum.

Pierce, G. R., Sarason, B. R., & Sarason, I. G. (1992). General and specific support expectations and stress as predictors of perceived supportiveness: An experimental study. *Journal of Personality and Social Psychology, 63,* 297–307.

Pierce, G. R., Sarason, B. R., & Sarason, I. G. (1996). *Handbook of social support and the family.* New York: Plenum.

Pierce, T., Baldwin, M., & Lydon, J. (1997). A relational schema approach to social support. In G. R. Pierce, B. Lakey, I. G. Sarason, & B. R. Sarason (Eds.), *Sourcebook of social support and personality* (pp. 19–48). New York: Plenum.

Procidano, M. E., & Heller, K. (1983). Measures of perceived social support from friends and from family: Three validation studies. *American Journal of Community Psychology, 11,* 1–24.

Rabkin, J. G., & Struening, E. L. (1976). Life events, stress, and illness. *Science, 194,* 1013–1020.

Repetti, R. L. (1987). Individual and common components of the social environment at work and psychological well-being. *Journal of Personality and Social Psychology, 52,* 710–720.

Rook, K. S. (1984). The negative side of social interaction: Impact on psychological well-being. *Journal of Personality and Social Psychology, 46,* 1097–1108.

Rook, K. S. (1987). Social support versus companionship: Effects on life stress, loneliness, and evaluations by others. *Journal of Personality and Social Psychology, 52,* 1132–1147.

Ross, L. T., Lutz, C., & Lakey, B. (in press). Perceived support and attributions for failed support attempts. *Personality and Social Psychology Bulletin.*

Rowlison, R. T., & Felner, R. D. (1988). Major life events, hassles, and adaptation in adolescence: Confounding in the conceptualization and measurement of life stress and adjustment revisited. *Journal of Personality and Social Psychology, 55,* 432–444.

Rudolph, K. D., Hammen, C., & Burge, D. (1995). Cognitive representations of self, family, and peers in school-age children: Links with social competence and sociometric status. *Child Development, 66,* 1385–1402.

Sandler, I. N., & Barrera, M., Jr. (1984). Toward a multimethod approach to assessing the effects of social support. *American Journal of Community Psychology, 12,* 37–52.

Sarason, B. R., Pierce, G. R., Sarason, I. G., Waltz, J. A., & Poppe, L. (1991). Perceived social support and working models of self and actual others. *Journal of Personality and Social Psychology, 60,* 273–287.

Sarason, B. R., Sarason, I. G., & Pierce, G. R. (1990). Traditional views of social support and their impact on assessment. In B. R. Sarason, I. G. Sarason, & G. R. Pierce (Eds.), *Social support: An interactional view* (pp. 9–25). New York: Wiley.

Sarason, B. R., Shearin, E. N., Pierce, G. R., & Sarason, I. G. (1987). Interrelations of social support measures: Theoretical and practical implications. *Journal of Personality and Social Psychology, 52,* 813–832.

Sarason, I. G., Levine, H. M., Basham, R. B., & Sarason, B. R. (1983). Assessing social support: The Social Support Questionnaire. *Journal of Personality and Social Psychology, 44,* 127–139.

Selye, H. (1956). *The stress of life.* New York: McGraw-Hill.

Shavelson, R. J., & Webb, N. M. (1991). *Generalizability theory: A primer.* Newbury Park, CA: Sage.

Smith, C. E., Fernengel, K., Holcroft, C., Gerald, K., & Marien, L. (1994). Meta-analysis of the associations between social support and health outcomes. *Annals of Behavioral Medicine, 16,* 352–362.

Stryker, S. (1980). *Symbolic interactionism: A social structural version.* Menlo Park, CA: Benjamin/Cummings.

Swindle, R. W., Cronkite, R. C., & Moos, R. H. (1989). Life stressors, social resources, coping, and the 4-year course of unipolar depression. *Journal of Abnormal Psychology, 98,* 468–477.

Thoits, P. A. (1985). Social support and psychological well-being: Theoretical possibilities. In I. G. Sarason & B. R. Sarason (Eds.), *Social support: Theory, research and application* (pp. 51–72). Dordrecht, The Netherlands: Martinus Nijhoff.

Uchino, B. N., Cacioppo, J. T., & Kiecolt-Glaser, J. K. (1996). The relationship between social support and physiological processes: A review with emphasis on underlying mechanisms and implications for health. *Psychological Bulletin, 119,* 488–531.

Valentiner, D. P., Holahan, C. J., & Moos, R. H. (1994). Social support, appraisals of event controllability, and coping: An integrative model. *Journal of Personality and Social Psychology, 66,* 1094–1102.

Vaux, A. (1988). *Social support: Theory, research, and intervention.* New York: Praeger.

Wethington, E., & Kessler, R. C. (1986). Perceived support, received support and adjustment to stressful life events. *Journal of Health and Social Behavior, 27,* 78–89.

Wiggins, J. (1973). *Personality and prediction: Principles of personality assessment.* Reading, MA: Addison-Wesley.

Winstead, B. A., Derlega, V. J., Lewis, R. J., Sanchez-Hucles, J., & Clarke, E. (1992). Friendship, social interaction, and coping with stress. *Communication Research, 19,* 193–211.

Wyer, R. S., & Carlston, D. E. (1994). The cognitive representation of persons and events. In R. S. Wyer Jr. & T. K. Srull (Eds.), *Handbook of social cognition* (Vol. 1, pp. 41–98). Hillsdale, NJ: Erlbaum.

11

DYSFUNCTIONAL RELATIONSHIPS

ROWLAND S. MILLER

People's interpersonal relationships substantially affect their well-being. People who maintain contented closeness with others also tend to enjoy psychological and physical health, exhibiting high self-esteem (Leary & Downs, 1995), low psychopathology (Bloom, Asher, & White, 1978), efficient immune system responses (Kiecolt-Glaser et al., 1993), and longer life (House, Robbins, & Metzner, 1982). Successful relationships with others are pervasively linked to individual adjustment, so that

> there is no simple recipe for producing happiness, but all of the research indicates that for almost everyone one necessary ingredient is some kind of satisfying, intimate relationship . . . people who are lucky enough to be happy in love, sex, and marriage are more likely to be happy with life in general than any other people. (Freedman, 1978, p. 48)

Indeed, Baumeister and Leary (1995) posited that the motive to establish and maintain a minimal level of satisfying closeness to others is an inborn, fundamental human need to belong; when it remains unfulfilled, a variety of deleterious psychological and physical outcomes follow.

Of course, a simple correlation between relational satisfaction and good health does not necessarily mean that dysfunctional relationships cause ill health or even that personal maladjustment causes relational distress. However, the results of various longitudinal studies suggest that both of those causal pathways do in fact exist: When personal problems develop, people become poor relational partners and their relationships suffer (e.g., Davila, Bradbury, Cohan, & Tochluk, 1997; Fincham, Beach, Harold, & Osborne, 1997); in addition, disturbances in one's relationships can cause a variety of personal difficulties (e.g., Barnett, Raudenbush, Brennan, Pleck, & Marshall, 1995; Beach & O'Leary, 1993; Burman & Margolin, 1992; Kiecolt-Glaser et al., 1993). A destructive cycle of deterioration and distress may even occur as relationship dysfunction and personal maladjustment each reciprocally exacerbate the other (see Davila, Bradbury, et al., 1997).

These processes are consequential, in part, because they are so common. The base rate of problematic partnerships people encounter is surprisingly high. Most people have been greatly troubled by an intimate partner within the past 5 years (Levitt, Silver, & Franco, 1996). Moreover, in the United States, it is more likely that one's marriage will fail than that it will succeed. The divorce rate in the United States continues to hover near 50% (U.S. Bureau of the Census, 1995), and if one also counts as "broken" marriages in which the spouses separate—or are simply miserable—without actually divorcing, the current failure rate of U.S. marriages is close to 70% (Martin & Bumpass, 1989). Studies of close relationships—and the manners in which they may falter—are thus essential foci for social and clinical psychology. In this chapter, I discuss the influences of both social and clinical relevance that may undermine the quality of close relationships, specifically examining three sources of trouble in relationships: (a) personal dysfunctions that debilitate one member of a dyad; (b) interactive dysfunctions that impair the moment-to-moment interactions of a particular couple; and (c) relational dysfunctions that spoil the long-term transactions of a couple.

The boundaries between these categories are sometimes fuzzy. Furthermore, as noted above, difficulties at one level may promote the emergence of problems at another level. Nevertheless, this tripartite scheme can be a useful way to organize the many ways relationships can founder.

PERSONAL DYSFUNCTIONS

My concern here is with those problems in relationships that stem from the perceptions or behavior of one of its participants and that may cause distress despite desirable behavior from the other partner. The complaints I address—insecure attachment, maladaptive expectations, jealousy, loneliness, and depression—often exemplify the reciprocal causation described above, both resulting from and causing troubled relationships.

Insecure Attachment

Many people hold romanticized views of close relationships as soulful unions in which two compatible partners open their lives to each other, but psychologists know better. Studies demonstrate that, although many people want closeness with others and are genuinely comfortable in intimate, interdependent partnerships, some people are chronically anxious, uncomfortable, or both in intimate situations. People differ in *attachment styles*, the internal working models that guide their orientations to and emotions and behavior in close relationships. A person's style of attachment is thought to emerge from past experiences with intimacy and reflects the individual's beliefs about whether he or she is worthy of love and whether other people can be trusted to reliably provide it (Bartholomew & Horowitz, 1991).

Many people—about 60% according to U.S. national surveys (Mickelson, Kessler, & Shaver, 1997)—have a *secure* style of attachment: They are comfortable depending on others, readily develop close attachments, and willingly trust their partners (Brennan & Shaver, 1995). However, many people are typically unsettled and *insecure*. Some of them (about 25% of all lovers; Mickelson et al., 1997) want closeness but constantly worry that their partners do not love them enough in return; as a result, they seem possessive, jealous, and clingy and are said to have an *anxious* style of attachment. In contrast, in another type of insecurity, people do not like being close to others very much; they do not trust others and are uncomfortable depending on them, and they are said to have an *avoidant* attachment style.

Infants display parallel patterns of diverse attachments to their major caregivers (and in fact these relational orientations were first noticed by developmental psychologists, e.g., Bowlby, 1982), but there is little reason to believe that such styles are genetic predispositions (see Waller & Shaver, 1994). Instead, these expectations are thought to develop straightforwardly from one's experiences in important relationships. An anxious style may result when one is met with inconsistent or unpredictable reactions from a caregiver or lover, and an avoidant style may follow when one is continually snubbed or spurned (Bowlby, 1982). Retrospective data support these assumptions. For instance, insecure adults remember their parents as having been less affectionate and more rejecting than do secure people (Frazier, Byer, Fischer, Wright, & DeBord, 1996), and they also recall more difficult separations, such as parental divorce, during their childhoods (Gerlsma, Buunk, & Mutsaers, 1996).

Being learned, adult attachment styles can presumably be unlearned and changed, and indeed about 30% of a sample is likely to change attachment orientations over a period of several months (Baldwin & Fehr, 1995; Fuller & Fincham, 1995). Insecure people are especially prone to fluctuations in style, however (Davila, Burge, & Hammen, 1997), and most other people probably evidence substantial cross-situational consistency in attachment tendencies over long lengths of time (Scharfe & Bartholomew, 1994). Moreover, attachment styles are correlated with other—stable—individual differences, so that anxious people tend to be high in neuroticism and avoidant people tend to be low in extraversion and agreeableness (Carver, 1997). Although they can change, attachment orientations are enduring predispositions in most people.

These stylistic differences are important because attachment tendencies appear to influence one's thoughts, feelings, and behavior in one's relationships. Compared with those who are securely attached, insecure people read more hostility and thoughtlessness into the ambiguous behavior of their partners (Collins, 1996) and exhibit more pessimistic and sour reactions to disagreement and conflict (Fuller & Fincham, 1995). After a disagreement, they perceive their partners and their relationships less positively than do secure people (Simpson, Rholes, & Phillips, 1996) and behave in less constructive ways: Whereas secure people tend to voice their concerns and remain loyal to their relationships, insecure people tend to passively neglect their partners or distance themselves from the relationship (Scharfe & Bartholomew, 1995). Insecure attachment is even correlated with abusiveness and psychological maltreatment of women (Dutton, Saunders, Starzomski, & Bartholomew, 1994).

Given these patterns, it should be no surprise that people with insecure attachment styles tend to be less satisfied with their close relationships than are secure people (Feeney, 1994; J. T. Jones & Cunningham, 1996). Indeed, the anxiousness, mistrust, or both that underlie insecure styles may not be well suited to calm contentment over time. In one study of premarital relationships, secure people generally stayed satisfied and committed over a 4-month period, but insecure people reported decreasing satisfaction, trust, and commitment and described more frustrations and disappointments (Keelan, Dion, & Dion, 1994). Worse, such patterns may be chronic: Over longer spans of time, insecure people tend to have more short-term relationships (i.e., more breakups) over time than do those who have a secure attachment style (Kirkpatrick & Hazan, 1994). Then, once their relationships have ended, they may suffer more; in an Israeli sample, insecure people evidenced lower levels of psychological well-being after a divorce than did secure ex-spouses (Birnbaum, Orr, Mikulincer, & Florian, 1997).

These differences between people who are securely and insecurely attached are especially notable in situations in which an individual encounters stress. Whereas secure people often derive genuine solace from the presence of a loved one in an anxiety-provoking situation, insecure people display *more* arousal and distress when their romantic partners are present than when they are absent (Carpenter & Kirkpatrick, 1996). If one is insecure, one's lover is apparently not a source of succor and consolation but is instead another embodiment of quiet threat.

Thus, people with insecure attachment styles appear to be relatively poorly equipped to maintain comfortable, contented, close relationships. If they are avoidant, their deep-seated lack of faith in others makes it difficult for them to placidly accept the interdependency from which intimacy springs. If they are anxious, they openly seek such closeness but fret that it will not last. Both styles burden people with pessimistic or nervous expectations that cause them either to "look a gift horse in the mouth" or refuse the gift altogether.

Of course, simply labeling people as "secure" or "insecure" is simplistic. These categories are used in research because they are convenient, but they do tend to confuse the fact that security, anxiousness, and avoidance seem to operate as continuous dimensions in interpersonal relations, with individuals ranging from low to high on each of the three tendencies (e.g., Carver, 1997). Moreover, many people have moderate amounts of each tendency, so that the actual differences among people who are labeled *secure* and those labeled as *insecure* may occasionally be trivial (Bartholomew, 1997). Nevertheless, an attachment perspective provides the useful reminder that there are meaningful individual differences among people—there are different types of lovers—with only some people really ready and able to contentedly embrace both the joys and uncertainties of a close relationship.

Dysfunctional Beliefs

Attachment styles are relational orientations that emerge from global judgments of self and other. People also hold a variety of specific beliefs and standards about how relationships are supposed to work, and sometimes these are so unrealistic, or even irrational, that they doom partners to disappointment and distress. Several such beliefs are risky (Eidelson & Epstein, 1982): People who believe that (a) a partner who misunderstands his or her lover does not love him or her, (b) disagreements are destructive, (c) men and women are much different from each other, (d) people never change, or (e) sex should be perfect every time or one's love is faulty tend to be less satisfied with their relationships than are people who do not hold such assumptions (Moller & Van Zyl, 1991). A major reason for their discontent appears to be the impaired problem solving that follows from such beliefs (Metts & Cupach, 1990); when disagreements do occur, people who endorse these notions are less likely to take any constructive action to rectify the problem. They also tend to think that relationship therapy is unlikely to do them any good. Ironically then, such beliefs not only guarantee inevitable disappointment but also leave a person curiously unwilling to try to fix their problems when they occur.

Jealousy

Unlike insecure attachment or maladaptive beliefs, intermittent jealousy seems to be a universal experience; it is hard to find someone who has never been jealous (Pines & Aronson, 1983). Some people *are* more prone to jealousy than others (Greenberg & Pyszczynski, 1985), so that people with strong desires for sexual exclusivity (Buunk, 1982), traditional sex roles (Hansen, 1985), and insecure attachment styles (Radecki-Bush, Farrell, & Bush, 1993; Sharpsteen & Kirkpatrick, 1997) are at greater risk. However, jealousy also depends in large part on the nature of the relationship people share with their partners and the nature of the threat to that relationship. Anyone, it seems, can become jealous.

The basis for jealousy, of course, is the fear that a desirable relationship may be usurped by a rival. The more valuable the relationship is and the more irreplaceable it seems, the more jealousy it is likely to evoke (Buunk, 1995). It is not just the threatened end of a relationship that induces jealousy, however, but people's perception of *why* the threat exists that causes them pain. When young adults imagine a romantic partnership ending because of an accidental death or a job transfer to a distant city, they envision distress and misery but little jealousy. In contrast, if they imagine losing a lover to a rival, they still think that they will be sad, but anger and jealousy flare up as well (Mathes, Adams, & Davies, 1985). Other particulars matter too. Rivals who are accomplished in domains that are relevant to one's own identity cause more jealousy than do competitors who possess skills and characteristics about which one does not care (DeSteno & Salovey, 1996b). Similarly, if a lover seems to be leaving because of dissatisfaction with a partner or because of a desire for better sex, the partner is likely to be much more jealous than he or she would be if the lover is leaving to find commitment that the partner chooses not to provide (Buunk, 1984; White, 1981).

As the foregoing suggests, jealousy depends on people's interpretations of the situations they face and seems to emerge from jolts to *relational self-esteem*, a person's evaluation of his or her adequacy and worth as a partner in a particular relationship. Global self-esteem is inconsistently related to jealousy, so people who generally devalue themselves are not necessarily any more susceptible to jealousy than anyone else (White & Mullen, 1989). Instead, the specific perception that one is becoming incapable of eliciting enough attention and devotion from a desired partner triggers jealousy (Sharpsteen, 1995). Although the loss of a desired relationship is always unsettling, jealousy stems from the double-edged sword of wanting a partner but feeling inadequate to the task of keeping him or her from straying to someone else.

Jealousy is an unpleasant emotion, with roots in both anger and anxiety (Sharpsteen, 1991), so it is notable that people sometimes try to *induce* jealousy in their romantic partners to "test" the relationships or to get more attention. Women are more likely to do this than are men (White, 1980), especially when they seek more control over their partners (Brainerd, Hunter, Moore, & Thompson, 1996). This may be a dangerous strategy, however, because the sexes tend to respond differently to jealousy when it occurs. When they were shown a jealousy-evoking videotape of a person unexpectedly encountering her (or his) current partner sharing a kiss of greeting with an ex-lover, women reported that they would usually feign indifference to such a situation but work to make themselves more attractive to their partners (Shettel-Neuber, Bryson, & Young, 1978). Women, then, generally said they would react to jealousy by trying to repair the damaged relationship. Men, however, said they would repair their egos. Men reported that they would threaten the rival, get drunk, and start chasing other women. Clearly, a woman who intentionally induces jealousy in her partner in the hope that he will pay her more attention may be sorely mistaken.

Another provocative sex difference in jealousy appears to fit the prediction from evolutionary social psychology that for maximal reproductive success, women should seek men who will devote resources to shelter their children whereas men should seek women who are faithful and fertile (Buss, 1995). In this view, women should be especially concerned by a threat that foretells a man's withdrawal of his resources, whereas men should be wary of the risk that they will devote their resources to another man's child. In fact, around the world (Buunk, Angleitner, Oubaid, & Buss, 1996; Geary, Rumsey, Bow-Thomas, & Hoard, 1995), if they have to choose between the threat of a partner's sexual infidelity or "emotional infidelity" (i.e., falling in love without having sex), men are more likely than women to choose sex as the source of the greater jealousy. In contrast, more women than men consider emotional infidelity the more worrisome act. The relevance of these data to an evolutionary model is arguable, and opposing viewpoints exist (e.g., DeSteno & Salovey, 1996a). Still, it does seem that women tend to fret even more than men do about the possibility that a partner may form a deep emotional attachment to someone else (Harris & Christenfeld, 1996).

Emerging from fearsome prospects like these and rooted in insecurity and dependency, jealousy is a common complaint among partners seeking relationship therapy (Geiss & O'Leary, 1981). It is one of the marital stressors that meaningfully predicts subsequent divorce (Amato & Rogers, 1997). Fortunately, several approaches may help alleviate troublesome jealousy. First, clear communication about expectations and limits can help partners avoid mdisunderstanding and prevent jealousy from occurring at all (White & Mullen, 1989). Second, one can combat catastrophizing appraisals of the situation that exaggerate either the threat to the relationship or the harm that its loss would entail (Ellis, 1977; Salovey & Rodin, 1988).

Finally, interventions can focus directly on the emotional components of jealousy, desensitizing the sufferer and rewarding calm and poise (Jacobson & Margolin, 1979).

Loneliness

Jealous people at least have valued relationships that they stand to lose. Another personal dysfunction, loneliness, afflicts those who feel that the relationships they have are not enough. Loneliness occurs when one confronts a frustrating discrepancy between the social relations one has and the relations one wants (Perlman & Peplau, 1981), and it appears to have two interrelated but discrete components. First, loneliness always involves a lack of pleasurable engagement that leaves people feeling less fulfilled by their interactions than they want to be. Second, it usually, but not always, also includes a painful, aching sense of disconnection from others (Joiner, Catanzaro, Rudd, & Rajab, in press). This latter aspect of loneliness is its more unpleasant component, routinely involving self-deprecation, impatient boredom, desperation, and depression (Rubenstein, Shaver, & Peplau, 1979).

Unfortunately, loneliness is a common experience (Rubenstein & Shaver, 1982) that can result from any adverse change in one's opportunities for interaction, such as the end of a marriage through death or divorce or the physical separation that accompanies graduation or a career move (Peplau & Perlman, 1982). Even marriage can cause surprising shrinkage of one's social network, leaving one at an unanticipated loss (Milardo, Johnson, & Huston, 1983).

Once these changes occur, they can be regrettably persistent. Loneliness seems to cause undesirable changes in people's interactive styles that make them less inviting to others, potentially perpetuating their loneliness. For instance, lonely people have *negative outlooks* about themselves and others (Rotenberg, 1994). They consider themselves to be relatively unlikable people surrounded by unappealing people, and they interact with others expecting the worst (W. H. Jones, Sansone, & Helm, 1983). They also display *social skill deficits*, interacting with others in superficial, inattentive, self-absorbed ways that can be unrewarding.

In fact, lonely people often have considerable contact with others but simply seem to extract less intimacy and meaning from their interactions than do nonlonely people. They engage in less self-disclosure, have shallower friendships, and spend more time with acquaintances and less time with their friends than do those who are less lonely (W. H. Jones, Freemon, & Goswick, 1981; Wheeler, Reis, & Nezlek, 1983).

Thus, loneliness is a prototypical but ironic example of the manner in which personal dysfunction can damage relationships. Lonely people are often surrounded by others but are ill-equipped for rich, gratifying transactions with them; their dissatisfaction with the insubstantial nature of their contact with others leaves them pessimistic and inept and thereby unlikely to attract the intimacy they crave. How does such a problem ever go away? Situational interventions that provide a person new opportunities for social contact can be useful (Rook, 1984), but efforts to modify both a client's cognition and social skills may be necessary (Rook & Peplau, 1982). In one study of first-year college students, those who overcame their initial loneliness did so by gradually growing closer to—making friends with— the people they already had around them, whereas those who stayed lonely felt that finding a romantic partner was the only way their loneliness would subside (Cutrona, 1982). Setting one's standards too high and insisting that one be loved by someone else may be likely to keep a lonely person dissatisfied.

Depression

A similar sort of "self-perpetuating interpersonal system" (Coyne, 1976) may beset the social lives of depressed people, who—like lonely people—engage in pessimistic cognition and exhibit impaired social skills. (Loneliness and depression have much in common but are nevertheless discrete, different states, e.g., Weeks, Michela, Peplau, & Bragg, 1980.) Depressed people are often unpleasant partners. They judge others negatively (McCabe & Gotlib, 1993) and issue few rewards (Assh & Byers, 1996), but they are especially sensitive to signs of rejection (Nezlek, Kowalski, Leary, Blevins, & Holgate, 1997) and seek constant reassurance (Katz & Beach, 1997), overreacting when they do not get it (Beach & O'Leary, 1993). This gloomy, needy style of interaction may not be overly detrimental in short-term transactions (Marcus & Nardone, 1992), but it is unquestionably aversive over the long haul. As a semester proceeds, for instance, the roommates of depressed college students gradually become more hostile, withdrawn, and dissatisfied with their dysphoric roommates (Hokanson & Butler, 1992). Depression also goes hand-in-hand with marital distress: Depressed spouses are 10 times more likely to have troubled marriages than they are to have happy marriages (O'Leary, Christian, & Mendell, 1994).

Depression also provides a regrettable but unmistakable example of the manner in which personal well-being and relational functioning can *reciprocally* influence one another. Not only does depression help cause marital dissatisfaction, but it can also result from marital woes (Davila, Bradbury, et al., 1997). In particular, women are especially likely to become depressed when they encounter persistent dissatisfaction, whereas men are notably likely to become dissatisfied when they or their partners are depressed (Fincham et al., 1997). Indeed, the link between depression and discord is robust enough that some clinicians advocate marital therapy as a first choice for depressed spouses (O'Leary et al., 1994).

Thus, personal dysfunctions that contribute to troubled relationships are no small matter. I focused on personal attributes or states that are either temporary or learned because they are undoubtedly more amenable to therapeutic change. Nevertheless, I should also acknowledge that lasting personalities are influential, too. Traits such as agreeableness (Botwin, Buss, & Shackelford, 1997; Graziano, Jensen-Campbell, & Hair, 1996) and hostility (Newton, Kiecolt-Glaser, Glaser, & Malarkey, 1995) have an obvious impact on the chronic nature of one's interactions with a partner. Impressively and eerily, surveys of adult twins suggest that about one third of a person's risk of divorce is heritable, influenced by genetic factors that underlie personality (Jockin, McGue, & Lykken, 1996). Many predispositions affecting relationship success vary during one's lifetime, but some people are chronically more likely than others to find happiness nevertheless.

INTERACTIVE DYSFUNCTIONS

Idiosyncratic states such as insecure attachment, jealousy, loneliness, or depression not only create painful emotions in those who experience them but are also deleterious influences on a person's behavior in close relationships. Each of them may substantially and negatively affect the interactions one shares with others. I have classed them as *personal dysfunctions*, however, because they clearly originate in one or the other partner in a relationship. In contrast, there are other components of interaction that do not cause individuals distress but that do cause problems for a couple's interaction. The average attributes of two normal people can combine to create awkward, unsatisfying interactions that are unique to that dyad. A troubled relationship can thus emerge from the interactive, joint contributions of two people who have no apparent personal dysfunctions and who can (and do) enjoy satisfactory relationships with others. These are *interactive dysfunctions*; they lie not in the individuals but in their interactions with each other. They include frustrations stemming from gender differences, betrayals, problematic attributions, and maladroit nonverbal communication.

Nonverbal Communication

The patterns of people's movements, facial expressions, eye contact, and interpersonal distances, in combination with the sounds of their voices (e.g., loudness, pitch, and rate), constitute a nonverbal language that underlies and regulates interactions with others. Vital information about people's moods and meaning may be conveyed through nonverbal means; the paralinguistic cues of how something is said, for example, communicate whether it was meant to be sarcastic. Nonverbal cues also facilitate smooth turn taking and synchrony in interaction (Patterson, 1983). Obviously, two people who have difficulty communicating well nonverbally are likely to encounter frequent misunderstandings, irritation, and conflict, and nonverbal deficiencies may contribute to troubled relationships.

In fact, a couple's satisfaction is often tied to their nonverbal adequacy (Gottman & Porterfield, 1981). Not only do unhappy couples communicate more negative affect to each other than do happy couples (Escudero, Rogers, & Gutierrez, 1997; Levenson & Gottman, 1983), but they also *misinterpret* one another's messages more often. In distressed marriages, both husbands and wives typically read the nonverbal messages of total strangers more accurately than they read each other (Noller, 1981). They are also more likely to send discrepant messages in which the sender's nonverbal behavior conflicts with what he or she is saying (Noller, 1982). It is important to note, however, that their communication deficit is an interactive dysfunction that appears to be specific to their marital relationship; each partner may engage in adequate nonverbal communication with others but fails to implement it with his or her spouse.

Communicative deficiencies like these may merely be symptoms of prior dissatisfaction that do not precipitate poor adjustment; for instance, spouses who are already unhappy with each other are likely to become inattentive to subtleties in the other's behavior. However, evidence suggests that nonverbal dysfunction does lead to dissatisfaction (Noller, 1987); the aggravating mistakes and confusion that result from poor nonverbal communication are costs that erode contentment.

Thus, by communicating poorly with each other, two individually skilled partners can create an interactive, nonverbal dysfunction that undermines their relationship. Because they are competent communicators in other settings, skills training will often be unwarranted; instead, therapy may be more effective if it addresses the relational problems that discourage clear communication.

Gender Differences

When a couple's nonverbal adequacy falters, at least clinicians can see that they are making mistakes. Another interactive dysfunction can exist when partners are behaving just as they are expected to and cannot be conceived to be doing anything "wrong." In particular, masculine men and feminine women who adhere to cultural stereotypes of typical male and female behavior often pride themselves on being perfectly normal. But they should not expect to get along with each other very well.

A man who fits traditional notions of masculinity possesses predominantly instrumental traits; he is likely to be competitive, independent, self-reliant, and assertive but not especially sensitive, kind, gentle, or tender. In contrast, a traditionally feminine woman is everything the traditional man is not: warm, nurturant, dependent and compliant, and emotionally expressive. Although American women are slowly becoming more instrumental with each new generation (Twenge, 1997), many men and women still fit these classic molds. This is unfortunate because instead of making men and women more compatible, these gender differences "may actually be responsible for much of the *incompatibility*" (Ickes, 1985, p. 188) that causes relationships to fail.

From the moment they meet, traditional men and women like each other less than do partners who transcend stereotypical roles and thus have more in common. For instance, in a classic study, Ickes and Barnes (1978) compared dyads that paired an instrumental man with an expressive woman with other dyads that contained at least one partner who was *androgynous*, a term describing people who are adept at both instrumental and expressive behaviors, being both assertive *and* warm, self-confident *and* kind. After establishing that the members of each dyad had never met, the researchers simply left them alone together for 5 min and covertly videotaped their interaction. The results were striking. The traditional couples talked less, looked at each other less, laughed and smiled less, and said they liked each other much less than did those couples in which at least one person transcended tradition. With their different domains of expertise, masculine men and feminine women simply do not enjoy each other very much when they first meet.

Worse, surveys of marital satisfaction (e.g., Antill, 1983) suggest that their interactions do not improve. Expressive women who have traditional, instrumental husbands—who after all are not very warm, tender, sensitive people—are generally less content than are women who are married to androgynous men.

Perhaps this should not be surprising. People who are low in expressivity—like traditional men—routinely conduct interactions that are more superficial, less meaningful, and less supportive than the associations shared by people who are more expressive (Reis, 1986). This style may work perfectly well among acquaintances, but an intimate partner may be distressed, particularly over time, by its lower affection and warmth (Ickes, 1993). Traditional couples also establish a more stereotypical and more rigid division of labor in their households, so that idiosyncratic interests and strengths are less likely to be accommodated (Huston & Geis, 1993).

Altogether, unyielding adherence to cultural expectations of appropriate male and female behavior is likely to have deleterious rather than desirable effects on close relationships (Bradbury, Campbell, & Fincham, 1995). Over the long haul, both men and women prefer relational partners who are warm, thoughtful, and tender to those who are not (Lamke, Sollie,

Durbin, & Fitzpatrick, 1994), so men in particular should be encouraged to be androgynous. Indeed, when they are instructed to do so in laboratory studies, men are generally capable of intimate, sensitive interaction (Reis, Senchak, & Solomon, 1985), so they are not actually incapable of such behavior. For that reason, people's respect and support of those who try to transcend socially prescribed sex roles may be highly important, allowing more men and women to enjoy rewarding interactions as fully realized people rather than as stereotyped specialists.

Attributional Processes

A variety of potential explanations may be possible for most events (see chap. 2 in this book), but attributions for episodes in relationships can be especially complex. The interdependence that underlies intimacy often means that both partners are partially responsible for some event. Moreover, intimacy may make each partner the other's "most knowledgeable *and* least objective observer" (Sillars, 1985, p. 280), equipping partners with unique detailed information but occasionally making them less willing to face the facts. In particular, through their attributions, relational partners can cast each other's actions in either a desirable or damning light, implicitly forgiving or begrudging each other their inevitable transgressions. For this reason, relational attributions are often a barometer of the health of a relationship and can either help maintain or destroy a partnership.

Three attributional phenomena are probably especially important to relationship functioning. First, partners are affected by robust actor–observer biases despite their intimate knowledge of each other (Orvis, Kelley, & Butler, 1976). Although they are acutely aware of the situational pressures that have shaped their own behavior, they tend to attribute the partner's behavior to his or her intentions and personality. In particular, this leads both partners to overlook how they may provoke the behavior they observe in the other. During an argument, for instance, if one partner thinks, "She infuriates me so when she acts that way," the other is likely to be thinking, "He has a real problem with his anger." What is more, the two partners are unlikely to be aware of the discrepancies in their attributions, with each person believing that the other sees things his or her way (Sillars et al., 1994).

Despite genuine affection for each other, partners are also likely to be self-serving in their views. Even in close relationships, both partners are likely to overestimate their own responsibility for positive events while denying their culpability for negative outcomes. Spouses usually attribute momentous importance and meaning to the extramarital affairs of their partners, for instance, but consider their own affairs to be relatively innocuous, passing dalliances (Buunk, 1987). In a similar fashion, when conflict occurs, both partners are likely to see it as the other person's fault (Sillars, 1985).

Finally, the general pattern of a couple's attributions helps determine how happy they will be with their relationship. In general, contented partners give each other credit for their kindnesses, perceiving them to be intentional and deliberate; they also tend to excuse one another's misdeeds, seeing them as accidental and unusual (Bradbury & Fincham, 1990). In comparison, the attributions of distressed couples are mirror opposites. They see each other's negative actions as deliberate and routine and kindnesses as inadvertent. Thus, the attributions of unhappy partners are of a sort that is likely to keep them dissatisfied regardless of how the partner behaves. More important, pejorative attributions like these can create dissatisfaction and distress when none exists (Horneffer & Fincham, 1996). Obviously, when kindnesses seem accidental and hurts seem deliberate, contentment must be hard to come by.

In summary, partners' personal perspectives allow them to have better excuses for their mistakes than their partners have, to cast those partners as the source of most disagreements and conflict, and to claim more credit than the partners would allow for the success of the relationship. These egocentric judgments may be adaptive for the individual, but they are hardly adaptive for the relationship, and in distressed couples such attributions cause and sustain trouble in the relationship. Thus, attributions are another potential source of interactive dysfunction, a fact duly recognized by some marital therapists; in fact, interventions specifically aimed at changing spouses' perceptions of each other's behavior are often a component of cognitive–behavioral marital therapy (e.g., Berley & Jacobson, 1984).

Betrayal

A final source of interactive dysfunction includes the inevitable instances in which partners violate the rules of their relationships by lying, revealing confidences, breaking promises, spending time elsewhere, or otherwise engaging in actions that would hurt a partner's feelings if he or she knew of them (Metts, 1994). Across time and situations, some people are less trustworthy than others, telling more lies (Kashy & DePaulo, 1996) and betraying their families, friends, and lovers more often than do other people (W. H. Jones & Burdette, 1994). However, I classify betrayal as an interactive, rather than personal, dysfunction for several reasons. First, although there are ordinarily some guilty psychic costs involved in keeping secrets from one's partner (Wegner & Lane, 1995), many small betrayals do not trouble their perpetrators as long as the partner never learns of them (DePaulo, Kashy, Kirkendol, Wyer, & Epstein, 1996). Moreover, the perpetrator sometimes has honorable intentions; for instance, lies told to a partner are often intended to benefit or protect the partner in some way (Buller & Burgoon, 1994; DePaulo et al., 1996). Most important, because people normally try to be loyal simultaneously to several different relationships, competing demands are inescapable and occasional violations of the rules in a given relationship are unavoidable. Betrayal then is an inevitable fact of relational life (Baxter et al., 1997).

Still, that does not make such events any easier to swallow. When betrayals become known to the person who is betrayed, they almost always have a negative—and sometimes lasting—effect on the relationship (Amato & Rogers, 1997). This may seem self-evident, but it is often a surprise to the perpetrator, who is usually inclined to perceive his or her misbehavior in a less negative light. In their surveys of recalled betrayals, W. H . Jones and Burdette (1994) found that those who were betrayed almost never believed that such events had had a favorable influence on the relationship; instead, 93% of the time, they felt harm had been done. In contrast, the betrayers acknowledged harm only half the time, and they actually thought the relationship had improved as a result of their transgression in one of every five such instances. One may feel better believing that one's betrayal of a partner is relatively innocuous, but it may be more adaptive to face the facts: Betrayals are costly events that are often the central complaint of couples seeking therapy or divorce (Geiss & O'Leary, 1981).

RELATIONSHIP DYSFUNCTION

One broad source of trouble in relationships remains. Over time, a relationship may deteriorate because a couple's interactions simply fail to be rewarding enough for the participants. Both partners may be free of personal dysfunction, and they may be capable of smooth, error-free interactions but may still find themselves ultimately discontented. In this case, the locus of disorder may be the pattern and type of their long-term transactions (i.e., the relationship itself). Perhaps the partners have gotten so used to each other that they no longer find pleasure in each other's company, or perhaps one partner is exploiting the other and the relationship seems unfair. Whatever the particulars, such concerns can doom a relationship. I discuss two types of such dysfunction, dealing in turn with partners' desires to maximize reward and to be treated fairly.

Rewarding Interdependence

It is not a romantic view, but if one assumes that people greedily seek interaction with each other only when it is to their advantage to do so, one gains powerful insights into the course of human relationships. Interdependence theory holds that people seek to maximize their interpersonal rewards and minimize their costs, so that a couple must be able to exchange rewards that are adequate for both partners or interaction is unlikely to continue (Rusbult & Van Lange, 1996).

This perspective has several broad advantages. First, it reminds one that no matter what their history, relationship partners must continue to be pleasant, polite, generous, and enjoyable to each other or they will ultimately seek new, alternative partners. This may seem self-evident, but being nice to an intimate partner over time may nevertheless be a surprisingly elusive process that requires conscious attention and effort. Once a relationship is established, novelty wanes, illusions fade, and reality intrudes; partners work less hard at impressing each other and, with their intimate knowledge of each other, are equipped to do each other more harm—accidental or otherwise—than anyone else can (Miller, 1997). Despite its potent rewards, closeness also brings conflict, as intimate partners confront problems of coordination and compromise that mere acquaintances do not face.

Thus, close relationships often present unanticipated costs (e.g., Felmlee, 1995; McGonagle, Kessler, & Schilling, 1992), and "one of the first things to go in a marriage is politeness" (Gottman, 1994, p. 65). Over time, criticism, contempt, defensiveness, and stonewalling come to pervade the interactions of many couples, so that the partners may actually be more impolite to each other than they are to total strangers (Gottman, 1994). This is a perilous state; Gottman and Levenson (1992) found that couples who did not maintain a 5:1 ratio of positive-to-negative behaviors toward each other, even during disagreements, were much more likely to have divorced 4 years later than were those couples who maintained high levels of positive regard. Communicating continual respect, interest, concern, and affection to an intimate partner is not always easy to do, especially during periods of conflict, but these rewarding responses appear to be essential components of satisfying partnerships (Gottman, 1993a, 1993b; Heavey, Layne, & Christensen, 1993).

Interdependence theory also explicates several subtleties of relationship functioning. For instance, it asserts that people are satisfied to the extent their current outcomes exceed their expectations (Rusbult & Van Lange, 1996). However, people who are lucky enough to obtain high relational rewards are likely to gradually grow accustomed to such treatment; as their expectations slowly rise, satisfaction subsides. Relationships may typically become less satisfying (as they tend to; see Kurdek, 1993) not (just) because they become more costly but because people come to take them for granted.

Still, if dissatisfaction sets in, the relationship may not end. Another instructive contribution of interdependence theory is the proposition that regardless of whether they are happy, people decide whether to leave a relationship by comparing it with other alternatives they have. Only when people genuinely believe that they can do better elsewhere, the theory asserts, will they leave an existing partnership. This explains those puzzling situations in which a miserable partner clings to a broken, disastrous relationship; such a person must believe that his or her next best alternative would be even worse. Several factors, including individual differences (e.g., low self-esteem), situational variables (e.g., unemployment), and cultural influences (e.g., religious sanctions against divorce), may affect such calculations; indeed, the worse their finances, the less likely battered women are to leave their abusive partners (Rusbult & Martz, 1995).

The flip side of this coin, of course, is that even if people are reasonably happy with a particular partner, they may be lured away if a better alternative presents itself. Arguably, Western culture encourages people to insist on bliss, rather than mere contentment, in their romantic relationships and then challenges them with abundant alternatives that are easy to obtain (Attridge & Berscheid, 1994). That is not a climate that fosters relational permanence. In fact, American divorce rates are highest in those areas where the numbers of possible partners are highest (South & Lloyd, 1995).

Altogether outcomes that are too low, expectations that are too high, or alternative attractions that are too tempting lead to unsatisfying, unstable relationships and thus can constitute relationship dysfunctions. Fortunately, the interdependence perspective also provides a conceptual base for several aspects of behavioral marital therapy that attempt to reestablish positive, mutually desirable exchanges between distressed spouses (see Follette & Jacobson, 1985). It also informs preventive interventions that help couples avert dissatisfaction in the first place (Markman, Renick, Floyd, Stanley, & Clements, 1993). Although most people are perfectly capable of being polite and accommodating to anyone for short periods of time, many people find that they need some help and instruction in maintaining such pleasantries for decades in a close relationship.

Equitable Relationships

It is one matter to ask whether one is gaining satisfactory reward from a relationship and another matter to ask whether the available reward is apportioned *fairly* between the two partners. "Equity" theorists suggest that people are most content in relationships in which there is proportional justice, with each person gaining benefits from the partnership that are in fair proportion to his or her contributions to it (Sprecher & Schwartz, 1994). Equity exists when

$$\frac{\text{one's outcomes}}{\text{one's inputs}} = \frac{\text{one's partner's outcomes}}{\text{one's partner's inputs}}.$$

Note that equity does not depend on partners gaining equal outcomes from their interaction; indeed, when their inputs are different, equality would be inequitable. Instead, this perspective suggests that one should be rewarded relative to one's efforts and that the relative amounts of net profit participants receive are just as influential as their absolute amounts.

These judgments are important, according to equity theory, because it is distressing to find oneself in an inequitable relationship. When inequity exists, one partner is "underbenefited," receiving less than he or she deserves, and thus is likely to be angry and resentful; the other partner is "overbenefited" and probably feels somewhat guilty. It is better to be over- than underbenefited, of course, but any departure from an equitable relationship is thought to cause some discomfort, if only because such situations are inherently unstable: People are thought to dislike unfairness and so are motivated to change or escape it (Sprecher & Schwartz, 1994).

This perspective thus suggests the intriguing subtlety that even if their rewards are lower than those that would be obtained by exploiting a partner, people are more content in fair relationships than in unfair ones. In fact, this appears to be true. In a survey of 373 spouses representing all phases of the family life cycle, Feeney, Peterson, and Noller (1994) demonstrated that overbenefited partners are typically happier with their marriages than underbenefited spouses are, but participants in equitable marriages are the most satisfied of all. Inequity erodes commitment (Floyd & Wasner, 1994), so that, for instance, wives in inequitable marriages are more likely to have extramarital affairs than are wives who feel they are treated fairly (Prins, Buunk, & Van Yperen, 1993).

Thus, chronic inequity appears to be a relationship dysfunction that puts a partnership at some risk, even when the relationship is otherwise fairly rewarding. In short, "despite the popular notion that 'true love is unselfish,' for both men and women, the best kind of love relationship seems to be one in which everyone feels that he or she is getting what they deserve" (Utne, Hatfield, Traupmann, & Greenberger, 1984, pp. 331–332). Because working mothers tend to do twice as many family chores as their husbands do (Huppe & Cyr, 1997), one general admonition for modern couples is for men "to do more housework, child care, and affectional maintenance if they wish to have a happy wife" (Gottman & Carrère, 1994, p. 225). Equity is ultimately in the eye of the beholder, however, so intimate couples will always have to decide for themselves what is fair and what is not.

CONCLUSION

I identified a variety of factors that contribute to troubled relationships, but my list is far from complete (see, e.g., Amato & Rogers, 1997).

I hope, however, that the personal, interactive, and relational sources of dysfunction identified here provide an indication of the enormous intricacy of happy relationships and the number of levels at which they can break down. I offer my tripartite scheme as a handy organizing device, but I am reluctant to make too much of these distinctions because these personal, interactive, and relational factors are often interrelated, routinely influencing, and sometimes causing, each other. It is the diversity of these influences, ranging from intrapersonal to interpersonal, cognitive to behavioral (and back again), that I wish to highlight.

With all these pitfalls, why should people take the risks intimacy presents? Perhaps because, as a highly social species, affiliation and intimacy are in people's blood; it really is better to love and lose than never to love at all. In any case, given the fundamental importance of close relationships in people's lives, understanding the processes of both healthy and unhealthy relationships is an essential focus for social and clinical psychology.

REFERENCES

Amato, P. R., & Rogers, S. J. (1997). A longitudinal study of marital problems and subsequent divorce. *Journal of Marriage and the Family, 59,* 612–624.

Antill, J. K. (1983). Sex role complementarity versus similarity in married couples. *Journal of Personality and Social Psychology, 45,* 145–155.

Assh, S. D., & Byers, E. S. (1996). Understanding the co-occurrence of marital distress and depression in women. *Journal of Social and Personal Relationships, 13,* 537–552.

Attridge, M., & Berscheid, E. (1994). Entitlement in romantic relationships in the United States: A social-exchange perspective. In M. J. Lerner & G. Mikula (Eds.), *Entitlement and the affectional bond: Justice in close relationships* (pp. 117–147). New York: Plenum.

Baldwin, M. W., & Fehr, B. (1995). On the instability of attachment style ratings. *Personal Relationships, 2,* 247–261.

Barnett, R. C., Raudenbush, S. W., Brennan, R. T., Pleck, J. H., & Marshall, N. L. (1995). Change in job and marital experiences and change in psychological distress: A longitudinal study of dual-earner couples. *Journal of Personality and Social Psychology, 69,* 839–850.

Bartholomew, K. (1997, October). *The merits of interviews in attachment research.* Paper presented at the meeting of the Society for Experimental Social Psychology, Toronto, Ontario, Canada.

Bartholomew, K., & Horowitz, L. M. (1991). Attachment styles among young adults: A test of a four-category model. *Journal of Personality and Social Psychology, 61,* 226–244.

Baumeister, R. F., & Leary, M. R. (1995). The need to belong: Desire for interpersonal attachments as a fundamental human motivation. *Psychological Bulletin, 117*, 497–529.

Baxter, L. A., Mazanec, M., Nicholson, J., Pittman, G., Smith, K., & West, L. (1997). Everyday loyalties and betrayals in personal relationships. *Journal of Social and Personal Relationships, 14*, 655–678.

Beach, S. R. H., & O'Leary, K. D. (1993). Marital discord and dysphoria: For whom does the marital relationship predict depressive symptomatology? *Journal of Social and Personal Relationships, 10*, 405–420.

Berley, R. A., & Jacobson, M. S. (1984). Causal attributions in intimate relationships: Toward a model of cognitive–behavioral marital therapy. In P. C. Kendall (Ed.), *Advances in cognitive–behavioral research and therapy* (Vol. 3, pp. 1–60). Orlando, FL: Academic Press.

Birnbaum, G. E., Orr, I., Mikulincer, M., & Florian, V. (1997). When marriage breaks up: Does attachment style contribute to coping and mental health? *Journal of Social and Personal Relationships, 14*, 643–654.

Bloom, B. L., Asher, S. J., & White, S. W. (1978). Marital disruption as a stressor: A review and analysis. *Psychological Bulletin, 85*, 867–894.

Botwin, M. D., Buss, D. M., & Shackelford, T. K. (1997). Personality and mate preferences: Five factors in mate selection and marital satisfaction. *Journal of Personality, 65*, 107–136.

Bowlby, J. (1982). *Attachment and loss: Vol. 1. Attachment* (2nd ed.). New York: Basic Books.

Bradbury, T. N., Campbell, S. M., & Fincham, F. D. (1995). Longitudinal and behavioral analysis of masculinity and femininity in marriage. *Journal of Personality and Social Psychology, 68*, 328–341.

Bradbury, T. N., & Fincham, F. D. (1990). Attributions in marriage: Review and critique. *Psychological Bulletin, 107*, 3–33.

Brainerd, E. G., Hunter, P. A., Moore, D., & Thompson, T. R. (1996). Jealousy induction as a predictor of power and the use of other control methods in heterosexual relationships. *Psychological Reports, 79*, 1319–1325.

Brennan, K. A., & Shaver, P. R. (1995). Dimensions of adult attachment, affect regulation, and romantic relationship functioning. *Personality and Social Psychology Bulletin, 21*, 267–283.

Buller, D. B., & Burgoon, J. K. (1994). Deception: Strategic and nonstrategic communication. In J. A. Daly & J. M. Wiemann (Eds.), *Strategic interpersonal communication* (pp. 191–223). Hillsdale, NJ: Erlbaum.

Burman, B., & Margolin, G. (1992). Analysis of the association between marital relationships and health problems: An interactional perspective. *Psychological Bulletin, 112*, 39–63.

Buss, D. M. (1995). Psychological sex differences: Origins through sexual selection. *American Psychologist, 50*, 164–168.

Buunk, B. (1982). Anticipated sexual jealousy: Its relationship to self-esteem, dependency, and reciprocity. *Personality and Social Psychology Bulletin, 8*, 310–316.

Buunk, B. (1984). Jealousy as related to attributions for the partner's behavior. *Social Psychology Quarterly, 47,* 107–112.

Buunk, B. (1987). Conditions that promote breakups as a consequence of extra-dyadic involvements. *Journal of Social and Clinical Psychology, 5,* 271–284.

Buunk, B. P. (1995). Sex, self-esteem, dependency and extradyadic sexual experience as related to jealousy responses. *Journal of Social and Personal Relationships, 12,* 147–153.

Buunk, B. P., Angleitner, A., Oubaid, V., & Buss, D. M. (1996). Sex differences in jealousy in evolutionary and cultural perspective: Tests from the Netherlands, Germany, and the United States. *Psychological Science, 7,* 359–363.

Carpenter, E. M., & Kirkpatrick, L. A. (1996). Attachment style and presence of a romantic partner as moderators of psychophysiological responses to a stressful laboratory situation. *Personal Relationships, 3,* 351–367.

Carver, C. S. (1997). Adult attachment and personality: Converging evidence and a new measure. *Personality and Social Psychology Bulletin, 23,* 865–883.

Collins, N. L. (1996). Working models of attachment: Implications for explanation, emotion, and behavior. *Journal of Personality and Social Psychology, 71,* 810–832.

Coyne, J. C. (1976). Toward an interactional description of depression. *Psychiatry, 39,* 28–40.

Cutrona, C. E. (1982). Transition to college: Loneliness and the process of social adjustment. In L. A. Peplau & D. Perlman (Eds.), *Loneliness: A source book of current theory, research, and therapy* (pp. 291–309). New York: Wiley.

Davila, J., Bradbury, T. N., Cohan, C. L., & Tochluk, S. (1997). Marital functioning and depressive symptoms: Evidence for a stress generation model. *Journal of Personality and Social Psychology, 73,* 849–861.

Davila, J., Burge, D., & Hammen, C. (1997). Why does attachment style change? *Journal of Personality and Social Psychology, 73,* 826–838.

DePaulo, B. M., Kashy, D. A., Kirkendol, S. E., Wyer, M. M., & Epstein, J. A. (1996). Lying in everyday life. *Journal of Personality and Social Psychology, 70,* 979–995.

DeSteno, D. A., & Salovey, P. (1996a). Evolutionary origins of sex differences in jealousy? Questioning the "fitness" of the model. *Psychological Science, 7,* 367–372.

DeSteno, D. A., & Salovey, P. (1996b). Jealousy and the characteristics of one's rival: A self-evaluation maintenance perspective. *Personality and Social Psychology Bulletin, 22,* 920–932.

Dutton, D. G., Saunders, K., Starzomski, A., & Bartholomew, K. (1994). Intimacy-anger and insecure attachment as precursors of abuse in intimate relationships. *Journal of Applied Social Psychology, 24,* 1367–1386.

Eidelson, R. J., & Epstein, N. (1982). Cognition and relationship maladjustment: Development of a measure of dysfunctional relationship beliefs. *Journal of Consulting and Clinical Psychology, 50,* 715–720.

Ellis, A. (1977). Rational and irrational jealousy. In G. Clanton & L. G. Smith (Eds.), *Jealousy* (pp. 170–178). Englewood Cliffs, NJ: Prentice Hall.

Escudero, V., Rogers, L. E., & Gutierrez, E. (1997). Patterns of relational control and nonverbal affect in clinic and nonclinic couples. *Journal of Social and Personal Relationships, 14,* 5–29.

Feeney, J. A. (1994). Attachment style, communication patterns, and satisfaction across the life cycle of marriage. *Personal Relationships, 1,* 333–348.

Feeney, J., Peterson, C., & Noller, P. (1994). Equity and marital satisfaction over the family life cycle. *Personal Relationships, 1,* 83–99.

Felmlee, D. H. (1995). Fatal attractions: Affection and disaffection in intimate relationships. *Journal of Social and Personal Relationships, 12,* 295–311.

Fincham, F. D., Beach, S. R. H., Harold, G. T., & Osborne, L. N. (1997). Marital satisfaction and depression: Different causal relationships for men and women? *Psychological Science, 8,* 351–357.

Floyd, F. J., & Wasner, G. H. (1994). Social exchange, equity, and commitment: Structural equation modeling of dating relationships. *Journal of Family Psychology, 8,* 55–73.

Follette, W. C., & Jacobson, N. S. (1985). Assessment and treatment of incompatible marital relationships. In W. Ickes (Ed.), *Compatible and incompatible relationships* (pp. 333–361). New York: Springer-Verlag.

Frazier, P. A., Byer, A. L., Fischer, A. R., Wright, D. M., & DeBord, K. A. (1996). Adult attachment style and partner choice: Correlational and experimental findings. *Personal Relationships, 3,* 117–136.

Freedman, J. (1978). *Happy people: What happiness is, who has it, and why.* New York: Harcourt Brace Jovanovich.

Fuller, T. L., & Fincham, F. D. (1995). Attachment style in married couples: Relation to current marital functioning, stability over time, and method of assessment. *Personal Relationships, 2,* 17–34.

Geary, D. C., Rumsey, M., Bow-Thomas, C. C., & Hoard, M. K. (1995). Sexual jealousy as a facultative trait: Evidence from the pattern of sex differences in adults from China and the United States. *Ethology and Sociobiology, 16,* 355–383.

Geiss, S. K., & O'Leary, K. D. (1981). Therapist ratings of frequency and severity of marital problems: Implications for research. *Journal of Marital and Family Therapy, 7,* 515–520.

Gerlsma, C., Buunk, B. P., & Mutsaers, W. C. M. (1996). Correlates of self-reported adult attachment styles in a Dutch sample of married men and women. *Journal of Social and Personal Relationships, 13,* 313–320.

Gottman, J. M. (1993a). A theory of marital dissolution and stability. *Journal of Family Psychology, 7,* 57–75.

Gottman, J. M. (1993b). The roles of conflict engagement, escalation, and avoidance in marital interaction: A longitudinal view of five types of couples. *Journal of Consulting and Clinical Psychology, 61,* 6–15.

Gottman, J. M. (1994). *Why marriages succeed or fail.* New York: Simon & Schuster.

Gottman, J. M., & Carrère, S. (1994). Why can't men and women get along?: Developmental roots and marital inequities. In D. J. Canary & L. Stafford (Eds.), *Communication and relational maintenance* (pp. 203–229). San Diego, CA: Academic Press.

Gottman, J. M., & Levenson, R. W. (1992). Marital processes predictive of later dissolution: Behavior, physiology, and health. *Journal of Personality and Social Psychology, 63,* 221–233.

Gottman, J. M., & Porterfield, A. L. (1981). Communicative competence in the nonverbal behavior of married couples. *Journal of Marriage and the Family, 43,* 807–824.

Graziano, W. G., Jensen-Campbell, L. A., & Hair, E. C. (1996). Perceiving interpersonal conflict and reacting to it: The case of agreeableness. *Journal of Personality and Social Psychology, 70,* 820–835.

Greenberg, J., & Pyszczynski, T. (1985). Proneness to romantic jealousy and responses to jealousy in others. *Journal of Personality, 53,* 468–479.

Hansen, G. L. (1985). Perceived threats and marital jealousy. *Social Psychology Quarterly, 48,* 262–268.

Harris, C. R., & Christenfeld, N. (1996). Gender, jealousy, and reason. *Psychological Science, 7,* 364–366.

Heavey, C. L., Layne, C., & Christensen, A. (1993). Gender and conflict structure in marital interaction: A replication and extension. *Journal of Consulting and Clinical Psychology, 61,* 16–27.

Hokanson, J. E., & Butler, A. C. (1992). Cluster analysis of depressed college students' social behaviors. *Journal of Personality and Social Psychology, 62,* 273–280.

Horneffer, K. J., & Fincham, F. D. (1996). Attributional models of depression and marital distress. *Personality and Social Psychology Bulletin, 22,* 678–689.

House, J. S., Robbins, C., & Metzner, H. L. (1982). The association of social relationships and activities with mortality: Prospective evidence from the Tecumseh Community Health Study. *American Journal of Epidemiology, 116,* 123–140.

Huppe, M., & Cyr, M. (1997). Division of household labor and marital satisfaction of dual income couples according to family life cycle. *Canadian Journal of Counseling, 31,* 145–162.

Huston, T. L., & Geis, G. (1993). In what ways do gender-related attributes and beliefs affect marriage? *Journal of Social Issues, 49,* 87–106.

Ickes, W. (1985). Sex-role influences on compatibility in relationships. In W. Ickes (Ed.), *Compatible and incompatible relationships* (pp. 187–208). New York: Springer-Verlag.

Ickes, W. (1993). Traditional gender roles: Do they make, and then break, our relationships? *Journal of Social Issues, 49,* 71–86.

Ickes, W., & Barnes, R. D. (1978). Boys and girls together—And alienated: On enacting stereotyped sex roles in mixed-sex dyads. *Journal of Personality and Social Psychology, 36,* 669–683.

Jacobson, N. S., & Margolin, G. (1979). *Marital therapy: Strategies based on social learning and behavior exchange principles*. New York: Brunner/Mazel.

Jockin, V., McGue, M., & Lykken, D. T. (1996). Personality and divorce: A genetic analysis. *Journal of Personality and Social Psychology, 71*, 288–299.

Joiner, T. E., Jr., Catanzaro, S. J., Rudd, M. D., & Rajab, M. H. (in press). The case for a hierarchical, oblique, and bidimensional structure of loneliness. *Journal of Social and Clinical Psychology*.

Jones, J. T., & Cunningham, J. D. (1996). Attachment styles and other predictors of relationship satisfaction in dating couples. *Personal Relationships, 3*, 387–399.

Jones, W. H., & Burdette, M. P. (1994). Betrayal in relationships. In A. L. Weber & J. H. Harvey (Eds.), *Perspectives on close relationships* (pp. 243–262). Boston: Allyn & Bacon.

Jones, W. H., Freemon, J. R., & Goswick, R. A. (1981). The persistence of loneliness: Self and other determinants. *Journal of Personality, 49*, 27–48.

Jones, W. H., Sansone, C., & Helm, B. (1983). Loneliness and interpersonal judgments. *Personality and Social Psychology Bulletin, 9*, 437–442.

Kashy, D. A., & DePaulo, B. M. (1996). Who lies? *Journal of Personality and Social Psychology, 70*, 1037–1051.

Katz, J., & Beach, S. R. H. (1997). Romance in the crossfire: When do women's depressive symptoms predict partner relationship dissatisfaction? *Journal of Social and Clinical Psychology, 16*, 243–258.

Keelan, J. P. R., Dion, K. L., & Dion, K. K. (1994). Attachment style and heterosexual relationships among young adults: A short-term panel study. *Journal of Social and Personal Relationships, 11*, 201–214.

Kiecolt-Glaser, J. K., Malarkey, W. B., Chee, M., Newton, T., Cacioppo, J. T., Hsiao-Yin, M., & Glaser, R. (1993). Negative behavior during marital conflict is associated with immunological down-regulation. *Psychosomatic Medicine, 55*, 395–409.

Kirkpatrick, L. A., & Hazan, C. (1994). Attachment styles and close relationships: A four-year prospective study. *Personal Relationships, 1*, 123–142.

Kurdek, L. A. (1993). Nature and prediction of changes in marital quality for first-time parent and nonparent husbands and wives. *Journal of Family Psychology, 6*, 255–265.

Lamke, L. K., Sollie, D. L., Durbin, R. G., & Fitzpatrick, J. A. (1994). Masculinity, femininity and relationship satisfaction: The mediating role of interpersonal competence. *Journal of Social and Personal Relationships, 11*, 535–554.

Leary, M. R., & Downs, D. L. (1995). Interpersonal functions of the self-esteem motive: The self-esteem system as sociometer. In M. H. Kernis (Ed.), *Efficacy, agency, and self-esteem* (pp. 123–144). New York: Plenum.

Levenson, R. W., & Gottman, J. M. (1983). Marital interaction: Physiological linkage and affective exchange. *Journal of Personality and Social Psychology, 45*, 587–597.

Levitt, M. J., Silver, M. E., & Franco, N. (1996). Troublesome relationships: A part of human experience. *Journal of Social and Personal Relationships, 13*, 523–536.

Marcus, D. K., & Nardone, M. E. (1992). Depression and interpersonal rejection. *Clinical Psychology Review, 12*, 433–449.

Markman, H. J., Renick, M. J., Floyd, F. J., Stanley, S. M., & Clements, M. (1993). Preventing marital distress through communication and conflict management training: A 4- and 5-year follow-up. *Journal of Consulting and Clinical Psychology, 61*, 70–77.

Martin, T. C., & Bumpass, L. (1989). Recent trends in marital disruption. *Demography, 26*, 37–51.

Mathes, E. W., Adams, H. E., & Davies, R. M. (1985). Jealousy: Loss of relationship rewards, loss of self-esteem, depression, anxiety, and anger. *Journal of Personality and Social Psychology, 48*, 1552–1561.

McCabe, S. B., & Gotlib, I. H. (1993). Interactions of couples with and without a depressed spouse: Self-report and observations of problem-solving situations. *Journal of Social and Personal Relationships, 10*, 589–599.

McGonagle, K. A., Kessler, R. C., & Schilling, E. A. (1992). The frequency and determinants of marital disagreements in a community sample. *Journal of Social and Personal Relationships, 9*, 507–524.

Metts, S. (1994). Relational transgressions. In W. R. Cupach & B. H. Spitzberg (Eds.), *The dark side of interpersonal communication* (pp. 217–239). Hillsdale, NJ: Erlbaum.

Metts, S., & Cupach, W. R. (1990). The influence of relationship beliefs and problem-solving responses on satisfaction in romantic relationships. *Human Communication Research, 17*, 170–185.

Mickelson, K. D., Kessler, R. C., & Shaver, P. R. (1997). Adult attachment in a nationally representative sample. *Journal of Personality and Social Psychology, 73*, 1092–1106.

Milardo, R. M., Johnson, M. P., & Huston, T. L. (1983). Developing close relationships: Changing patterns of interaction between pair members and social networks. *Journal of Personality and Social Psychology, 44*, 964–976.

Miller, R. S. (1997). We always hurt the ones we love: Aversive interactions in close relationships. In R. Kowalski (Ed.), *Aversive interpersonal behaviors* (pp. 11–29). New York: Plenum.

Moller, A. T., & Van Zyl, P. D. (1991). Relationship beliefs, interpersonal perception, and marital adjustment. *Journal of Clinical Psychology, 47*, 28–33.

Newton, T. L., Kiecolt-Glaser, J. K., Glaser, R., & Malarkey, W. B. (1995). Conflict and withdrawal during marital interaction: The roles of hostility and defensiveness. *Personality and Social Psychology Bulletin, 21*, 512–524.

Nezlek, J. B., Kowalski, R. M., Leary, M. R., Blevins, T., & Holgate, S. (1997). Personality moderators of reactions to interpersonal rejection: Depression and trait self-esteem. *Personality and Social Psychology Bulletin, 23*, 1235–1244.

Noller, P. (1981). Gender and marital adjustment level differences in decoding messages from spouses and strangers. *Journal of Personality and Social Psychology, 41,* 272–278.

Noller, P. (1982). Channel consistency and inconsistency in the communications of married couples. *Journal of Personality and Social Psychology, 43,* 732–741.

Noller, P. (1987). Nonverbal communication in marriage. In D. Perlman & S. Duck (Eds.), *Intimate relationships: Development, dynamics, and deterioration* (pp. 123–147). Newbury Park, CA: Sage.

O'Leary, K. D., Christian, J. L., & Mendell, N. R. (1994). A closer look at the link between marital discord and depressive symptomatology. *Journal of Social and Clinical Psychology, 13,* 33–41.

Orvis, B. R., Kelley, H. H., & Butler, D. (1976). Attributional conflict in young couples. In J. Harvey, W. Ickes, & R. Kidd (Eds.), *New directions in attribution research* (Vol. 1, pp. 353–386). Hillsdale, NJ: Erlbaum.

Patterson, M. L. (1983). *Nonverbal behavior: A functional perspective.* New York: Springer-Verlag.

Peplau, L. A., & Perlman, D. (Eds.). (1982). *Loneliness: A sourcebook of current theory, research, and therapy.* New York: Wiley.

Perlman, D., & Peplau, L. A. (1981). Toward a social psychology of loneliness. In S. Duck & R. Gilmour (Eds.), *Personal relationships: 3. Personal relationships in disorder* (pp. 31–56). London: Academic Press.

Pines, A., & Aronson, E. (1983). Antecedents, correlates, and consequences of sexual jealousy. *Journal of Personality, 51,* 108–136.

Prins, K. S., Buunk, B. P., & Van Yperen, N. W. (1993). Equity, normative disapproval and extramarital relationships. *Journal of Social and Personal Relationships, 10,* 39–53.

Radecki-Bush, C., Farrell, A. D., & Bush, J. P. (1993). Predicting jealous responses: The influence of adult attachment and depression on threat appraisal. *Journal of Social and Personal Relationships, 10,* 569–588.

Reis, H. T. (1986). Gender effects in social participation: Intimacy, loneliness, and the conduct of social interaction. In R. Gilmour & S. Duck (Eds.), *The emerging field of personal relationships* (pp. 91–105). London: Academic Press.

Reis, H. T., Senchak, M., & Solomon, B. (1985). Sex differences in the intimacy of social interaction: Further examination of potential explanations. *Journal of Personality and Social Psychology, 48,* 1204–1217.

Rook, K. S. (1984). Promoting social bonding: Strategies for helping the lonely and socially isolated. *American Psychologist, 39,* 1389–1407.

Rook, K. S., & Peplau, L. A. (1982). Perspectives on helping the lonely. In L. A. Peplau & D. Perlman (Eds.), *Loneliness: A source book of current theory, research, and therapy* (pp. 351–378). New York: Wiley.

Rotenberg, K. J. (1994). Loneliness and interpersonal trust. *Journal of Social and Clinical Psychology, 13,* 152–173.

Rubenstein, C. M., & Shaver, P. (1982). *In search of intimacy.* New York: Delacorte Press.

Rubenstein, C. M., Shaver, P., & Peplau, L. A. (1979). Loneliness. *Human Nature*, 2, 58–65.

Rusbult, C. E., & Martz, J. M. (1995). Remaining in an abusive relationship: An investment model analysis of nonvoluntary dependence. *Personality and Social Psychology Bulletin*, 21, 558–571.

Rusbult, C. E., & Van Lange, P. A. M. (1996). Interdependence processes. In E. T. Higgins & A. W. Kruglanski (Eds.), *Social psychology: Handbook of basic principles* (pp. 564–596). New York: Guilford Press.

Salovey, P., & Rodin, J. (1988). Coping with envy and jealousy. *Journal of Social and Clinical Psychology*, 7, 15–33.

Scharfe, E., & Bartholomew, K. (1994). Reliability and stability of adult attachment patterns. *Personal Relationships*, 1, 23–43.

Scharfe, E., & Bartholomew, K. (1995). Accommodation and attachment representations in young couples. *Journal of Social and Personal Relationships*, 12, 389–401.

Sharpsteen, D. J. (1991). The organization of jealousy knowledge: Romantic jealousy as a blended emotion. In P. Salovey (Ed.), *The psychology of jealousy and envy* (pp. 31–51). New York: Guilford Press.

Sharpsteen, D. J. (1995). The effects of relationship and self-esteem threats on the likelihood of romantic jealousy. *Journal of Social and Personal Relationships*, 12, 89–101.

Sharpsteen, D. J., & Kirkpatrick, L. A. (1997). Romantic jealousy and adult romantic attachment. *Journal of Personality and Social Psychology*, 72, 627–640.

Shettel-Neuber, J., Bryson, J. B., & Young, L. E. (1978). Physical attractiveness of the "other person" and jealousy. *Personality and Social Psychology Bulletin*, 4, 612–615.

Sillars, A. L. (1985). Interpersonal perception in relationships. In W. Ickes (Ed.), *Compatible and incompatible relationships* (pp. 277–305). New York: Springer-Verlag.

Sillars, A. L., Folwell, A. L., Hill, K. C., Maki, B. K., Hurst, A. P., & Casano, R. A. (1994). Marital communication and the persistence of misunderstanding. *Journal of Social and Personal Relationships*, 11, 611–617.

Simpson, J. A., Rholes, W. S., & Phillips, D. (1996). Conflict in close relationships: An attachment perspective. *Journal of Personality and Social Psychology*, 71, 899–914.

South, S. J., & Lloyd, K. M. (1995). Spousal alternatives and marital dissolution. *American Sociological Review*, 60, 21–35.

Sprecher, S., & Schwartz, P. (1994). Equity and balance in the exchange of contributions in close relationships. In M. J. Lerner & G. Mikula (Eds.), *Entitlement and the affectional bond: Justice in close relationships* (pp. 11–41). New York: Plenum.

Twenge, J. M. (1997). Changes in masculine and feminine traits over time: A meta-analysis. *Sex Roles*, 36, 305–325.

U.S. Bureau of the Census. (1995). *Statistical abstracts of the United States* (115th ed.). Washington, DC: U.S. Government Printing Office.

Utne, M. K., Hatfield, E., Traupmann, J., & Greenberger, D. (1984). Equity, marital satisfaction, and stability. *Journal of Social and Personal Relationships, 1,* 323–332.

Waller, N. G., & Shaver, P. R. (1994). The importance of nongenetic influences on romantic love styles: A twin–family study. *Psychological Science, 5,* 268–274.

Weeks, D. G., Michela, J. L., Peplau, L. A., & Bragg, M. E. (1980). The relation between loneliness and depression: A structural equation analysis. *Journal of Personality and Social Psychology, 39,* 1238–1244.

Wegner, D. M., & Lane, J. D. (1995). From secrecy to psychopathology. In J. W. Pennebaker (Ed.), *Emotion, disclosure, and health* (pp. 25–46). Washington, DC: American Psychological Association.

Wheeler, L., Reis, H., & Nezlek, J. (1983). Loneliness, social interaction, and sex roles. *Journal of Personality and Social Psychology, 45,* 943–953.

White, G. L. (1980). Inducing jealousy: A power perspective. *Personality and Social Psychology Bulletin, 6,* 222–227.

White, G. L. (1981). Jealousy and partner's perceived motives for attraction to a rival. *Social Psychology Quarterly, 44,* 24–30.

White, G. L., & Mullen, P. E. (1989). *Jealousy: Theory, research, and clinical strategies.* New York: Guilford Press.

12

GROUP DYNAMICS AND PSYCHOLOGICAL WELL-BEING: THE IMPACT OF GROUPS ON ADJUSTMENT AND DYSFUNCTION

DONELSON R. FORSYTH AND TIMOTHY R. ELLIOTT

Groups are the setting for most social activities. All but an occasional recluse or exile belong to groups, and those who insist on living their lives apart from others, refusing to join any groups, are considered curiosities, eccentrics, or even mentally unsettled (Storr, 1988). Nearly all human societies are organized around small groups, such as families, clans, communities, gangs, religious denominations, and tribes, and the influence of these groups on individual members is considerable. Virtually all social activities—working, learning, worshiping, relaxing, playing, socializing, chatting in cyberspace communities, and even sleeping—occur in groups rather than in isolation from others.

Groups exert a ubiquitous, unrelenting influence over their members, shaping both their psychological adjustment and their dysfunction. Those who study mental health—clinical psychologists, counseling psychologists, community psychologists, health psychologists, social workers, and psychiatrists—have long recognized the relationship between groups and members' psychological well-being. Pratt (1922), as early as 1905, found that patients suffering from tuberculosis improved when they took part in small-group discussions and listened to inspirational lectures. When Moreno (1932) used sociometric methods to create cohesive subgroups in an institutionalized population, he documented increases in adjustment and decreases in interpersonal conflict. Freud (1922), in an insightful rebuttal to the idea that people in groups become a mob or lose their individual identities, argued that groups are essential to most adults' mental health. Lewin (1936) founded the scientific field of group dynamics, and his training groups, "T-groups," provided the template for a wide variety of interpersonal, group-based training techniques.

In this chapter we seek, in a limited way, to reestablish the link between the social psychology of groups and the application of group dynamics to understand clinical and interpersonal dysfunction. We begin our analysis by asking some fundamental questions: Are groups real, in a psychological sense? Are individuals who are members of groups influenced, in fundamental ways, by these memberships? Can their adjustment, health, and dysfunction be understood if these memberships are ignored? If groups are not real, then little can be gained from examining their influence on the psychological adjustment of individuals.

THE REALITY OF GROUPS

Groups lie at the center of one of the great debates in the field of psychology and sociology: Are groups real? Durkheim (1897/1966), for example, argued that his analysis of suicide provided clear evidence of the reality of groups because it explained psychological despair in purely group-level terms. Durkheim also endorsed the conclusions of Le Bon (1895/1960) and other crowd psychologists, going so far as to conclude that people in large groups can become so deindividuated that they act with a single, and somewhat delusional, mind. Durkheim believed that the collective conscious can be so powerful that it blots out the group members' will.

Although McDougall (1908) agreed with many of Durkheim's (1897/1966) conclusions—and traced much of the influence of groups over individuals back to humanity's instinctive gregariousness—most psychologists questioned the significance of groups and group-level processes. Allport (1924) argued forcefully against the scientific legitimacy of group concepts when he concluded that "the actions of all are nothing more than the sum of the actions of each taken separately" (p. 5). Groups, according to Allport, were not real entities, and he felt that the behavior of individuals in groups could be understood by studying the psychology of the group members.

Few contemporary psychologists would agree with Allport's (1924) radical rejection of the importance of studying groups, but vestiges of this antigroup orientation continue to influence theorists' and researchers' willingness to consider group-level concepts when explaining maladaptive and adaptive processes. Asked why an individual is depressed, addicted, or engages in aberrant actions, many psychologists would focus on internal, psychological determinants of behavior. Extant clinical conceptualizations and intervention models adopt this so-called "psychogenic perspective" when they emphasize personality traits, genetic factors, past events, and biological processes as causes of dysfunction (Forsyth & Leary, 1991). This bias has been summarized unabashedly by Urban (1983), who argued that when psychologists look for causes outside of the individual, they "deny and distort the essential quality of human existence. Everything of significance with regard to this entire process occurs within the inner or subjective experience of the individual" (p. 163). Psychogenic approaches assume that psychological states mediate the relationship between the external world and the person's reaction to it.

This psychogenic perspective slights the very real impact of groups on individual members. Even Allport (1962) admitted that people sometimes act differently when they are in groups. Some of these changes are subtle. Moving from isolation to a group context can reduce people's sense of uniqueness while also enhancing their ability to perform simple tasks rapidly (Triplett, 1898). Interacting with other people can also prompt individuals to gradually change their attitudes and values as they come to agree with the overall consensus of the group (Newcomb, 1943). In groups, individuals acquire a sense of shared identity, social support, and most of their values. Groups also can change people more dramatically. Milgram's (1963) studies of obedience, for example, placed participants in three-person groups. The experimenter, who has much of the authority in the setting, told the participant to deliver painful electric shocks to another person. The shocks were bogus, but the harm seemed real to the participants. Nonetheless, fewer than 35% of the participants were able to resist the demands of their role by refusing to follow orders. More recently, Insko and his colleagues have verified the discontinuity effect: People are much more competitive when they are in groups responding to other groups rather than individuals responding to other individuals (Pemberton, Insko, & Schopler, 1996). Groups may just be collections of individuals, but this collective experience changes the members.

Groups also possess characteristics that go beyond the characteristics possessed by individual members of the group. A group's cohesiveness, for example, is more than the mere attraction of each individual member for one another (Hogg, 1992). Individuals may not like each other on a personal level, yet when they form a group they experience powerful feelings of unity and *esprit de corps*. Groups seem to possess supervening qualities "that cannot be reduced to or described as qualities of its participants" (Sandelands & St. Clair, 1993, p. 443). Group membership can transcend place and collapse space, so that the sense of community and belongingness connects each participating member with unseen others who share and subscribe to the salient features of the group. As Lewin's (1951) gestalt orientation argues, a group is greater than the sum of its parts.

Individuals also readily hypostatize groups: They perceive them to be real and assume that their properties are influential ones. Not all collections of individuals are groups, but the perceiver considers an aggregate with certain qualities to be a group. Campbell's (1958) analysis of *entitativity* (perceived groupness), for example, argues that perceptual factors such as common fate, proximity, and similarity influence both members' and nonmembers' perceptions of a group's unity. Other investigators have shown that observers, once they decide that they are observing a group rather than a collection of individuals, no longer monitor which person said what, only which group said what (Brewer, Weber, & Carini, 1995, Experiment 1). Groups are as real as individuals, at least at a perceptual level (Hilton & von Hippel, 1990; McConnell, Sherman, & Hamilton, 1994a, 1994b).

In summary, a group-dynamics approach to psychological well-being and dysfunction rejects the idea that analyses that focus on individual-level mechanisms are superior to ones that emphasize group-level mechanisms. Groups possess features that go well beyond the characteristics of individual members, and observers' impressions of people differ when they think the people they are watching are members of a unified group. Groups also influence their members in both subtle and dramatic ways, and some of these influences affect their mental health. We review some of these relationships between groups and psychological adjustment, but our review is a selective one. We provide examples of the relationship between groups and mental health rather than a comprehensive cataloging of all linkages. Also, whereas Levine and Moreland (1992) examined the impact of particular types of groups (e.g., families, work groups, school groups) on mental health, we examine how group processes (e.g., social support, socialization) influence health. We also focus on nontherapeutic groups and refer interested readers to other treatments of the relationship between group dynamics and group psychotherapy (e.g., Forsyth, 1991).

GROUPS, REJECTION, AND LONELINESS

James Pelosi made many friends when he first entered West Point, but all that changed when he was charged with an honor code violation. He was exonerated by a student court, but his fellow cadets believed he was guilty. They sentenced him to The Silence: No student spoke to him or interacted with him in any way for nearly 2 years. He felt lonely and depressed much of the time and lost 26 lb during the period. (adapted from Steinberg, 1975)

Theory and research suggest that people need to be connected to other people and that they experience significant psychological distress if these connections are severed. Baumeister and Leary's (1995) belongingness hypothesis, for example, argues that "human beings have a pervasive drive to form and maintain at least a minimum quantity of lasting, positive, and impactful interpersonal relationships" (p. 497). They likened the need to belong to other basic needs, such as hunger or thirst. Just as an inadequate diet can undermine one's health, separation can lead to pronounced psychological discomfort.

Groups play an essential role in satisfying the need to belong. Years ago, Freud (1922) argued that membership in groups promotes mental health because groups take the place of childhood families when people reach adulthood. Freud developed the concept of *transference* when he observed that some of his patients reacted to him as if they were children and he was their parent. He theorized that a similar transference occurs in groups when individuals accept leaders as authority figures. This transference leads to identification with the leader, and other group members come to take the place of siblings. Group membership may be an unconscious means of regaining the security of the family, and the emotional ties that bind members to their groups are like the ties that bind children to their family (Kohut, 1984).

Freud's (1922) replacement hypothesis is speculative, but it nonetheless underscores the importance of groups for members. Indeed, some members of long-term, emotionally intensive groups—therapeutic groups, support groups, combat units, and high-demand religious organizations—act in ways that are consistent with Freud's hypotheses. They respond to leaders as if they were parents, treat one another like siblings (e.g., they may even refer to each other as "brother" or "sister"), and show pronounced grief and withdrawal when someone leaves the "family" (Wrong, 1994). Freud's theory is also consistent with evidence that suggests groups (a) provide a sense of security like that of a nurturing parent and (b) make relations with others who are similar in affective tone to siblings possible (Lee & Robbins, 1995).

Freud may have exaggerated people's need to return to the shelter of their childhood families, but his arguments for the importance of group membership for mental health have been borne out by studies of the effects of social isolation and loneliness. Individuals who have been isolated from others for too long, such as stranded explorers or prisoners in solitary confinement, report fear, insomnia, memory lapses, depression, fatigue, and general confusion. Suedfeld (1997) noted that these negative consequences of isolation become more intense when the isolation is unintended and undesirable rather than when people voluntarily seek solitude.

Studies of people who are socially isolated from others also attest to the distress caused by too-few connections to others. Loneliness is so commonly reported by individuals suffering from psychological problems that it has been called the "common cold of psychopathology" (Jones, quoted in Meer, 1985, p. 33). Loneliness is a profoundly negative experience, so negative that people often seek professional help simply to alleviate their discomfort. Loneliness also tends to be present whenever people suffer from depression, anxiety, personality disorders, and interpersonal hostility (Jones & Carver, 1991). Prolonged periods of loneliness have been linked to physical illnesses such as cirrhosis of the liver (brought on by alcohol abuse), hypertension, heart disease, and leukemia (Hojat & Vogel, 1987). Loneliness may also attack the immune system. Individuals who are extremely lonely have higher levels of Epstein–Barr virus and lower levels of B lymphocytes. Both of these physical characteristics are associated with reductions in immunity and increased vulnerability to mononucleosis (Kiecolt-Glaser, Ricker, et al., 1984; Kiecolt-Glaser, Speicher, Holliday, & Glaser, 1984).

Weiss (1973) drew an interesting distinction between social loneliness, which occurs when people lack ties to other people in general, and emotional loneliness, which is the absence of a meaningful, intimate relationship with another person (DiTommaso & Spinner, 1997; Russell, Cutrona, Rose, & Yurko, 1984). Transitory groups do little to prevent either social or emotional loneliness, but more "involving" groups are sufficient to prevent social loneliness. A tight-knit group of friends or a family may be so emotionally involving that members never feel the lack of a dyadic love relationship. Indeed, people who belong to more groups and organizations report less loneliness than those who keep to themselves (Rubenstein & Shaver, 1980, 1982). Groups with extensive interconnections among all the members provide a particularly powerful antidote to loneliness (Kraus, Davis, Bazzini, Church, & Kirchman, 1993; Stokes, 1985), as do groups that are cohesive or unified (Anderson & Martin, 1995; Hoyle & Crawford, 1994; Schmidt & Sermat, 1983). People who belong to groups are healthier than individuals who have few ties to other people, because they suffer fewer psychological problems and physical illnesses (Stroebe, Stroebe, Abakoumkin, & Schut, 1996). They even live longer (Stroebe & Stroebe, 1996; Sugisawa, Liang, & Liu, 1994).

Membership in a cohesive group can, however, sometimes undermine rather than sustain health. Janis's (1963) classic analysis of the "old sergeant syndrome," for example, describes how soldiers who come to depend too much on their units sometimes suffer psychological problems. Although the cohesiveness of the unit initially provides psychological support for the individual, the loss of comrades during battle causes severe distress. Furthermore, when the unit is reinforced with replacements, the original group members are reluctant to establish emotional ties with the newcomers, partly in fear of the pain produced by separation. Hence, they begin restricting their interactions, and a coalition of old versus new begins to evolve. In time, the group members can become completely detached from the group.

Some highly cohesive groups may also purposefully sequester members from other groups in attempts to keep members away from a corrosive and hostile "outside world" (J. P. Elliott, 1993). In such cases, in-group/out-group perceptions stress similarities between members and the differences with those nonmembers outside the group. Contact with outsiders may be discouraged in these high-demand groups because such interaction may potentially corrupt the member's belief system or worldview; contact with nonmembers may be limited to the superficial civilities required of everyday life and to highly structured attempts to persuade or debate nonmembers with scripted or rehearsed material (J. P. Elliott, 1993).

These dynamics embue members with a clear sense of identity, value, and purpose, but they can restrict individuals' self-conceptions and complicate social interactions with nonmembers. If members' identities are defined in large part by their membership in the group, their self-concept may become oversimplified. As the results of studies of self-complexity suggest, they may respond more negatively when their group fails or their relationship with the group is threatened (Linville, 1985, 1987; Niedenthal, Setterlund, & Wherry, 1992). Individuals who leave high-demand religious groups because of changes in beliefs or social mobility may experience a "shattered faith syndrome" that may be marked by loneliness, chronic guilt and isolation, a lingering distrust of other people and groups, and anxiety about intimate relationships (Yao, 1987). Others who are disciplined for violating group norms and beliefs may face "shunning" or "disfellowship," in which guilty members are ostracized, alienated, and left alone to confront the consequences of their actions without the comfort of the peer group.

GROUPS AND SOCIAL SUPPORT

> Ricky's husband committed suicide, leaving her to care for their two small children. For months she relied on tranquilizers and her family for help, but she could not overcome her grief. Then she joined a self-help group of about 10 people who were recently widowed. The group helped her climb out of her despair, providing her with friends, support, and a place to talk. She explained, "I can't tell you how important that group was to me in terms of making me live with myself, live with my grief, and get through the pain." (Lieberman, 1993, pp. 294–295)

When people find themselves in stressful, difficult circumstances, they often cope by forming or joining a group. In times of trouble, such as illness, divorce, or loss, people seek out other people (Dooley & Catalano,

1984). When students first go to college, they cope by forming extensive social networks of peers and friends (Hays & Oxley, 1986). People who have been diagnosed with serious illnesses often take part in small discussion groups with other patients (Jacobs & Goodman, 1989). People who have personal problems, such as a general feeling of unhappiness or dissatisfaction, seek help from friends and relatives before turning to mental health professionals (Wills & DePaulo, 1991). Individuals experiencing work-related stress, such as layoffs, time pressures, or inadequate supervision, cope by joining with coworkers (Caplan, Vinokur, Price, & Van Ryn, 1989; Cooper, 1981).

Groups counter stress by providing members with social support: personal actions and resources that help them cope with minor aspects of everyday living, daily hassles, and more significant life crises (Coyne & Downey, 1991; Finch et al., 1997). Group members provide emotional support when they compliment and encourage one another, express their friendship for others, and listen to others' problems without offering criticism or suggestions. They offer informational support when they give directions, offer advice, and make suggestions about how to solve a particular problem. They also offer task support and tangible assistance to one another. Moreover, as noted above, most groups offer their members a sense of belonging: The need to belong is satisfied when people join groups (Sarason, Pierce, & Sarason, 1990). For others, group support may reinforce a sense of worthiness and reassure the unique worth of the person under times of duress (Cutrona & Russell, 1987); such support has often been associated with decreased levels of distress and depressive behavior (e.g., T. Elliott, Marmarosh, & Pickelman, 1994).

Some groups fail to deliver on their promise of support. They add stressors by stirring up conflicts, increasing responsibilities, and exposing members to criticism (Hays & Oxley, 1986; Seeman, Seeman, & Sayles, 1985). Overall, however, groups are more frequently supportive than burdensome. People who are deeply involved in a network of friends and families tend to be healthier than more isolated individuals. Although the benefits of relationships do not emerge in all studies, many show that people with more ties to other people suffer fewer physical (e.g., tuberculosis, heart disease) and psychological (e.g., depression, anxiety) illnesses. In one long-term study, 7,000 people were asked to describe their social relationships. Nine years later, the researchers found that people who did not have many ties to other people were more likely to have died than people with many ties (Berkman & Syme, 1979). Having a network of friends helps people return to health more quickly should they become ill. Heart patients, stroke victims, and kidney patients all recovered more rapidly when their friends and loved ones visited them regularly (Wallston, Alagna, DeVellis, & DeVellis, 1983). One review of 17 studies shows that people who received support from others tended to experience less stress in their lives (Barrera, 1986).

Social support is particularly valuable when stress levels increase. Stressful life circumstances increase the risk of psychological and physical illness, but groups can serve as protective buffers against these negative consequences (Herbert & Cohen, 1993; Uchino, Cacioppo, & Kiecolt-Glaser, 1996; Wills & Cleary, 1996). This buffering effect argues that individuals who are part of a group may not be able to avoid stressful life events but that they respond more positively when these stressors befall them. Individuals who experience a high level of stress, for example, may cope by taking drugs if they are not part of a strong social network (Pakier & Wills, 1990). Similarly, individuals trying to recover from a devastating crisis (e.g., death of a spouse or child) who were part of a social network of friends, relatives, and neighbors were less depressed than people who were not integrated into groups (Norris & Murrell, 1990).

Social support processes are formalized and deliberately manipulated in so-called "self-help groups." As defined by Jacobs and Goodman (1989), a self-help group's members share a common problem and meet for the purpose of exchanging social support. Most support groups are guided by the members themselves with little or no assistance from mental health professionals. Self-help groups tend to (a) develop norms that emphasize autonomy and self-governance, with members rather than external authorities determining activities; (b) emphasize democratic processes, in that the group provides methods for ensuring equality of treatment and advocates freedom of expression; (c) include people who face a common predicament, problem, or concern (participants are "psychologically bonded by the compelling similarity of member concerns"; Jacobs & Goodman, 1989, p. 537); (d) emphasize reciprocal helping (both giving and receiving assistance); and (e) impose minimal fees on members.

Self-help groups exist for nearly every major medical, psychological, or stress-related problem, including groups for sufferers of heart disease, cancer, liver disease, and AIDS; groups for people who provide care for those suffering from chronic disease, illness, and disability; groups to help people overcome addictions to alcohol and other substances; groups for children of parents overcome by addictions to alcohol and other substances; and groups for a variety of problems in living, such as helping people with money or time management problems.

Jacobs and Goodman (1989) noted that many practicing psychologists are neutral about, or even openly opposed to, self-help groups because they misunderstand their value. Self-help groups are not substitutes for psychotherapy but instead are designed to provide members with social support. Jacobs and Goodman estimated that self-help groups are growing in terms of numbers and members, with perhaps as many as 7 million people belonging to such groups. They attributed this growth to changes in the family, an increase in the number of people still living with significant diseases, an erosion of confidence in care providers, the lack of mental health services, an increasing faith in the value of social support as a buffer against stress, and the increased media attention provided by TV docudramas.

GROUPS AS SOCIALIZING AGENTS

In 1976, David Moore joined a group of forward-thinking young people who were interested in personal development, religion, and space travel. He studied and worked with the group for years and over time his ideas became arguably bizarre: He dressed only in black, he shaved his head, he cut himself off from contact with his family, and he became convinced that a comet was actually a spacecraft. In 1997, he and 38 other members of Heaven's Gate committed suicide.

Cooley (1909) drew a broad distinction between two types of groups: primary groups and secondary groups (or complex groups). Primary groups are small, close-knit groups, such as families, friendship cliques, or neighborhoods. Secondary groups are larger and more formally organized than primary groups. Such groups—religious congregations, work groups, clubs, neighborhood associations, and the like—tend to be shorter lived and less emotionally involving. Secondary groups, however, continue to define individuals' places in the social structure of society (Parsons, Bales, & Shils, 1953).

Both of these types of groups provide members with their attitudes, values, and identities. These groups teach members the skills they need to contribute to the group, provide them with the opportunity to discover and internalize the rules that govern social behavior, and let them practice modifying their behavior in response to social norms and others' requirements. Groups socialize individual members.

In most cases, group norms are consistent with more general social norms pertaining to work, family, relations, and civility. In other cases, however, norms emerge in groups that are odd, atypical, or unexpected. Cults such as Heaven's Gate condone mass suicide. Norms in gangs encourage members to take aggressive actions against others. Adolescent peer cliques pressure members to take drugs and commit illegal acts. Fraternities insist that members engage in unhealthy practices, such as drinking excessive amounts of alcohol. Work groups develop such high standards for productivity that members experience unrelievable amounts of stress.

Crandall (1988) described how bulimia—a cycle of binge eating followed by self-induced vomiting or other forms of purging—can be sustained by group norms. Bulimia is considered by society at large to be an abnormal behavior, yet it is prevalent in certain groups, such as cheerleading squads, models, dance troupes, women's athletic teams, and sororities. Crandall suggested that such groups, rather than viewing these actions as a threat to health, accept purging as a normal means of controlling one's weight. In the sororities he studied, he found that the women who were popular in the group were the ones who binged at the rate established by the group's norms. Also, as time passed, those who did not binge began to binge. Thus, even norms that run counter to society's general traditions can establish a life of their own in small subgroups within that society.

These emergent group norms are sustained by a common set of group-level processes (Forsyth, 1990). Informational influence occurs when the group provides members with information that they can use to make decisions and form opinions. People who spend years and years in a group that explains things in terms of UFOs, for example, will in time also begin to explain things in that way. Normative influence occurs when individuals tailor their actions to fit the group's norms. People take norms such as "Do not tell lies" and "Help other people when they are in need" for granted, but some societies and some groups have different norms that are equally powerful and widely accepted. Normative influence accounts for the transmission of religious, economic, moral, political, and interpersonal attitudes, beliefs, and values across generations. Interpersonal influence is used in rare instances when someone violates the group's norms. The individual who publicly violates a group's norm will likely meet with reproach or even be ostracized from the group.

The operation of these three factors—informational, normative, and interpersonal influence—can be readily observed in groups as diverse as military units, street gangs, college fraternities, and religious denominations. All of these groups have a relatively exclusive membership; all subsequently provide members with a unique sense of identity. In addition, all use signs and symbols to mark their territory and to communicate nonverbally to group members and, to some extent, to outsiders. Forms of dress, grooming, and personal appearance may be espoused and regulated to some degree within each group, so that the exclusiveness, identity, and values of the group are reinforced and displayed.

Speech, in particular, may be highly jargonized in these groups. Montgomery (1989) observed that the group's discourse serves to dichotomize the speaking world into insiders and outsiders. J. P. Elliott (1993) noted the dual, if not ironic, function of group jargon:

> While one normally thinks of language as a communicative system employed to bridge semantic gaps, this jargonized discourse is equally effective at excluding and repelling, generating limits and maintaining boundaries. The discriminating power of language exalts and assures those inside this rhetorical space, while rejecting and offending discursive Others. (p. 3)

Members understandably and typically rely on the group for guidance and answers to personally important questions. They often conform to group norms that encourage friendliness, cooperation, and total acceptance of the principles of the group. In some situations, these effects may be relatively benign or positive: For example, people who regularly go to church generally are more socially conservative, conforming, and acquiescent, and they exhibit fewer behavioral problems than those who do not go to church (Spilka, Hood, & Gorsuch, 1985). However, in demanding religious groups, the pressure to conform and suppress individual expression may have more deleterious effects. Participants in one study of high-demand religious movements reported changes in their personality as a function of participation in the religious group, with much of the change in the direction advocated by the principles of the group (Yeakley, 1988). Studies of related groups describe similar dynamics across all the groups: intense cohesiveness, public statements of principles, pressure placed on anyone who dissents, ostracism from the group for disagreement, and strong rewards for agreement with the group's ideals (Gallanter, 1989).

GROUPS, PANIC, AND DELUSIONS

The citizens of Mattoon, Illinois, were certain that a mysterious gasser was on the loose. After one woman reported that someone had sprayed a poison gas into her bedroom window, the local paper published the headline "Anesthetic Prowler on the Loose." The police received dozens of calls for the next week but could find no perpetrator. The conclusion was that the town suffered from a mild form of hysteria. (adapted from Johnson, 1945)

In most cases, groups are a source of emotional, interpersonal, and informational stability. Groups satisfy members' needs to belong and provide members with social support when they are stressed or experience trauma. They are also a rich source of social comparison data when group members face ambiguous situations (Festinger, 1954). When physical reality and conventional sources of information do not provide enough information, group members often compare their personal viewpoint with the views expressed by other members of groups to determine whether they are "correct," "valid," or "proper" (Goethals & Darley, 1987; Wills, 1991).

Groups can, however, also be a major source of emotional, interpersonal, and informational instability. Indeed, instances of mass hysteria—the spontaneous outbreak of atypical thoughts, feelings, or actions in a group or aggregate, including psychogenic illness, common hallucinations, and bizarre actions—can often be traced back to the communication of faulty and misleading information among group members (Pennebaker, 1982; Phoon, 1982). In June 1962, for example, workers at a garment factory began complaining of nausea, pain, disorientation, and muscular weakness; some actually collapsed at their jobs or lost consciousness. Rumors spread rapidly that the illness was caused by "some kind of insect" that had infested one of the shipments of cloth from overseas, and the owners began making efforts to eradicate the bug. No bug was ever discovered, however, and experts eventually concluded that the "June bug incident" had been caused by mass hysteria (Kerckhoff & Back, 1968; Kerckhoff, Back, & Miller, 1965). In 1974, a team of occupational safety investigators were called to a garment plant in the southwest United States to investigate the cause of an epidemic of nausea, dizziness, and fainting among nearly one third of the plant workers. Despite the severity of the symptoms, no toxic agent could be found and the researchers were forced to conclude that the illness "involved psychogenic components, e.g., stress or anxiety" (Colligan & Murphy, 1982, p. 34).

These outbreaks of a contagious psychogenic illness are not that rare. Although such incidents are difficult to document conclusively, one team of researchers identified 23 separate cases that involved large numbers of individuals afflicted with "physical symptoms . . . in the absence of an identifiable pathogen" (Colligan & Murphy, 1982, p. 35). More than 1,200 people were affected by these outbreaks, with most reporting symptoms that are often associated with anxiety, panic, and stress (e.g., headaches, nausea, dizziness, and weakness). Many were women working in repetitive, routinized jobs, and the illness often spread through friendship networks.

Because of the scarcity of information, experts are reluctant to offer recommendations to prevent the problem. Some suggest that as soon as the possibility of a physical cause is eliminated, medical experts should tell workers that their problems are caused by stress rather than physical illness. An alternative, however, lies in removing the negative environmental conditions that encourage such epidemics. Research indicates that in many of the cases, the affected employees work under highly stressful conditions. In some instances, the outbreaks occur when employees have been told to increase their productivity or have been working overtime. Poor labor–management relations have also been implicated, as have negative environmental factors, such as noise, poor lighting, and exposure to dust, foul odors, or chemicals. These findings suggest that psychogenic outbreaks can be reduced by improving working conditions (Colligan, Pennebaker, & Murphy, 1982).

GROUPS, IDENTITY, AND SELF-ESTEEM

R., an 18-year-old African American man, joined three friends robbing stores, beating bystanders, and vandalizing storefronts during a riot in Harlem. R. expresses no remorse for his actions, and interviewers conclude he is exhibitionistic, delusional, defiant, and emotionally restricted. They suggest that his personality reflects his attempt to protect his self-esteem from negative experiences as a minority in a White-majority culture. (adapted from Clark & Barker, 1945)

Just as Freud (1922) believed that identification causes children to bond with and imitate their parents, identification with a group prompts members to bond with and take on the characteristics of their groups. According to social identity theory (Tajfel, 1981; Turner, 1981), when people identify with a group their sense of self changes. Their unique, individualistic qualities—traits, beliefs, skills, and so on—make up their personal identity. All those qualities that spring from membership in social groups, such as families, cliques, work groups, neighborhoods, tribes, cities, countries, and region, make up the collective self or social identity.

People who identify with their groups experience a strong sense of belonging in their groups and take pride in their membership. They are more involved in the group's activities and willingly help the group meet its goals (Abrams, 1992; Deaux, 1996). However, with the increased identification with the group comes the tendency to engage in self-stereotyping: the integration of stereotypes pertaining to the group in one's own self-descriptions (Biernat, Vescio, & Green, 1996). Social identity is also connected to feelings of self-worth. People who belong to prestigious groups tend to have higher self-esteem than those who belong to stigmatized groups (Rosenberg, 1979). High school students who are members of the most prestigious groups generally report feeling highly satisfied with themselves and their group. Students who want to be a part of an in-crowd but are not accepted by that clique, in contrast, are the most dissatisfied (Brown & Lohr, 1987). People who were members of prestigious or satisfying groups in high school have higher levels of self-esteem later in life (Wright & Forsyth, 1997). Sports fans' moods swing up and down as their favorite team wins and loses. After a loss, they feel depressed and rate themselves more negatively, but after a win they feel elated and rate themselves more positively (Hirt, Zillmann, Erickson, & Kennedy, 1992). Crocker and Luhtanen reported that individuals who have positive collective self-esteem also have more positive personal self-esteem (Crocker & Luhtanen, 1990; Crocker, Luhtanen, Blaine, & Broadnax, 1994; Luhtanen & Crocker, 1992).

As Crocker and Major (1989) noted in their seminal analysis of the relationship between self-esteem and membership in a stigmatized or negatively valued group, even membership in a socially denigrated group can sustain self-esteem. In many cases members of stigmatized groups and minority groups protect their personal appraisals of their groups from the unfair negative stereotypes about their groups held by nonmembers by rejecting the disparaging elements of their group's label. Adolescents with learning disabilities who did not negatively rate the social category of "special education students" had higher self-esteem than did those who self-stereotyped (Stager, Chassin, & Young, 1983). Conversely, incarcerated adolescents who attributed negative qualities to the category of "delinquents" had lower self-esteem than did delinquents who did not hold negative stereotypes about their group (Chassin & Stager, 1984).

Crocker et al. (1994) also found that members of racial minorities who reject the majority's stereotypes about their group do not display low self-esteem. They discovered that African Americans were more positive about being Black than Anglo Americans were about being White. African Americans, however, were much less likely to agree that "others' respect African Americans as a group" (Crocker et al., 1994, p. 503). This incongruence between the perceptions of the subgroup's "culture of origin" and the majority's "culture at present" can result in distress, self-derogation, and loss of group identity (T. Elliott & Sherwin, 1997). Crocker et al., however, found that in most cases, African Americans' perceptions of their group's value were not correlated with their private self-esteem. As long as individuals believe the groups they belong to are valuable, then they will experience a heightened sense of personal self-esteem.

The identity-sustaining aspect of group memberships has a downside, however. Membership in a group or social category may provide members with a social identity, but it can set in motion the tendency to derogate members of other groups. As social identity theorists Tajfel and Turner argued, categorization sows the seeds of conflict by creating a cognitive distinction between "us" and "them." They wrote that the "mere perception of belonging to two distinct groups—that is, social categorization per se—is sufficient to trigger intergroup discrimination favoring the in-group" (Tajfel & Turner, 1986, p. 13). Groups thus sustain individual members' self-esteem but at the cost of creating animosity toward those who belong to other groups.

THE IMPORTANCE OF GROUPS

Groups have the capacity both to sustain and to undermine mental health. Groups make possible connections between individuals, and so they can protect them from loneliness. Groups are also a critical source of social support, which becomes particularly beneficial when people experience trauma or other forms of stress. Groups are also critical socializing agents, providing members with values, attitudes, roles, activities, and behavioral skills that are sometimes health promoting. Groups can also contribute directly to the development of identity and self-esteem.

Groups are not all benefit with no cost. As we have discussed, groups can demand great investments of time and energy from their members, who can become too committed to their groups. Although groups provide social support, they are also the source of considerable stress for their members. Groups, too, can socialize members in ways that are not healthy and set social identity processes in motion that increase conflict between groups.

Their checkered impact in no way, however, detracts from their significance in shaping mental health. A social psychological approach to adjustment traces both dysfunction and adjustment back to interaction between people, and in most cases these interactions unfold in groups. Researchers and practitioners across many disciplines are shifting their sights to focus more on group-level processes rather than individual-level ones. As organizations become more multicultural, issues of group composition and diversity increase in importance. In therapeutic settings, shifts in health care have created practical advantages for those who can use groups to achieve change. Indeed, group dynamicists and practitioners who work with groups likely share more similarities than social psychologists and clinicians in general. Both recognize the causal power of a group and have seen the change that it can produce. Clinicians, with their emphasis on personality and assessment, often focus on each person's uniqueness. Group therapists, in contrast, are struck by the way in which surprisingly different individuals change when they become part of a group that changes. Both the social psychologist and the mental health professional who understands groups agree with basic assumptions such as "A group is greater than the sum of its parts," "Groups are real," and "It is easier to change individuals formed into a group than individuals who are alone." Given this shared perspective, social psychologists and clinical psychologists should join together to answer the fundamental questions about groups as well as the practical questions about the relationship among group membership, mental health, and well-being.

REFERENCES

Abrams, D. (1992). Processes of social identification. In G. M. Breakwell (Ed.), *Social psychology of identity and self-concept* (pp. 57–99). New York: Surrey University Press.

Allport, F. H. (1924). *Social psychology*. Boston: Houghton Mifflin.

Allport, F. H. (1962). A structuronomic conception of behavior: Individual and collective. I: Structural theory and the master problem of social psychology. *Journal of Abnormal and Social Psychology, 64*, 3–30.

Anderson, C. M., & Martin, M. M. (1995). The effects of communication motives, interaction involvement, and loneliness on satisfaction: A model of small groups. *Small Group Research, 26*, 118–137.

Barrera, M., Jr. (1986). Distinctions between social support concepts, measures, and models. *American Journal of Community Psychology, 14*, 413–422.

Baumeister, R. F., & Leary, M. R. (1995). The need to belong: Desire for interpersonal attachments as a fundamental human motivation. *Psychological Bulletin, 117,* 497–529.

Berkman, L. F., & Syme, S. L. (1979). Social networks, host resistance, and mortality: A nine-year followup study of Alameda County residents. *American Journal of Epidemiology, 109,* 186–204.

Biernat, M., Vescio, T. K., & Green, M. L. (1996). Selective self-stereotyping. *Journal of Personality and Social Psychology, 71,* 1194–1209.

Brewer, M. B., Weber, J. G., & Carini, B. (1995). Person memory in intergroup contexts: Categorization versus individuation. *Journal of Personality and Social Psychology, 69,* 29–40.

Brown, B. B., & Lohr, M. J. (1987). Peer group affiliation and adolescent self-esteem: An integration of ego-identity and symbolic-interaction theories. *Journal of Personality and Social Psychology, 52,* 47–55.

Campbell, D. T. (1958). Common fate, similarity, and other indices of the status of aggregates of persons as social entities. *Behavioral Science, 3,* 14–25.

Caplan, R. D., Vinokur, A. D., Price, R. H., & Van Ryn, M. (1989). Job seeking, reemployment, and mental health: A randomized field experiment in coping with job loss. *Journal of Applied Psychology, 74,* 759–769.

Chassin, L., & Stager, S. F. (1984). Determinants of self-esteem among incarcerated delinquents. *Social Psychology Quarterly, 47,* 382–390.

Clark, K. B., & Barker, J. (1945). The zoot effect in personality: A race riot participant. *Journal of Abnormal and Social Psychology, 40,* 143–148.

Colligan, M. J., & Murphy, L. R. (1982). A review of mass psychogenic illness in work settings. In M. J. Colligan, J. W. Pennebaker, & L. R. Murphy (Eds.), *Mass psychogenic illness: A social psychological analysis* (pp. 35–52). Hillsdale, NJ: Erlbaum.

Colligan, M. J., Pennebaker, J. W., & Murphy, L. R. (Eds.). (1982). *Mass psychogenic illness: A social psychological analysis.* Hillsdale, NJ: Erlbaum.

Cooley, C. H. (1909). *Social organization.* New York: Scribner.

Cooper, C. L. (1981). Social support at work and stress management. *Small Group Behavior, 12,* 285–297.

Coyne, J. C., & Downey, G. (1991). Social factors and psychopathology: Stress, social support, and coping processes. *Annual Review of Psychology, 42,* 401–425.

Crandall, C. S. (1988). Social contagion of binge eating. *Journal of Personality and Social Psychology, 55,* 588–598.

Crocker, J., & Luhtanen, R. (1990). Collective self-esteem and ingroup bias. *Journal of Personality and Social Psychology, 58,* 60–67.

Crocker, J., Luhtanen, R., Blaine, B., & Broadnax, S. (1994). Collective self-esteem and psychological well-being among White, Black, and Asian college students. *Personality and Social Psychology Bulletin, 20,* 503–513.

Crocker, J., & Major, B. (1989). Social stigma and self-esteem: The self-protective properties of stigma. *Psychological Review, 96,* 608–630.

Cutrona, C., & Russell, D. (1987). The provisions of social relationships and adaptation to stress. In W. H. Jones & D. Perlman (Eds.), *Advances in personal relationships* (Vol. 1, pp. 37–67). Greenwich, CT: JAI Press.

Deaux, K. (1996). Social identification. In E. T. Higgins & A. W. Kruglanski (Eds.), *Social psychology: Handbook of basic principles* (pp. 777–798). New York: Guilford Press.

DiTommaso, E., & Spinner, B. (1997). Social and emotional loneliness: A re-examination of Weiss' typology of loneliness. *Personality and Individual Differences, 22,* 417–427.

Dooley, D., & Catalano, R. (1984). The epidemiology of economic stress. *American Journal of Community Psychology, 12,* 387–409.

Durkheim, E. (1966). *Suicide.* New York: Free Press. (Original work published 1897)

Elliott, J. P. (1993). Language and diversity at the Kingdom Hall: The discursive strategies of the Watchtower Society. *Excursus: A Review of Religious Studies, 6,* 3–13.

Elliott, T., Marmarosh, C., & Pickelman, H. (1994). Negative affectivity, social support, and the prediction of distress and depression. *Journal of Personality, 62,* 299–319.

Elliott, T., & Sherwin, E. (1997). Developing hope in the social context: Alternative perspectives of motive, meaning, and identity. *Group Dynamics: Theory, Research, and Practice, 1,* 119–123.

Festinger, L. (1954). A theory of social comparison processes. *Human Relations, 7,* 117–140.

Finch, J. F., Barrera, M., Jr., Okun, M. A., Brant, W. H. M., Pool, G. J., & Snow-Turek, A. L. (1997). The factor structure of received social support: Dimensionality and the prediction of depression and life satisfaction. *Journal of Social and Clinical Psychology, 16,* 323–342.

Forsyth, D. R. (1990). *Group dynamics.* Pacific Grove, CA: Brooks/Cole.

Forsyth, D. R. (1991). Change in therapeutic groups. In C. R. Snyder & D. R. Forsyth (Eds.), *Handbook in social and clinical psychology: The health perspective* (pp. 664–680). Elmsford, NY: Pergamon Press.

Forsyth, D. R., & Leary, M. R. (1991). Metatheoretical and epistemological issues. In C. R. Snyder & D. R. Forsyth (Eds.), *Handbook of social and clinical psychology: The health perspective* (pp. 757–773). Elmsford, NY: Pergamon Press.

Freud, S. (1922). *Group psychology and the analysis of the ego* (J. Strachey, Trans.). London: Hogarth.

Gallanter, M. (1989). *Cults.* New York: Oxford University Press.

Goethals, G. R., & Darley, J. M. (1987). Social comparison theory: Self-evaluation and group life. In B. Mullen & G. R. Goethals (Eds.), *Theories of group behavior* (pp. 21–47). New York: Springer-Verlag.

Hays, R. B., & Oxley, D. (1986). Social network development and functioning during a life transition. *Journal of Personality and Social Psychology, 50,* 304–313.

Herbert, T. B., & Cohen, S. (1993). Stress and immunity in humans: A meta-analytic review. *Psychosomatic Medicine, 55,* 364–379.

Hilton, J. L., & von Hippel, W. (1990). The role of consistency in the judgment of stereotype-relevant behaviors. *Personality and Social Psychology Bulletin, 16,* 430–448.

Hirt, E. R., Zillmann, D., Erickson, G. A., & Kennedy, C. (1992). Costs and benefits of allegiance: Changes in fans' self-ascribed competencies after team victory versus defeat. *Journal of Personality and Social Psychology, 63,* 724–738.

Hogg, M. A. (1992). *The social psychology of group cohesiveness: From attraction to social identity.* New York: New York University Press.

Hojat, M., & Vogel, W. H. (1987). Socioemotional bonding and neurobiochemistry. *Journal of Social Behavior and Personality, 2,* 135–144.

Hoyle, R. H., & Crawford, A. M. (1994). Use of individual-level data to investigate group phenomena: Issues and strategies. *Small Group Behavior, 25,* 464–485.

Jacobs, M. K., & Goodman, G. (1989). Psychology and self-help groups: Predictions on a partnership. *American Psychologist, 44,* 536–545.

Janis, I. L. (1963). Group identification under conditions of external danger. *British Journal of Medical Psychology, 36,* 227–238.

Johnson, D. M. (1945). The "phantom anesthetist" of Mattoon: A field study of mass hysteria. *Journal of Abnormal and Social Psychology, 40,* 175–187.

Jones, W. H., & Carver, M. D. (1991). Adjustment and coping implications of loneliness. In C. R. Snyder & D. R. Forsyth (Eds.), *Handbook of social and clinical psychology: The health perspective* (pp. 395–415). Elmsford, NY: Pergamon Press.

Kerckhoff, A. C., & Back, K. W. (1968). *The June bug: A study of hysterical contagion.* New York: Appleton-Century-Crofts.

Kerckhoff, A. C., Back, K. W., & Miller, N. (1965). Sociometric patterns in hysterical contagion. *Sociometry, 28,* 2–15.

Kiecolt-Glaser, J. K., Ricker, D., Messick, G., Speicher, C., Holliday, J., Garner, W., & Glaser, R. (1984). Urinary cortisol levels, cellular immunocompetency, and loneliness in psychiatric inpatients. *Psychosomatic Medicine, 46,* 15–24.

Kiecolt-Glaser, J. K., Speicher, C. E., Holliday, J. E., & Glaser, R. (1984). Stress and the transformation of lymphocytes by Epstein–Barr virus. *Journal of Behavioral Medicine, 7,* 1–11.

Kohut, H. (1984). *How does analysis cure?* Chicago: University of Chicago Press.

Kraus, L. A., Davis, M. H., Bazzini, D. G., Church, M., & Kirchman, M. M. (1993). Personal and social influences on loneliness: The mediating effect of social provisions. *Social Psychology Quarterly, 56,* 37–53.

Le Bon, G. (1960). *The crowd.* New York: Viking Press. (Original work published 1895)

Lee, R. M., & Robbins, S. B. (1995). Measuring belongingness: The Social Connectedness and the Social Assurance Scales. *Journal of Counseling Psychology, 42,* 232–241.

Levine, J. M., & Moreland, R. L. (1992). Small groups and mental health. In D. N. Ruble, P. R. Costanzo, & M. E. Oliveri (Eds.), *The social psychology of mental health* (pp. 126–165). New York: Guilford Press.

Lewin, K. (1936). *A dynamic theory of personality.* New York: McGraw-Hill.

Lewin, K. (1951). *Field theory in social science.* New York: Harper.

Lieberman, M. A. (1993). Self-help groups. In H. I. Kaplan & M. J. Sadock (Eds.), *Comprehensive group psychotherapy* (3rd ed., pp. 292–304). Baltimore: Williams & Wilkins.

Linville, P. W. (1985). Self-complexity and affective extremity: Don't put all of your eggs in one cognitive basket. *Social Cognition, 3,* 94–120.

Linville, P. W. (1987). Self-complexity as a cognitive buffer against stress-related depression and illness. *Journal of Personality and Social Psychology, 52,* 663–676.

Luhtanen, R., & Crocker, J. (1992). A collective self-esteem scale: Self-evaluation of one's social identity. *Personality and Social Psychology Bulletin, 18,* 302–318.

McConnell, A. R., Sherman, S. J., & Hamilton, D. L. (1994a). Illusory correlation in the perception of groups: An extension of the distinctiveness-based account. *Journal of Personality and Social Psychology, 67,* 414–429.

McConnell, A. R., Sherman, S. J., & Hamilton, D. L. (1994b). On-line and memory-based aspects of individual and group target judgments. *Journal of Personality and Social Psychology, 67,* 173–185.

McDougall, W. (1908). *Introduction to social psychology.* London: Methuen.

Meer, J. (1985, July). Loneliness. *Psychology Today,* pp. 28–33.

Milgram, S. (1963). Behavioral study of obedience. *Journal of Abnormal and Social Psychology, 67,* 371–378.

Montgomery, S. L. (1989). The cult of jargon: Reflections on language in science. *Science as Culture, 6,* 46–55.

Moreno, J. L. (1932). *Who shall survive?* Washington, DC: Nervous and Mental Disease.

Newcomb, T. M. (1943). *Personality and social change.* New York: Dryden.

Niedenthal, P. M., Setterlund, M. B., & Wherry, M. B. (1992). Possible self-complexity and affective reactions to goal-relevant evaluation. *Journal of Personality and Social Psychology, 63,* 5–16.

Norris, F. H., & Murrell, S. A. (1990). Social support, life events, and stress as modifiers of adjustment to bereavement by older adults. *Psychology and Aging, 5,* 429–436.

Pakier, A., & Wills, T. A. (1990, August). *Life stress and social support predict illicit drug use among methadone clients.* Paper presented at the 98th Annual Convention of the American Psychological Association, Boston, MA.

Parsons, T., Bales, R. F., & Shils, E. (1953). *Working papers in the theory of action.* New York: Free Press.

Pemberton, M. B., Insko, C. A., & Schopler, J. (1996). Memory for and experience of differential competitive behavior of individuals and groups. *Journal of Personality and Social Psychology, 71,* 953–966.

Pennebaker, J. W. (1982). Social and perceptual factors affecting symptom reporting and mass psychogenic illness. In M. J. Colligan, J. W. Pennebaker, & L. R. Murphy (Eds.), *Mass psychogenic illness: A social psychological analysis* (pp. 139–153). Hillsdale, NJ: Erlbaum.

Phoon, W. H. (1982). Outbreaks of mass hysteria at workplaces in Singapore: Some patterns and modes of presentation. In M. J. Colligan, J. W. Pennebaker, & L. R. Murphy (Eds.), *Mass psychogenic illness: A social psychological analysis* (pp. 21–31). Hillsdale, NJ: Erlbaum.

Pratt, J. H. (1922). The principle of class treatment and their application to various chronic diseases. *Hospital Social Services, 6,* 401–417.

Rosenberg, M. (1979). *Conceiving the self.* New York: Basic Books.

Rubenstein, C. M., & Shaver, P. (1980). Loneliness in two northeastern cities. In J. Hartog, J. R. Audy, & Y. A. Cohen (Eds.), *The anatomy of loneliness* (pp. 319–337). Madison, CT: International Universities Press.

Rubenstein, C. M., & Shaver, P. (1982). The experience of loneliness. In L. A. Peplau & D. Perlman (Eds.), *Loneliness: A sourcebook of current theory, research, and therapy* (pp. 206–223). New York: Wiley Interscience.

Russell, D., Cutrona, C. E., Rose, J., & Yurko, K. (1984). Social and emotional loneliness: An examination of Weiss's typology of loneliness. *Journal of Personality and Social Psychology, 46,* 1313–1321.

Sandelands, L., & St. Clair, L. (1993). Toward an empirical concept of group. *Journal for the Theory of Social Behaviour, 23,* 423–458.

Sarason, I. G., Pierce, G. R., & Sarason, B. R. (1990). Social support and interactional processes: A triadic hypothesis. *Journal of Social and Personal Relationships, 7,* 495–506.

Schmidt, N., & Sermat, V. (1983). Measuring loneliness in different relationships. *Journal of Personality and Social Psychology, 44,* 1038–1047.

Seeman, M., Seeman, T., & Sayles, M. (1985). Social networks and health status: A longitudinal analysis. *Social Psychology Quarterly, 48,* 237–248.

Spilka, B., Hood, R. W., & Gorsuch, R. L. (1985). *The psychology of religion: An empirical approach.* Englewood Cliffs, NJ: Prentice Hall.

Stager, S. F., Chassin, L., & Young, R. D. (1983). Determinants of self-esteem among labeled adolescents. *Social Psychology Quarterly, 46,* 3–10.

Steinberg, R. (1975). *Man and the organization.* New York: Time-Life Books.

Stokes, J. P. (1985). The relation of social network and individual difference variables to loneliness. *Journal of Personality and Social Psychology, 48,* 981–990.

Storr, A. (1988). *Solitude: A return to the self.* New York: Free Press.

Stroebe, W., & Stroebe, M. (1996). The social psychology of social support. In E. T. Higgins & A. W. Kruglanski (Eds.), *Social psychology: Handbook of basic principles* (pp. 597–621). New York: Guilford Press.

Stroebe, W., Stroebe, M., Abakoumkin, G., & Schut, H. (1996). The role of loneliness and social support in adjustment to loss: A test of attachment versus stress theory. *Journal of Personality and Social Psychology, 70,* 1241–1249.

Suedfeld, P. (1997). The social psychology of "invictus": Conceptual and methodological approaches to indomitability. In C. McGarty & S. A. Haslam (Eds.), *The message of social psychology* (pp. 328–341). Cambridge, MA: Blackwell.

Sugisawa, H., Liang, J., & Liu, X. (1994). Social networks, social support, and mortality among older people in Japan. *Journal of Gerontology, 49,* 3–13.

Tajfel, H. (1981). *Human groups and social categories.* Cambridge, England: Cambridge University Press.

Tajfel, H., & Turner, J. C. (1986). The social identity theory of intergroup behavior. In S. Worchel & W. G. Austin (Eds.), *Psychology of intergroup relations* (2nd ed., pp. 7–24). Chicago: Nelson-Hall.

Triplett, N. (1898). The dynamogenic factors in pacemaking and competition. *American Journal of Psychology, 9,* 507–533.

Turner, J. C. (1981). The experimental social psychology of intergroup behavior. In J. C. Turner & H. Giles (Eds.), *Intergroup behavior* (pp. 144–167). Oxford, England: Blackwell.

Uchino, B. N., Cacioppo, J. T., & Kiecolt-Glaser, J. K. (1996). The relationship between social support and physiological processes: A review with emphasis on underlying mechanisms and implications for health. *Psychological Bulletin, 119,* 488–531.

Urban, H. B. (1983). Phenomenological-humanistic approaches. In M. Hersen, A. E. Kazdin, & A. S. Bellack (Eds.), *The clinical psychology handbook* (pp. 155–175). Elmsford, NY: Pergamon Press.

Wallston, B. S., Alagna, S. W., DeVellis, B. M., & DeVellis, R. F. (1983). Social support and physical health. *Health Psychology, 2,* 367–391.

Weiss, R. S. (1973). *Loneliness: The experience of emotional and social isolation.* Cambridge, MA: MIT Press.

Wills, T. A. (1991). Social comparison in coping and health. In C. R. Snyder & D. R. Forsyth (Eds.), *Handbook of social and clinical psychology: The health perspective* (pp. 376–394). Elmsford, NY: Pergamon Press.

Wills, T. A., & Cleary, S. D. (1996). How are social support effects mediated? A test with parental support and adolescent substance use. *Journal of Personality and Social Psychology, 71,* 937–952.

Wills, T. A., & DePaulo, B. M. (1991). Interpersonal analysis of the help-seeking process. In C. R. Snyder & D. R. Forsyth (Eds.), *Handbook of social and clinical psychology: The health perspective* (pp. 350–375). Elmsford, NY: Pergamon Press.

Wright, S. S., & Forsyth, D. R. (1997). Group membership and collective identity: Consequences for self-esteem. *Journal of Social and Clinical Psychology, 16,* 43–56.

Wrong, D. H. (1994). *The problem of order: What unites and divides society.* New York: Free Press.

Yao, R. (1987). *An introduction to fundamentalists anonymous.* New York: Fundamentalists Anonymous.

Yeakley, F. R. (1988). *The discipling dilemma.* Nashville, TN: Gospel Advocate.

13

SOCIAL–CLINICAL PSYCHOLOGY: PAST, PRESENT, AND FUTURE

JOHN H. HARVEY, JULIA OMARZU, AND BRIAN E. PAUWELS

One achieves mental health to the extent that one becomes aware of one's interpersonal relations. (Harry Stack Sullivan, 1953, p. 26)

In this chapter, we provide a 20-year retrospective of developments at the juncture of social and clinical psychology. This social–clinical interface encompasses social–counseling and social–health psychology as well as social–clinical psychology. Also, on most occasions when the term *social* is used in reference to this interface, readers should recognize that *social–personality* is often the more accurate label for the type of work being described. A distinctive genre of research and theory, which characterizes this interface, builds on the theme of this book regarding the social psychological base of many emotional and behavioral problems. This book includes a number of strands of that genre of work, and in this chapter we note other representative directions.

There is the question of why it may be argued that social psychological knowledge is so essential for understanding emotional and behavioral problems. We propose that the answer may be found both in the intrinsically social nature of human problems and the vigorous scholarly milieu of social psychological theory and research. In this chapter, we also address

---

The editors of this book contributed to the concluding section.

the question of formal doctoral training at this interface posed by various writers about 2 decades ago (e.g., Harvey & Weary, 1979), a question that continues to be debated in the 1990s (e.g., Harvey & Stein, 1995). In light of the vitality of this interface, why have so few formal doctoral programs reflecting this integration been attempted or carried out for any appreciable period of time? Before addressing developments in the past 20 years, however, we briefly note historical events that have led to the social–clinical psychology literature.

KEY HISTORICAL DEVELOPMENTS

In 1921, Morton Prince and Floyd Allport changed the title of the *Journal of Abnormal Psychology* that Prince had begun in 1906 to the *Journal of Abnormal and Social Psychology (JASP)*. They made this change to reflect the key role of interpersonal processes in psychopathology and psychotherapy. Those scholars had observed the pivotal role of interpersonal relations in various aspects of psychopathology during World War 1 and believed that the study of social behavior benefited from research on abnormal mental processes (see Hill & Weary, 1983). *JASP* was split into the *Journal of Abnormal Psychology* and the *Journal of Personality and Social Psychology* in 1965.

Work at the social–clinical interface has been represented by other major historical developments. Many scholars deepened the understanding of the role of social processes in clinical psychology during this period. Various neo-Freudians, including Harry Stack Sullivan and Karen Horney in the 1920s and 1930s, emphasized social processes in phenomena that psychoanalysts previously had interpreted without much reference to interpersonal relations. In the 1930s and 1940s, Kurt Lewin (see Patnoe, 1988), who is often regarded as the founder of experimental social psychology, promoted his ideas about an action psychology that involved the application of theory to the solution of interpersonal and group system problems. Later, Jerome Frank (1961), whose training was in medicine rather than psychology, wrote about persuasion and healing.

As described by Strong, Welsh, Corcoran, and Hoyt (1992), counseling psychology's use of social psychological logic and theory began with Francis Robinson's work at Ohio State University in the 1950s. Robinson conceived of the counseling interview as an expression of social psychology in terms of how the moment-by-moment interaction adjustments between counselor and client might affect the process and outcome of the counseling session. Stanley Strong's own work represented a pioneering effort to apply social psychological work on attitudes and attitude change to counseling processes (e.g., Strong, 1968). Subsequently, a host of scholars authored or edited books that both analyzed and stimulated integrations of social and clinical psychology, including Goldstein, Heller, and Sechrest (1966); Brehm (1976); Strong and Claiborn (1982); Leary and Miller (1986); Maddux, Stoltenberg, and Rosenwein (1987); and Snyder and Forsyth (1991).

In the early 1980s, the *Journal of Social and Clinical Psychology (JSCP)*, explicitly representing this interface, was begun and has succeeded as a reputable forum for integrative work. This journal was founded on the earlier logic of *JASP*, which acknowledged that social–personality processes are inherently involved in psychopathology and human problems in general (Harvey, 1983). Early in the development of this journal, some scholars expressed the view that such a forum was not necessary. They believed that the interface between social and clinical psychology was adequately represented by existing journals.

This early concern about redundancy did not prove to be an obstacle in the growth of the journal. Influential scholars in the community of social–clinical psychology readily supported *JSCP* by serving as editors, reviewers, and submitters of manuscripts. A second concern raised by Harvey (1987) as the founding editor of *JSCP* was that the field of social-personality psychology had been represented in about one fourth of the articles published during his initial 4-year term, due in part to the greater numbers of scholars in clinical and counseling psychology. He voiced concern that the percentage of social psychologists represented would decline even further. Fortunately, that has not happened. In the tenure of C. R. Snyder as editor of *JSCP* (from 1987 to the present), the journal has maintained a nice balance among the constituent fields. The journal now is well established in terms of scholarly reputation, subscription base, and indexing by journal citation services.

This high degree of interdisciplinary activity between social and clinical psychology has been most vividly demonstrated in the 1990s in the research published in leading journals in each area. Perusal of the work published in these journals reveals regular publication of articles showing considerable integration and cross-referencing of work at this interface. These journals include the *Journal of Personality and Social Psychology, Personality and Social Psychology Bulletin, Journal of Personality, Journal of Abnormal Psychology, Journal of Counseling Psychology,* and *The Counseling Psychologist.*

IS SOCIAL PSYCHOLOGY NECESSARY TO UNDERSTAND EMOTIONAL AND BEHAVIORAL PROBLEMS?

Obviously, our answer to that question is *yes*. This conclusion may sound a bit arrogant, but a practical, logical defense supports it. As many of the authors in this book have implied or directly shown, emotional and behavioral problems in human life are often wrapped up in a complex skein of interpersonal relations. Social factors, including one's close relationships with others, can play pivotal roles in determining how these problems unfold.

Social–personality psychology is a vehicle to study both social psychological and individual-difference processes in thought, feeling, and behavior. Gordon Allport's (1985) definition of social psychology suggests how daunting the task is and, by implication, how fallible any vehicle for studying it may be: "an attempt to understand and explain how the thought, feeling, and behavior of individuals are influenced by the actual, imagined, or implied presence of others" (p. 3). That definition certainly embraces many of the questions clinical and counseling psychologists ask. Allport (1985) also suggested that the breadth of social psychology made it the "queen of the social sciences" (p. 4). That breadth was championed by the pioneers in social psychology, including both Floyd and Gordon Allport, Kurt Lewin, and Fritz Heider. It is a breadth of inquiry that sheds light on the complex, nuanced nature of psychopathology as well as the everyday problems of living. Whether in therapy or research, this inquiry into the nature of human problems is most likely endless, given the depth and breadth of social psychological processes and their inexorable roles in emotional and behavioral problems.

Many forms of therapy, and many of those who provide therapy, are at least partially dependent on the literature and wisdom of social–personality psychology, however extensive or limited that literature and wisdom may be. Perhaps the clinical interdependence with social–personality psychology is no stronger than it is with other fields such as developmental and biological psychology, but it is a fundamental link that has been part of the American Psychological Association's (APA) necessary bases for accreditation of practitioners of psychology. Programs that the APA accredits in clinical, counseling, and school psychology must require students to take at least one doctoral-level course in the social bases of behavior. This course varies depending on a curriculum's focus, but it might be a course such as advanced social psychology or a seminar in social perception and attribution.

At the practical level, the social–clinical interdependence is found in the abundance of social psychological research relevant to clinical psychology and inspired by clinical psychologists. This literature runs the gamut of major social psychological topics and includes attitudes and attitude change, attribution, social cognition and perception, the self and self-presentation, prejudice, aggression, helping behavior, groups, and individual differences. Evidence relevant to clinically applied questions is found throughout this work. In commenting on research by social–personality psychologists at the interface, Jacobson and Weary (1996) suggested that by far the largest number of *PsycLIT* references in the past 2 decades have focused on applications of attribution theory and research to clinical phenomena, particularly to the emotional disorders of depression and anxiety.

As well as advancing knowledge of human behavior and problems, research at the interface requires careful consideration of experimental methods and designs to ensure that results will be useful for both social–personality psychologists and clinical practitioners. Several methodological issues have special relevance for interface research, creating a number of questions that sometimes are approached through different methods in social and clinical psychology. It is important that researchers in each area appreciate the advantages and disadvantages of these different methods and not be too quick to dismiss the other's preferred paradigms. These questions include the following:

1. *What are the pros and cons of laboratory versus field research?* Social psychologists traditionally have been the more laboratory oriented; however, many social psychologists now work in field settings, whereas clinical psychologists often conduct laboratory research.
2. *What are the pros and cons of experimental versus nonexperimental research?* Social psychologists traditionally have been more experimentally oriented. As their research foci have broadened, they increasingly have been more willing to adopt nonexperimental research approaches.
3. *What are the pros and cons of relying on research populations of young college students versus other groups of people representing different ages, socioeconomic backgrounds, and experiences?* Researchers in both fields most likely do too little research with diverse populations.
4. *What are the pros and cons of linking research on emotional and behavioral problems with therapy for the participants?* (See Rubin & Mitchell, 1976, for a relevant discussion.) This linkage has a strong recent history, especially in the work of clinical psychologists pursuing close-relationships topics (e.g., Fincham & Bradbury, 1991).
5. *What are the pros and cons of specializing in cross-sectional versus longitudinal methodologies?* Again, psychologists from all sectors of the interface might consider embarking on more longitudinal work because cross-sectional work has been the norm.

These are multifaceted issues, and social–clinical psychologists do not necessarily have to consistently endorse one side as opposed to the other, but each question may pose dilemmas for scholars attempting to blend their work and ensure its relevance to both fields. Debate about these questions is likely to continue as research at this interface continues to gain interest and popularity among current and prospective scholars.

Social–personality psychology is a field containing perhaps as many as 7,000–10,000 workers in various settings but mostly in teaching and research positions (Franzoi, 1996). Many universities have strong master's and doctoral programs in social psychology, and students continue to flock to social psychology introductory and specialty courses. Estimates of total enrollment in social psychology introductory courses are in the hundreds of thousands in the United States alone. Social psychology as a discipline is also growing in many European countries as well as in Japan, Australia, and New Zealand.

At the same time, hundreds of thousands of practitioners may be found in the fields of clinical and counseling psychology in the United States. For almost 4 decades, these fields have been tremendously attractive to both graduate and undergraduate students. The questions stirred up by the work of such an army of applied workers will necessarily make social–personality psychology an important source of information and this interface an important connection to the profession for years to come.

THE INTERFACE IN DOCTORAL TRAINING: UNFULFILLED PROMISE?

Although scholarship at the interface has been vigorous in the past 20 years, formal integrative training efforts at the doctoral level have been less successful. At various points in the history of the social–clinical interface, it has made sense to educators in the constituent fields to try to combine training efforts to produce doctoral graduates with substantial training in both areas.

Harvey and Weary (1979) articulated a rationale for such a joint program based on their experience at Vanderbilt University, where Harvey was a social psychologist and Weary, with other doctoral students, worked on social psychological research while training in the APA-accredited clinical program. Weary has subsequently made major contributions to the interface (e.g., Weary & Mirels, 1982) and is the director of the social psychology program at Ohio State University.

Harvey and Weary's (1979) primary argument for a formal integration was that each area could learn from the other. A focus on clinical problems could structure research agendas, and social psychological theory and research could facilitate the clinician's approach to various mental health problems. Harvey and Weary argued that many people were already being trained in both disciplines informally, as at Vanderbilt, and that a formal recognition of such training would give it national credibility and enhance various scholarly and professional developments at the interface. The possibilities of the influence of this integrative concept can be seen in the many authored and edited books and journals that now represent the interface, including JSCP, and in a series of interdisciplinary conferences funded by the National Science Foundation and APA at various universities and a National Institute of Mental Health–funded postdoctoral program that blended training in social and developmental psychology at Vanderbilt between 1982 and 1986.

Despite the success of the informal training approach at Vanderbilt and the attempts to create a more formal integration, such a program never materialized there. Since the mid-1980s, in fact, the field of social psychology has been deemphasized overall in the foci of training at Vanderbilt's Arts and Sciences Psychology Department. The loss of social psychology faculty combined with the comparatively rich funding for work in the neurosciences and cognitive sciences were factors involved in the deemphasis on social psychology at Vanderbilt and in the resulting loss of much of the thrust for the social–clinical integrative research and training activities.

At Vanderbilt, a key faculty person participating in these integrative activities was social–health psychologist Barbara Wallston, whose stellar career ended with her untimely death in the mid-1980s. One lesson of the Vanderbilt experience is that integrative training activities may not be sustainable within the constraints of typical academic units unless there are faculty to lead the charge for their implementation.

Leary and Maddux (1987) also provided a strong case for more collaborative work among scholars from related fields at the social–clinical psychology interface. Their argument had further implications for considerations about joint-track training. For example, Leary and Maddux argued that graduate training programs sometimes are hindered by professional territoriality and factionalism. They also suggested that collaborative scholarly exchanges in research activity, and in the classroom, would help redress such territoriality and factionalism. They did not, however, call for formal joint training programs per se.

Some doctoral programs have tried joint-track training. In such cases, student applicants interested both in social psychological research and in applying that knowledge as a licensed clinician–counselor apply to the joint-track program. For example, the Department of Psychology at the University of Iowa experimented with a social–clinical track in the late 1980s and 1990s, and the Department of Psychology at Texas Tech University did likewise with a social–counseling track in the 1980s (see Hendrick, 1995). In these joint programs, the students' applications were evaluated by admission committees representing both faculties (social–clinical and social–counseling). During their program, students were typically responsible for fulfilling virtually all the requirements of both training areas.

For example, a social–clinical student would be required to meet research requirements (e.g., first- and second-year research papers, empirical dissertations) as well as comprehensive examinations representing both social and clinical areas of work. Furthermore, such students had to complete the requisite amount of on-campus practicum work and an APA-accredited internship before being awarded their doctorate.

We have found that these doctoral joint-track program efforts usually serve about one or two generations of doctoral students before being discontinued. The general reason for the short tenure of these programs is that students think that too much additional work is required, with too little demonstrable payoff for them. Faculty also often become disenchanted if extra work reduces their time for research and writing. At these schools, the faculty in the different areas often collaborated in research and writing, but collaboration in teaching was not common (typically because departments and programs tend to have teaching needs that preclude collaborative arrangements, as might be found in proseminars). The joint-track program thus created a teaching burden for faculty in both the social and clinical–counseling areas.

One of the more thoughtful and practical analyses of issues in interface doctoral training was provided by Hendrick and Hendrick (1991). They described their own work toward a blended training program at Texas Tech University. Their analysis also involved a set of resolutions and recommendations for implementing joint training. They pointed to health psychology as a model for such development.

There has been a long-lasting master of arts program in social–counseling at Ball State University in Indiana. This program appears to have been successful because two counseling psychologists with major interests in social psychological approaches have taken responsibility for administering the program and promoting it to other members of their academic unit. It is a small program in terms of the number of students. Some of the students do go on to doctoral training at Ball State, choosing mainly the APA-accredited program in counseling psychology (S. Stein, personal communication, May 1, 1997).

In addition, as described well by Hart (1991), social psychologists at many universities have developed graduate courses that reflect this interface well and that serve students across the constituent areas. Social–personality psychologists frequently teach the APA-required courses in social processes to students from clinical, counseling, and school psychology. This no doubt inspires some students in these health service delivery fields to use social–personality knowledge and methods in their work.

Overall, we believe there is unfulfilled potential at the social–clinical interface in the lack of formal training approaches that are effective and widespread among doctoral programs. However, that potential remains viable for new generations of educators to consider in light of their own philosophies and situations.

A NEW INTEGRATIVE TOPIC FOR INTERFACE WORK: INTERPERSONAL LOSS

Before concluding, we would like to pose a new perspective on work at the social–clinical interface. By posing this different way of looking at some of the interface phenomena, scholars may be stimulated to ask new research questions and to advance new ideas that may have a reverberating effect on interface work.

We believe that a promising unifying theme for much of the social–clinical interface involves real, anticipated, and imagined loss in interpersonal relations. We define *interpersonal loss* as reductions in the social resources to which a person attaches considerable emotional investment. These resources may be tangible or intangible. Interpersonal loss involves not only clear-cut mental and physical health problems, but it also pertains to human problems posed by social phenomena, including prejudice and stigmata (e.g., Jones et al., 1984); disability and its impact on relationships (e.g., Lyons, Sullivan, Ritvo, & Coyne, 1995); romantic rejection and termination (e.g., Vaughn, 1986); dissolution of friendships (e.g., Matthews, 1986); loss of identity due to illness and aging (e.g., Greenberger, 1993); loss of assumptions about the positive qualities of the world and others (e.g., Janoff-Bulman, 1992); loss of home or employment (e.g., Morse, 1998); and the losses experienced by children who are homeless because of parental neglect and abuse (e.g., Coates, 1990).

"Loss logic" is found in a significant portion of the theory and practice of clinical–counseling psychology. It serves as a unifying concept that may facilitate social–clinical psychologists' greater involvement with the problems of individuals as well as broad cultural phenomena such as genocide (e.g., Staub, 1996). Although loss may be constantly on or in the back of people's minds and a part of the daily barrage of TV and newspaper images of loss that confront people, it is strange that the topic has received so little formal attention in psychology overall. The social–clinical interface, broadly construed, is the natural meeting ground for analysis of and research and practice on questions of interpersonal loss.

Several arguments support the importance of loss research to the social–clinical interface. First, whether the mental health problem is depression, anxiety, or personality disorder, the etiology of the individual's problem is often linked to interpersonal events that the person frames in terms of an existing or potential loss of esteem and meaning (Baumeister & Leary, 1995; Harvey, 1996; Leary & Kowalski, 1995). As Baumeister and Leary (1995) suggested, "from our standpoint, a great deal of people's psychological difficulties reflects emotional and behavioral reactions to perceived threats to social bonds" (p. 521). People who feel threatened in this way are reacting to the experience or the fear of a potential loss—a loss of social support, identity, esteem, and so on. This diminishing of the social self often begins early in life and, at any point in life, may become so pronounced that it challenges the individual's ability or willingness to go on with his or her roles and responsibilities. This compounding sense of interpersonal loss is too often neglected as a powerful contributing factor in people's plunges into psychopathology (Styron, 1990).

The topic of interpersonal loss is similar to the agenda of work often pursued in health psychology, which, as Hendrick (1983) noted, is a natural arena for interface collaboration and one that has been enriched with many substantial contributions from social and clinical psychologists. Loss research, though, is even broader in scope than health psychology, including and addressing human problems that are only tangentially related to traditional health issues as well as those that are directly and obviously health related. Loss theory specifically suggests that to help people adjust to or resolve negative experiences, clinicians need to focus on whatever it is that people feel they have lost or are losing that is affecting their health, relationships, and general welfare.

There is a final and extremely important argument about the value of conceiving and studying loss at the interface. Major losses will occur in everyone's life. That is inevitable. Thus, people can benefit from psychological inquiry into the loss experience. Furthermore, if people have compassion for life in general, they will regularly feel to some degree the losses that others whom they encounter are experiencing. That is the nature of empathy (Batson, Duncan, Ackerman, Buckley, & Birch, 1981), a state that is desirable for humans to seek.

Loss is not always unremittingly negative, however. As Ernest Hemingway suggested, people often seem to be strongest at the broken places. Loss, whether one's own or someone else's loss, may be a powerful motivator to understand the experience or to dedicate oneself to relieving the suffering of others, a type of generativity or giving back (Erikson, 1963). There are many examples of such motivation and behavior, including Viktor Frankl's (1959) book Man's Search for Meaning, the work of Elizabeth Neeld, and the Pan Am 103 organization of surviving families. Frankl wrote his book and developed logotherapy as a way of helping people who experience major losses to find meaning, instill will in their behavior, and reach out to others. Elizabeth Neeld (1990) wrote eloquently of her journey from English professor to counselor dedicated to helping grieving others after the sudden death of her young husband from a heart attack while jogging. The Pan Am 103 organization of surviving families was created after the 1988 terrorist bombing of that airplane. This organization's efforts have led to more stringent airline screening of luggage and passengers, and it has lobbied the U.S. Congress for a more aggressive pursuit of terrorists. The Pan Am 103 Families Organization gives annual scholarships to students at Syracuse University, where many of the young people on Pan Am 103 went to school. One member of this organization, the mother of a crash victim, has created a sculpture garden at Syracuse University titled Dark Elegy, which displays sculptured forms depicting the grief reactions of mothers of the Syracuse students aboard Pan Am 103 at the moment they heard of their children's deaths. Great strength, selflessness, and beauty can rise from the ashes of great losses. Social and clinical psychology seem naturally suited to collaborate in helping to more fully understand how this transformation occurs.

CONCLUSIONS

Despite the fact that the integration of social–personality and clinical–counseling psychology has not been reflected in formal doctoral training (as it was theorized it might 2 decades ago), the interface between social and clinical psychology has been a vibrant one during this time period. The interface has already proved to be a fertile ground for exchanges on many topics, including those discussed in this book, and the interface currently represents one of the most active cross-disciplinary boundaries in psychology.

The future of the interface is bright. Scholarly and professional work that incorporates aspects of social–personality psychology and clinical–counseling psychology has the potential to continue for decades to come. As we have discussed, interpersonal processes have many complex and varied effects on psychological well-being and dysfunction, and the topics that can be fruitfully examined from an integrative perspective are virtually infinite. However, to achieve an optimal interface that benefits behavioral science, psychological practice, and the public (who are the ultimate benefactors of both basic psychological knowledge and mental health services), we hope to see three developments in the coming years.

First, like many writers, we hope that the factionalism that has plagued psychology for many years—the division between researchers and practitioners generally and the division between social and clinical psychologists specifically—will continue to erode. This is essential to widespread cross-fertilization of the fields.

Second, for reasons that we described earlier, we hope to see more formal and informal alliances formed between social–personality and clinical–counseling psychologists who are involved in graduate training. Research in social and personality psychology will surely benefit from having a corps of behavioral scientists who are specialists in both basic science and psychological practice, and the practice of psychology will be enhanced by the informed inclusion of perspectives from social–personality psychology by practitioners who are trained in both social–personality and clinical or counseling psychology. At present, too many social and personality psychologists have a naive view of psychological problems and their treatment, and too many clinical and counseling psychologists have an uninformed (or, worse, misinformed) view of fundamental processes in social and personality psychology.

Finally, we hope that researchers and practitioners alike will continue to explore new avenues of inquiry. During the past 20 years, most of the perspectives in social and personality psychology that were applied to the study and treatment of emotional and behavioral problems involved concepts, theories, and lines of research that had existed for some time. Thus, there has been a great deal of social–clinical research on attribution, social perception and cognition, attitude change, self-disclosure, social support, the self, and individual differences. As Kowalski and Leary pointed out in chapter 1 of this book, many other topics and perspectives in social psychology could be incorporated into the study of psychological problems with fruitful results. In addition, psychologists should look for new perspectives involving basic interpersonal processes that will inform their understanding of emotional and behavioral problems. As just one example, we discussed earlier how the topic of interpersonal loss may represent an important new phenomenon for social–clinical exploration. Similarly, other, yet-unidentified perspectives will emerge that like interpersonal loss, embody the necessary breadth and relevance to promote the synergistic integration of social and clinical psychology.

REFERENCES

Allport, G. W. (1985). The historical background of social psychology. In G. Lindzey & E. Aronson (Eds.), *Handbook of social psychology* (Vol. 1, 3rd ed., pp. 1–46). New York: Random House.

Batson, C. D., Duncan, B. D., Ackerman, P., Buckley, T., & Birch, K. (1981). Is empathic emotion a source of altruistic motivation? *Journal of Personality and Social Psychology, 40*, 290–302.

Baumeister, R. F., & Leary, M. R. (1995). The need to belong: Desire for interpersonal attachments as a fundamental human motivation. *Psychological Bulletin, 3*, 497–529.

Brehm, S. S. (1976). *The application of social psychology to clinical practice.* Washington, DC: Hemisphere.

Coates, R. (1990). *A street is not a home.* Buffalo, NY: Prometheus Books.

Erikson, E. (1963). *Childhood and society* (2nd ed.). New York: Norton.

Fincham, F. D., & Bradbury, T. N. (1991). Cognition in marriage: A program of research on attribution. In W. H. Jones & D. Perlman (Eds.), *Advances in personal relationships* (Vol. 2, pp. 159–203). London, UK: Kingsley.

Frank, J. D. (1961). *Persuasion and healing*. Baltimore: Johns Hopkins University Press.

Frankl, V. E. (1959). *Man's search for meaning*. New York: Washington Square.

Franzoi, S. L. (1996). *Social psychology*. Madison, WI: Brown & Benchmark.

Goldstein, A. P., Heller, K., & Sechrest, L. B. (1966). *Psychotherapy and the psychology of behavior change*. New York: Wiley.

Greenberger, D. (1993). *Duplex planet*. New York: Faber & Faber.

Hart, K. E. (1991). *A graduate course at the social–clinical–counseling psychology interface*. Unpublished manuscript, Hofstra University.

Harvey, J. H. (1983). The founding of the *Journal of Social and Clinical Psychology*. *Journal of Social and Clinical Psychology, 1,* 1–3.

Harvey, J. H. (1987). JSCP: An established forum and a season of change. *Journal of Social and Clinical Psychology, 5,* 143–145.

Harvey, J. H. (1996). *Embracing their memory: Loss and the social psychology of storytelling*. Needham Heights, MA: Allyn & Bacon.

Harvey, J. H., & Stein, S. K. (1995). Social and counseling psychology: Progress and obstacles. *The Counseling Psychologist, 23,* 697–702.

Harvey, J. H., & Weary, G. (1979). The integration of social and clinical psychology training programs. *Personality and Social Psychology Bulletin, 5,* 511–515.

Hendrick, S. S. (1983). Ecumenical (social and clinical and x, y, z . . .) psychology. *Journal of Social and Clinical Psychology, 1,* 79–87.

Hendrick, S. S. (1995). Close relationships research: Applications to counseling psychology. *The Counseling Psychologist, 23,* 649–665.

Hendrick, S. S., & Hendrick, C. (1991). Education at the interface. In C. R. Snyder & D. R. Forsyth (Eds.), *Handbook of social and clinical psychology* (pp. 774–787). Elmsford, NY: Pergamon Press.

Hill, M. G., & Weary, G. (1983). Perspectives on the *Journal of Abnormal and Social Psychology*: How it began and was transformed. *Journal of Social and Clinical Psychology, 1,* 4–14.

Jacobson, J. A., & Weary, G. (1996). The application of social psychology to clinical practice: A catalyst for integrative research—Review of S. S. Brehm's *The application of social psychology to clinical practice*. *Contemporary Psychology, 41,* 1173–1176.

Janoff-Bulman, R. (1992). *Shattered assumptions: Towards a new psychology of trauma*. New York: Free Press.

Jones, E. E., Farina, A., Hastorf, A. H., Markus, H., Miller, D. T., & Scott, R. A. (1984). *Social stigma: The psychology of marked relationships*. New York: Freeman.

Leary, M. R., & Kowalski, R. M. (1995). *Social anxiety*. New York: Guilford Press.

Leary, M. R., & Maddux, J. E. (1987). Progress toward a viable interface between social and clinical–counseling psychology. *American Psychologist, 47,* 904–911.

Leary, M. R., & Miller, R. (1986). *Social psychology and dysfunctional behavior: Origins, diagnosis, and treatment.* New York: Springer-Verlag.

Lyons, R. F., Sullivan, M. J. L., Ritvo, P. G., & Coyne, J. C. (1995). *Relationships in chronic illness and disability.* Thousand Oaks, CA: Sage.

Maddux, J. E., Stoltenberg, C. D., & Rosenwein, R. (Eds.). (1987). *Social processes in clinical and counseling psychology.* New York: Springer-Verlag.

Matthews, S. H. (1986). *Friendship through the life course.* Beverly Hills, CA: Sage.

Morse, G. A. (1998). Homelessness and loss: Conceptual and research considerations. In J. H. Harvey (Ed.), *Perspectives on loss: A sourcebook* (pp. 269–280). Washington, DC: Taylor & Francis.

Neeld, E. (1990). *Seven choices: Taking the steps to a new life after losing someone you love.* New York: Delta.

Patnoe, S. (1988). *A narrative history of experimental social psychology: The Lewin tradition.* New York: Springer-Verlag.

Rubin, Z., & Mitchell, C. (1976). Couples research as couples counseling: Some unintended effects of studying close relationships. *American Psychologist, 31,* 17–25.

Snyder, C. R., & Forsyth, D. R. (Eds.). (1991). *Handbook of social and clinical psychology.* Elmsford, NY: Pergamon Press.

Staub, E. (1996). Breaking the cycle of violence: Helping victims of genocidal violence heal. *Journal of Personal and Interpersonal Loss, 1,* 191–197.

Strong, S. R. (1968). Counseling: An interpersonal influence process. *Journal of Counseling Psychology, 15,* 215–224.

Strong, S. R., & Claiborn, C. D. (1982). *Change through interaction: Social psychological processes of counseling and psychotherapy.* New York: Wiley Interscience.

Strong, S. R., Welsh, J. A., Corcoran, J. L., & Hoyt, W. T. (1992). Social psychology and counseling psychology: The history, products, and promise of an interface. *Journal of Counseling Psychology, 39,* 139–157.

Styron, W. (1990). *Darkness inside: A memoir of madness.* New York: Random House.

Sullivan, H. S. (1953). *Conceptions of modern psychiatry.* New York: Norton.

Vaughn, D. (1986). *Uncoupling.* New York: Oxford University Press.

Weary, G., & Mirels, H. L. (Eds.). (1982). *Integrations of clinical and social psychology.* New York: Oxford University Press.

AUTHOR INDEX

Numbers in italics refer to listings in the reference sections.

377

Solomon, L. K., 42, 64
Solomon, S., 207, 218, 221
Sommer, K., 153, 165, 178, 193
Sorman, P. B., 204, 206, 220
Soucherman, R., 259, 276
South, S. J., 327, 337
Sowards, B. A., 207, 221
Specker, S. M., 149, 166
Speicher, C., 344, 357
Spiegel, D., 228, 247
Spilka, B., 350, 359
Spinner, B., 344, 356
Spinoza, B., 171, 193
Spranca, M., 82, 95
Sprecher, S., 327, 328, 337
St. Clair, L., 342, 359
Stager, S. F., 353, 355, 359
Stanley, M. A., 51, 67
Stanley, S. M., 327, 335
Stark, H. A., 264, 277
Starzomski, A., 314, 331
Staub, E., 371, 376
Steele, C. M., 86, 95, 159, 166
Stegge, H., 170, 179, 190
Steiger, H., 157, 166
Stein, D. J., 145, 154, 155, 166
Stein, M. B., 85, 95
Stein, S. J., 54, 62
Stein, S. K., 364, 370, 375
Steinberg, R., 343, 359
Steinmetz, J. L., 80, 94
Stiles, W. B., 226, 227, 229, 247
Stillwell, A. M., 178, 189
Stilwell, C. D., 74, 91
Stipek, D. J., 51, 66
Stires, L. D., 258, 276
Stokes, J. P., 344, 359
Stoltenberg, C. D., 13, 14, 27, 31, 365, 376
Storms, M. D., 85, 95
Storr, A., 339, 360
Stowe, M. L., 52, 60
Strauman, T. J., 145, 150, 166
Strauss, C., 200, 221
Strausser, K. S., 124, 132, 212, 219
Strenta, A., 256, 276
Striegel-Moore, R., 183, 192
Stroebe, M., 344, 360
Stroebe, W., 344, 360
Strong, S. R., 11, 14, 18, 30, 33, 364, 365, 376
Struening, E. L., 284, 289, 307

Stryker, S., 287, 308
Stuart, C., 160, 166
Stucky, R. J., 19, 33, 252, 276
Stull, D. E., 239, 244
Styron, W., 372, 376
Suarez, L., 54, 60
Suedfeld, P., 343, 360
Sugisawa, H., 344, 360
Suhr, J. A., 289, 304
Suinn, R. M., 31
Sullaway, M., 71, 91
Sullivan, H. S., 363, 376
Sullivan, P. F., 162
Sullivan, M. J. L., 371, 376
Sussman, S., 264, 276
Swallow, S., 98, 100, 101, 103, 105, 108, 114, 116, 133, 134
Swann, W. B., Jr., 21, 33, 43, 66, 102, 103, 106, 134, 260, 276
Sweeney, P. D., 53, 62
Swindle, R. W., 282, 285, 286, 288, 297, 305, 308
Syme, S. L., 282, 283, 303, 346, 355
Szapocznik, J., 241, 247

Tafoya, D., 234, 245
Tajfel, H., 352, 353, 360
Tambor, E. S., 208, 210, 212, 220
Tanenbaum, R. L., 66
Tangney, J. P., 50, 65, 66, 168, 169, 172, 175–179, 181–183, 185–187, 189, 191–195
Tannock, R., 148, 165
Taylor, D. A., 231, 242
Taylor, K. L., 109, 113, 135
Taylor, S. E., 4, 41–43, 62, 66, 101, 102, 104, 110, 117, 120–127, 131, 132, 134, 201, 203, 206, 213, 221
Tchividjian, L. R., 19, 31, 269, 274
Teasdale, J., 17, 28, 40, 58, 99, 130
Teglasi, H., 54, 66
Templeton, J. L., 179, 192
Tennant-Clark, C. M., 201, 221
Tennen, H., 203, 221
Terdal, S. J., 208, 220
Tesser, A., 122, 126, 134, 173, 195
Testa, M., 99, 132
Teti, L. O., 146, 162
Tetlock, P. E., 214n, 221
Thissen, D., 158, 163

SUBJECT INDEX

Self-esteem, 197–216
    assumptions about, 198–208
    and attribution, 49
    benefits–liabilities of, 200–201,
        210–211
    clinical implications, 214–216
    consequences of raising, 201–202,
        211–213
    and feedback, 207
    functionality of, 205–207
    and group membership, 352–353
    motivation for maintaining–
        enhancing, 198–200, 209–210
    negative aspects of, 202–205
    relational, 316
    and social acceptance, 299–300
    social comparisons in persons with low.
        See Social comparison
    sociometer theory of, 208–216
    threats to, 199, 213–214
Self-evaluation, 99–100, 298–299
Self-evaluation maintenance (SEM) the-
    ory, 173–175
Self-exacerbating syndromes, 84–86
Self-handicapping, 254–256
Self-help groups, 347–348
Self-interest, 76
Self-perception, disclosure and, 234–235
Self-presentation, 18–19
Self-protection, 100–101, 113–115
Self-regulation, 139–161
    and adaptive functioning, 145
    and attention deficit hyperactivity dis-
        order, 147–149
    definition of, 139
    and eating disorders, 155–159
    failure of, 143–145
    and mood disorders, 149–152
    and obsessive–compulsive disorder,
        152–155
    requirements for successful, 141
    strength model of, 141–143
    and substance-related disorders, 159–
        160
    theoretical background, 140–141
    treatment implications, 145–147
Self-stereotyping, 352
Self-validation, 101
SEM theory. *See* Self-evaluation mainte-
    nance theory
Sexual abuse, 265
Sexual aggression, 20

Sexual harassment, and illusion of trans-
    parency, 88
Sexual interest, 268
Sexual promiscuity, 158, 253–254, 264
Shakespeare, William, 261
Shame, 172
    adaptive function of, 177–179
    and anger, 185–187
    guilt vs., 168–170, 187
    interpersonal context of, 175–177
    and jealousy, 187–188
    as problematic emotion, 181
    and psychopathology, 182–183
Shame and Guilt in Neurosis (Lewis), 182
Shyness, and attribution, 53–54
"Sight of adultery" cases, 185
Similarity hypothesis, 98
Social anxiety
    and attribution, 53–54
    and illusion of transparency, 86
Social–clinical psychology, 20–22
Social cognition, 5
Social-cognitive processes, 16–18
    See also Attribution
    attitudes, 17–18
    perception, social, 17
Social comparison, 97–130, 173
    affiliation studies of, 116–119
    comparative rating measures of, 107–
        109
    and degree of comparison seeking,
        103–106
    in depression and low self-esteem,
        98–99
    effects of, 119–126
    and envy, 180
    Festinger's theory of, 97–98
    laboratory studies of, 112–116, 122
    mood measures of, 122–126
    self-reports of, 110–112, 119–122
    specific comparison targets, 106–119
    theoretical perspectives on, 99–102
Social emotions, problematic, 167–189
    adaptive functions of, 177–181
    and aggression, 184–187
    common aspects of, 171–177, 187–
        188
    coping with, 181–182
    distinguishing among, 167–171
    and psychopathology, 182–184
Social identity, 352
Social influence, 18

ABOUT THE EDITORS

Robin M. Kowalski, PhD, is an associate professor of psychology at Western Carolina University in Cullowhee, NC. She obtained her PhD in social psychology from the University of North Carolina at Greensboro. Her research interests include social anxiety; social psychological factors in health and illness, gender, and aggression; and aversive interpersonal behaviors, specifically complaining and teasing. She is the editor of *Aversive Interpersonal Behaviors* and coauthor of *Social Anxiety*. Her research on complaining brought her international attention, including an appearance on NBC's *Today Show*.

Mark R. Leary, PhD, is a professor of psychology at Wake Forest University in Winston-Salem, NC. He obtained his PhD in social psychology from the University of Florida and has held faculty positions at Denison University and the University of Texas at Austin. His research interests focus on social motivation and emotion, particularly processes involving self-presentation, social anxiety, and self-esteem. He is the author or coauthor of six books, including *Social Psychology and Dysfunctional Behavior, Self-Presentation, Social Anxiety,* and *Selfhood: Identity, Esteem, Regulation*.